In Bitterness and in Tears

In Bitterness and in Tears

*Andrew Jackson's Destruction of the
Creeks and Seminoles*

Sean Michael O'Brien

THE LYONS PRESS
Guilford, Connecticut
An imprint of The Globe Pequot Press

Copyright © 2003 by Sean Michael O'Brien

First Lyons Press paperback edition, 2005

In Bitterness and in Tears: Andrew Jackson's Destruction of the Creeks and Seminoles by
Sean Michael O'Brien, originally published by Praeger, an imprint of Greenwood Press.
Copyright © 2003 by Sean Michael O'Brien. Published in paperback by arrangement with
Greenwood Publishing Group, Inc., Westport, CT. All rights reserved.

The Lyons Press is an imprint of The Globe Pequot Press.

10 9 8 7 6 5 4 3 2 1

Printed in the United States of America

Library of Congress Cataloging-in-Publication Data

O'Brien, Sean Michael, 1944-
 In bitterness and in tears : Andrew Jackson's destruction of the Creeks and Seminoles /
Sean Michael O'Brien.
        p. cm.
   Originally published: Westport, Conn. : Praeger, 2003.
   Includes bibliographical references and index.
   ISBN 1-59228-681-X (trade pbk.)
 1. Jackson, Andrew, 1767-1845—Relations with Creek Indians. 2. Jackson, Andrew,
    1767-1845—Relations with Seminole Indians. 3. Indians of North America—Wars—
    1815-1875. 4. Indians of North America—Government relations—1789-1869. 5.
    United States—Politics and government—1829-1837. 6. United States—Race relations.
    I. Title.
 E381.O27 2005
 323.1197'385073'09034--dc22
                                                        2005040736

When the first white man came over the wide waters, he was but a little man...very little. His legs were cramped by sitting long in his big boat, and he begged for a little land.

When he came to these shores the Indians gave him land, and kindled fires to make him comfortable.

But when the white man had warmed himself at the Indian's fire, and had filled himself with the Indian's hominy, he became very large. He stopped not at the mountain tops, and his foot covered the plains and the valleys. His hands grasped the eastern and western seas. Then he became our Great Father. He loved his red children, but he said: "You must move a little farther, lest by accident I tread on you."

—Speckled Snake, Muscogee chief, 1829

Contents

An illustration essay follows p. 112

Prologue:
"A Most Bloody Butchery"

As the blazing August sun arced high in the sky, the center of the wooden stockade was a beehive of activity. Fort Mims, as it was called, was an acre-sized frontier palisade casually thrown up around the big frame home of local settler Samuel Mims and a few smaller cabins. The day had been hot and steamy, typical for the backcountry along the Alabama River. On this day, August 30, 1813, a group of some 275 to 300, made up of white settlers, Muscogee (Creek) Indians, mixed-blood Muscogees, and soldiers—along with an unknown number of black slaves—milled about informally in the crowded fort, some busy at their work, others talking of the rumored threat of an attack by hostile Red Stick Muscogees. Practically no one anticipated that the threat was real.

The beating of a military drum summoned the fort's inhabitants to their noontime meal. Soldiers laid aside their weapons and ambled toward the serving line. Waiting their turn to eat, young men and women passed the time dancing, while small children played and older men and women discussed the day's activities. A game of cards held the attention of a party of soldiers. Everyone was unaware of any danger. Fort Mims was a microcosm of frontier America going about its way of life.

The attack came suddenly and swiftly, with no warning, as 750 Red Stick warriors poured out of a tree-covered ravine a hundred yards from the stockade. The attackers surged toward the fort, but only when they were thirty paces from the main gate did the sentry, who was watching the party of soldiers at their card game, become aware of the sounds of running feet and turn to see the angry swarm—terrifying in their red and black war paint and feathers—thundering toward him. "Indians!" cried the sentry, discharging his weapon and stumbling into the fort. "Indians!" (Owsley, 35–36; Griffith, 102–104; Owen, 107; L. Thompson, 342).

Major Daniel Beasley, the fort's commander, drew his sword and ran toward the main gate, which was wide open. Doubled over by a gunshot to the gut, Beasley pulled with all his might in a frenzied attempt to close the gate. But the heavy gate had been left ajar for so long that drifting sand had jammed it, and the major couldn't make it budge. The attackers were already upon him. Several warriors pounded him savagely with their clubs. Beasley managed to crawl behind the gate where, as he lay dying, he summoned the last of his strength to implore his soldiers to make a stand (L. Thompson, 342).

Four Red Stick prophets, covered in feathers and black war paint, were first to enter the fort, with their warriors close behind. Confident that the bullets of the white men would simply pass harmlessly around their bodies, the prophets marched boldly through the gate. Three of them fell dead at once as the soldiers mustered their courage and opened fire. Although momentarily stunned, the rest of the war party, led by the mixed-blood renegade Peter McQueen, renewed their attack and pushed their way into the stockade (Griffith, 105–106).

Inside the fort, all was disorder as terrified men, women, and children scrambled for cover and soldiers desperately tried to mount a defense. Officers' orders were drowned out by the screams of women and children and the bloodcurdling cries of the warriors. Captain Hatton Middleton's soldiers, posted near the main gate in the fort's eastern wall, attempted to form a ragged firing line and were annihilated almost immediately as Red Stick warriors poured into the fort and swarmed over them, hacking and stabbing. Captain William Jack's company, taking up their position along the south wall of the fort, rushed to assist Middleton and also fell early in the fighting. Lieutenant Peter Randon with a detachment of soldiers defended the western wall, where the guardhouse and the fort's one blockhouse—not yet completed—stood. The soldiers fought desperately. They discharged muskets into the surging horde of warriors, and when unable to reload, they used bayonets, swords, anything they could grab.

Captain Dixon Bailey, whose militia company held the northern wall, took command of the resistance, and the defenders scattered in groups into or behind the buildings inside the compound. Half Muscogee himself, as were his men, Bailey encouraged his troops to hold on, since the Muscogees generally did not fight for long periods at a time. He sought a volunteer to climb the wall and run to bring help from Fort Pierce, about two miles away, but all were too afraid to try. Finally the captain began to scale the wall himself, but friends and family members took hold of him and pulled him back (Griffith, 106; Owsley, 37; L. Thompson, 345–347).

The Red Sticks quickly gained control of most of the fort. Their leaders had prepared well for this moment. While McQueen's war party storming the main gate kept up pressure on that front, the rest of the Creeks, led by William Weatherford—Red Eagle—rushed the remaining three walls and took control of the loopholes in the pickets. Circumstances again favored the attackers. The defenders had cut the loopholes low, and the Red Sticks were able to fire their weapons through them into the fort. They kept up a murderous fire (Owsley, 37).

Only from the Mims house itself, in the center of the compound, and from the loom house near the northern wall, where Bailey and his mixed-blood company held out, did the Red Sticks encounter effective resistance. Most of the fort's women and children fled into the Mims house, which was partially surrounded by a protective wall. Two of Dixon Bailey's brothers sniped at the attackers from the attic of the Mims house, and other defenders fired out of the windows on the ground floor. The women fought too, many reloading muskets and bringing up water from the fort's well.

The loom house became known as the "bastion." With plenty of guns and powder, Bailey and his men kept up a steady fire, and for a while it looked as if they might hold out all day. The Red Sticks charged them again and again but were thrown back each time with heavy losses. The mixed-bloods still held some of the loopholes in the northern wall, and a partial wall attached to the loom house gave them some protection, but at the same time the defenders were exposed to fire from the loopholes held by the Red Sticks firing into the fort. At some of the loopholes, a defender and an assailant would fire through the same hole at each other. Inside the bastion, Major Beasley's wife loaded weapons and urged the men not to surrender, and when a sick sergeant would not get up and fight, she became so enraged that she stabbed him with a bayonet (Owsley, 37–38; L. Thompson, 348–349; E. Rowland, 43).

The fighting had gone on for three hours, and the Red Sticks—still unable to overwhelm the last pockets of resistance—tired of the combat and suspended the assault. Word spread among them that their principal chief, Hopie Tustunnuggee (Far-Off-Warrior), was dead. The warriors began plundering the captured portion of the fort, particularly the officers' quarters, and dragged off their spoils to a house about 300 yards from the stockade. A hasty meeting of the subchiefs chose William Weatherford as the new chief. Red Eagle immediately rallied the warriors for a renewed assault on the stockade; black renegades in their party also favored continuing the attack. The Red Sticks were too close to victory to quit now, and, emboldened by the persuasiveness of their chief, they took up their muskets, clubs, and tomahawks again (Owsley, 37–38; L. Thompson, 347–348; Martin, 157; Stiggins, 112).

The warriors renewed their attacks on the bastion, and still Bailey's men stubbornly held out despite repeated assaults. But Red Eagle had another tactic in mind. He ordered a heavy assault on the western wall of the fort. The warriors now broke through the back gate with axes and poured into the compound. Weatherford entered the fort running at the head of his warriors and cleared a pile of logs nearly as high as he was. His eyes fell on Bailey, a man he hated. "Dixon Bailey," he cried out, "today one or both of us must die." By now the fires the attackers had set when they captured the eastern part of the fort had begun to spread to the other buildings inside, and Bailey and his men knew the end was coming (L. Thompson, 350; Griffith, 106).

Now the Mims house fell, as burning arrows set it ablaze. The women and children who had taken refuge there fled toward the bastion, but warriors cut them down as soon as they ran from the house. David Mims made a break for the loom house but was overtaken by Red Sticks. One clubbed him in the neck, and blood spurted out as Mims fell to the ground. "Oh, God," he cried, "I am a dead man." The warrior quickly sliced around Mims's scalp with his knife and tore off the top of his head. He held it in the air as he screamed a cry of triumph. Soon the roof of the Mims house gave way, and the two Bailey brothers fell to their death. The interior was a blazing inferno, and those left inside were burned alive. Shortly afterward, a terrific blast rent the air as the fort's powder magazine exploded (L. Thompson, 351–353; Pickett, 535).

The last of the defenders went down. A single soldier fought on in the unfinished blockhouse, holding the Creeks off until he was down to his last musket ball. He had killed several of the assailants. Finally one of the warriors succeeded in shooting him in the head, and he slumped over, his brains splattering the inside of the blockhouse. Between the Mims house and the loom house, a husky black man stubbornly kept swinging his ax, laying low several Red Sticks before tomahawks and clubs finally brought him down. A loyal Muscogee named Johomohtee succeeded in shooting down three Red Sticks before being killed. Near the fort's well, several Spanish deserters from the military post at Pensacola huddled together, cowering and making the sign of the cross. The Red Sticks beat them to death with their tomahawks and clubs (L. Thompson, 349–353; E. Rowland, 49–51).

Badly wounded and losing blood, Bailey cringed at the cries of men, women, and children being burned alive. There was nothing left to do but either be killed in the stockade or make a break for freedom. The fort's assistant surgeon, Dr. Thomas G. Holmes, used his ax to chop through some of the logs in the fort's wall. Then he helped the wounded Bailey, along with the captain's black slave, Tom—bearing Bailey's thirteen-year-old son, sick with a fever—and a black woman named Hester, through the opening. As soon as they were beyond the wall, Red Sticks outside the fort opened fire on them and began a pursuit. Bailey and Holmes fired back, but they failed to see Tom—who was terrified and confused—rush back into the fort with the boy. A warrior grabbed the child and smashed in his head with a war club. Miraculously, the three escapees reached a swamp nearby, but Bailey was too badly wounded to go on. He died there in the marsh. Holmes hid out in the swamp, and Hester, although wounded herself, managed to walk twelve miles to Fort Stoddert, where she reported the details of the massacre to the troops there (Griffith, 108).

Only a handful of defenders made it out of the fort alive. Lieutenant Randon and his father broke through the picket wall and ran for the swamp, but the older man gave out and fell. When the young officer stooped to help him up, he waved his son on, urging him to save himself. Sorrowfully, the young officer abandoned him and ran toward the swamp. Behind him came the sound of a gunshot where he had left his father (L. Thompson, 354–355).

Nehemiah Page, an overnight visitor at the fort, made his escape from a hiding place in the stables, where he had slept off a drunken episode during the previous night only to awaken to the terrifying sounds of the Creek assault. Page bolted from the stable door after one of the war parties passed, and he raced from the fort like a rabbit. He never looked back or even slowed down until he was away from the stockade and headed for the Alabama River. The sounds of something in pursuit came up from behind him, and despite his best exertions Page couldn't outrun it. The young man lost his footing, sprawled to the ground, and instinctively cringed in anticipation of an expected blow from the enemy. What he felt instead was the wet muzzle of a small dog that had chased him from the stockade. Breathing a huge sigh of relief, Page was on his feet again and speeding toward the river with the little dog still in pursuit. With difficulty Page managed to swim the river and reach safety on the far bank, but he found his canine friend had kept up with him all the way. Man and dog became fast companions from then on (L. Thompson, 343–344).

The Red Sticks battered down the doors to the loom house and dragged the remaining whites and mixed-bloods out into the compound, where they were slaughtered. Once the killings began, not even Weatherford could stop them. Although he urged his warriors not to kill the women and children, angry voices shouted him down and war clubs were raised in his face. The way they died was ghastly. Small children were taken by the feet and dashed against the walls of the fort, splattering the walls with brains and blood. Women were stripped, scalped, and mutilated. Pregnant women were ripped open and their unborn babies killed before their eyes (Owsley, 38).

Weatherford had wanted a victory for the Red Sticks, but not a massacre. Some of his own relatives were among the fort's inhabitants. He could not force himself to stay and watch. As the orgy of killing unfolded, he was filled with remorse, took to his horse, and rode twelve miles to the home of David Tate, his half-brother. There—away from the killing—he poured out the story of the fate of Fort Mims, a story that would haunt him for the rest of his life (Griffith, 108).

Susan Hatterway saw her husband shot down by the Red Sticks. As the fort was overrun, she realized the inevitable. They were all going to die. She grabbed the hands of two children nearby—a white child named Elizabeth Randon and a black child named Lizzie—and told them, "Let us go out and be killed together." As they stepped forward to meet their death, one of the Red Stick warriors seemed to pick them out from among the terrified civilians and motioned them to his side. Susan recognized him as Dog Warrior, a young man whom she had known when he was a boy. Dog Warrior made them understand that they were now his captives. They were spared the worst of the terror (Griffith, 106; L. Thompson, 356–357).

One of the fiercest of the Muscogee warriors, Sanota, also spotted a familiar face among the captives. She was Vicey McGirth, a half Creek, with her seven daughters. Sanota remembered her as the woman who had taken him in when he was a small lad and had cared for him as one of her children. He was able to stop his comrades from slaughtering the McGirth women and claimed them as his captives (Griffith, 109).

No amount of pleading could save the rest of the fort's inhabitants. The warriors were out of control—worked up to a fever pitch by their hatred of the whites and turncoat mixed-bloods, angered by the losses of so many of their own men that day, and inflamed by a need for revenge. Many of them had former friends or kin among the fort's people, but their rage overrode reason and compassion. What happened at Fort Mims had been building up for a long time, a fratricidal civil conflict gone mad. Of the fort's inhabitants, the Red Sticks killed or captured 250 to 275. Twenty to forty of the defenders escaped. The attackers spared most of the black slaves and took them away with them. The day had cost the Red Sticks dearly as well; as many as half of their warriors were killed or wounded in the onslaught (Owsley, 38–39; Martin, 157; Stiggins, 114).

Ten days after the massacre, Major Joseph P. Kennedy's column arrived from the Fort Stoddert garrison. As they approached the smoldering ruins of Fort Mims, the soldiers were sickened at what greeted them. A swarm of vultures darkened the sky overhead, and as the soldiers drew closer to the fort they could see hundreds of wild dogs tearing at the remains of human bodies. Scalped, dismembered corpses of men, women, and children—many of them charred black from the fires—littered the ground with entrails and body parts scattered everywhere. Every building had been burned to the ground, with the exception of the unfinished blockhouse and part of the wooden picket wall. The mutilation of the dead was hardest to take—"a most bloody butchery," Tennessee frontiersman David Crockett remarked on hearing the news later. Kennedy's soldiers buried 247 victims of the massacre. They also found one hundred corpses of Red Stick warriors that the rebels had not taken time to bury (Griffith, 108; Owsley, 38–39; Crockett, 51).

Fort Mims was the worst frontier massacre in U.S. history, and the incident held tragic consequences for the Muscogee nation as well. Burning for vengeance, white settlers in Mississippi, Tennessee, and Georgia began raising troops for a retaliatory campaign. The massacre at Fort Mims released a river of blood that would not cease until the Red Sticks paid dearly for what they had done. For the whites, revenge would come seven months later at a place called the Horseshoe.

CHAPTER 1

Two Nations

The Muscogee land is become very small.... What we have left we
cannot spare, and you will find we are distressed.
—Hopoithle Miko, Muscogee chief, 1805 (Martin, 121)

To the Muscogees, nature was godly, and humans were part of nature. The
ultimate good was to be in balance with nature; lack of balance was something unnatural and wrong. The Muscogees' need to maintain equilibrium in their world underscored the essential difference between them
and their Anglo-American neighbors, who regarded nature as something
to be tamed, dominated, and exploited commercially (Martin, 17–18, 92).

The Muscogees were a Native American people who dwelt along the
creeks and rivers of present-day Georgia and Alabama. Early English settlers had called them "Creeks," but the people more commonly referred to
themselves by the name of the town in which they resided. The generic
name they used was Muskogee (or Muscogee)—"people of the lowland."
Most of the tribes spoke the Muskogean language. They were hardy people, nimble and active, powerfully built, about medium height, with
reddish-copper skin color. European observers had noted their proud and
independent nature. "As moral men," traveler William Bartram wrote of
them in 1791, "they certainly stand in no need of European civilization.
They are just, honest, liberal, and hospitable to strangers" (Martin, 7, 11, 17;
Barnard and Schwartzman, "Trail," 697–698; Brown and Owens, 81–82).

The Muscogees lived in towns (*italwa*) and smaller satellite villages
(*talofa*). Larger towns contained as many as one hundred homes and typi-
cally centered on a town square—a group of open buildings around a

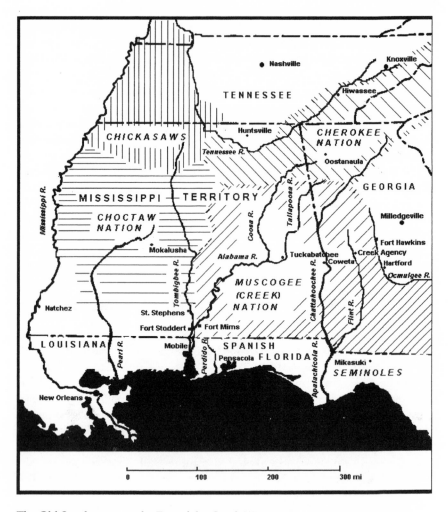

The Old Southwest, on the Eve of the Creek War, 1813

sacred fire. The home of the chief (*miko*) stood there, as well as a round council house where town leaders met and where members of the tribe assembled for dances and other ceremonies. There were sturdy winter houses as well as summer houses that were more like thatched-roof pavilions (Martin, 11; Brown and Owens, 83–84).

Tradition guided the lives of the Muscogees. Boys trained to be hunters and warriors. Hunters brought the town venison, turkey, or bear meat, while rivers and streams provided fish. Muscogee women tended the vegetable gardens that yielded corn, beans, squash, and sweet potatoes. A favorite staple dish was hominy (*sofkee*) (Brown and Owens, 83–84; Hudson, 302–305).

The clan was the main unit of social organization among the Muscogee. Important clans were the Wind, Bear, Bird, Raccoon, Deer, and Panther. The system demanded loyalty of clan members to each other and transcended loyalty to the town or tribe. Injury done to any member of the clan must be avenged by other clan members in an eye-for-an-eye manner. Balance was always to be maintained. Europeans and Anglo Americans persisted in treating the Native Americans as one people, or as a single tribe, when in fact allegiance to the clan was the overriding factor that often determined their conduct (Covington, 7).

The Muscogee nation was really a confederacy of tribes divided into two branches called the Upper Creeks and the Lower Creeks. The Upper Creek towns lay along the Alabama, Coosa, and Tallapoosa Rivers in present-day Alabama and included Autauga, Coosada, Tallassee, Autossee, Hillabee, and Okfuskee. The Lower Creeks inhabited the towns along the Chattahoochee and Flint Rivers in Georgia, with Coweta, Cusseta, and Eufaula some of their most important settlements. Muscogee towns were either white towns (peace towns) or red towns (war towns). The former served as centers for religious ceremonies such as the annual green corn festival and for ball games; the latter served as centers for war. A central tribal council, representing the confederacy as a whole, met at the capital of Tuckabatchee, an Upper Creek town on the Tallapoosa not far from present-day Montgomery (Brown and Owens, 81–83; Martin, 11).

More warlike than their neighbors, the Choctaws to the west and the Cherokees to the north, the Muscogees had a history of conflict with other tribes, and their relations with white settlers had not always been cordial, either. More than the other southeastern Native American tribes, the Muscogees seem to have borne the brunt of white encroachments. They had fought on the side of the British during the Revolutionary War and had continued an intermittent guerrilla war against the Americans until 1794 (Davis, 286–287; McLoughlin, 186).

Still the Muscogees were tolerant of the white men who chose to live among them. Many of these "Indian countrymen" were former military men like Captain William McIntosh and Timothy Barnard, Loyalist officers during the Revolutionary War who operated trading posts among the Creeks, or James McQueen, a Scottish sailor who deserted from a British ship to live among the Muscogees. Others were Scottish or Irish immigrant traders like Lachlan McGillivray; horse lover Charles Weatherford, who ran a trading post and racetrack at Coosawda; and David Francis, a silversmith who sold trinkets at Autauga. When such men took Muscogee women as their wives—in genuine marital commitments, rather than casual liaisons—they gained the support of their wives' clans. The mixed-blood offspring of such unions—like William McIntosh (Tustunnuggee Hutkee, or White Warrior), Timpoochee Barnard, Peter McQueen (Talmuches Hadjo), Alexander McGillivray, William Weatherford (Red Eagle), and Josiah Francis (Hillis Hadjo)—were accepted and accorded respect. Muscogees traced a child's lineage through the female, and the father's ethnic background was not important, so mixed-bloods also received the support of their mother's clans (Griffith, 1–5; Martin, 78–79; Owen, 9–10, 20, 35, 37–38, 81–82).

In the Muscogee nation, there was a growing influence of the mixed-bloods, who were bilingual and had adopted the white civilization's view of agriculture and wealth. Many were well educated, such as Alexander McGillivray, who attended a fine school in Charleston. Mixed-bloods lived like the whites, raising cotton, herding cattle, and keeping black slaves. William McIntosh, who lived in Coweta, became a powerful Lower Creek chief and headed the Muscogee nation's police force. William Weatherford owned a grand plantation on the Alabama River in present-day Lowndes County (Rogers, 46; Martin, 79–81; Owen, 37–38, 82).

The Muscogee nation was not the savage place that many uninformed eastern whites portrayed it to be. After Hannah Hale, a white girl, fell captive to a Muscogee war party raiding on the Georgia frontier, she was taken to a village on the Tallapoosa where she eventually was accepted into the tribe, married a local headman, and acquired a prominent position. In time, she gave birth to five children and became the proud owner of a substantial amount of property that included sixty cattle, some hogs, horses, and even one black slave. When her white family finally located her in 1799, Hannah chose to stay with the Muscogees (Martin, 70).

Many African Americans also dwelt in the Muscogee nation. Some were runaway slaves who had escaped the reach of the white man's law. Others came to the Muscogee country with their white masters. There were close to 1,900 slaves in the Muscogee nation by the 1790s. Many African Americans were carpenters, blacksmiths, and tanners, and they taught these skills to the Muscogees. Slavery as practiced by the mixed-blood Muscogees was less harsh than that of the white planters in Georgia and the Carolinas. African American slaves of Muscogees could own property and even marry into their owners' families. And free blacks in the Muscogee nations had none of the restraints on their movements and freedoms that they would have encountered in white society. Historian Joel Martin believes that the apocalyptic teachings of African American religion influenced the Muscogee prophetic movement (Martin, 71–76; Braund, 625–626; Davis, 73).

Muscogees and African Americans intermarried more frequently than in other southeastern Native American tribes. In an old joke a Muscogee says to a Cherokee, "You Cherokees are so mixed with whites we cannot tell you from whites." The Cherokee answers, "You Creeks are so mixed with Negroes we cannot tell you from Negroes." For the mixed-blood children of African American men and Muscogee women, their ethnicity carried no stigma as it would have in white society. As in the case of

Muscogee-white mixed-bloods, the child's lineage was traced through the mother and was accorded the respect of her clan. The prominent Muscogee chief Cusseta Hadjo (also called Cusseta Tustunnuggee, Jim Boy, or High Head Jim) was said to be part African American (Martin, 73, 126, 205, n. 8; Littlefield, 60).

For over 130 years—since the English settled Charleston—the Muscogees had traded with the white man. Two deerskins brought a yard of cloth, four an ax, twenty-five a flintlock musket. Soon the Muscogees' economy was dependent upon the deerskin trade. From the white trading posts—such as Fort Hawkins on the Ocmulgee River (present-day Macon, Georgia)—the Muscogees obtained knives, scissors, mirrors, needles and thread, blankets—all at low prices, to demonstrate the United States's goodwill toward the red man. But by the beginning of the nineteenth century, the deer herds had been overhunted, and the traditional hunting lands of the Muscogee were dwindling rapidly. It was unfortunate for the Muscogees that while they faced this economic crisis, they also encountered the first expansionist pressures of the young United States (Martin, 44; Barber, 163–164; Davis, 288).

In 1805, the Muscogees had surrendered nearly three million acres of land between the Oconee and Ocmulgee Rivers in Georgia. Within no time at all, white squatters were crossing the Ocmulgee in violation of the treaty. A principal chief, Hopoithle Miko, complained to President Thomas Jefferson, pointing out that it was the whites who had broken the agreement. While federal officials expressed sympathy for the Muscogees, it soon became apparent that the government lacked the means to remove the interlopers. Federal troops actually ran off 1,700 squatters from Muscogee and Chickasaw lands in 1809, but this failed to stem the tide (Martin, 121–122; Davis, 65).

In 1796, veteran North Carolina politician Benjamin Hawkins became the federal agent to the Muscogees. From his government agency on the Flint River in Georgia, the capable Hawkins encouraged the Muscogees to adopt white civilization. Hawkins utilized the Muscogee national council—originally conceived as a committee of "beloved men" to negotiate trade agreements for the whole confederacy, with a "speaker" appointed to serve as chief diplomat—as a tool for social change. The goal was to teach the Muscogees to become farmers instead of hunters, to raise livestock and cotton, and to assimilate into white civilization. The Muscogees would become loyal American citizens, and large tracts of their former hunting grounds—which they would no longer need, since they would be farmers—would become available for white settlement (Barber, 165–166; Braund, 626–627; Davis, 287; Martin, 97–98).

Hawkins believed that the best way to achieve rapid assimilation lay in the development of commercial cotton raising. He encouraged the Muscogees to adopt the plantation system as practiced by whites in the South and the efficient use of black slaves. At his agency, he demonstrated practical farming methods to the Muscogee men and urged them to take up the plow, while Muscogee women were to learn the efficient use of the spinning wheel and loom (Barber, 166; Braund, 627).

But although Hawkins was proud of the progress that the Creeks had made toward white civilization, many Muscogees resisted his new program. Hawkins failed to grasp the red man's deep-rooted communal concept of land ownership and the traditional division of labor between males and females. There was widespread resentment of what many Muscogees perceived to be a hostile plan to destroy their way of life (Braund, 630; Martin, 111–113).

But one group of Muscogees had already embraced the way of life Hawkins promoted, and they had done so even before the federal agent had begun his ambitious program. The small but influential group of Muscogee mixed-blood planters had already adopted the white man's concepts of agriculture and land ownership. Hawkins could point to the example of Alexander Cornells (Oche Hadjo), who owned nine slaves. "He is very attentive to all improvements," Hawkins reported, "and has now prepared a field of two acres for cotton." Cornells became a subagent under Hawkins and exercised considerable political clout in the Muscogee nation. Mixed-blood Muscogees lived like whites, and—having become capitalists in the white tradition—they did not share their wealth with the tribe as a whole. The largest concentration of these entrepreneurs dwelt among the white pioneers in the growing settlements of the lower Tombigbee and Tensaw Rivers, south of the Upper Creek towns. There they raised cotton and cattle, and the river gave them easy access to the port of Mobile. Mixed-blood planter David Tate was one of the most successful farmers in the area (Braund, 630–631; Martin, 80, 94, 102–106).

The problem with the mixed-bloods' economic and social successes was that—as in the broader white population—most Muscogees failed to benefit from it. As hunters, Muscogee men had a fairly equal chance to acquire trade goods. But commercial agriculture was based on wealth, and the breach was widening between the rich and the poorer Muscogees, who, lacking the means to acquire land, could not compete with the mixed-blood planters. This introduced class differences for the first time in Muscogee society and marked a real challenge to traditional Muscogee religious thought. As with Hawkins's reform program, it also intensified differences between Upper Creeks, who tended to be more traditional, and Lower Creeks, who were closer to the white frontier and who had more quickly taken to white ways (Martin, 107–108; Barber, 173; Heidler and Heidler, "Between," 268).

After the Revolutionary War, mixed-bloods assumed a commanding role in Muscogee politics. Alexander McGillivray—son of Scottish trader Lachlan McGillivray and Sehoy Marchand, a French-Muscogee woman—

dominated the Muscogee nation for many years. A skillful diplomat, McGillivray successfully played competing European nations against one another in order to obtain multiple outlets for Muscogee deerskins, while dodging reliance on any one power. McGillivray utilized his father's economic ties with the British trading firm of Panton, Leslie, and Forbes operating out of Spanish Pensacola and the support of his mother's powerful Wind clan. An opposition faction led by Hopoithle Miko of Tallassee preferred developing the nation's trade with the American settlers in Georgia (Martin, 81; Brown and Owens, 92).

In a bitter power struggle, McGillivray's faction won out. Using his economic connections, McGillivray could reward loyal chiefs with gifts. A key element in his political victory was his success in elevating the "war chiefs" over the "peace chiefs" in Muscogee towns. Traditionally the war chiefs exercised power in time of war but always relinquished it once the conflict was over. But after the Revolutionary War, the war chiefs refused to surrender their authority. Hopoithle Miko opposed the centralization of power in the Muscogee nation, but McGillivray had his homes burned and his property destroyed. McGillivray and Hopoithle Miko finally set aside their differences, because both realized the need for unity in the face of U.S. expansion. The two leaders traveled to New York in 1790 and negotiated an important treaty with President George Washington. After McGillivray's death in 1793, the United States exerted a much stronger role in Muscogee politics (Martin, 81–84).

In the first two decades of the nineteenth century, the Muscogee national council became the forum for ambitious chiefs seeking to resist white demands for more land concessions while maintaining tribal sovereignty and remaining at peace with the United States. A series of power struggles rocked the council, the main contenders being Hopoithle Miko—McGillivray's old enemy, who had withdrawn from the council in an unsuccessful attempt to form a rival government—and Tustunnuggee Thlucco (Big Warrior) of Tuckabatchee. Hopoithle Miko was hostile to Hawkins's plan of civilization, but he was far more acceptable to the federal agent than Big Warrior, who favored a "Four Nations" plan of cooperation between the Muscogees, Choctaws, Cherokees, and Chickasaws to resist white encroachments—a plan that seemed dashed in 1808 when the Choctaws agreed, without consulting the other tribes, to cede land east of the Tombigbee River—land also claimed by the Muscogees (Martin, 119; Barber, 166–169).

Hawkins's support helped win the speakership for Hopoithle Miko in 1808, and now it was Big Warrior who was the outsider, trying to form a rival government. And as with Hopoithle Miko, his attempt failed, because the council controlled the purse strings of the Muscogee nation, thanks to the annual payments from earlier land cessions. But by 1811, the council—disappointed in Hopoithle Miko's inability to put a stop to white infringements on Creek lands—replaced him with Big Warrior. To Hawkins, Big Warrior was "avaricious, ambitious, and intriguing," but the new speaker proceeded with his ambitious plan to kick off his Four Nations proposal (Barber, 169–170).

The opening of the Federal Road through the Muscogee nation caused bitter resentment and had political repercussions in the council. Hopoithle Miko firmly refused permission for such a road in 1811. "You ask for a path and I say no," he wrote President James Madison. "What land we have left is but large enough to live on and walk on." But he could not stop the road, and he lost favor with the council. Although some Lower Creek chiefs—notably Hawkins's ally William McIntosh—encouraged their fellow chiefs to support the federal agent's program, the Upper Creek chiefs remained unconvinced and sullenly opposed (Barber, 169–170; Martin, 120; Griffith, 65).

But it was not from the council that the road to war would come. Smoldering below the surface in the Muscogee nation was widespread popular discontent with both Hawkins's program of civilization and the national council's inability to stop the steady erosion of Muscogee land to white settlement. In the face of confusing economic, social, and political crisis, many Muscogees began to turn to their village shamans, a class of spiritual leaders who so far had largely been excluded from council government but who exercised great influence over the nation's religious life. The shamans preached that traditional religion would succeed where the council had failed, that the faithful would restore the right balance in a world gone awry and renew Muscogee tribal sovereignty. Soon Hawkins would face not only the rejection of his social program but the overthrow of the council as well. The salvation of the Muscogees seemed to lie in a spiritual revival and a holy war to drive back the white invaders (Barber, 170–171; Martin, 18, 44–45).

The Alabama Feaver rages here with great violence and has carried off vast numbers of our Citizens.... There is no question that this feaver is contagious.

—North Carolina resident, 1817 (Rogers et al., 54)

The Muscogees called them *Ecunnaunuxulgee*—"people greedily grasping after all lands." The whites were drawn by the vast land on the frontier just waiting for cultivating, land seemingly unused by the Native Americans. A steady stream of white settlers would become a flood of land seekers after 1814. The flood would sweep aside the Muscogees and the other Native American peoples of the southeastern United States (Martin, 122).

The land between the Chattahoochee and Mississippi Rivers—what Americans called the Old Southwest or the Mississippi Territory—witnessed the early stages of U.S. westward expansion, later called manifest destiny. The frontier served as a safety valve for the rapidly growing population in the eastern states. The land was the fertile black soil that became the "Black Belt" of Alabama and Mississippi, land perfectly suited to growing cotton, plenty of land for raising cattle, forests of elms and red oaks, peach trees and magnolias. The civilization of the Old Southwest was a blend of the Native American, French, Spanish, English, and American cultures. The area was claimed by three European powers prior to the independence of the United States, and the first significant numbers of American immigrants began moving in after the Revolutionary War. Many were Loyalist refugees seeking a new life on the frontier; others were Patriot settlers from Georgia and the Carolinas. Congress first established a land policy for the new territory, recognizing older British and Spanish grants and providing up to 640 acres each to settlers who could show that they had been living on and cultivating their farms when the Spanish evacuated the area in 1797. There were two main settlements, one on the lower Mississippi River at Natchez, the other on the lower Tombigbee River at St. Stephens (Davis, 11–12, 63–64, 129; Abernethy, 17–18).

Many white settlers were squatters. Land was cheap at $2.00, and later $1.25, an acre. It was simpler to just move in without paying, hoping that the Muscogees and Choctaws would leave them alone as long as they didn't bother them. Frontier men and women were a tough lot, uneducated, self-sufficient, anxious to make a better life for themselves. They were restless, generally staying just long enough in a place to get in one good crop before moving on to more attractive lands further west (Abernethy, 37; Davis, 65–66, 82).

Frontier society was a rough society. Settlers lived hard and played hard. One popular pastime, a game called "snick-a-snack," had participants hitting each other on the hands, head, and shoulders with their knives until the other cried quit. Milder forms of recreation included dancing and music played on the harmonica or fiddle. Corn liquor was plentiful, and frontier men and women generally drank it straight. Alcoholism was rampant, as was gambling, prostitution, and crime. There never were enough peace officers. Duels were common, even among frontier aristocrats, although the territorial legislature had outlawed the practice. Even squatters sometimes used force to resist eviction attempts, and more dangerous fugitives often sought safety across the border in Spanish Florida (Davis, 124, 193, 245–246, 254–256, 266).

Frontier behavior was often raucous. By 1823 the little frontier community of Marion, Alabama, had grown into a town with three hotels, three stores, and a dozen or so saloons, one of which—displaying a prominent sign boasting the slogan "Dum Vivimus, Vivimus" ("while we live, let us live it up")—stood across the street from the courthouse, a frame building on large wooden blocks that looked like a "smoke house with windows." One night a group of local rowdies removed the wooden blocks from one end of the courthouse, and the structure fell to the earth. The culprits were never prosecuted (Harris, 16–18).

Many federal officials and military officers stationed in the Mississippi Territory had a low opinion of the settlers and their wild lifestyle. General James Wilkinson, the department military commander at New Orleans, referred to them as "semi-Christians." Ephraim Kirby, appointed by President Thomas Jefferson to serve as territorial judge, gave this caustic assessment of the settlers on the lower Tombigbee and Tensaw Rivers:

This section of the United States has long afforded an assylum to those who prefer voluntary exile to punishments ordained by law for heinous offences. The present inhabitants (with few exceptions) are illiterate, wild and savage, of depraved morals, unworthy of public confidence or private esteem; litigious, disunited, and knowing each other, universally distrustful of each other. The magistrates without dignity, respect, probity, influence or authority. The administration of justice, imbecile and corrupt. The militia, without discipline or competent officers. (Haynes, 188; Doster, 87)

Although they may have been a crude and uncouth people themselves, the white settlers had an even lower opinion of Native Americans. The settlers viewed all red men as the same. After some Upper Creeks murdered two Georgia settlers in 1787, the Georgians retaliated by killing several Lower Creek hunters. When the Lower Creeks protested that they were not the guilty party—"You always promised that the innocent should not suffer for the guilty"—the Georgians replied that they would hold them accountable for acts done by the Upper Creeks. "Should any act of hostility, or depredations be committed on our people by your nation," they warned, "be perfectly assured we will not hesitate to do our selves ample justice by carrying War into your Country burning your Towns and staining your land with blood" (Martin, 7–8).

Except for the relatively few traders and "Indian countrymen" who had lived among them and knew better, white frontier settlers were almost universally hostile to Native Americans, regarding them as less than human, as a race of savages unworthy to occupy the bountiful land that nature had provided them. The hand of friendship—and the promise of equality as U.S. citizens—that had first been extended to the red man by early American leaders like Washington and Jefferson was gradually withdrawn as more and more white settlers moved into the frontier coveting the Native Americans' lands.

Historian William G. McLoughlin sees these negative frontier attitudes as a product of the "romantic nationalism" on the rise in the United States in the first decades of the nineteenth century. White Americans were reevaluating what it meant to be an American, and their redefinition excluded Native Americans and African Americans. In the view of the majority in the United States, the fruits of this land were destined to be enjoyed by Protestant Anglo Americans. Indeed, many frontier whites considered the red man not only uncivilized, but also incapable of being civilized, and some of them, Cherokee agent Return J. Meigs noted, "would not spend a dollar towards their improvement." Many southeastern white settlers simply saw the Native American as "a red nigger" (McLoughlin, xv-xvii, 48, 54).

White settlers also seemed to have no regard for the sovereignty of Native Americans over their own land. White leaders were constantly pressuring the southeastern tribes into surrendering more large tracts of land. In the 1790s, the Tennessee legislature wrote President John Adams that it considered the Cherokees "tenants at will" and that white settlers willed them to yield more of their lands. When the Cherokees refused, the government pushed ahead and finally wrangled away 90,000 acres in eastern Tennessee and 376,000 acres in western North Carolina, for which they paid the Cherokees $5,000 in cash and a yearly annuity of $1,000 (McLoughlin, 46).

From their homes in Georgia and the Carolinas, the pioneer families loaded their possessions into wagons and—with their slaves driving their herds of cattle and hogs—made the difficult journey overland to the Mississippi Territory, where, according to historian Thomas P. Abernethy, "the small farmer of the piedmont region became the pioneer planter of the Southwest." After reaching their destination, the family constructed a home, usually a log cabin—actually two rooms connected by a passageway. They used puncheons—split logs with the flat sides up—for the floors and chinked them in with clay. The frontier families grew cotton, corn, potatoes, and beans; tended herds of cattle and hogs; and supplemented their diet with venison, wild turkey, and bear (Abernethy, 36–37; Davis, 93–96).

For the white settlers, cotton was their key to prosperity—cotton and slavery. Planters introduced the cotton gin to the Alabama country in the first decade of the nineteenth century, and by 1810 nearly 40 percent of the population of the Tombigbee settlements was slave. The incentive for potential cotton growers was a powerful one, because an ambitious and hardworking man could make himself a successful planter almost overnight. But an ambitious man required slaves and plenty of them (Abernethy, 18–19, Davis, 73).

Trade with eastern cities was difficult, with no road across the Appalachians. The only practical outlets were the ports of New Orleans at the mouth of the Mississippi and Mobile at the mouth of the Alabama and Tombigbee river system. But Spain controlled Mobile, and New Orleans didn't become an American city until 1803. American merchants chafed at the high duties the Spanish required them to pay. Many pioneer settlers followed the practice of one entrepreneur who sailed his goods down the

Tennessee River to near Muscle Shoals, portaged them overland, and then brought them down the Tombigbee to St. Stephens (Abernethy, 19–20).

The first real road through the Mississippi Territory, the Natchez Trace, completed in 1809, connected Nashville, Tennessee, with Natchez on the Mississippi. The pioneers generally did not settle on the Trace but quickly branched out to the creeks and bottomlands. Natchez became a bustling and prosperous town where one could find genuine Southern aristocrats like Ferdinand L. Claiborne, a Virginian and former army officer who served as a member of the territorial legislature and brigadier general of the territorial militia. Guests at his fine mansion enjoyed Madeira wine with their meals of salad, meats, pastries, cheese, and apples (Abernethy, 20; Davis, 34, 91, 119).

While the population in the area around Natchez grew fairly rapidly, with over 31,000 people by 1811, the Tensaw-Tombigbee settlements (or the 'Bigbee settlements, as they were called)—with only about 3,000 people—were slower to develop. In 1804 there were some sixty families on the Tensaw and 140 families on the Tombigbee, mainly planters and cattlemen, their families, and slaves. Also living and farming in the area were a significant number of Muscogee mixed-blood planters (Davis, 104–106; Gaines, 143).

The only real town in the 'Bigbee was St. Stephens, built by the Spanish as a frontier outpost on the bluff of the river and abandoned in 1799. In 1805, the Americans were still using one of the blockhouses of the old Spanish fort as a store, and the former Spanish officers' quarters was now the home of the U.S. factor. Two companies of U.S. soldiers were stationed in St. Stephens. A large frame building housed the land office, and the homes of the white settlers were log cabins. By 1816 St. Stephens boasted 250 homes; fifteen stores; a newspaper; and the Washington Academy, the first public school in Alabama. To the south of St. Stephens on the west bank of the Mobile River was Fort Stoddert, built by U.S. troops in 1799 to mark the southernmost outpost of the United States at that time (Gaines, 140–141; Davis, 115).

With Spanish Mobile just thirty miles to their south and the Muscogee nation to their north—but with the nearest American settlement at Natchez 240 miles away—the 'Bigbee settlers felt isolated from the United States. Since the Alabama and Tombigbee Rivers furnished their only connection with the world at large, the settlers considered themselves vulnerable as long as Spain controlled Mobile. They were as suspicious of the Muscogees as the Creeks were of white intentions. And they felt neglected by the remote government of the United States. Ephraim Kirby believed that the isolation of the 'Bigbee had much to do with the poor moral climate of the frontier settlement. It is no wonder that many of the 'Bigbee settlers were inclined to take the law into their own hands (Doster, 86; Haynes, 184).

The Tensaw-Tombigbee settlers were men like prosperous farmer and herdsman Samuel Mims, who also operated a ferry, and New Englanders John and William Pierce, who ran a store. A familiar fixture at St. Stephens was the U.S. factor, George S. Gaines, who operated the government trading house for the Choctaws, whom, he observed, "were not such savages as I had imagined." Gaines was an honest man who dealt fairly with the Choctaws and the few Muscogees who came there to trade with him. And there was Big Sam Dale, who came to the 'Bigbee settlements from Georgia, where he was wanted for allegedly smuggling slaves and coffee into the state from Spanish Pensacola. Like many settlers, Sam enjoyed relative safety from prosecution on the frontier. The rugged six-foot-two frontiersman traded with the Choctaws and Muscogees and guided many white settlers into the territory (Doster, 86, 90; Haynes, 187, 190; Gaines, 141; L. Thompson, 197).

John and James Caller represented the rougher elements in the 'Bigbee settlements. John Caller, a Virginian who arrived in the settlements with his large family and slaves, became colonel of the local militia and created what amounted to his own private army. Judge Harry Toulmin, who replaced Ephraim Kirby on his death in 1804, worked to try to curb illegal military activity, but the Callers enjoyed considerable popular support. Toulmin was aware that a number of the local militia officers and justices of the peace had shady backgrounds; two of the justices were wanted for murder and another was wanted for helping a convicted murderer break out of jail (Doster, 88–90, 92).

The 'Bigbee settlements marked the end of the Federal Road, begun as a post road in 1805, widened in 1810, and expanded to a military road in 1811. From Augusta, Georgia, the road ran to Fort Hawkins on the Ocmulgee, through Hawkins's agency on the Flint, and on to Fort Stoddert. The Federal Road carried 3,700 people to the frontier in the first six months of operation, and Hawkins wrote in 1811 that it "is now crowded with travelers moving westward." The gateway to the Alabama country, it hardly rated as anything like a modern highway; as late as 1831 a British traveler described it as "positively, comparatively, and superlatively, the very worst I have ever treaded" (Davis, 53; Rogers et al., 45, 55; Southerland, 102).

White settlers were also steadily moving into the Muscogee nation from Tennessee. An 1806 land cession from the Cherokees led to the opening up of the Tennessee River Valley of present-day northern Alabama. The first pioneer, John Hunt, made his home near what became Huntsville, the main hamlet in the region. The Tennessee settlers—many of them squatters—called the area "Happy Valley" (Abernethy, 18; Hunt, 88–89; Davis, 61).

As early as 1809, cotton planters from Georgia began moving into the Tennessee Valley, attracted by the area's rich soil, and they quickly superseded the first settlers, who were mainly yeoman farmers. The number of slaves in the area increased from 300 in 1809 to 4,200 in 1816, and planters owning twenty slaves or more soon made up a small but powerful segment of the population. The valley continued to attract new residents. "It is not merely a rude frontier," a local planter noted in a July 4 speech in 1811, "thinly peopled with hunters and herdsmen, the mere precursors of the tillers of the earth, but it is the tillers of the earth themselves, who bring with them the pleasures of social life, the arts of industry, the abundant means of easy and comfortable subsistence" (Abernethy, 19, 24, 39; Dupre, 219–220).

Fort Hawkins on the Ocmulgee marked the entrance into the Muscogee nation from the east. Although the treaty of 1805 limited whites to settlements on the eastern side of the Ocmulgee, squatters relentlessly pushed into the Muscogee nation, first hunting and fishing or grazing their livestock, and later clearing and cultivating land. Fifty miles south of Fort Hawkins, whites had settled the village of Hartford (present-day Hawkinsville), which became an important trading center. Benjamin Hawkins's agency among the Muscogees lay westward on the Flint River, and about forty miles to the south along the Flint was Timothy Barnard's trading post (Chalker, 77, 81, 83–86).

The scattered white settlements on the fringes of the Muscogee nation contained the embryo of what would become the Cotton Kingdom. The lure of the cheap land and rich black soil of central Alabama and Mississippi attracted thousands of white pioneers between 1810 and 1820. The quest for wealth thrust a wedge among the rough-hewn pioneers and yeoman farmers who settled the Mississippi Territory and divided them into a society of rich and poor. Historian William C. Davis observes that "out of a virtually classless society in the 1780s, the Old Southwest grew into a class-ridden culture in a span of two to three generations." The land awaited the dominion of cotton. The only potential obstacle in the path of the Cotton Kingdom was the Muscogee nation (Abernethy, 18–19, 24, 35; Martin, 2; Rogers et al., 54; Davis, 73).

CHAPTER 2

The Catalyst

From 1811 to 1813, a charismatic spiritual movement swept through the Muscogee land. As many Muscogees turned increasingly to the shamans for direction in the face of confusion and crisis, traditional religious myths and rituals seemed to point the way to a new cosmology revealed in visions and prophecies. The shamans taught that a new world creation was about to take place. Only by seeking to restore the delicate balance that Muscogees held so sacred could the nation survive, maintain its identity, and rid itself of white intrusion.

Key spiritual leaders—medicine makers (*hilis hayaki*) and knowers (*kithlas*)—guided the Muscogee in this quest. The medicine makers, the priests or shamans of Muscogee towns, wielded great influence and power. A high seer commanded the respect and confidence of the Muscogee people, who believed he could cure illnesses, predict rain or drought, summon spirits, and turn back armies. Where political systems had failed, spiritual power would succeed in restoring a right balance and order in the world (Martin, ix–x, 123, 127).

The impending revolt that burned through the Muscogee nation was a fusion of religious spiritualism and political zeal. But while political and social discontent played a major role—exacerbated by increasing friction with white settlers over land—the essential element of the new movement was religious. Historian Joel Martin calls it "an anticolonial movement empowered by contact with spirits of earth, water, and sky" (6).

The Muscogee revolt was not simply a rebellion of traditionalists against the supporters of acculturation. The rebels were renouncing the ineffectual tactics of the Muscogee national council—which also opposed accultura-

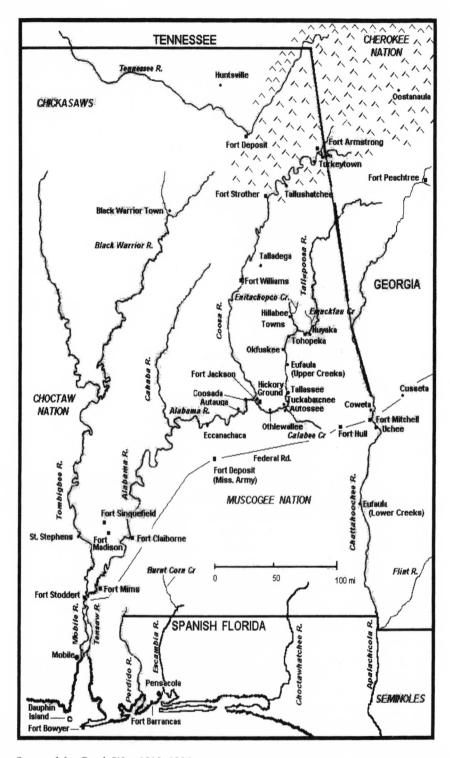

Scene of the Creek War, 1813–1814

tion—and were looking for a stronger weapon with which to fight white encroachment, a weapon they believed lay in religion. "The sharpest division in Creek politics," historian Douglas Barber writes, "was not between advocates of competing cultures but between advocates for competing strategies for maintaining Creek sovereignty in the face of trade dependence" (173).

And their leaders were not only conservative full-bloods. Well-to-do mixed-bloods such as Peter McQueen, Josiah Francis, and ultimately William Weatherford took a conspicuous part in the movement. Their participation may have been a matter of expediency. The bilingual Francis, already a powerful medicine maker in Autauga, carried on a profitable trade with the British in Pensacola, was heavily in debt—as were many other Muscogee leaders—and feared that the United States would use the debt as leverage to force the Creeks to cede more land. There was resentment by many traditional Muscogees against the material wealth of the mixed-bloods. With the Muscogee nation poised on the brink of class warfare, many of the mixed-bloods may have chosen to become conduits for the radicals' anger rather than the targets of it (Barber, 172–173; Martin, 126).

Nativist sentiments were also stirring elsewhere. In the Appalachian foothills to the north lay the great Cherokee nation. The proud Cherokees called themselves "the principal people," but the Muscogees called them "people of a different speech," since they spoke an Iroquoian language rather than Muskogean. Once white settlers had been in awe of Cherokee military power. Armed by their British allies, the "principal people" had fought the Americans in the Revolutionary War. But although their nation was still large, the Cherokees were beset by a declining economy and increasing white pressures to give up more land as the nineteenth century opened (Brown and Owens, 102–105).

Like the Muscogee, the Cherokee nation was a confederation of towns with a central council, but in fact it was on the verge of becoming a true nation-state. Benjamin Hawkins's counterpart among the Cherokees, agent Return J. Meigs, encouraged them to become farmers and adopt white civilization. There was also a minority of wealthy mixed-bloods who dominated Cherokee politics and who practiced commercial agriculture and slavery. The young Cherokee mixed-blood elite firmly believed that their nation's survival lay in imitating white civilization and winning acceptance and equality. "We want to do the best we can for ourselves and our Nation," a delegation of the young chiefs told Jefferson in 1808. "If we follow the old customs of our old people, we will never do well." Cherokee efforts toward this goal were so successful that their nation came closer than any other Native American tribe to meeting the standards of civilization set by whites (Ehle, 34; McLoughlin, xvii, 109, 177).

As in the Muscogee nation, an undercurrent of unrest also ran through the Cherokee lands. The Cherokees were experiencing a religious revival or "ghost dance movement" not unlike the Muscogees' spiritual upheaval and were struggling to retain their identity and the traditions of their past while adopting the white man's ways, which seemed to be the way of the future. Like the Muscogees, they sought a means to restore balance in their world, and many Cherokees began to turn to their shamans to point the way. As economic crisis loomed and increasing friction with white squatters caused discontent throughout the land, some shamans urged their followers to reject white civilization and turn back to traditional tribal practices, to cast off and burn their white clothing and destroy their plows, spinning wheels, and other implements of white culture (Ehle, 94–95; McLoughlin, 168, 178–179).

In February 1811, a Cherokee man and two women appeared before the national council at Oostanaula (near present-day Calhoun, Georgia) to recount a remarkable vision that came to them while traveling in northern Georgia. In this vision a multitude of ghost horsemen had descended from the sky to deliver a message to the Cherokees: The "principal people" were to restore balance in their world by returning to the traditional ways of the past and by expelling dishonest whites who had cheated the Cherokees. If any rejected this message, it would "not be well" for them. The report provoked heated debate in the council, and mixed-blood leader Ridge, a prominent planter, was quick to respond. Ridge sneered at the vision, pronounced it a false vision that would lead to a war with the United States, and defied death to come upon him if he spoke wrongly. Angered by Ridge's impertinence, other council members fell on him, and in a violent melee the chief very narrowly escaped with his life. After fighting off his attackers with the help of his friends, Ridge declared that he had proved that the message was a sham, because he still lived (Ehle, 97–99; McLoughlin, 179–181).

The radicalism of the Muscogee prophets and shamans had much in common with another Native American tribe, the Shawnees, who occupied land in the Ohio River Valley. The Muscogees and Shawnees shared a common historical connection. There had been much contact between the two tribes, and a Shawnee colony had once existed among the Muscogees on the Tallapoosa River. Both tribes had witnessed the loss of millions of acres of land to the pressure of white settlers moving west, and both were experiencing economic problems because of the collapse of the deerskin trade. Young warriors in both the Muscogee and Shawnee nations felt the same sense of rage and helplessness at the destruction of their national pride and identity. And in both tribes there was a strong pro-British tradition (Martin, 116–117).

Into the complex mix of spiritual confusion and sociopolitical unrest in the Shawnee nation stepped a truly charismatic leader, the war chief Tecumseh. He was the son of a Muscogee woman and a Shawnee man who had lived among the Creeks, and his name ("The Panther Passing Across") was given him when his father witnessed a bright meteor streak through the sky on the night that he was born. Forty-three years old in 1811, Tecumseh was athletic and vigorous, a skillful hunter and a respected warrior. Unlike most of his contemporaries, he refused to mistreat prisoners or to make war on women and children. He was a spellbinding speaker whose reputation for eloquence was legendary (Edmunds, 19, 23–33, 178, 220–225; Barnard and Schwartzman, "Tecumseh," 491–493).

The steady loss of lands to the United States dismayed Tecumseh, who believed that "all the land belonged to all the Indians, and that not even the whole membership of a single tribe could alienate the property of the race." The Shawnee chief preached that Native Americans had only one hope of survival: red unity. The tribes must set aside past differences and form a confederacy to resist white expansion. While Tecumseh provided the charisma and political leadership to spur many discontented young warriors to his banner, his younger brother Tenskwatawa (The Prophet) helped transform his mission into a religious crusade. The brothers and their recruits built Prophet's Town, their stronghold on Tippecanoe Creek, a branch of the Wabash River in the southern Indiana Territory. By 1811, Tecumseh had preached his message of unity to northern tribes such as the Chippewas, Ottawas, and Kickapoos, and in the summer of that year he crossed the Ohio River with his interpreter, Sikaboo, and twenty mounted warriors and embarked on an ambitious trip south (Edmunds, 145–146; Barnard and Schwartzman, "Tecumseh," 491–493; Martin, 118–119).

Tecumseh first visited the Chickasaws, one of the smaller southeastern tribes, who lived in present-day northern Mississippi and northwestern Alabama. The Chickasaws were highly regarded as warriors, but they had been at peace with the Americans for some time, and the Natchez Trace ran through their nation. As in the Muscogee and Cherokee nations, mixed-blood Chickasaw planters and slave owners—such as George Colbert, who operated a ferry on the Tennessee River in present-day northwestern Alabama—played a dominant role in the nation's political affairs. A man of considerable clout in the Chickasaw nation and a shrewd entrepreneur, Colbert also ran a profitable inn, where one could buy a twenty-five-cent quart of whiskey for a dollar. Cherokee agent Return J. Meigs called him "extremely mercenary" (Gibson, 4, 64–65; Davis, 29–30).

Tecumseh's meeting with the Chickasaw chiefs took place in August 1811 at Colbert's home. After listening respectfully to his talk, Colbert rejected the Shawnee chief's plan. Many of the northern tribes affiliated with Tecumseh were former enemies of the Chickasaws, and they wanted nothing to do with them. The Chickasaws intended to remain at peace with the whites. The chiefs supplied Tecumseh with a mounted escort through their nation, but they made it clear that they would not join his confederacy (Gibson, 96; Edmunds, 146).

Undaunted, Tecumseh and his party continued southward into the large Choctaw nation. Scattered among some fifty towns (*okla*) in the flatlands of present-day Mississippi and southwestern Alabama and with a population of 20,000 people, the Choctaws (sometimes called Longhairs) were more farmers than warriors. They could be fierce in battle, and even Choctaw women were known to take up the war club if their homes were threatened. But they had always been friendly with the whites and were more staunchly loyal to the United States than any other tribe in the Old Southwest. The Choctaws were rapidly adopting white ways, raising corn as well as hogs and other livestock on their small farms. Like the Muscogees and Cherokees, they had a sophisticated political structure and were divided into three districts, each with a principal chief, or *mingo,* elected by the men of each district. A national council made decisions for the whole nation. And like their neighbors, the Choctaws were alarmed by increasing demands by white settlers for more and more of their land (DeRosier, 6–12; Hudson, 202; Rogers et al., 9–11; Davis, 280–283; Edmunds, 146–147).

The Shawnee and his party spent several days in September at the home of Mushulatubbee, the respected chief of the northeastern Choctaw district, near present-day Mashulaville, Mississippi. Mushulatubbee was very pro-American, and Tecumseh made no headway with him. But the most ardent opponent of the Shawnee chief was Pushmataha, chief of the southern Choctaw district. A celebrated warrior, Pushmataha won fame—and the name Eagle—while still a teenager when he took five scalps during a raid against the Osage west of the Mississippi. Wherever Tecumseh went in the Choctaw country, Pushmataha dogged his trail, urging local headmen to reject the Shawnee's message (Halbert and Ball, 41–42; Davis, 283; Edmunds, 147; Owen, 67–69).

Tecumseh spoke to the Choctaw council at Mokalusha, their main town, near present-day Philadelphia, Mississippi. Through his interpreter, Sikaboo—an excellent linguist who spoke Shawnee, English, Choctaw, and Muskogean—the war chief gave an impassioned talk, summarizing the history of the United States's policy toward the Native Americans and the gradual acquisition of tribal lands. Tecumseh proposed a confederacy of tribes and an alliance with Britain and preached a holy war against the whites (Edmunds, 147; Griffith, 71).

Choctaws viewed the land in the same way that the Muscogees and Cherokees did, that it belonged to the tribe in common and that it could not be ceded by individual chiefs. (When a Spanish negotiator had reminded one chief in 1792 that Britain had ceded the Choctaw lands to Spain after the Revolutionary War, the chief replied that the land had not been Britain's to give anyway.) But the Choctaws had seen a steady erosion of their territory to the whites. When the tribe incurred $46,000 in debts to the British firm of Panton, Leslie, and Forbes in 1805—debts that they were unable to pay—the United States agreed to assume payment of the debt in return for more than four million acres of Choctaw land. The Choctaw chiefs were sensitive about the loss of lands, and many of them liked the idea of cooperation with other tribes, but they were distrustful of an alliance with the British and especially wanted to remain at peace with the Americans. Pushmataha spoke vehemently against the Shawnee's message. "Be not deceived with illusive hopes," he cautioned the chiefs. "…Listen to the voice of prudence, ere you rashly act" (Davis, 282; DeRosier, 31–34; Halbert and Ball, 44–45).

Also opposing Tecumseh was John Pitchlynn, the federal interpreter for the Choctaws for more than forty years, whose home was in present-day Lowndes County, Mississippi. Pitchlynn was fiercely loyal to the United States, and one official wrote of him, "I do not believe that he has been or can be corrupted by any man acting against the government." Pitchlynn argued from the Bible "that the day of prophecy had passed," and urged the chiefs to reject the Shawnee and his message. Pushmataha threatened Tecumseh and any Choctaw who joined him with death if they returned to the nation. With hostility growing against him, especially among the younger Choctaws, the Shawnee chief thought it prudent to leave for the Muscogee nation (Baird, 10–11; Owen, 146–147; Griffith, 71; Edmunds, 147–148).

Tecumseh expected a much friendlier reception from the Muscogees, and he was not disappointed. The Shawnee party traveled up the Alabama River and gradually made their way into the Upper Creek towns, stopping at Autauga and Hickory Ground. Numbers of younger Muscogees seemed receptive to Tecumseh's talk, and several threw in their lot with the Shawnees.

The Muscogee capital at Tuckabatchee was teeming with activity when Tecumseh arrived there on September 20, 1811. The national council was in session, with Big Warrior, Hopoithle Miko, and many other prominent chiefs in attendance. Also on hand was agent Benjamin Hawkins, come to address the council on the necessity of running the Federal Road through the Muscogee nation. There were white traders as well, including Sam Dale from the 'Bigbee settlements; a few African Americans; and representatives from the Choctaw, Chickasaw, and even the Seminole tribes who were anxious to hear what the famous Shawnee war chief had to say. From the Cherokee nation came a delegation of forty-six observers led by the skeptical Ridge. As many as 5,000 people had gathered for what promised to be a memorable address, and Tecumseh's timing for his talk could not have been better (Edmunds, 149; Barnard and Schwartzman, "Tecumseh," 493; Ehle, 99; McDaniel, 5–6; Martin, 120; L. Thompson, 213).

Tecumseh and his party made an impressive appearance as they rode into Tuckabatchee. The twenty warriors who had accompanied their chief from the north were all dressed alike in fringed and beaded buckskin hunting shirts and leggings. Each wore a red headband with hawk and eagle feathers, and all had silver bands on their arms and wrists. Their hair hung in three long braids in back with temples shaved, and their faces bore red war paint under each eye. All carried rifles, tomahawks, and scalping knives. Tecumseh wore two long crane feathers, one red—for war to the Americans—and one white—for peace among the red tribes. The men dismounted and solemnly approached the town square where Big Warrior— who was as large in physical stature as he was in political influence—offered his pipe to Tecumseh. The Shawnee chief then passed the pipe to each of his warriors. Big Warrior indicated a large cabin near the edge of town that had been provided for the Shawnees' lodging, and the party made their way there to rest. That night Tecumseh and his warriors—stripped to their loincloths—electrified their audience by performing the Shawnees' Dance of the Lakes, a passionate and compelling exhibition (Ehle, 99–100; Griffith, 73; Halbert and Ball, 42–43).

Tecumseh seemed surprised to see Hawkins among the dignitaries in town, and he apparently preferred to wait until the agent had left Tuckabatchee before addressing the formal council. Each day he managed to find some excuse to put off the meeting, and another week passed while Hawkins and the other leaders waited for him to speak. Sam Dale was suspicious and warned Hawkins that "the Shawnees intended mischief," but the agent did not take Tecumseh seriously. Publicly the Shawnee chief spoke of the Native American tribes associating together in friendship while remaining at peace with the whites. In private meetings his message was more extreme, urging the Muscogees to throw off all trappings of white civilization (Barnard and Schwartzman, "Tecumseh," 493; Edmunds, 149; Griffith, 73–74; McDaniel, 6; Owsley, 11–12).

Unwilling to wait any longer, Hawkins addressed the council on the controversial matter of the Federal Road. He insisted that the whites must have a road through the Muscogee nation, that it was essential for marketing their goods and for national defense. The chiefs were angry, but Hawkins made them understand that the road was going through whether they wanted it or not, and he finally persuaded them to give in by promising them payments of goods. Hawkins returned to his agency on the Flint, but he asked his ally William McIntosh to keep an eye on Tecumseh and report what he was up to (Martin, 120–121; Edmunds, 149).

Tecumseh's big moment arrived on September 30. The Shawnee party left their lodge at noon and made their way in single file to the council house. Naked except for their loincloths and smeared with black paint, they carried red war clubs and wore expressions of anger—"like a procession of devils," Dale reported. They marched three times around the central square, and Tecumseh scattered tobacco and sumac at each corner and finally on the town's sacred flame as a purification ritual. Still in single file, they strode into the council house, where they gave a ferocious war cry that shattered the afternoon calm. Tecumseh proffered a wampum bag and a peace pipe to Big Warrior, and the speaker smoked and then passed the pipe to the other chiefs. "Every thing was still as death," Dale recalled, "...only the gentle rustle of the falling leaves" (Griffith, 74; McDaniel, 7; L. Thompson, 232).

All eyes were turned on the Shawnee war chief and all ears attentive as he spoke. Through the interpreter, Sikaboo, Tecumseh gave one of the most stirring talks of his career. He reminded his audience of the greed of the white settlers for the red man's land, a greed that soon would reduce the Muscogees to the status of black slaves. Only radical measures would save the Native Americans. All tribes must return to their traditional way of life and seek spiritual guidance from their shamans and holy men. They must join forces for a war to drive out the Americans. He predicted that the United States and Britain would soon go to war with one another and that the British would help the tribes to regain their lands. "Oh, Muscogees!" Tecumseh cried. "Brethren of my mother! Brush from your eyelids the sleep of slavery, and strike for vengeance and your country!" The effect on the chiefs was electrifying, Dale reported, and "a thousand tomahawks were brandished in the air." It moved even Big Warrior, although the Tuckabatchee chief was not a supporter of Tecumseh. The younger Muscogee warriors seemed especially impressed (Edmunds, 150; Ehle, 101; Griffith, 74; McDaniel, 7–8; Owsley, 12–13).

First to respond to the Shawnee's talk was William Weatherford. He asked the Shawnee why—if so eager for a war with the whites—he was not already leading the northern tribes into battle. Tecumseh was quick to reply to this question. "All Indians must work under the same yoke," he explained. "...There has already been too much partisan warfare. It must be made general." But Weatherford was not convinced, and he flatly rejected Tecumseh's message. For the Muscogees to follow the Shawnee's advice would bring war with the United States, he warned, and that would mean the ruin of their nation. As for the British, they cared no more for the red man than the Americans, and to depend on them for military aid was sheer folly (Griffith, 77; L. Thompson, 237).

Also clearly hostile to Tecumseh's talk was the Cherokee delegation led by Ridge. Meeting later that night in private with the Shawnee, Ridge told him that the Cherokee nation was at peace with the United States and intended to remain so. And he warned Tecumseh that if he came to the Cherokee country, he would kill him (Barnard and Schwartzman, "Tecumseh," 494; Ehle, 102).

But there were those who were visibly impressed with what Tecumseh was saying. Sikaboo reinforced this with a promise that those who accepted the Shawnee's message would receive spiritual power. The Shawnees assured their listeners that the spirits would protect them if they fought against the whites, that the earth would swallow up white armies if they approached the Muscogee towns. Younger mixed-bloods Hillis Hadjo (Josiah Francis) of Autauga and Cusseta Hadjo (Jim Boy) of Autossee took all this in eagerly. Tallassee chiefs Hopoithle Miko and Peter McQueen (Talmuches Hadjo) also seemed very interested. But Big Warrior, William McIntosh, and the Lower Creek chiefs were committed to supporting the Americans (Edmunds, 151; McDaniel, 9; Martin, 126; McLoughlin, 188; Owsley, 13).

Tecumseh visited several more Muscogee towns before returning to Tuckabatchee to speak once more before the council on November 14. Again he argued passionately for the Muscogees to join with him in his confederacy of tribes. Big Warrior was reluctant to endorse his plan, and Tecumseh was clearly angered. The Shawnee threatened serious consequences for anyone who took his message lightly. He would stamp his foot when he returned to the Shawnee country, and the earth would shake, rattling the Muscogee land to its foundations. When he left Tuckabatchee, about thirty Muscogee warriors, including Tustunuggachee (Little Warrior), went with him. Sikaboo remained in the Muscogee nation to cultivate more recruits (Barnard and Schwartzman, "Tecumseh," 494; Edmunds, 151; McDaniel, 9; L. Thompson, 239).

When Tecumseh reached the Indiana country, he was dismayed to learn that a major setback had taken place during his absence. Brigadier General William Henry Harrison, governor of the Indiana Territory, had advanced his soldiers against Prophet's Town, the Shawnees' camp on Tippecanoe Creek, and Tenskwatawa—acting against Tecumseh's instructions to avoid armed conflict until the intertribal confederacy had solidified—had decided to attack. On November 8, 1811, the Shawnees launched a dawn attack on Harrison's troops, who turned back the assault and then routed the Prophet's warriors. When the smoke had cleared at Tippecanoe, red corpses littered the field. Harrison went on to burn Prophet's Town. The defeat was a serious reversal for Tecumseh but in no way ended his attempts to foment a war against the whites. Harrison's victory at Tippecanoe, while lauded by frontier whites, did not really alter events shaping up in the Muscogee nation.

As if to fulfill Tecumseh's prophecy, nature seemed to be speaking to the Muscogees. On December 16, 1811, a major earthquake shook the area near New Madrid, Missouri, on the Mississippi—an area that, by a remarkable coincidence, Tecumseh and his party had passed through on his trip back to the Indiana Territory. Startled citizens rolled out of bed in the predawn hours as the earth thundered—"a most tremendous noise," according to one resident. Settlers at St. Stephens felt the ground rumble "so as to shake the fowls off their roosts, and made the houses shake very much." The Muscogee nation experienced these effects, too, and there were reports of tremors in the Cherokee nation, with homes rocked from their foundations and sinkholes as large as thirty yards wide formed.

Aftershocks continued for the next two months and were felt as far away as Baltimore and New Orleans (Dean, 164–166; McLoughlin, 182; Martin, 114–115).

Some Muscogees also believed that a fiery comet visible in the heavens in the fall of 1811 recalled Tecumseh's words that "you shall see my arm of fire stretched athwart the sky." Such signs coming on the heels of Tecumseh's visit enhanced the credibility of the Muscogee shamans and prophets. Josiah Francis, who was especially taken with the Shawnee's talk, soon became a prophet himself, claiming visions of his own and winning over many followers, and he began to take an active role in the Muscogee religious revival. Prominent shaman Paddy Walsh—who was fluent in English, Muscogee, and Choctaw—also was quick to embrace the new movement. The religious revival took on greater political strength when Hopoithle Miko, Big Warrior's rival, and the Okfuskee chief Menawa, a bitter enemy of William McIntosh, joined the fray (Owsley, 13–15; Martin, 122–128).

The rebels became known as Red Sticks, because of their red war clubs (a symbol of justice) and because of the chiefs' traditional practice of marking time by discarding one stick from a bundle of small sticks each day until the arrival of an important event such as an assembly of warriors. The sticks were painted red in wartime. It is possible that Tecumseh may have intended this system to better coordinate the movements of the tribes in his confederacy (Martin, 129, 187; Owsley, 13–14; Saunt, 250).

The movement spread rapidly in the Upper Creek towns during the early months of 1812. The radicals intimidated, beat, and even murdered those who opposed them. There was an element of fanaticism among the Red Sticks that alarmed frontier whites, and the prophets' zeal often took on physical manifestations. William Weatherford's brother-in-law Sam Moniac described a meeting with Cusseta Hadjo (Jim Boy). "He shook hands with me," Moniac wrote, "and immediately began to tremble and jerk in every part of his frame, and the very calves of his legs would be convulsed and he would get entirely out of breath with agitation" (Owsley, 15).

The earthquake late in 1811 added fuel to the growing religious revival in the Cherokee nation, but the movement's anger was blunted by young mixed-blood leaders like Ridge. Many Cherokees sought meaning in the signs and visions that had visited their nation. While some saw in them the Great Spirit's displeasure for embracing the ways of the whites, others believed them to be a sign to show them their own spiritual weakness. As in the Muscogee nation, a number of minor prophets claimed power but lost face when their prophecies did not come to pass. As the movement peaked in mid-1812, the young mixed-bloods sought to persuade their people that they could appease the Great Spirit by returning to their warrior traditions and by winning glory—not in a war with the Americans, but as their allies in the coming war against the British (McLoughlin, 182–185).

Hawkins, who underestimated the strength of the Red Sticks, still considered the movement the work of a handful of fanatics. He trusted the Lower Creek chiefs, who, he reported, "unanimously refused to smoke the [war] pipe." But things turned uglier as the radicals began to attack whites. In May 1812, Red Sticks murdered settler William Lott in an unprovoked attack near his home. Citing the 1790 Treaty of New York, which required the Muscogees to punish their own people who had committed crimes against whites, Hawkins called on Big Warrior for justice. Big Warrior entrusted this task to William McIntosh, head of the Muscogees' national police force. McIntosh and his warriors carried out their mission and executed the murderers, one of whom had sought sanctuary in Hopoithle Miko's town. McIntosh shot the man dead in the town square. An angry Hopoithle Miko considered the incident an offense to his sovereignty, widening the rupture between the Upper Creeks and Lower Creeks and threatening to plunge the Muscogee nation into civil war. The danger became even more ominous as the Red Sticks looked to the British for arms (Barnard and Schwartzman, "Tecumseh," 494–495; Martin, 125; Owsley, 15).

CHAPTER 3

The Opportunists

In the 1790s William Augustus Bowles, a former British military officer, plotted to detach part of the southern United States border region and create an independent state—with the backing of Britain. Married to a Muscogee woman, Bowles gained great influence among the Muscogees and Seminoles and even proclaimed himself king of the independent nation of Muscogee. Bowles also attempted to take over the profitable operations of the British trading firm of Panton, Leslie, and Forbes. At the head of an armed force of Muscogees and Seminoles, he captured the Spanish outpost of St. Marks and the Panton store. Finally, fed up with Bowles-incited border raids and intrigues, Spanish agents convinced a group of Upper Muscogees including William Weatherford to capture Bowles in 1803. Bowles died a prisoner in Cuba, and his dream of an independent state of Muscogee collapsed.

The Bowles affair illustrates just how vulnerable was the United States frontier, an area not firmly controlled by any one nation. Adventurers and opportunists were always ready and eager to create enclaves for themselves by appealing to the competing colonial powers. The Old Southwest was the back door to control of the Gulf Coast and New Orleans. The nation that controlled New Orleans held the gateway to the interior of North America. Both Britain and Spain were anxious to reoccupy the Old Southwest and had much to gain in their involvement with the Native American tribes. There was always an international dimension to events on the frontier.

The 1795 Treaty of San Lorenzo (or Pinckney's Treaty) clarified a long-running boundary dispute between Spanish Florida and the United States, and Spain relinquished control of territory north of the thirty-first parallel. The Spanish actually did not evacuate their small post at St. Stephens—formerly in the disputed zone—until February 1799, when their commander there—weary of waiting—simply entrusted the keys to the fort to a neighbor and withdrew with his soldiers to Mobile. Later that year American soldiers moved in and constructed Fort Stoddert on the Mobile River to the south. Congress organized American lands south of Tennessee and north of the thirty-first parallel into the Mississippi Territory.

The situation on the southern frontier became more precarious in 1800, when Spain transferred the vast Louisiana Territory to French control. Although Spain had been antagonistic to U.S. interests, the presence of France—a far stronger military threat—gravely concerned American leaders. For Thomas Jefferson, New Orleans was "on the globe one single spot, the possessor of which is our natural and habitual enemy." The potential threat resolved itself in 1803 when France sold the Louisiana Territory to the United States. Americans now controlled New Orleans and the mouth of the Mississippi. On the other hand, the eastern boundary of the Louisiana Territory with Spanish Florida was unclear. James Monroe and Robert R. Livingston, who represented the United States in negotiations with France for Louisiana, both maintained that Spanish West Florida, which included Mobile and Pensacola, was part of the purchase. Spain denied that this was the case (G. A. Smith, 4–5).

The cession of Muscogee lands was a linchpin in the western land policy of the United States, a newly independent and weak power with much to fear from British, Spanish, and French imperial aims. The territory in the Old Southwest contained few Anglo American settlers. What was needed was rapid American settlement to create a barrier against the Europeans, to "[p]lant on the Mississippi a population equal to its own defense," Secretary of War Henry Dearborn urged in 1803. The sooner the Muscogee lands were opened up, the sooner this goal would be achieved, and a southwest available for settlement would act as an outlet for the expanding U.S. population as well (Davis, 296).

Meanwhile, tensions between the United States and Britain were escalating. War nearly broke out in June 1807 following the British capture of a U.S. warship, the *Chesapeake*, during which several American sailors were killed and four alleged British deserters were removed. "War Hawks" in Congress demanded war with Britain and an invasion of Canada. The war scare passed, but the causes of the difficulty—the impressment of American seamen and the threat of British-instigated Native American unrest on the frontier—continued. In 1808 Jefferson, anticipating a coming conflict with Britain, encouraged American settlement of the Mississippi Territory to bolster it against enemy attack. "It is now," he wrote in a message to the U.S. Senate, "perhaps, become as interesting to obtain footing for a strong settlement of militia along our southern frontier, eastward of the Mississippi, as on the west of that river" (Guice, 168).

Many white settlers in the Mississippi Territory welcomed a war with the British, whom they accused of encouraging unrest among the Native Americans. In 1809 George Gaines wrote, "In case of a war with G. B. we expect to have warm work here, and should she land many Troops in the W. Floridas we shall not be disappointed, for the Creeks, a most powerful Nation of Indians, often express a partiality for the B. Government." Gaines recognized the vulnerability of white settlers on the frontier. "Surrounded as we will be by enemies on all sides," he wrote, "we can only hope to save ourselves by gathering together in Forts & until we get help from Georgia Tennessee & Kentucky." "[T]he Govt of the U.S. has many Enemys[,]" John Adair wrote from Natchez in 1809, "and but few warm friends here." Some white settlers were inclined toward Britain, and "British agents are now amongst these people" (Davis, 308).

Fear of a war with Great Britain motivated U.S. officials to push for a road through the Muscogee country. The road would be needed for the movement of troops and supplies to protect the vitally important Gulf Coast and New Orleans. At the Muscogees' national council in September 1811 Hawkins informed the chiefs that despite their opposition, the road must be built. By November 1811 the military road from the Flint to Fort Stoddert was open. The Muscogees bitterly resented both the road and the manner in which it was forced on their nation, and the issue was a major grievance leading to the Creek War.

From Spanish Pensacola, the powerful British trading company of Panton, Leslie, and Forbes (later John Forbes and Company) continued to trade with the Muscogees long after Britain was forced to give up Florida at the end of the Revolutionary War. Although many Americans, including leading politicians, believed the British were using Pensacola as a base to furnish the southeastern tribes with arms, there is no real evidence of such, at least not of official aid. As for individual British traders operating out of the Apalachicola area, they probably were secretly encouraging the tribes to make trouble for the Americans. British officials more than likely knew about this and did nothing to suppress it. Native American chiefs and traders in the South often visited Nassau, the lively British port in the nearby Bahamas, and American officials believed British merchants there were supplying the tribes with weapons. British warships frequently put in at Pensacola and Mobile, and Indian leaders sometimes met with officers from these ships (Owsley, 2, 8–9, 18–19).

As for the Spanish, they had much to be worried about—namely, their colonies of East and West Florida, coveted by the United States. The Napoleonic Wars had weakened Spain's military presence there, and the isolated territories were hard to defend. The Spanish were wary of relying on British military assistance, so an alliance with the red men remained the only card they had left to play. Spain had promised the Muscogees and Seminoles arms and supplies should war break out. At the same time, the Spanish realized that in a major conflict between the United States and the

Indians, the tribes would certainly be the losers. Their strategy was to provide them with enough aid to help them defend themselves, but not
enough to encourage an all-out attack on the Anglo-American settlers,
which would provoke a war (Owsley, 2–3, 9–10, 20–21, 24).

Both Jefferson and his presidential successor, James Madison, regarded
Spanish Florida as a potential problem should war with Britain erupt.
There was the danger that Spain, an ally of Britain in the wars with
Napoleon, would allow the redcoats to use Florida as a staging area for
operations against the Americans, to use the Gulf ports as bases for British
ships, and to incite the Indians to raid across the border. Even without official or covert Spanish cooperation, the local authorities in Florida lacked
the means to patrol the border and prevent the raids that Americans
feared. The solution seemed to be somehow—peacefully if possible, but
by force if necessary—for Florida to become a U.S. possession. Underlying
strategic considerations, Florida was a prize for land-hungry settlers.

In the fall of 1810, American filibusters led by Reuben Kemper seized
Baton Rouge and part of West Florida between the Mississippi and Pearl
Rivers. Proclaiming independence for all of West Florida, they requested
that Congress annex this area to the United States. Madison was uneasy
lest the insurrection set off conflict with Spain and jeopardize diplomatic
efforts to secure all of Florida. But he felt prompt action was called for, and
on October 27 he issued a proclamation annexing the West Florida region
between the Perdido and Mississippi.

It soon became clear that the Americans were not strong enough to seize
the area of West Florida between the Pearl and Perdido, which included
Mobile. Madison hoped to get it through negotiation, but more hotheaded
leaders contemplated resorting to force. Kemper met at Fort Stoddert in
late 1810 with local militia officers John and James Caller and Joseph P.
Kennedy. The men discussed an expedition against Mobile, but Judge
Harry Toulmin was able to convince the commander of the Fort Stoddert
garrison not to support them.

The issues simmering between the United States and Britain finally
boiled over in the spring of 1812, and Congress declared war on June 19.
American officials worried about possible British contact with the Muscogees. "War is declared against Great Britain," Secretary of War William
Eustis wrote to Benjamin Hawkins on June 19. "Your vigilance and attention are rendered particularly necessary in your agency at this time, and
no exertions or reasonable Expenses will be spared to keep the Indians
quiet and friendly" (Creek Letters).

But many whites in the Old Southwest welcomed the news of the declaration of war. "None, as it seems to me, was ever juster," one man wrote.
"And we never make peace, till our rights at sea, as well as at land, are
acknowledged." And a territorial delegate promised, "[W]e really do
intend to pull John Bull by the nose" (Davis, 308; McLemore, 227).

The first year of the conflict went badly for the United States. A poorly executed three-pronged invasion of Canada failed miserably, even though—with Britain deeply engaged in war with Napoleon—the only forces available for its defense were a small number of regulars, Canadian militia, and Native American allies. Fort Dearborn (present-day Chicago) fell to the British on August 15, 1812. On the following day, the American commander at Detroit, confronted by a much smaller enemy force—600 Shawnee warriors under Tecumseh, who had joined the British as he had promised, and 730 Canadian militia—surrendered the outpost without putting up a fight.

On January 22, 1813, Colonel Henry Proctor's army of British regulars, Canadian militia, and Shawnees attacked the American base at French-town on the Raisin River, near Monroe, Michigan. About 550 American troops, largely Kentucky militia, surrendered to Proctor after he assured them that they would not be mistreated. Instead, Proctor failed to control his allies—among them Tustunuggachee and the Red Sticks who had joined Tecumseh—who massacred many of the wounded prisoners, some of whom were burned to death in their cabins. The incident, known as the River Raisin Massacre, inflamed American settlers along the northwestern frontier, and they cried out for revenge (Freehoff, 32; Elting, 161).

Proctor and Tecumseh attacked American troops at Fort Meigs on the Maumee River in Ohio on May 6, 1813. Around 600 Americans either died or fell captive, and again Proctor failed to check the Shawnees, who fell on the prisoners and scalped twenty before Tecumseh arrived and put a stop to it. "Are there no men here?" the Shawnee chief demanded. He confronted Proctor and demanded to know why the British commander had let the warriors get out of hand. "Your Indians cannot be controlled," Proctor responded, "cannot be commanded." "You are not fit to command," the disgusted Tecumseh shot back. "Go put on your petticoats." Tecumseh became more and more disillusioned with his British allies as the campaign wore on (Freehoff, 32).

American expansionists had failed in their attempt to conquer Canada, and the first year of the war with Britain brought them no closer to acquiring the Floridas either. Sporadic troubles had flared up for some time along the U.S. border with Spanish Florida. It was in this area that the Seminole nation existed. The first Seminoles were actually Muscogees who had migrated into Florida in the eighteenth century to form permanent settlements as they expanded their deer hunting activities. They brought with them the political and social organization of the Muscogees, including the clans, warrior hierarchy, and town governments. But, joining the descendants of other Native American tribes who had never been conquered by the Spanish, the independent Seminoles became a nation unto themselves. "They do not follow our rules," the Muscogee speaker Big Warrior said, "and dont go by our orders" (Covington, 5–11; Saunt, 241).

To the forests and swamps of the Seminole lands came escaped slaves from Georgia seeking freedom among the renegade tribes. Encouraged by the Spanish, who granted them sanctuary, African Americans formed their own free settlements—sometimes called Maroon towns—in Florida. "The Negroes dwell in towns apart from the Indians," a white observer wrote, "and are the finest looking people I have ever seen. They dress and live pretty much like the Indians, each having a gun, and hunting a portion of his time. Like the Indians, they plant in common, and farm an Indian field apart, which they attend together." He also commented on the Seminoles' humane treatment of their slaves: "The Negroes uniformly testify to the kind treatment they receive from their Indian Masters, who are indulgent, and require but little labour from them" (Covington, 29–30).

The Seminoles also had a hierarchy of mixed-bloods who exercised considerable political power in their nation. William Augustus Bowles's father-in-law, mixed-blood chief Thomas Perryman (also known as Kinache), was chief of the Mikasuki settlement at Lake Miccosukee. He was a slave owner and trader, and he owned herds of cattle and horses. King Payne, chief of Payne's Town or Alachua (near present-day Gainesville, Florida), was a prosperous planter who owned 1,500 head of cattle, 400 horses, herds of sheep and goats, and twenty slaves. The mixed-bloods traded with merchants at Panton's store in Pensacola, and they enjoyed fair relations with the Spanish, who sought to represent themselves as protectors of the tribes while portraying the Americans as the enemy (Covington, 20, 22, 25, 29; Saunt, 236; Wright, 126).

U.S. tension with the Seminoles increased when American plans to wrest East Florida away from Spain began to unfold. With the support of Congress, Madison commissioned elderly ex–Georgia governor George Mathews to try to obtain Florida peacefully, in order to beat stronger powers to the punch. Georgians considered their state especially vulnerable—with Spanish Florida and the Seminoles to the south, the Muscogees and Cherokees to the west, and a long coastline open to possible British attack—and many saw a valuable opportunity in acquiring Florida. Trouble had plagued the Florida border for years, as white settlers and squatters from Georgia—just as they were doing along the Muscogee frontier to the west—intruded on Seminole lands, grazing their cattle and sometimes raiding Seminole towns.

When the Spanish rebuffed his diplomatic overtures, Mathews decided to attempt an armed takeover of the weak colony. With the tacit support of Colonel Thomas A. Smith's U.S. troops who had occupied the St. Marys River crossings at the Georgia border, Mathews invaded Florida with a small "Patriot Army"—some 200 men—and seized the Spanish post of Fernandina on Amelia Island in March 1812. But to take the heavily defended Spanish bastion at St. Augustine, the Patriots needed the support of the Seminoles and Maroons, both of whom had strong reasons for remaining loyal to Spain. The Seminoles feared what their kinsmen the Muscogees feared in Georgia and the Alabama country—the takeover of their lands by white settlers. Spain had given the blacks a safe haven in Florida, and they realized that they would be reduced to slavery if the area came under U.S. control.

The aged Payne, who at first preferred neutrality, finally gave in to the demands of his younger warriors—incited by Spanish promises of ten dollars per scalp—and declared war on the Americans. In July and August of 1812, the Seminoles struck at isolated plantations along the St. Johns River, killed eight white settlers, and captured over a hundred slaves, as well as cattle that they drove to St. Augustine—to the welcome relief of the hungry Spanish garrison. Prince, a free black, led a largely African American force in a September 12 attack on an American wagon train escorted by twenty U.S. marines that severed the Patriots' supply line. As deaths and sickness took their toll, the Patriots abandoned their position near St. Augustine and retreated north (Covington, 29; Saunt, 238, 239; Mahon, "Newnan," 149).

The Patriot defeat was followed by an incursion by Colonel Daniel Newnan's Georgia militia volunteers, called into the field in June but quickly hamstrung by lack of supplies and horses and by short-term enlistments that expired in September—familiar problems that would also plague American forces in the Creek War. Newnan could persuade only 117 soldiers to extend their enlistments, and he crossed the St. Johns River with this small force on September 24 and moved toward Alachua. On September 27, the Georgians encountered Payne and his Seminoles, who held them off for several hours while 200 more Seminoles and blacks led by Payne's younger brother Bowlegs hit the rear of Newnan's column after sunset. Newnan's troops dug in, and for seven days the Seminoles and blacks had them under siege. When their supplies gave out, Newnan's soldiers were down to eating horse meat and alligators before pulling back eight miles to a more secure position, where they dug in again (Covington, 29–30; Mahon, "Newnan," 149–151; Quimby, 150–155).

Moving out the next afternoon, the Georgians made only five more miles before heavy gunfire forced them to take cover again. They experienced the nightmare of combat with the Seminoles on the Seminoles' home ground, and the comments of some of the Georgian officers mirror those of white soldiers fighting the Muscogee Red Sticks later. The Seminoles had methodically picked off the soldiers' remaining horses. Ambushes plagued Newnan's starving, exhausted troops as they slogged their way through the swamp, sometimes plunging into water waist-deep, sweating and cursing, to free wagons from the mud. Especially terrifying to them was the Seminoles' war dance, similar to that performed by the Red Sticks. "They commenced the most horrid yells imaginable," a fever-ridden Newnan wrote, "imitating the cries of almost every animal of the forest, their chiefs advancing in front in a stooping, serpentine manner, and making the most wild and fanatic gestures." Demoralization quickly set in. A sick and disgusted Georgia militia officer bemoaned the "woeful state of this province which we are harassing by our inexplicable political and military manoeuvers" (Mahon, "Newnan," 150–151; Fredriksen, 83, 107).

Bogged down in the swamp, pinned down by Seminole snipers, the Georgians were debilitated and nearly famished when a relief column finally reached them. Newnan was elated just to get his troops out of the swamp alive. He had lost nine men killed and eight wounded; eight more men were missing. The Seminoles had also suffered casualties. Payne had been wounded in the first encounter, and his warriors had now used up most of their ammunition (Mahon, "Newnan," 151; Saunt, 240; Covington, 30).

Payne envisioned a confederation of the Florida tribes, much as Tecumseh proposed for the northern tribes. He suggested such a plan to a general council attended by most of the major chiefs. Payne believed that the Seminoles could also count on the blacks—"their best soldiers," according to Colonel Newnan—to fight on their side, and on the Spanish, who would provide supplies. Together they would expel the whites from Florida. But most of the chiefs rejected Payne's plan, and the old chief died soon after from his wounds received in the recent fighting. The Seminoles assured agent Benjamin Hawkins that they would restore the property (and slaves) that they had taken from the Georgia planters if he would guarantee peace (Covington, 31; Saunt, 240).

The next phase in the Florida border war injected a new element—the Tennessee militia—into the mix. Colonel John Williams, the Tennessee adjutant general, left Knoxville in December 1812 and entered the Seminole country with 240 mounted volunteers. Governor David B. Mitchell of Georgia was planning another offensive into Florida, as well. Williams's Tennesseans crossed the St. Marys River and rendezvoused with 220 Georgia troops, led by regular army officer Colonel Thomas Smith, for a three-week offensive into Seminole country.

The combined militia force marched on Payne's Town on February 8, 1813, but the Seminoles had deserted it and withdrawn, so they pushed forward ten or twelve miles to Bowlegs Town (near present-day Micanopy, Florida), where they engaged in a firefight with Bowlegs's warriors that lasted several hours. The troops established a base for their operations and conducted daily raids on nearby Seminole villages, where they burned homes and crops. They were unable to engage the Seminole warriors, who temporarily retreated to the safety of the swamps. The white soldiers finally withdrew from Seminole country on February 24. They left behind twenty Seminoles killed, 386 houses burned, and some 2,000 bushels of corn and 2,000 deerskins destroyed. They took with them 300 horses, 400 head of cattle, and nine Seminole and black prisoners. Bowlegs led part of the Seminoles from Alachua westward to the Suwannee River, where he established a new settlement near Suwannee Old Town, a colony of the Upper Muscogee. There he set about rebuilding his herds of cattle and horses (Covington, 31–33; Saunt, 246; Quimby, 157–158).

The soldiers' tactics against the Seminole towns—systematically destroying their homes and food supplies—was typical of those used by white troops against Native Americans in earlier conflicts. The Seminoles' response—withdrawing to the swamps and avoiding open battle—was also characteristic. The 1812–1813 Florida border war between the Seminoles and blacks and the American troops was only the first phase of a larger conflict between Native Americans and the United States in the War of 1812 period (Sugden, 273).

The eager participation of African Americans in the war alarmed the Georgia settlers, who feared the outbreak of a bloody slave insurrection like the one that had devastated Haiti a decade earlier. The Seminoles also realized that the Georgians would never agree to peace unless they returned all the fugitive slaves within their nation. Thomas Perryman summed up American motivations in a letter to the Spanish governor at Pensacola: "Am[e]rica want[s] [to] take negro[es] belong[ing] to the Ind[i]ans." The blacks realized this too. After the February 1813 American offensive, the African Americans separated from the Seminoles and operated on their own, but still fighting as their allies. Although the war on the Florida frontier had subsided for now, as the focus of military activity shifted elsewhere, the conflict was far from over (Saunt, 237, 247).

In February 1813, the Madison government ordered General James Wilkinson, U.S. commander for the Seventh Military District at New Orleans, to move against Spanish-occupied Mobile. At the head of 600 troops of the Third and Seventh U.S. Infantry Regiments, Wilkinson arrived before the Gulf City on April 10. Lieutenant Colonel John Bowyer with 400 soldiers from Fort Stoddert moved south to sever land communications between Mobile and Pensacola. Wilkinson and his troops landed south of Fort Charlotte, the Spanish bastion guarding Mobile, on the morning of April 12. Bowyer's troops arrived that same morning and placed five artillery pieces north of the fort (Elting, 158–159; G. A. Smith, 14).

Wilkinson sent a dispatch to Captain Cayetano Perez, the Spanish commander, assuring him that the American troops had not come as enemies of Spain but were there to "relieve the brave garrison which you so worthily command, from the occupancy of a post within the legitimate limits of the United States." Despite his anger at such a galling message—to which he submitted a formal protest—Perez knew that his sixty ill-fed soldiers were in no position to fight. The garrison at Pensacola, fifty-five miles to the east, was in no better shape and was unable to provide reinforcements. Total Spanish forces in West Florida numbered less than 300 men (Elting, 158–159; G. A. Smith, 15).

Faced with an impossible defense, Perez surrendered Fort Charlotte on April 15. The Spanish garrison marched out and boarded American ships bound for Pensacola. Without any bloodshed and without a gun being fired, U.S. troops had occupied Mobile, the only territorial gain for the United States during the War of 1812, taken from a country with which America was not officially at war. Mobile was an American city now, and for the first time the United States controlled the mouth of the Alabama river system. Wilkinson decided that he could better defend the Gulf City by fortifying Mobile Point thirty miles south of the city where a new fort could command the entrance into Mobile Bay. Engineers began work on the new outpost, and in June 1813 Bowyer took over the work of finishing it. American troops began moving cannon from old Fort Charlotte to the new fort, called Fort Bowyer, now the city's main defense.

Now the Spanish were becoming increasingly worried about an American offensive against Pensacola, and the governor of West Florida, Mauricio Zuniga, decided to provide aid to the Red Sticks. He felt that by inciting a Muscogee-American conflict, he might force the Americans to cancel their plans to move on Pensacola and possibly withdraw from Mobile as well. Although he later denied doing so, evidence indicates that Zuniga actually issued an invitation to the Red Stick leaders to come to Pensacola. The problem for Zuniga was that he had no arms or supplies to give the Muscogees, at least not at this time. He probably intended to summon the Red Stick leaders to Pensacola for a preliminary planning session, but the Muscogees believed they were going to receive immediate aid. When about sixty of them arrived in Pensacola in May 1813—expecting to meet with Zuniga and be furnished with arms and supplies—they found that he had been replaced by Don Mateo Gonzalez Manrique, who dismissed them and provided them with nothing (Owsley, 24–25).

Shortly afterward, Gonzalez Manrique came around to Zuniga's way of thinking and decided to arm the Indians after all. He notified the captain general of Cuba, Juan Ruiz Apodaca, that he feared an American attack on Pensacola and that he could not hope to defend the town without the aid of the Indians. Ruiz Apodaca enthusiastically approved providing arms to the Muscogees. Gonzalez Manrique requisitioned arms from Cuba, but before they arrived in Pensacola, a second group of Muscogees was already there, and he would have to turn them away empty-handed as well (Owsley, 25–26).

Although sympathetic to the aims of the Red Sticks, neither Britain nor Spain was prepared to provide military aid to them in the critical summer of 1813. The war that broke out that summer was premature and would have serious negative consequences for the war faction of the Muscogees.

CHAPTER 4

Collision Course

In late February 1813, Red Sticks savagely murdered seven white families in the Ohio River region. Led by Tustunuggachee, the culprits were from the party that had gone north with Tecumseh and were on their way back to enlist more recruits among the Muscogees. James Robertson, agent to the Chickasaws, wrote of the incident to Hawkins: "Seven families have been murdered near the mouth of the Ohio, and most cruelly mangled, showing all the savage barbarity that could be invented. One woman cut open, a child taken and stuck on a stake." A horrified Hawkins again called on Big Warrior for justice (Griffith, 84–85).

Again William McIntosh commanded the party sent out to apprehend the murderers. According to their intelligence, Tustunuggachee and his party were at Hickory Ground, a town near the confluence of the Coosa and Tallapoosa, and after an all-night ride, McIntosh and his men reached and surrounded the house where the murderers slept. During the gun battle that followed, the Red Sticks inside the barricaded home exhausted their ammunition but refused to surrender. McIntosh ordered the house set afire, and five fugitives were all either burned to death or were killed while trying to escape. Tustunuggachee was absent from the home, but the following day the "law menders" located and killed him too (Griffith, 86).

McIntosh, Big Warrior, and Alexander Cornells hoped that the execution of Tustunuggachee and his party would help alleviate any doubts about their own loyalty. "You think that we lean to the Shawnee tribes," they wrote Hawkins, "because you saw Tecumseh and his party dance in our square, around our fire, and some of our foolish people believed their foolish talk.... You need not be jealous that we shall take up arms against the United States: we mean to kill all our red people that spill the blood of our white friends" (Griffith, 86).

But instead of helping to quell the Red Stick rebellion, the actions of McIntosh and Big Warrior seemed only to make things worse. In a final attempt to suppress the insurgent movement, the chiefs challenged the prophets to come to Tuckabatchee and demonstrate their powers—to prove that they indeed were what they claimed to be. When the Red Sticks in the Alabama towns received this summons, they were so enraged that they killed the messenger and scalped him. The news shocked Hawkins, who had regarded the Alabamas as "the most industrious and best behaved of all our Indians." Now it seemed that the towns along the Alabama had become a hotbed of fanaticism (Griffith, 80, 87).

As the Red Sticks' anger boiled over, they began a wave of reprisals against the peace faction. The rebels sought out and killed nine of McIntosh's law menders who had taken part in the executions of Tustunuggachee's group. They burned and pillaged all along the Alabama River, killing livestock and destroying plows and other implements of white civilization. The prophets proclaimed a march on Tuckabatchee and Coweta and threatened to destroy the two towns and everyone in them. It was what Hawkins had dreaded but hoped would never happen. He had downplayed the spread of the Red Stick movement in his reports to his superiors, and now the Muscogee nation was torn by civil war.

Twenty-nine of the thirty-four Upper Creek towns were firmly in the Red Stick camp. The rebellion spread from the Alabamas to towns on the Coosa and Tallapoosa Rivers. As many as 9,000 people may have joined the movement at its peak. Included were Autauga (Josiah Francis's town), Autossee (Jim Boy's town), Tallassee (Hopoithle Miko's town, where Peter McQueen ranked as the chief warrior), Emuckfau, Okfuskee (Menawa's town), Coosada, and Hillabee. The Red Sticks also built three new strongholds—sacred sites for spiritual purification and protection—for each of the main subdivisions of the Upper Muscogees (the Alabamas, Tallapoosas, and Abekas). Their prophets and warriors left their main towns and moved to these settlements at Eccanachaca (Holy Ground) on the Alabama River near William Weatherford's plantation, at Othlewallee near Autossee on the lower Tallapoosa, and at Tohopeka on the middle Tallapoosa (Martin, 133–137, 144; Owen, 12, 16, 45).

Tuckabatchee remained in the camp of the peace faction led by Big Warrior, as did Lower Creek towns on the Chattahoochee, particularly Cusseta and Coweta. A few towns far up the Coosa also opposed the Red Sticks, but those nearer to the rebel towns risked their wrath. Red Sticks pillaged the dissident towns of Kailugee and Hatchechubba in July 1813, murdering several people and forcing many to flee to Tuckabatchee. But even in the Chattahoochee country, many Muscogees found the prophets' message appealing. Red Stick prophets courted Eufaula, fifty miles south of Coweta, and for a while it seemed on the verge of joining the rebellion

(Martin, 135–138).

The leadership of the two factions also had taken shape. At the head of the Red Sticks were the major prophets and leading military men of the Upper Creeks. They were men of considerable ability, education, and wealth. The prophet Hillis Hadjo (Medicine Crazy), or Josiah Francis, was described by an American officer as "a handsome man...of pleasing manners; conversed well in English and Spanish; humane in his disposition; by no means barbarous—withal a model chief." Peter McQueen (Talmuches Hadjo) was "shrewd, sanguinary, and deceitful," according to Sam Dale. While one witness described Cusseta Hadjo (Jim Boy or High-Head Jim) as handsome and decisive, another wrote that he combined "all the vices of white, Indian, and negro, without the virtues of any." Menawa and Hopoithle Miko, two men with powerful political grudges against McIntosh and Big Warrior, were also in the war faction's camp. In an attempt to put the white settlers at ease, the wily ex-speaker professed to have no intentions of making war on them. "I am not at war with any nation of people," Hopoithle Miko explained. "I am settling an affair with my own chiefs" (Martin, 131; Owen, 23; L. Thompson, 265; Griffith, 89; Littlefield, 60–61).

Big Warrior may have flirted with the idea of joining the rebels. A white trader described him as "hostile as any" to the white settlers and "inclined to take the talk" of Tecumseh. But for all his rhetoric against white expansion, Big Warrior was a willing recipient of gifts from Hawkins, with financial interests in the Federal Road, and as he became more of a target for the Red Stick dissidents, he was forced into leadership of the peace faction. Lower Creek chiefs William McIntosh, also a beneficiary of the Federal Road, and Tustunnuggee Hopoi (Little Prince) of Coweta also remained firmly committed against the radicals, whose views threatened their property and position. "The Prophets are enemies to the plan of civilization," Alexander Cornells wrote, "and advocates for the wild Indian mode of living" (Martin, 136; Edmunds, 150; Saunt, 254).

African Americans in the Muscogee nation found themselves faced with a particularly hard choice. Which side would they support? Most slaves were caught in the middle of a tragic situation, and many were torn between loyalty to their white or mixed-blood masters and their desire for freedom. And like African Americans among the Seminoles, many embraced the Red Stick cause (Braund, 632; Littlefield, 58–59).

In July 1813, the Red Sticks made two provocative moves that led to war. On July 10, at the head of at least one hundred warriors, Peter McQueen, Hillis Hadjo, and High-Head Jim left the Red Stick camp at Eccanachaca and rode south for Pensacola, where they expected to receive arms from the Spanish as Tecumseh had promised. It was also clear, McQueen would reveal to the Spanish governor, that the Red Sticks intended to use the arms to make war on the Americans as well as on their mixed-blood Muscogee enemies (Griffith, 89; Owen, 96; Saunt, 262).

While they waited for McQueen to return, the Red Sticks laid siege to Tuckabatchee on July 22. The war faction was not well armed, but Big Warrior's defenders were short of food and ammunition as well. Tuckabatchee contained close to 200 people, but only about thirty were fighting men. Big Warrior held out for eight days. In answer to his appeal for aid, about 200 Lower Creek warriors from Coweta and Cusseta arrived to break the siege. Big Warrior and his followers evacuated Tuckabatchee, sought shelter in Coweta, and appealed to Hawkins for military aid. The Red Sticks put Tuckabatchee to the torch. Georgia's governor, David Mitchell, mobilized 1,500 militia to defend the frontier. The militias in Tennessee and the Mississippi Territory also were on alert. "The American soldiers are now your friends," Hawkins warned the Red Stick chiefs, "and I hope will always be so. Take care how you make them your enemy" (Barnard and Schwartzman, "Tecumseh," 497–498; McDaniel, 12; Griffith, 91; Martin, 132; Saunt, 256).

On their way to Pensacola, McQueen's men beat and intimidated a number of Muscogees who refused to join the war faction. The Red Sticks reached the plantation of Alexander Cornells's brother James at Burnt Corn Spring (about ten miles east of present-day Monroeville, Alabama), where they beat a white man and a black slave. After ransacking and burning the home, they abducted Cornells's wife and carried her with them to Pensacola. Cornells, away from home, returned to find his property in ruins and spread the word to the white settlements. The Red Sticks also burned the homes of other mixed-bloods, including Sam Moniac, and destroyed their livestock and cotton.

When the Red Sticks arrived in Pensacola, they were disappointed at not finding the muskets and rifles that they expected. The Spanish governor still had no arms to give them, and he stalled for time as McQueen became more belligerent. The size and hostile mood of the McQueen party made Gonzalez Manrique uneasy, and he feared that if the Red Sticks became too dangerous, the Spanish garrison might have to deal with them. The governor finally provided McQueen with about 1,000 pounds of gunpowder, some lead, and a supply of food and blankets. McQueen was incensed and threatened to kill the Spaniards; Gonzalez Manrique ordered the soldiers to deploy to defend the town. The war party backed down and left Pensacola with their gunpowder and supplies. It is probable that a few of the independent merchants in Pensacola provided them with a small quantity of firearms (Owsley, 26–27).

Word of McQueen's activities in Pensacola reached the 'Bigbee settlements, where Colonel James Caller mustered the local militia and rode out to intercept the Red Sticks as they returned. Caller fired off a message to Brigadier General Ferdinand L. Claiborne, the territorial militia commander.

Only decisive action, he wrote, could stop the rebels from disrupting the 'Bigbee communities. Meanwhile, settlers in the area reacted to the alarming news by building defenses, and log forts or stockades sprang up all along the Tensaw and Tombigbee. "The people have been fleeing all night," Judge Harry Toulmin wrote on July 23 (Griffith, 95; Halbert and Ball, 129).

Caller and his troops left St. Stephens on July 22, crossed the Tombigbee, and rendezvoused with Sam Dale (armed with a double-barreled shotgun) and his company of fifty men at Fort Glass, near present-day Jackson. The next day they reached David Tate's farm, where Captain Dixon Bailey and his mixed-blood company of volunteers joined up with them. Bailey, a mixed-blood Muscogee from Autossee, was an able officer, educated in Philadelphia. Caller now had about 180 men. The party also included James Cornells—clearly out for blood after what McQueen had done to his home and to his wife—and numbers of the mixed-bloods from the Tensaw settlements. The troops moved on until they reached the Pensacola road and camped for the night on July 26. Caller's scouts went out the next morning and spotted the Red Sticks camped just several miles down the road at Burnt Corn Creek (Griffith, 92, 95–96, 106; Martin, 151).

Unaware of any danger, McQueen had not posted scouts. His men were cooking their food and were busy eating. Caller's scouts observed a small group of Red Sticks on the bank of the creek with most of their ammunition-laden packhorses. The majority of the party was on the other side of the creek in the swamp, where they had halted. At about 11 A.M., Caller's scouts reported back to him, and the colonel and his officers decided to attack. The militia wheeled away from the road into the woods, dismounted, and moved across a low hill north of the Red Stick camp. Then they charged down the hill and came out of the woods firing. The alarmed Red Sticks, after returning fire, ran for cover and raced to the rear across the creek. An African American cook decided not to run, believing the whites would spare him since he was a slave and carried no arms, but Caller's men shot him down and seized the packhorses (Griffith, 96; Owsley, 31; Elting, 162–163; Littlefield, 60).

The whites and mixed-bloods had caught the Red Sticks napping; but instead of pressing the attack, they stopped to inspect and to divide up the captured baggage. The delay gave the Red Sticks on the other side of Burnt Corn Creek time to regroup and counterattack. Although only a dozen or so of the warriors had guns—most in fact had only war clubs and bows and arrows—they opened fire on Caller's men from the woods. Panic seized the militia who fled. But about eighty men under Sam Dale, Dixon Bailey, and Benjamin Smoot stood their ground, holding off the rebels for nearly an hour. The militia and Red Sticks sniped at each other from the cover of the trees. Dale, hit in the side, was vomiting blood while one of his men reloaded his rifle for him. Then the militia pulled back (Griffith, 96–97; Owsley, 31–32; Elting, 163–164).

The Red Sticks recovered their packhorses but lost part of the gunpowder and lead they had brought from Pensacola. The confusing skirmish at Burnt Corn Creek brought the first casualties of the Creek War. Two of Caller's militia were killed, with fifteen wounded. Two Red Sticks lay dead, and five more were wounded (Owsley, 32; Elting, 163–164).

Forced to fall back in disorder, most of the militiamen were unable to find their horses where they had left them. The retreat became a rout as Caller's men stumbled northward through the woods that night. Rather than reassembling to fight again, the men simply headed for their homes. Caller became separated from the rest of his troops. Fifteen days later a search party led by Dixon Bailey, Sam Moniac, and David Tate found him and another officer—exhausted, raving, and nearly starved—wandering in the woods. The affair at Burnt Corn Creek was a major embarrassment for the whites (Griffith, 97).

Some of the Muscogees reported that the militia mutilated the bodies of the dead Red Sticks at Burnt Corn Creek. This infuriated McQueen's party, who burned for revenge. The Red Sticks gained boldness from their win at Burnt Corn, certain that they could take on the white army and defeat it. The warriors exaggerated their victory, which seemed to demonstrate the truth of the prophets' claims of spiritual protection. Burnt Corn helped solidify the Red Stick faction. "It gave them an exalted opinion of their own valor and prowess," mixed-blood George Stiggins wrote, "and a most contemptible opinion of the Americans." The conflict was escalating from a civil war within the Muscogee nation to a general war between the Red Sticks and the United States (Griffith, 97–98; Owsley, 32–33; Martin, 151–152; Stiggins, 101).

The peace faction among the Muscogees was also active at this time. In late August, Big Warrior launched a retaliatory raid against Peter McQueen's village, Chattucchufaulee. William McIntosh, at the head of 375 warriors, attacked the town but found it deserted. The Red Sticks had left much property there, including a large store of salt, and McIntosh set the town ablaze and destroyed the town's corn crop. He then withdrew with some cattle and much of the property remaining there. At about the same time as McIntosh's raid, one of Big Warrior's war parties brought in the scalps of three Red Sticks whom they had killed in a separate action. McIntosh also wanted to neutralize the threat of the rebellion's spread to the Cherokee nation. At the end of August he was on his way to meet with Ridge and other Cherokee leaders to seek their aid against the Red Sticks (Griffith, 99).

It was about this time that William Weatherford joined the Red Sticks. Weatherford had been opposed to Tecumseh's plan for Native American confederation, and it is still uncertain just how willing he was to join the war faction. Weatherford was caught in the middle of a civil conflict that divided families and clans. Most of his family—including his half-brother

David Tate, his brother Jack, and a number of his mixed-blood friends in the Tensaw settlements—were all in the peace faction. Both George Stiggins, who would become Weatherford's brother-in-law, and Thomas S. Woodward, who knew him, maintained that the Red Sticks coerced Red Eagle into joining them. Stiggins reported that while Weatherford was away on a business trip, the Red Sticks removed his family and much of his property to Othlewallee, one of their strongholds on the Tallapoosa River. With his family held hostage, Weatherford resolved to cast his lot with the war faction. The peace faction already considered him an enemy, and some of its leaders were threatening to kill him on sight. According to Woodward's account, Weatherford—"a man of fine sense, great courage, and knew much about our government and mankind in general"—chose to remain with the Red Sticks despite their threats to his family. He thought the warriors' course of action was doomed, but they were his people and he would share their fate (Griffith, 94, 99–100; Owsley, 33; Stiggins, 103–105; T. Woodward, 82–84).

Whatever his true motivation, Weatherford became the most able military strategist and leader that the Red Stick faction had. Weatherford was a realist and apparently gave little credence to the prophets. Even with his own abilities, he doubted the war party could win without help from the British, the Spanish, and other tribes. Red Eagle conducted a mission to the Choctaws in July to seek an alliance for the Red Sticks. But the Choctaw chiefs, still under the sway of Pushmataha, flatly declined (Griffith, 99–100; Owsley, 33).

About thirty-two years old in 1813, Red Eagle (Lamochattee) was the son of Scottish trader Charles Weatherford, who ran the trading post at Coosada, and Sehoy Durant, half-sister to Alexander McGillivray. Weatherford benefited greatly from connections with his mother's Wind clan. He also was close to his uncle and often accompanied McGillivray on diplomatic missions. Weatherford never learned to read and write, but he was fluent in Muscogee and English. He picked up his father's love of horses and often was spotted on Arrow, his black war steed. Red Eagle was a skilled horseman, hunter, and athlete, and his plantation on the Alabama River was the envy of many. Since 1803, when he accompanied the Upper Creeks who captured William Augustus Bowles, he had exercised considerable clout in the Muscogee nation (Griffith, 4–5, 11, 18, 52–53; Owen, 81–82; Brown and Owens, 96).

Whites and mixed-bloods in the Tensaw settlements, alarmed by the debacle at Burnt Corn Creek and fearful of Red Stick attack, flocked into a series of hastily erected wooden stockades for protection. One of these was Fort Mims, built around Samuel Mims's home near the Alabama River. Brigadier General Ferdinand Claiborne had mobilized the territorial militia, but he had few troops with which to launch an attack on the Red Sticks. Instead, he divided his forces into relatively small detachments, stationed them in the forts, and encouraged frontier families to seek shelter there.

Although they had planned an offensive against Coweta, the rebels now targeted Fort Mims as their next objective. The Red Sticks knew that many of the "half breeds and their assistants" who had attacked at Burnt Corn were at Fort Mims, and clan vengeance called for retaliation against them. The wealthy mixed-bloods in the Tensaw settlements had been a source of irritation to the Upper Muscogees for a long time. The Red Sticks wanted to send a powerful message to the white settlers and the mixed-bloods who had taken the side of Big Warrior and his peace faction. This would be a bold move, because the white settlers would not expect the red men to assault a garrisoned fort. But the Red Sticks knew the strengths and weaknesses of the fort, because runaway slaves had passed on the information. Weatherford made one more attempt to turn the war chiefs' collision course around. He was unsuccessful. He proposed that the war chiefs at least agree to send their women and children to Spanish Florida while the warriors waged war on the whites; but the chiefs vetoed this idea as well. They asked his counsel in planning the attack on Fort Mims, and Weatherford described a plan that he felt would work (Owsley, 34; Martin, 155–156; Griffith, 100; T. Woodward, 84–85).

The various Red Stick war parties rendezvoused at Flat Creek (in present-day Monroe County, Alabama), where they danced the war dance and moved out on foot and on horseback. They divided into two major parties. The larger group of 750, led by the prophet Paddy Walsh—along with Peter McQueen, William Weatherford, Jim Boy, and Hopie Tustunnuggee (Far-Off-Warrior), a respected elder chief—would attack Fort Mims. At the same time, Josiah Francis, with Menawa and Hopoithle Miko, would lead a smaller force of 125 warriors in an assault on Fort Sinquefield, a small stockade west of the Alabama River. Francis's movements would help to mask the location of the main Red Stick army. Ironically, several white settlers spotted the war parties moving across country, but no one believed they actually had plans to attack (Stiggins, 107–108; Owen, 21; L. Thompson, 315, 363).

About six miles from Fort Mims on the afternoon of August 29, the larger war party—hidden in the woods—spotted two militia scouts riding down the road. The Red Sticks feared discovery and worried that the men might see tracks the war party had left in crossing a nearby stream. But the militiamen were too engrossed in conversation to take notice. Some of the warriors made ready to attack the scouts, but Weatherford and Walsh advised restraint. If they killed the scouts, who then failed to return to the fort, the garrison would be alert and expect an attack (Stiggins, 109; Owsley, 35).

That night, Weatherford and two warriors conducted a clandestine inspection of the stockade's defenses. Stealing up to the very walls of Fort

Mims without being spotted, they discovered three interesting things. First, the stockade was not carefully guarded. Second, there was no defensive ditch around the fort. And third, the stockade's wooden wall, or picket, contained loopholes that the defenders could shoot through, but they were cut low, only about four feet from the ground, and this meant that the attackers could fire through them as well—at the defenders inside (Stiggins, 109–110; Owsley, 36).

Weatherford returned to the Red Sticks' camp and shared the results of his reconnaissance with the war leaders, and they finalized their plan of attack. Weatherford's strategy was sound. A mobile assaulting column of warriors directed by Peter McQueen would storm the main gate. Hopie Tustunnuggee, as senior chief, would have the honor of leading the attack. The rest of the Red Sticks, under Weatherford's leadership, would rush the stockade walls, take possession of the loopholes, and fire through them into the fort before the defenders could man them. Paddy Walsh assured the warriors that the spirits would protect them and deliver the fort into their hands. Four chosen men were to march through the gate into the stockade, raise the war cry, and demonstrate that the enemy's guns could not harm them, inspiring the other warriors to attack. Weatherford implored the warriors not to harm the women and children in the fort (Stiggins, 110; Griffith, 101).

As Weatherford had guessed, the garrison was woefully unprepared for an attack. The fort's commander, Major Daniel Beasley, an attorney in civilian life, was brave but overconfident. Beasley's superior, Brigadier General Claiborne, said that "although often warned he turned a deaf ear to all idea of danger." Beasley's 206 soldiers at Fort Mims included 120 of his own First Regiment of Mississippi Infantry, Captain Dixon Bailey's seventy mixed-blood volunteers, and sixteen soldiers from Fort Stoddert. The civilians who had taken refuge there included close to a hundred white settlers and mixed-bloods, as well as their black slaves. Beasley had failed to complete Fort Mims before the Red Stick attack. The soldiers had started work on one blockhouse but had not finished it, and although their orders were to build at least one additional blockhouse, no work had started (Griffith, 102; Elting, 164).

Beasley disregarded warnings that a war party was in the area, even on the afternoon prior to the attack. On the morning of August 30, Zachariah McGirth left the fort with two of his slaves and headed by river to his plantation near present-day Claiborne, Alabama. He left his wife, Vicey (who was part Muscogee), and their seven children in the fort. McGirth was planning on returning with supplies from his plantation, and his boat would be well up the Alabama River before he would learn of the Red Sticks' attack on the fort (Griffith, 109; L. Thompson, 342).

Just before noon, James Cornells, scouting for Beasley, rode up to the fort and shouted for the major to come to the gate. He warned Beasley that

Red Sticks were nearby and were preparing to attack the fort. Beasley suggested that Cornells had seen only a herd of red cattle, not a war party of red men, and some witnesses said the major was intoxicated. Cornells, angered, shot back that those red cattle would "give him a hell of a kick before night." The hostile exchange between the two men escalated, as other officers became involved. Finally, after Beasley threatened to have him arrested, Cornells galloped away, still shouting that the foolish garrison had better prepare for an attack. The whole scene was taken in by Weatherford and his warriors, watching and listening from a ravine nearby (T. Woodward, 86; Griffith, 104).

The fort's gate was open. The Red Sticks probably knew that it was jammed with sand, and Weatherford and his men may even have done it themselves on the night before the attack. The warriors waited breathlessly for the moment to strike, but they held off until after the noontime drum sounded inside the stockade. A few minutes more passed, and the Red Sticks knew that the garrison's noon meal was well under way. And then McQueen's warriors sprang from cover and rushed through the gate. Weatherford's party charged toward the walls of the fort (Owsley, 36).

"No one was ready," reported George Stiggins, a member of Dixon Bailey's mixed-blood company who was on furlough in Mobile on the day of the attack. "As they got ready and came out of their houses, they were mostly killed by the Indians from the portholes." Beasley and his militia soldiers died within a few minutes, but Bailey and his mixed-bloods—perhaps realizing their fate if captured—fought to the bitter end. "Though the Indians made their assault with steadiness and seeming desperation," Stiggins wrote, "they were twice repelled by the brave white men and Indians within" (Stiggins, 111; Quimby, 438 n. 48).

The Red Sticks set fire to the houses inside the stockade. Still, the defenders in the Mims house and in the loom house at the fort's northern wall held out for three hours before the warriors suddenly suspended their attack. The death of their old chief Hopie Tustunnuggee early in the fighting required a brief council of war to name his replacement, and Weatherford was chosen. The next decision was whether to resume the attack. Weatherford felt that the warriors must overcome the remaining pockets of resistance in the fort in order to claim a complete victory. African Americans fighting with the Red Sticks agreed. Stiggins wrote, "[T]hey would not have commenced their attack anew, but the Negroes they had would not cease, urging them on by reciting that they thought it interested them to have the fort destroyed" (Stiggins, 111–112; Griffith, 106; Owsley, 37–38; L. Thompson, 346–348).

Red Eagle and his party assaulted the rear gate of the fort, battering it down with their axes, and as this fresh column of warriors swarmed into the stockade, the defenders' last hope of survival evaporated. Soon flames consumed the Mims house and the loom house, where Bailey and his men were, and the last strongholds of resistance fell. The warriors, completely out of control now, began butchering the survivors—men, women, and children (L. Thompson, 350–353).

The accounts of Stiggins and Woodward maintain that Weatherford made a passionate attempt to stop the massacre at Fort Mims. But despite his pleas, the Red Sticks were bent on revenge, and nothing could turn aside their wrath. Sick at heart, Weatherford rode to his half-brother Davy Tate's home. The warriors spent the balance of the afternoon in a frenzy of killing, hacking their victims to pieces and burning the remains of the fort (Stiggins, 113; T. Woodward, 80–81; Griffith, 107–108; Owsley, 38; L. Thompson, 355).

The prophets had assured the warriors that no more than three of their men would perish in the attack on Fort Mims. It came as a shock to learn that their losses amounted to over 200. They left their dead on the field and carried their wounded with them as they withdrew. Paddy Walsh's reputation suffered a serious setback after Fort Mims. Muscogee tradition was stern when it came to false prophets or "malicious conjurers." It is possible that they might have put Walsh to death, even though he had been wounded several times himself during the assault, but he was an important chief among the Alabamas, who shielded him from harm (Griffith, 110; Martin, 157; Stiggins, 114–115).

It was dawn by the time Zachariah McGirth made his way back to Fort Mims, and the stockade was a smoldering ruin. Daylight revealed a site covered with mutilated bodies, some of them still frying on the coals of the recent fires. McGirth began the grisly task of searching through piles of nearly unrecognizable corpses, but he found no trace of his wife and children. He was unaware that they had been carried off by the Red Stick warrior Sanota, who remembered Vicey and her act of kindness done to him as a child (Quimby, 109).

The atrocities committed at Fort Mims stunned even the most hardened frontiersmen. "The way that many of the unfortunate women were mangled and cut to pieces," wrote Dr. Thomas G. Holmes, the fort's assistant surgeon, "is shocking to humanity." Major Joseph P. Kennedy, commanding the relief column of Mississippi militia that arrived ten days later, made this report to Claiborne: "Indians, negroes, white men, women and children, lay in one promiscuous ruin. All were scalped, and the females, of every age, were butchered in a manner which neither decency nor language will permit me to describe. The main building was burned to ashes, which were filled with bones. The plains and the woods around were covered with dead bodies" (Griffith, 106; Pickett, 542).

Evidence suggests that African Americans in the fort may have aided the Red Sticks. A black survivor reported that "Siras, a negro man, cut down the pickets," and that black men were fighting on the side of the Red Sticks in the assault. Josiah Francis recalled that in the attack on the fort,

"[T]he blacks were the first in." African Americans were said to have taken an active part in firing the buildings in Fort Mims, and when the attack seemed to falter, it was the blacks who encouraged the Red Sticks to fight on. Some, Stiggins reported, joined the Red Sticks "to assist in exterminating the white people and be free." Following the Fort Mims massacre, rumors of slave uprisings flooded the frontier. However, blacks also helped the defenders at Fort Mims. Twenty slaves were killed there. Many were taken captive and carried off by the Red Sticks (Grant, 664; Martin, 156–157; Owsley, 39–40; Littlefield, 61–62; Saunt, 269; Braund, 632).

The Red Sticks canceled plans to assault Fort Pierce, a small stockade two miles from Fort Mims. At the first reports of gunfire from Fort Mims, the Fort Pierce defenders evacuated and headed for the Alabama River. Most of the settlers could not swim the river, and Peggy Bailey (Dixon's sister) swam to the opposite bank, where she secured a flatboat to ferry the party across to safety. The Fort Pierce group traveled on to Fort Stoddert (L. Thompson, 359).

Josiah Francis and his war party—operating independently from Weatherford and McQueen—had been moving through the country on the west side of the Alabama River, where settlers had erected a cluster of forts in the central part of present-day Clarke County—Fort Glass, Fort Madison, Fort Landrum, Fort Sinquefield, Fort White, and Fort Mott. On September 1, they surprised two families away from Fort Sinquefield (five miles southeast of present-day Grove Hill) and killed twelve of them. One woman, wounded and scalped and left for dead, managed to struggle back to the fort with her infant child. The Red Sticks withdrew, taking the scalps of the dead and some of the family's slaves. They decided the time was right to take Fort Sinquefield (L. Thompson, 363–365; Owen, 109, 128).

The Red Sticks timed their attack for 11 A.M. on September 2, to coincide with the burial of their victims of the previous day, when numbers of people would be outside the fort. There also were some women outside at a nearby spring washing clothes and fetching water. Francis's party attempted to cut them off from the fort, but settlers spotted them and gave the alarm. All but one woman was able to retreat into the stockade (Owen, 109–110).

The garrison was better prepared than at Fort Mims. Only fifteen white, mixed-blood, and Muscogee men defended the fort, but eleven more men under Lieutenant James Bailey, Dixon's brother, had just arrived from Fort Stoddert, bringing the horrendous news of the Fort Mims massacre. The Red Sticks' 125 warriors were eager for blood. But the settlers were alerted to the danger of attack, and Francis was denied the element of surprise (Owen, 109–110; L. Thompson, 366–367).

Still, the Red Sticks launched an assault on Fort Sinquefield that lasted about two hours. The settlers—aware of the fate of the Fort Mims garrison—fought desperately. Lieutenant Bailey placed his best marksmen in the upper floor of the blockhouse where they could pick off advancing warriors as they took cover behind pine trees. Stephen Lacy, spotting a Red Stick emerge from behind a tree, took careful aim and dropped his red target. He stopped long enough to give a jubilant cry to his comrades and turned back to his porthole, when a Red Stick bullet hit him in the neck. Lacy fell back into the arms of his wife, who had climbed up into the loft to help him. Low on ammunition, the snipers yelled to those below for help. A ten-year-old boy brought more up to them and was wounded in the back as he climbed back down (L. Thompson, 370–372).

Francis was not able to gain entrance to the stockade. Forced to suspend his attack, he withdrew with his dead and wounded. Eleven of the warriors were killed and many more wounded. The garrison had lost one man killed (Lacy), one woman killed, and one boy wounded. Francis ordered a withdrawal across the Alabama. Fearing the return of the Red Sticks, the settlers evacuated Fort Sinquefield and withdrew to Fort Madison (Owen, 109–110, L. Thompson, 372–373).

Francis's party met Weatherford's warriors at Burnt Corn Spring. The Red Sticks spent several days in the Tensaw settlements burning and terrorizing the countryside. They had used up much of the ammunition they had brought from Pensacola and had suffered enormous casualties, but Red Eagle hoped to maintain their momentum before the whites regrouped. At his direction the war leaders drafted and sent a letter to the governor at Pensacola requesting more arms. Weatherford suggested that if the Spanish would aid him, he would stage an offensive against Mobile. The white settlers prepared first to defend the region, and then to launch a counteroffensive into the Muscogee nation. It was evident to all that there was no way back from full-scale war now (L. Thompson, 374–375).

CHAPTER 5

The Allies

The killings committed at Fort Mims were on a scale unknown on the frontier up to that time, and the news stunned the American public. The closer white settlers were to the actual scene of the massacre, the greater the horror. At Fort Stoddert, where settlers could see the winding smoke from what used to be Fort Mims just ten miles upriver, Judge Harry Toulmin wrote, "We are in a situation truly distressing, all the people have abandoned their houses and this unfortunate stoccade [sic] is crowded with women and children" (Lengel, 33).

At St. Stephens, George Gaines, the factor to the Choctaws, had moved his headquarters from the leaky old Spanish fort to a new brick building. Since the outbreak of trouble with the Red Sticks, he had also had a stockade built around the trading house. The town was flooded with a large influx of settlers who had built a new stockade called Fort Republic, and Gaines was at the fort late in the evening of August 31 when a messenger brought him news of the Fort Mims massacre. Gaines shared the contents of the letter with the anxious settlers gathered around him. "I saw it created a panic," he wrote (Gaines, 154, 157).

Gaines quickly composed two letters—one to Major General Andrew Jackson of the Tennessee militia and one to Tennessee governor Willie Blount—recounting the massacre at Fort Mims and appealing to them for troops to assist the settlements. He dispatched a young mounted volunteer for Nashville the next morning. The rider would make various stops through the Choctaw country and receive fresh mounts and provisions.

Horror gave way to calls for revenge. "[W]hen I heard of the mischief which was done at the fort," Tennessee volunteer David Crockett wrote, "I instantly felt like going, and I had none of the dread of dying that I expected to feel." When he received news of the massacre, Andrew Jackson vowed, "Long shall the Creeks remember Fort Mims in bitterness and in tears" (Crockett, 51; Jenkins, 175).

But avenging Fort Mims would not be easy. The nation already was in the second year of the war with Britain, a war that had not gone well for the Americans. The United States possessed far greater numbers and resources than the Red Sticks, but several serious obstacles stood in the way of a victory.

First was the problem of supply. American troops would need rations of beef, pork, and flour to last them through a winter campaign. They would be unable to rely on allied Muscogees to provide food, since most of the red men were merely subsistence farmers themselves. The white armies also would need wagons, pack animals, and boats to carry the supplies. State bureaucracies were unequal to the task. Lack of decent roads would also slow down the allied advance. The only road into the Muscogee nation was the Federal Road, such as it was, running from Fort Hawkins to Fort Stoddert.

Friction between the area military commanders also hampered an offensive. Sixty-three-year-old Major General Thomas Pinckney—a respected veteran officer of the Revolutionary War, former governor of South Carolina, and architect of Pinckney's Treaty of 1795—commanded the Sixth Military District, which included Georgia and the Carolinas. Major General Thomas Flournoy, a thirty-eight-year-old Georgian, had just replaced James Wilkinson as commander of the Seventh Military District, which encompassed Louisiana and the Mississippi Territory. The Muscogee lands lay between the two military districts. Britain's naval blockade of the United States restricted communications between the commanders at their headquarters at Charleston and New Orleans. Secretary of War John Armstrong attempted to resolve the problem of divided command by giving Pinckney, the senior general, overall command of the entire military operation. This idea made sense to Armstrong but did not set well with Flournoy, who was often uncooperative and obstinate.

The nature of the available military forces themselves also presented problems. The United States had very few regular troops on the southern frontier, since most were committed in the war effort in the north. That left the militia and volunteers. The American militia in the early nineteenth century was not very reliable as a fighting force. There was very little actual training. Drilling was haphazard, discipline lax. Militia soldiers elected their officers, who usually were men from their local communities whom they knew and trusted. They brought their own arms from home, generally rifles and shotguns, and many reported for duty with no weapons at all. Some did not even know how to use a firearm. There were no uniforms, and men turned out in hunting shirts and all manner of headgear. They enlisted for ninety days, expecting to whip the red savages and be back home before Christmas. It would not be as simple as many of them believed.

Nevertheless, Secretary of War Armstrong and Major General Pinckney worked out a strategy for crushing the Red Sticks. Their plans called for three American armies to invade the Muscogee nation. The Georgia army would cross the Chattahoochee and hit Red Stick strongholds from the east. The Mississippi Territory's army would move north up the Alabama River into Creek country. The Tennessee army would march down from the north. The three armies would build military roads and forts along their communications route. They would destroy Red Stick towns and burn their crops, and they would rendezvous eventually in the heart of Upper Creek country at Hickory Ground near the confluence of the Coosa and Tallapoosa Rivers. Pinckney would supervise the entire campaign, which would involve some 10,000 soldiers.

Many whites welcomed a conflict with the Muscogees. A number of planter-politicians in Georgia and Tennessee saw a golden opportunity to dismember the Muscogee nation and make its fertile lands available for cotton. Tennessee governor Willie Blount expected that the war would "teach those barbarous sons of the woods their inferiority," destroy the Creek nation and open the area, and possibly Florida as well, to white set-tlement (Martin, 153, 158).

For planters and investors back east, the Creek War may have seemed a grand fortuity, but for whites on the frontier there was only sheer terror. Even before the Fort Mims massacre, settlers along the Ocmulgee had begun to dread for their safety. With nearly 200 miles of frontier to guard against Red Stick attacks, an unstable southern border with Spanish Florida, and the danger of British naval movements along the Atlantic coast, Georgians felt extremely uneasy. Major General David Adams, commanding the Georgia militia on the Ocmulgee, had received alarming reports of the Red Sticks' intentions and was on the verge of ordering the white settlers into defensive stockades like those in the Tensaw settle-ments. Adams worried about possible British and Spanish assistance to the Red Sticks, and he cautioned Georgia governor David B. Mitchell that the frontier settlers would hold him accountable for their security.

On the upper Ocmulgee above Fort Hawkins, settlers in Jones and Jasper Counties especially feared a Red Stick attack since they were clos-est to the Upper Creek towns. Mitchell authorized Adams to enlist a regi-ment of 500 to 1,000 militia volunteers to protect this vulnerable part of Georgia. Adams's army was to stage an aggressive drive against the Red Sticks independently of the main Georgia army under Brigadier General John Floyd that would invade Muscogee and link up with the Ten-nesseans and Mississippians—an army that was stalled now because of lack of supplies (Owsley, 51).

For settlers on the lower Ocmulgee, the main threat seemed to come from the Seminoles to the south. Along the lower Flint River, settlements of Lower Creeks overlapped with Seminole towns. Although the Lower Creeks were allies, Georgia settlers feared that the Seminoles would influence them to join the war against the Americans. A series of raids by hostile bands during the summer of 1813, coupled with the Red Stick attack on Tuckabatchee and the flight of Big Warrior and his party to Coweta, alarmed the Ocmulgee settlers. Already they had constructed a blockhouse at Hartford, and a company of mounted militia had conducted an unsuccessful search for marauders earlier in the year. What made things especially difficult for the white soldiers was that it was hard to distinguish between friendly Muscogees and Red Sticks in disguise.

Brigadier General David Blackshear reacted to the settlers' alarm by constructing a chain of ten small forts—stockades similar to those built by the Tensaw settlers—on the eastern side of the Ocmulgee from Fort Hawkins to the Oconee. Small detachments of fifteen to twenty men served as garrisons in each fort and also sent out mounted scouts across the river to watch for signs of hostile activity. Frontier families were glad to have this chain of little forts when news of the massacre at Fort Mims reached them (Chalker, 92–98).

Before Fort Mims, Benjamin Hawkins had sought to keep the civil war in the Muscogee nation as contained as possible. Even after the Red Sticks had forced Big Warrior from Tuckabatchee and the embattled chief called on him for aid, Hawkins had asked Governor Mitchell for only 300 soldiers. The agent still felt that he could handle the conflict without a large force of Georgia militia being turned loose on the Muscogee nation. Hawkins feared that Georgia whites would use the war as an excuse to seize more of the Muscogee lands, and he also believed that the federal government—not the state of Georgia—had the authority to handle Indian troubles (Pound, 107–108).

But after news of the Fort Mims massacre reached him, Hawkins had to admit that the Red Stick rebellion was far more serious than he had thought. As agent, he had the advantage of considerable intelligence from the friendly chiefs, and their reports now convinced him that the war faction was so strong that the Georgia frontier itself was in danger of Red Stick attack. "Our Chiefs are still under the influence of fear," he wrote Mitchell on September 6. Accordingly, Hawkins became much more cooperative with General Floyd, passing on information that he received on the activities of the Red Sticks. He also expected to help coordinate recruitment of the allied Muscogees under Big Warrior (Pound, 108; Grant, 660).

During the Creek War, Big Warrior's headquarters remained in Coweta, the Lower Creek capital on the Chattahoochee in present-day Russell County, Alabama. "I never expected a civil war among us," he wrote Hawkins on July 26. "[T]he Council house of the four Nation was appointed to preserve peace and friendship among us, and our white friends, But it is destroyed." As the troublesome summer of 1813 wore on and the bloody events at Fort Mims unfolded, Big Warrior became even more dismayed at the destructive schism within the Muscogee nation. The speaker was concerned about the strength of the Red Sticks and anxious to receive military aid from the Americans. "The red Club party says that you are afraid & cant come to our assistance," he wrote Hawkins on September 24. "The taking of Sam Mimms's fort & Dixon Bailey & Cutting of him to pieces has encouraged them that they think themselves above all the world" (Hawkins Papers).

No group of white settlers was more terrified after the Fort Mims attack than the 'Bigbee settlers. In the weeks following the massacre, Red Stick war parties prowled the land in the forks of the Tombigbee and Alabama Rivers, striking at isolated cabins. The white and mixed-blood settlers and soldiers crowded into frontier stockades such as Fort Glass, where Sam Dale—recovering from his wound suffered at Burnt Corn Creek—commanded eighty volunteers, and Fort Madison, where 1,000 people were packed into a space the size of an acre (E. Rowland, 42; Lossing, 761).

Brigadier General Ferdinand L. Claiborne, commander of the Mississippi territorial troops in the Tensaw-Tombigbee settlements, was unable to launch a retaliatory offensive against the Red Sticks. But while his own army waited for more manpower and supplies, he found an enthusiastic ally in the Choctaw chief Pushmataha. The Choctaws saw the actions of the Red Sticks as a breach of faith. By attacking Fort Mims, the radicals threatened to bring down the wrath of the United States on all of the southeastern tribes. Pushmataha also feared that if he didn't get his warriors into the war on the American side soon, many of them might be tempted to take up the way of the Red Sticks. The former agent to the Choctaws, John McKee, seemed to agree. "Indians cannot well support a state of neutrallity," he reflected in a letter to John Pitchlynn on September 14. "The young men fond of distinction will go to war however well the Chiefs may be disposed to prevent it." He went on to express his concern about a timely recruitment of the Choctaws. "I hope the Choctaws will pursue what I sincerely [believe] will be their true interest [to] take up the hatchet at once." he wrote. "If they do not, many of their young men will join the Creeks and finally draw the whole nation into their alliance" (DeRosier, 35; McKee Letters).

Despite the efforts of Pushmataha, McKee, and others, there were dissidents within the Choctaw nation that favored the Red Stick movement. At least sixty-five Choctaw warriors and their families from two small towns on the Tombigbee and Yahnubbee Creek joined the rebel Muscogees in their holy war against the Americans. Descendants of these rebel Choctaws—known today as the MOWA Choctaw—still live in the marshlands north of Mobile where the warriors and their families retreated after the conclusion of the Creek War. The renegade Choctaws regarded Pushmataha as a traitor. But the vast majority of Choctaws supported their war chief (Matte, 15, 22).

Although they had never attacked the Americans, the usually peaceful Choctaws had a reputation as tenacious fighters when they were provoked. They were proud people, and the most noble boast that a Choctaw warrior could make was "*Choctaw siah*" ("I am a Choctaw"). Comfortable in their farming communities, they preferred a war of defense and generally waited for the enemy to come to them. But small parties of warriors, or *tushka chipota* (little warriors), patrolled the woods during wartime. They could be expected to be formidable adversaries against the Red Sticks if they joined the conflict (DeRosier, 12; Halbert, 1).

Pushmataha first learned of the Fort Mims massacre when George Gaines's rider stopped in the Choctaw country on his way north to Tennessee. He quickly made his way to St. Stephens to meet with Gaines and offer his services. Gaines and Pushmataha saddled up and rode to Mobile, where they found General Flournoy at his headquarters in the former Spanish Fort Charlotte. Gaines introduced Pushmataha to the general, and through an interpreter the chief explained that the Choctaws wished to offer military aid. Flournoy replied that he had no authority to accept. Pushmataha explained that there were three things that he wanted to do: to protect the settlements; to seek revenge on his old enemy the Muscogees for the massacre of personal friends at Fort Mims; and to ensure that his warriors—who were "becoming excited," Gaines wrote, "and were desirous to be engaged in the war"—would fight on the right side. But Flournoy still was not interested (Gaines, 158–159).

Gaines could hardly believe his ears. He asked the general if he felt he had enough men to defend the settlements. Flournoy replied that he couldn't say. Gaines told him that if he had any doubts, then he should accept any aid offered to him. "I did not receive a very civil reply," Gaines wrote, "and remarked that I would hasten back to St. Stephens and do the best I could to prevent the public property from falling into the hands of the Creeks." He collected the Choctaw chief, and the two men rode back to St. Stephens (Gaines, 159).

Gaines and Pushmataha had barely reached the gate at Fort Republic and had not even dismounted before an anxious crowd surrounded them, eager to learn of their mission to Mobile. While Gaines was telling them the bad news and cursing Flournoy for his foolishness, a mounted rider from Mobile caught up with them and delivered a letter from Flournoy. The general had given the matter thought, had reconsidered, and now had decided to accept Pushmataha's offer of aid. He authorized Gaines to travel back to the Choctaw nation with the chief and help him recruit as many warriors as he could enlist (Gaines, 159–160).

Pushmataha scheduled a council at Kooncheto (near present-day Quitman, Mississippi), where the Choctaw chiefs and principal warriors would meet with him to consider going to war against the Red Sticks. Several thousand Choctaws were waiting for him, and the meeting was held under a large leafy oak tree. The chief dismounted from his horse, while his wife mixed with the other women on the rim of the crowd. Gaines observed silently from a log nearby. In a lengthy speech, Pushmataha explained to his audience how the British had provoked a war with the United States and how the Red Stick Muscogees had joined them (Gaines, 160–163; Griffith, 114).

Pushmataha, a powerful speaker in a nation that cherished persuasive rhetoric, brought his talk to a climax:

You know Tecumseh. He is a bad man. He came through our nation, but did not turn our heads. He went among the Muscogees and got many of them to join him. You know the Tensaw people. They were our friends. They played ball with us. They sheltered and fed us, whenever we went to Pensacola. Where are they now? Their bodies rot at Sam Mims' place. The people at St. Stephens are our friends. The Muscogees intend to kill them too.

"You can all do as you please," the Choctaw chief concluded, drawing his sword. "You are all freemen. I dictate to none of you. But I shall join the St. Stephens people. If you have a mind to follow me, I will lead you to glory and to victory!" Nearly every Choctaw warrior was on his feet, crying, "I am a man! I am a man! I will follow you!" (Pickett, 549).

Soon Pushmataha was back at St. Stephens with a number of his warriors and the promise of more as soon as they could arrive. Claiborne, relieved, welcomed him and provided his men with arms and equipment. Soon the Choctaw war parties were out in the 'Bigbee frontier. The chiefs of the two other Choctaw districts also enlisted some fighting men.

Meanwhile, John McKee had arrived as a special agent sent by Jackson and Blount to recruit warriors in the northern part of the Choctaw nation and in the Chickasaw country. Jackson wanted his red allies to mount an expedition against Muscogee towns on the falls of the Black Warrior River. McKee left the Choctaw country on October 24, along with some fifty warriors, and made his way to St. Stephens. He was disappointed at finding very little ammunition there and dismayed on learning that Flournoy was still reluctant to provide arms to the Choctaws because he doubted their loyalty. But McKee wrote, "I know that to shew doubts of their fidelity was to excite & justify their treachery." He decided to make his own arrangements to obtain the needed ammunition (Gaines, 160–161; McKee Journal, 2).

As McKee reported in a letter to John Coffee on October 15, 1813, the Choctaws wasted little time in seeking combat with the Red Sticks. A party of nine warriors scouted a Muscogee town on the Black Warrior on October 9. The town had a stockade and was rumored to have held 200

warriors, but now it was deserted. The Choctaws believed the main
enemy force had probably moved to the fork of the Coosa and Tallapoosa.

The Cherokee nation received the news of Fort Mims with alarm and
excitement. Like the Choctaws, Cherokees blamed the Red Sticks for trig-
gering a war that threatened to disrupt all of the tribes. The young mixed-
blood leaders saw the Creek conflict as an opportunity to channel the
energy of the ghost dance movement into a path to national glory
(McLoughlin, 191).

Taller than the Muscogees and lighter in color, the Cherokees also had a
fearsome reputation as warriors, although they had been at peace for two
decades. "The Cherokees," William Bartram wrote, "...are grave and
steady; dignified and circumspect in their deportment; rather slow and
reserved in conversation; yet frank, cheerful, and humane; tenacious of
their liberties and natural rights of man." The Cherokees' cleanliness far
surpassed that of their white frontier neighbors, and their level of civilization was at least its equal. They were proud of their heritage. "Many of
the Cherokees," agent Return J. Meigs observed, "think that they are not
derived from the same stock as whites, that they are favorites of the great
spirit" (McLoughlin, 1–2).

The Cherokees were near nation-state status and since 1810 had added
a new obligation to what it meant to be a Cherokee. Besides sharing common clan membership, kinship, and beliefs, members of the "principal
people" were now required to live within the Cherokee nation and to give
their loyalty to the national council and its laws. The Cherokees' remarkable social and political development was due to the leadership of a group
of progressive "young chiefs" that included Ridge, James Vann, and
Charles Hicks (McLoughlin, 109–110).

The young chiefs, all of them well-to-do planters, rose to power in 1807
when they deposed Chief Doublehead, also a planter and a supporter of
acculturation. After the chief, in addition to taking bribes, leased private
tribal lands to whites, the rebels determined to execute him. The assassins
cornered Doublehead in a furious tavern melee and put a bullet in his
head. When the old chief didn't die, they plunged a hatchet into his skull
the next day. Doublehead had signed a treaty giving iron ore rights to a
South Carolina entrepreneur. An armed party led by Ridge, Hicks, and
others intercepted and turned back the South Carolinians and their wagons (McLoughlin, 109–127; Ehle, 71–76).

Meigs described the leaders of the rebel party as ambitious men seeking
their own advantages at the expense of the older chiefs. But the young
chiefs were actually nationalists who sought to protect Cherokee autonomy and prevent the further loss of tribal lands to white settlers. They also
insisted on the right of the Cherokees to self-government. "We, as a free
People," the young chiefs asserted in 1808,"have a Right to claim for ourselves and our children" the privilege of "ratifying or rejecting treaties

after they are concluded." The young nationalists were coping with the same social, economic, and spiritual crises that had split the Muscogees, but while the Red Sticks chose a holy war to restore Muscogee independence, the Cherokee leaders saw their salvation in imitation of the white man's society and acceptance as equals (McLoughlin, 109–126).

The son of a Cherokee mixed-blood mother and a Scottish trader, Ridge was forty-two years old in 1813. Since the age of seventeen, he had been a fighting man, a veteran of the 1788–1794 border wars between the Cherokees and whites. The seasoned warrior settled at Pine Log in present-day Bartow County, Georgia, and was its representative at the national council at Oostanaula. Ridge played a major role in persuading the council to amend the nation's blood law to make accidental killings exempt from clan vengeance. Ridge's star rose in the Cherokee nation after the overthrow of Doublehead. He became the leader of one of two "light horse guards" or police forces in the nation, similar to William McIntosh's law enforcers for the Creeks. Ridge married ambitious, hardworking Susanna Wickett, and the couple became enormously successful. Ridge accumulated 250 acres of land, planted in cotton, corn, potatoes, tobacco, apples, and peaches. He owned many slaves and herds of cattle, horses, and hogs; and he operated a store and a ferry (Parins, 3–7; Ehle, 75–76, 207, 240).

Ridge's mixed-blood colleagues shared his progressive visions for the Cherokees, including imitation of the white economy. All were flourishing planters and slave owners. Highly literate, good-natured Charles Hicks, who walked with a crippled hip, lived near Pine Log and was an aide to agent Meigs. Twenty-three-year-old John Ross, called Little John, also was an assistant to Meigs and was fluent in English and Cherokee. Richard Brown, described by Meigs as "intelligent, vigilant, enterprising," lived near the Tennessee River in present-day Marshall County, Alabama (Ehle, 49, 127; Hood, 22–24).

Return J. Meigs, or White Eagle as the "principal people" called him, was the Cherokees' seventy-three-year-old agent. A native of Connecticut and a veteran of the Revolutionary War, he came to the Cherokee country in 1801 and served there until 1823. From his agency at Hiwassee, near present-day Dayton, Tennessee, Meigs sought to protect the Cherokees from white encroachment, but he was frustrated by a legal system that discriminated against them. Out of four murder cases in which whites had killed Cherokees in 1813, Meigs was unable to get a conviction by a white jury. He complained bitterly that "a jury impaneled in the frontier Counties dare not bring in a Verdict to take the life of a citizen for Killing an Indian." Meigs understood the anger of young Cherokee men, who had not had the opportunity to prove themselves in war: "The Indians steal horses from the white people," he explained, "and the white people steal their land; this is their way of expressing it" (Ehle, 49; McLoughlin, 47–48, 52, 55).

In his own way, Meigs tried to preserve Cherokee autonomy, but he also supported the same kind of civilization program that Hawkins was pushing on the Muscogees. Meigs urged the Cherokees to adopt white civilization, to become farmers and planters and slave owners, to divide up their tribal lands into 640-acre farms that would be owned by individual Cherokee families. The surplus land would be freed up for cession to the whites. He explained to the Cherokees that this was the best way for them to keep their land; since U.S. law protected private property, "[Y]ou will secure your land to your people forever." But Cherokee leaders wanted to maintain the nation-state, not just individual Cherokee farms. Convinced that acceptance by white Americans as equals was the key to sovereignty—and that the Cherokees could more quickly gain acceptance by proving their loyalty in time of war—the mixed-blood leaders enthusiastically embraced the opportunity to fight (McLoughlin, 112–113).

As early as May 1812, even before Congress declared war, three of the "young chiefs"—Ridge, John Lowrey, and John Walker—offered to raise warriors to fight against the British. Meigs urged the secretary of war to accept them, "because they are real horsemen" and "they love war; it has no terrors for them." The chiefs approached Meigs again in July 1813, when the Muscogee nation was embroiled in civil war. "The intelligence recd from the Creek Nation at this present crisis is very serious," a concerned John Ross wrote. "The hostile party is said to be numerous & it is apprehensive that they will be conquered from the Superior force of the rebels" (McLoughlin, 188–190; Moulton, 19).

Ridge had attended the council meeting of the Lower Creeks at Coweta, and he was in close contact with Big Warrior and William McIntosh. Arriving back in the Cherokee nation, he brought Big Warrior's plea for help before the council. After some serious deliberation, the members voted to stay out of the Muscogee mess. But Ridge pushed the issue, warning that—if not stopped now—the Red Stick movement would spread to their own nation, and he sought to enlist warriors to go and fight. The council members took a second vote. This time they were for sending warriors to aid the Muscogees (Ehle, 105–106).

Secretary of War Armstrong accepted Meigs's proposal for Cherokee warriors. They would receive the same equipment, rank, and pay as the white frontier militia. Meigs had enlisted 500 by late October. The Cherokees were organized into a regiment under Colonel Gideon Morgan, an Indian countryman who had lived among the Cherokees and was married to a mixed-blood woman. But their own officers—men such as John Lowrey, Ridge, Charles Hicks, Richard Brown, and John Ross—would serve at ranks of lieutenant colonel and below. Pathkiller, the Cherokees' principal chief, too old to fight, received the honorary rank of colonel (McLoughlin, 191–192; Wilkins, 68).

Meigs furnished the Cherokee volunteers with muskets, ammunition, flints, and other supplies. In his talk to the warriors, he urged them not to make war on women and children. "You will find the Army to be a school of instruction," he told them, "that will elevate and raise up your minds to sentiments unknown to barbarous nations." It was an ironic sermon, considering the standards of behavior of white frontier militia (McLoughlin, 192).

Meanwhile, the Red Sticks—bracing for a white counteroffensive—still counted heavily on aid from Britain and Spain. Governor Gonzalez Manrique wrote Weatherford and applauded his victory at Fort Mims. While promising him aid, he did not encourage Red Eagle to attack Mobile. In September 1813, Gonzalez Manrique received yet a third visit from southeastern Native Americans seeking arms, Seminoles and Lower Creeks led by Thomas and William Perryman and Alexander Durant. As with Peter McQueen's visit to Pensacola in July, the Spanish governor still had no arms to give the red men. The captain general of Cuba, Ruiz Apodaca, had instructed Gonzalez Manrique to provide the Muscogees with whatever arms and supplies he could spare; and Spain's policy of arming the Native Americans would be approved by royal decision in December 1813. But for now the Spanish, although sympathetic to the Muscogees, could provide no more than promises of aid (Owsley, 27).

The prospect of British aid was more favorable. The British warship *Herald* had put in at the harbor of Pensacola, and the Lower Creeks and Seminoles met on September 18 with Lieutenant Edward Handfield, who probably furnished them with a small amount of arms. Handfield had orders from Charles Cameron, governor of Nassau, to size up the volatile condition of the Muscogees and Seminoles, and he regretted missing McQueen's party in Pensacola a few weeks earlier. Even though the Lower Creeks and Seminoles were not under the sway of the Red Stick prophets, they equally felt the threat of U.S. expansion and expected that only with British aid could they hold on to their lands. The opportunity was encouraging to Handfield, who sailed from Pensacola with letters to Cameron from the Perrymans and Durant, as well as one of their interpreters, Henry Durgen (Owsley, 27–28).

After meeting with Durgen and reviewing the Perryman-Durant letters, Governor Cameron communicated with Lord Bathurst, Britain's secretary for war and colonies. Bathurst issued orders to British naval forces to provide aid to the Muscogees and Seminoles hostile to the United States. As the Creek War between the Red Sticks and the United States began in the fall of 1813, the Muscogees had two potentially powerful foreign allies—Spain and Britain. But neither of these foreign powers had really thought through a policy for actually arming the Red Sticks and had no immediate material aid to give. Any substantial assistance would require several months to provide (Owsley, 28).

So, as the war with the Americans got under way, the Red Sticks still were militarily unprepared. With no centralized supply system, they could not maintain any sizable force at any distance from their home towns. The Red Sticks had worsened the situation by killing livestock as they rampaged through Creek farms. With winter coming on, there was the grim danger of starvation for their people, since white armies would target their towns and crops, as they had done in the Seminole country. Although Weatherford lost some of the war leaders' confidence by trying to stop the massacre at Fort Mims, he was still their best strategist. He would now concentrate his forces at key strong points in the Muscogee nation and meet whatever forces the whites threw at him. The Red Sticks probably had no more than 2,500 fighting men. Only one in three was armed with a musket or rifle. The rest carried only war clubs, hatchets, bows and arrows—and the dubious promises of their prophets that they were invincible and that the white armies would fail. Such promises had done little good at Fort Mims (Owsley, 28–29; Elting, 166–167; Stiggins, 97, 123).

For the Red Sticks, news of the war in the north was not good. On October 5, 1813, Tippecanoe's victor, William Henry Harrison, with 4,500 men—mostly Kentucky militia volunteers eager to avenge their countrymen massacred at the River Raisin in January—smashed the British and Shawnee army at the Thames River (or Moraviantown) in Canada. "Butcher" Henry Proctor had less than a fourth the number of the Americans; and the night before, Tecumseh had told his own men, "Brother warriors, we are about to enter into an engagement from which I shall never return." Colonel Richard M. Johnson's Kentucky Mounted Riflemen, using tactics very similar to those that would be used against the Red Sticks in Alabama, charged Tecumseh's 500 warriors. The Shawnee chief, shot in the chest, fell dead. Thirty-three warriors and eighteen British soldiers were killed, while American losses were fifteen killed and thirty wounded. Moraviantown dealt the death blow to Tecumseh's confederacy and to the Native Americans on the northern frontier. It was a foreshadow of what was to come in the Muscogee nation (Edmunds, 212; Freehoff, 32–36).

CHAPTER 6

"Old Hickory"

In Nashville, Willie Blount read George Gaines's letter describing the Fort Mims massacre with shock and alarm. The state legislature was about to meet, and the governor wasted no time in appealing for a call to arms. The delegates passed an act on September 25 calling up 3,500 volunteers, in addition to the 1,500 already mobilized earlier in the summer. The troops were to assemble at Fayetteville, just north of the Mississippi Territory's border, on October 4. In their haste to report for duty, many soldiers left without making plans for harvesting their crops and without any supply of winter clothing.

Emotions ran high, and frontiersmen had to weigh the needs of their families against their burning urge to avenge Fort Mims. David Crockett's wife argued with him not to go, that he was needed more at home. But he wrote, "[M]y countrymen had been murdered, and I knew that the next thing would be, that the Indians would be scalping the women and the children all about there, if we didn't put a stop to it…. The truth is, my dander was up, and nothing but war could bring it right again" (Crockett, 51–52).

Andrew Jackson, the sandy-haired, stern-faced commander of the Tennessee militia army, received the news of Fort Mims at the Hermitage, his home near Nashville. Jackson was recovering from a bullet wound in his left shoulder—a wound received in a recent street fight with Thomas and Jesse Benton, two bitter enemies. Jackson's wife, Rachel, was caring for him, and the old warrior was really in no physical shape to lead an army on an active campaign into the wild backcountry of the Muscogees.

Jackson had long argued for a military strike against the Red Sticks and their British allies. "The late attack of the Creek Indians," he declared,

"…call a loud for retaliatory vengeance." Although some might have counseled delay, Jackson was eager to fight, writing, "It is no time for a patient to be sick when his country needs his services." The campaign against the Muscogees was Jackson's great opportunity for military fame and glory. "The health of your general is restored," he assured Tennesseans. "[H]e will command in person." Jackson arrived at Fayetteville on October 7, with his arm in a sling (Remini, *Jackson,* 1977, 190; Moore and Foster, 343–344).

The master of the Hermitage was a self-made frontier entrepreneur who had become the most eminent planter in the Cumberland River valley. Jackson was a tough and strong-willed politician and military leader. Choleric and mean-tempered, prone to temper tantrums laced with abusive language, he took offense easily and was quick to resort to the *code duello.* By nature Jackson was a competitor, and his autocratic personality tolerated no disagreement. To his enemies he was unforgiving and vindictive (Remini, *Jackson,* 1977, 7–9).

Raised among poor Scotch-Irish settlers on the Carolina frontier, Jackson never knew his father, who died just before Andy was born. Jackson was just eight years old at the outbreak of the Revolutionary War, a conflict that claimed his mother and two brothers. By age thirteen, he was active with the rebel partisans fighting against the British and was captured by enemy soldiers. Jackson carried physical scars of a sword-whipping given him by a British dragoon when the boy refused to shine an officer's boots. His wartime experiences left him with a lifelong hatred and distrust of the British. To Jackson, it was the British who were at the root of the Red Stick troubles (Faust, 202–203).

Jackson's opinion of Native Americans wasn't much better. He had fought them on the Cumberland frontier and believed that they responded not to reason, but only to force. Like most white frontiersmen, he saw the red man as inferior. But Sharp Knife, as the Native Americans called him, also believed that the tribes could be "civilized" and absorbed into white society. This did not mean they should not be forced to give up their rich lands to the sweep of white westward settlement. Even before the Creek War, he had already formed a rough plan in his mind for the removal of the southeastern tribes (Remini, *Jackson,* 1977, 71; Remini, *Legacy,* 46–47).

As a Nashville attorney who had also dabbled in politics and served a short term in Congress, Jackson had no real command experience. But he was a popular figure in Nashville's social world, and soon he was elected major general of the militia for Tennessee's western district. The forty-six-year-old Jackson had demonstrated his toughness in January 1813. Ordered to march his Tennessee militia south—to make ready either to seize Mobile or to defend against a suspected British move against New Orleans—he dispatched Colonel John Coffee's 670 cavalrymen to

Natchez, while he loaded his 1,830 foot militia on flatboats to carry them down the Cumberland River to the Ohio and from there down the Mississippi (Ehle, 106–107; Davis, 311).

With winter unusually severe that year, the timing was brutal for either a thousand-mile journey downriver or a 500-mile march overland along the Natchez Trace. Temperatures were freezing, roads were rivers of mud as Coffee's column rode south to the Tennessee River, and it took the colonel two days to move his men and horses over. Chickasaw mixed-blood chief George Colbert cheerfully ferried the troops across and fed them—at his usual price-gouging rate—and the soldiers received help from the Chickasaws they encountered along the Natchez Trace. Coffee reached Natchez on February 16 (Davis, 311–312; Elting, 157; Gibson, 97).

Coffee's men had made a difficult march, but he was more worried about Jackson: "I fear he will be froze up in the river." And in fact, he nearly had been. Jackson's expedition moved slowly downriver. Once into the Ohio, the boats encountered ice in the river so hazardous that Jackson had to hold up for three days, while his men shivered in the snow and the bone-chilling wind. Three soldiers died. The expedition continued down the Ohio and Mississippi Rivers, and one of the boats went down, but no lives were lost. It was a tired and irritated Jackson who rendezvoused with Coffee at Natchez (Davis, 311–312).

But this had been only the beginning of Jackson's frustrations. He waited with his army at Natchez, expecting orders to move on to New Orleans or Mobile, but no orders came. A month passed, and the Tennesseans still sat in Natchez—with no enemy in sight and no orders to move forward. Volunteers grew increasingly restless, eager to either do something or go home. Finally Jackson received word from Washington to abort the campaign; his expedition was being recalled to Nashville. The British had not moved on New Orleans; there was no enemy to engage. Jackson was livid. An exasperated Coffee wrote, "We had just begun to learn how to do duty when we shall be discharged." His men would have preferred at least "one stump of a fight" before being sent home. Fuming, Jackson marched his entire army out of Natchez on March 22 and headed them north on the Trace. He engaged wagons for the sick, and paid the expenses himself, vowing to take personal responsibility for the cost of paying and feeding his soldiers. Jackson made the trip on foot, refusing to ride as long as there were sick men who needed transportation. And out of this badly handled fiasco the old warrior received a new nickname: Old Hickory (Davis, 312–313; Elting, 158).

Now, in the fall of 1813, many were relieved to see Old Hickory moving against the Red Sticks. Major General John Cocke and his 2,500-man division of East Tennessee Militia, assembling at Knoxville, would join Jackson's army somewhere on the northern fringe of the Muscogee country, and Jackson would have overall command. From there, he would march

south, destroy the Red Stick strongholds, and eventually rendezvous with
the Georgia and Mississippi militias under Floyd and Claiborne.

Jackson's army assembled at Fayetteville both mounted and on foot.
His 1,000-man infantry force was composed of William Hall's brigade of
volunteers and Isaac Roberts's brigade of militia. Hall's men were veterans of Jackson's Natchez expedition—called up, since their twelve-month
term of enlistment would not expire until December 10 (Clayton, 78–79).

Jackson's cavalry arm was also filled with veterans of his earlier expedition. Now a brigadier general, John Coffee commanded 1,300 Tennessee
cavalry and mounted riflemen. In their brown woolen hunting shirts and
headgear made from raccoon or fox skins, or slouched hats, the mounted
volunteers did not cut a very military appearance. But armed with the
long rifles favored by frontiersmen, as well as hunting knives, they were
every bit as formidable as the Kentucky Mounted Riflemen who had
smashed the British and Tecumseh's Shawnee warriors at the Thames
(Chartrand, 81).

"John Coffee is a consummate commander," Jackson wrote. "He was
born so. But he is so modest that he doesn't know it." Coffee was Jackson's
best friend. Standing over six feet tall, weighing 216 pounds, the frontier
giant was brave and unassuming, and he had aided Old Hickory in the
fight with the Bentons. He was also Jackson's business partner and was
married to Jackson's niece. Coffee was forty-one years old in 1813. His
grandparents were Irish immigrants, and his father was a veteran of the
Revolutionary War. Coffee owned land along the Cumberland River near
Nashville, the wealthiest community in the area. Unlike most of Jackson's
acquaintances, both friends and enemies, Coffee had no interest in elected
office. Perhaps that was what made him such a trusted confidant. Once
when Jackson went overboard at a horse race, betting far more than he
could afford, Coffee physically picked up the six-foot, 140-pound Jackson
and carried him off to prevent his throwing away his savings. Coffee
expected the Creek campaign to be "short and vigorous" (Owen, 131;
Remini, *Jackson*, 1977, 135, 172, 185; Ratner, 41–44; Holland, 13).

One of Coffee's mounted volunteers was David Crockett, a twenty-
seven-year-old frontier settler who had just recently moved with his wife,
Polly, and their children to a cabin on Bean's Creek, a few miles north of
the Mississippi Territory boundary. Crockett enlisted in a company at
nearby Winchester, Tennessee. "Expecting to be gone only a short time,"
he wrote in his journal, "I took no more clothing with me than I supposed
would be necessary, so that if I got into an Indian battle, I might not be
pestered with any unnecessary plunder." Crockett clearly was proud of
the men he served with and wrote, "I verily believe the whole army was
of the real grit" (Hauck, 18–19; Crockett, 51–53).

Also riding with Coffee were several picked companies of mounted
rangers, or "spies." Their job was critical, for they would scout ahead of

the main army and scan the country for enemy war parties. They would work with Native American allies—Cherokees, friendly Muscogees, Choctaws, a few Chickasaws—and would provide Jackson with the intelligence he needed to plan his campaign against the Red Sticks. The captains of the spies included men who were well familiar with the frontier, men such as William Russell and John Gordon, a fifty-year-old veteran of Indian conflicts who operated a trading post where the Natchez Trace crossed the Duck River (Davis, 315).

At Jackson's side were several officers who had earned his trust. Major John Reid, his aide, was a twenty-nine-year-old Virginian, bright, loyal, and one of Old Hickory's favorites. Twenty-five-year-old Colonel William Carroll, Jackson's brigade inspector, was the son of Irish immigrants, his father an officer in the Continental Army during the Revolutionary War. Sharp and literate in spite of only a minimal formal education, Carroll settled in Nashville, where he met Jackson on joining the local militia. He quickly advanced in rank and in attachment to Old Hickory, and he was with Jackson in his Natchez expedition (Remini, *Jackson,* 1977, 172, 180–181; Ratner, 65–67).

Carroll was indirectly responsible for Jackson's trouble with the Benton brothers that resulted in Old Hickory's recent shoulder wound. Carroll, who was somewhat unpopular with other officers because they saw him as Jackson's pet, had been challenged to a duel by another young militia officer. When Carroll first declined to fight—on the grounds that the young man was not a gentleman—Jesse Benton took the other officer's place, forcing Carroll to fight. Carroll asked Jackson to be his second. Carroll's marksmanship was not good. He stalled for time while he practiced with a dueling pistol and insisted on shortening the distance between the two duelists to ten feet, something counter to the code of dueling. Jackson was unable to talk him out of it. The meeting on June 14, 1813, resulted in neither Carroll nor Benton being seriously hurt. But the incident triggered a bitter feud between Jackson and Benton, who along with his brother Thomas accused Old Hickory of favoritism and resented his becoming involved. The belligerent rhetoric between the men escalated (Ratner, 67).

Jackson himself was no stranger to dueling and was certainly not one to back down from any fight. After marrying Rachel Donelson Robards in 1791, he discovered that her divorce from her first husband was not actually final until 1793. Jackson and Rachel went through a second wedding ceremony. But this didn't quell the slanderous talk that his political enemies spread against him throughout his life in public office. The quick-tempered Jackson fought several duels rising from the matter and killed one man, a fellow lawyer, in 1806.

Finally, Jackson challenged Thomas Benton, but before the duel could take place the two men encountered each other on a Nashville street. There were angry words, and the hotheaded Jackson sprang on Benton with his sword cane. Rushing to help his brother, Jesse Benton fired his pistol and hit Jackson in the shoulder. So in October 1813, Jackson was still mending (Ratner, 68).

Other troops marched into the Muscogee country with Old Hickory. Captain David Deaderick's volunteer artillery company from Nashville signed up for six months. Deaderick was a veteran militia officer, and with him were young lieutenants Robert Armstrong and Joel Parish and fifty enlisted men. Artillery was considered the elite branch of the American army during the War of 1812, but lack of horses and adequate supplies was always a problem, especially on the frontier. Deaderick's men marched on foot. Field guns had an effective range of only 900 yards and had to be re-aimed after each round fired. A typical nine-man crew could fire one or two rounds per minute. Deaderick's company had only two small fieldpieces, but the Nashville artillerists would prove their worth to Jackson several times over during the Creek campaign (Heidler and Heidler, *Encyclopedia*, 17–19; Remini, *Jackson*, 1977, 200).

Finally, there were Jackson's red allies. Since distinguishing the Cherokees and Allied Creeks from the enemy might be a problem, Jackson instructed them to wear white feathers or deer's tails in their hair. The red allies were not to mutilate the dead. There was to be no killing of prisoners, but soldiers and allied tribesmen could take anything the prisoners had, including their women and children and their slaves (Owsley, 62; Ehle, 108–109).

Jackson envisioned a masterful strike deep into the Muscogee nation, crushing the Red Sticks and pushing on to Mobile. His army would construct a military road along his route of march, and this road could be used by white settlers moving into the Creek lands after the Red Stick menace was ended. Like Ferdinand L. Claiborne, Old Hickory's associate in Congress, he also believed that there would be no real peace in the Old Southwest until the Spanish were expelled from Florida, and he expected to move against Pensacola as soon as the Red Sticks were dealt with (Remini, *Jackson*, 1977, 191).

Jackson had already ordered Coffee with his 1,300 mounted troops to move out ahead of the main army. Coffee's command rode south to Huntsville, where many former Tennesseans had settled, and on to Beaty's Spring, a few miles farther south. Reliable information on the whereabouts of the enemy was difficult to come by. The Red Sticks had made no major offensive in the six weeks since Fort Mims. Their intentions were unclear, and the location of their main army was unknown. Coffee sent out scouts to gather intelligence. David Crockett led one of two mounted patrols that crossed the Tennessee River and returned with news that Red Stick warriors were heading north to attack Jackson's column (Clayton, 79; Crockett, 53–57).

Coffee reacted quickly. On October 11, he sent a dispatch to Jackson reporting what he had learned, and Jackson put his troops on the move, joining Coffee at Huntsville that night. When the enemy attack failed to materialize, Jackson marched his army south to Ditto's Landing on the Tennessee River where supplies were supposed to be waiting for him, brought down from Knoxville. The supplies weren't there, because the river was too shallow and the flatboats had been unable to move downriver (Clayton, 79).

Undeterred by the first of many setbacks in the campaign, Old Hickory determined to forge ahead. Jackson waited at Ditto's Landing until October 22, when it was evident that the supply boats would not show, then he marched his command twenty-four miles upriver, his troops cutting a crude military road across the rugged mountains. Reaching the bend in the Tennessee River at the mouth of Thompson's Creek (near present-day Guntersville, Alabama), the Tennesseans constructed Fort Deposit, Jackson's supply depot, where he expected to receive the boats from upriver. Meanwhile, Jackson sent Coffee's mounted volunteers westward to raid enemy towns on the Black Warrior River (Clayton, 79; Owsley, 64; Remini, *Jackson*, 1977, 192).

At the head of 600 to 700 of his mounted riflemen, Coffee rode through Huntsville on October 15 and moved west, crossing the Tennessee River near the head of Muscle Shoals. Coffee's objective was Black Warrior Town, the westernmost Red Stick settlement—actually located in Choctaw territory—at the Sipsey and Mulberry forks of the Black Warrior in present-day Walker County, Alabama. The Tennesseans expected to accomplish two things by their long ride to the southwest: to destroy a major Red Stick stronghold and to forage for food. Coffee's men braced for their first encounter with the dreaded Red Sticks, but when they struck Black Warrior Town they found that the enemy had evacuated it. This probably was the same town that the Choctaws had found deserted on October 9. The Tennesseans confiscated 300 bushels of corn and beans, then set the town ablaze. Then they pushed on to catch up with Jackson (Owsley, 64; Crockett, 58; Doss, 271, 274; L. Thompson, 412–413, 419–420).

At Fort Deposit, no supply boats had appeared, and Old Hickory wrote that he feared "an enemy whom I dread much more than I do the hostile Creek... 'Famine.'" Jackson's little army had already used up what rations they had, and it was a welcome relief when Coffee's troops rode into camp with corn captured from the Black Warrior towns (Bassett, vol. 1, 335; Clayton, 79; Owsley, 64).

The ease with which Coffee had destroyed Black Warrior Town led Jackson to feel that the Red Sticks might not offer resistance. This encouraged him to push on into enemy territory despite his lack of supplies. Jackson now had the cooperation of his Cherokee allies. Richard Brown, the mixed-blood chief who lived not far from Fort Deposit, joined the Tennesseans with some twenty of his warriors, who would guide Jackson into the Muscogee country (Owsley, 64; Hood, 28–29).

While Old Hickory stubbornly plowed ahead through the hills of northern Alabama, his counterpart, Major General John Cocke, left Knoxville and moved southwest through the Cherokee country. Brigadier General James White, a sixty-six-year-old North Carolina veteran of the Revolutionary War, commanded the 1,000-man advance mounted contingent, performing the same function for Cocke as Coffee did for Jackson. Colonel Gideon Morgan met White's column at Hiwassee with 200 Cherokee volunteers—including Ridge, mounted, armed with rifle and sword, and equipped for the campaign. There were full-bloods and mixed-bloods in the Cherokee contingent, and some warriors were as young as sixteen. White's soldiers were from the East Tennessee mountains. Their natural inclination was to be wary of the Cherokees, as the red men were suspicious of them. The Cherokees rode in front of White's army, moving at a slow pace through the mountains (Heidler and Heidler, *Encyclopedia*, 117; Moore and Foster, 345; McCown, vol. 11, 101; Hoig, 117; Ehle, 109–110).

White's troops continued down the Tennessee, and by October 17 they reached the trading post of John Ross's father at Lookout Mountain, near present-day Chattanooga, Tennessee. They were now just a few days' march from Jackson's army, and soon they halted at Turkeytown, Pathkiller's town in the bend of the Coosa, in present-day Cherokee County, Alabama. There they waited to rendezvous with the West Tennessee troops (Lossing, 760; Hood, 31–33; McCown, vol. 11, 101).

Like every other major army involved in the Creek War, Cocke's East Tennesseans were plagued by shortages of food and supplies, as well as the frustrations of military bureaucracy and petty rivalries of some of its officers. The forty-one-year-old Cocke, an attorney and a member of Tennessee's legislature, was a political rival of Old Hickory and had his own agenda. Cocke's 2,500 troops were scheduled to rendezvous with Jackson at his forward base in the Alabama country, where they would be under Jackson's command. Cocke was in no hurry and preferred to operate independently for as long as he could (Heidler and Heidler, *Encyclopedia*, 117).

Marching in Cocke's army was twenty-seven-year-old Captain Jacob Hartsell, whose widowed mother, along with her three sons, had migrated to present-day Washington County in the northeast corner of Tennessee. Civic-minded Jacob was the county tax assessor, and even though he had no military experience, he raised a local company whose 300-odd-mile trek to Alabama probably took them farther over rougher terrain than any other group of volunteers. Hartsell worked hard to make his company one of the best in Colonel William Lillard's Second Regiment of East Tennessee Volunteers. He kept a journal during the campaign and faithfully recorded details of camp life, the geography and plant life of the Cherokee country through which the troops passed, and the customs of the Cherokees themselves (McCown, vol. 11, 93–96).

By the end of October, Cocke's soldiers had constructed a supply base near the junction of the Coosa and Chattooga Rivers in present-day Cherokee County, Alabama. Fort Armstrong, as the stockade was called, occupied the site of an old British post during the Revolutionary War and was probably no more than fifty miles due east of Jackson's army. It would be mid-November before Colonel Lillard's regiment, with Jacob Hartsell's company, would reach there (McCown, vol. 11, 102; Heidler and Heidler, *Encyclopedia*, 117; Jenkins, 175).

Meanwhile, Jackson was preparing to move again. He received word from Pathkiller, the elderly Cherokee chief, that Red Stick war parties were massing in the Ten Islands area of the upper Coosa, near present-day Gadsden, Alabama, and that they planned an offensive against Coweta and other allied Muscogee towns. In his first major operation since Fort Mims, William Weatherford had marshaled his forces in this area to oppose Jackson and his allies. Red Eagle had spread the word in late October that the Red Sticks would retaliate against any Muscogees or Cherokees who aided the invaders (Owsley, 64; Griffith, 117; L. Thompson, 421).

Old Hickory now had about six days' rations of beef and two days' rations of bread for his army. But he was bound to press the campaign. "I am determined to push forward," he wrote, "if I have to live upon acorns." On October 25, he set out for Ten Islands, his troops again cutting a road through the rugged mountains, "almost as difficult as the Alps," according to an impressionable Major John Reid. Jackson was near his objective by November 1, although his troops had to stop often to forage for food. Coffee's rangers scouted vigilantly for signs of enemy activity (Bassett, vol. 1, 336; Clayton, 79; Remini, *Jackson*, 1977, 192–193; Griffith, 116; Elting, 167; Hauck, 22; Heiskell, 404).

Jackson sent out another mounted detachment, about 200 men led by Lieutenant Colonel Robert H. Dyer, to raid nearby villages for food. Before dawn on October 29, Dyer and his troops struck the village of Littafuchee on Canoe Creek in present-day St. Clair County. The Tennesseans achieved complete surprise; captured twenty-nine Creek prisoners, including some women and children; burned the village; and seized cattle and corn for Jackson's army (Owen, 131; L. Thompson, 422).

The hungry Tennesseans had reached Ten Islands and were busy constructing Jackson's new forward supply base, Fort Strother, on the Coosa River fifteen miles south of present-day Gadsden. Beyond the Coosa was the Muscogee nation. On November 7, an excited Creek runner came into the Tennesseans' camp with startling news. The friendly Creek town of Talladega, about thirty miles farther south, was under siege by a thousand Red Stick warriors. The messenger relayed an urgent appeal from the defenders, begging for help before it was too late (Elting, 167; Owsley, 65; L. Thompson, 432).

Old Hickory had already encouraged the Allied Creeks to hold out against the Red Sticks. He had written Chennabee, a friendly chief, "If one hair of your head is hurt, or of any who are friendly to the whites, or of your family, I will sacrafice a hundred lives to pay for it." Eager to do battle, Old Hickory spurred on his Tennesseans as well: "You have, at length, penetrated the country of your enemies.... If the enemy fly before us, we will overtake and chastise them" (Bassett, vol. 1, 334; Remini, *Jackson*, 1977, 193; Moore and Foster, 345–346).

Jackson pushed on to Talladega and his first major encounter with the Red Sticks. He expected glory. But the strike would have to be swift, since he still did not have sufficient rations for a lengthy campaign. And victory would also depend on the timely appearance of General Cocke's army. Would the East Tennesseans arrive in time? Meanwhile, at Talladega, Red Eagle was waiting.

CHAPTER 7

"Shot Them Like Dogs"

Even before the Talladegas' pressing appeal for help reached Fort Strother, Jackson had learned of a large concentration of Red Stick warriors at Tallushatchee, a small town just eight miles northeast, near present-day Jacksonville, Alabama. He needed to neutralize this enemy stronghold before he moved his army farther south, and he sent John Coffee with 900 troops from his mounted brigade to do the job.

Two friendly Muscogees led the way, and Cherokee warriors led by Richard Brown also rode with the Tennesseans. Coffee's men crossed the Coosa and made camp at the Fish Dams. Up and on the move before dawn on November 3, the horsemen reached within a mile of Tallushatchee, where Coffee halted them and divided the command into two columns, each led by one of the Muscogee guides. Coffee with Colonel Newton Cannon's mounted riflemen maneuvered around the northern side of the town, while Colonel John Alcorn's cavalry took the southern side (Quimby, 407; Griffith, 118; Crockett, 60).

The horsemen moved as silently as possible through the crisp autumn foliage and around the town until the head of each column met on the opposite side. Tallushatchee now was completely encircled. The sound of Red Stick drums and war cries told the soldiers that the warriors in the town had learned of their presence. Captain Eli Hammond's rangers and Lieutenant Andrew Patterson's mounted company touched off the action. Riding up to the town, the rangers quickly drew fire from the Red Sticks—who "raised the yell," David Crockett wrote, and came charging out "like so many red devils" (Quimby, 407; Griffith, 118; Crockett, 60).

The Red Sticks fired one volley with their muskets, then used their bows and arrows. The rangers fell back toward the lines of grim-faced riflemen waiting in position around the town. With the Creeks lured out into the open, Alcorn's cavalry discharged a volley, and Cannon's mounted riflemen followed suit. The ring of fire that Coffee had thrown up around Tallushatchee opened up, trapping the Red Sticks in a crossfire. The warriors returned fire and quickly fell back into the town for cover. The mounted troops closed in (Quimby, 408; Crockett, 60–61; Griffith, 118; Owsley, 65; Heidler and Heidler, *Encyclopedia*, 500).

It was clear that there could be no escape. Pockets of die-hard warriors headed to the houses for a last-ditch battle. Soldiers shot women and children as they mingled with the warriors, something that Coffee later said he regretted. Terrified women tried desperately to surrender. Crockett recalled seeing seven of them holding on to one soldier's shirttails. But some resisted fiercely. One woman—planted firmly in the doorway of a house held by nearly fifty warriors—used her feet to pull the bow she held in her hands and sent an arrow into a Tennessee lieutenant, killing him. Almost immediately, twenty musket balls cut her down, and the soldiers stormed into the house (Griffith, 120; Crockett, 61).

Crockett wrote, "We now shot them like dogs." The soldiers closed in on the warriors, shooting and bayoneting them inside and outside of the houses. The Red Sticks resisted furiously, with whatever weapons they could find. The Tennesseans set fire to the houses. The warriors trapped inside burned to death. Those who ran out were shot down. No one escaped. Crockett remembered one young boy, probably about twelve years old, crawling away from a burning house, his arm and thigh shattered and "the grease stewing out of him" but begging no quarter (Crockett, 61; Lossing, 763).

Coffee's soldiers killed 200 Red Stick warriors at Tallushatchee and took eighty-four women and children prisoner. The entire town was in flames. Five Tennessee soldiers were killed, and forty-one were wounded in the action. "We have retaliated for the destruction of Fort Mims," Jackson reported to Governor Blount (Elting, 167; Owsley, 65; Griffith, 119; Bassett, vol. 1, 341).

The mounted troops left the burning ruins of Tallushatchee and joined Jackson at Ten Islands. They had been on half rations for several days and were dismayed to find that no supplies had arrived there. Some of them returned to Tallushatchee the next day in an attempt to find something to eat. The stench and appearance of the dead in the smoldering village were appalling. Someone uncovered a potato cellar under one of the burned houses, and Coffee's soldiers—"hungry as wolves," according to Crockett—ravenously helped themselves. It was a grim meal, though. Crockett recalled that "the oil of the Indians we had burned up on the day before had run down on them, and they looked like they had been stewed with fat meat" (Crockett, 61–62).

"We found as many as eight or ten bodies in a single cabin," Lieutenant Richard Keith Call wrote. "[H]alf consumed bodies were seen amidst the smoking ruins. In other instances dogs had torn and feasted on the mangled bodies of their masters." Call was sickened by the sight. And when Jackson's young aide, Major John Reid, reached the Tallushatchee battle site, "the first I ever beheld," he wrote his wife, "it is impossible to conceive so horrid a spectacle" (Remini, *Jackson*, 1977, 193; Heiskell, 404).

Colonel Gideon Morgan's Cherokee warriors, wearing the white feathers and deer's tails that marked them as Jackson's allies, also rode into Tallushatchee, disappointed to find that Coffee's white soldiers had already destroyed the town. The group, which included Ridge and John Walker, had been released by Brigadier General James White of Cocke's East Tennessee army, but they arrived too late to take part in the fighting. All they found now was the smoking ruins of the town, a few Creek women and children who had emerged to sift through what was left of their homes, and piles of dead bodies. Anxious to vent their warlike passions on the Red Sticks, the Cherokees scalped any of the bodies that were not already scalped by the white soldiers. John Walker wrote that he was saddened at the sight of "women and children slaughtered with their fathers" (Wilkins, 69, 353 n. 50).

The pitiful cries of a small infant led soldiers to a baby, the body of his dead Muscogee mother nearby. They carried him back to Jackson's camp at Ten Islands, where somehow the child caught Old Hickory's attention. Jackson urged some of the captive Muscogee women to take care of him. "No," they shook their heads and declared, "all his relations are dead, kill him too." The tough frontiersman's heart suddenly went out to this infant, about ten months old—the same age as his adopted son, Andrew Jr. War had made this baby an orphan, as it had the general in his childhood. Jackson took the baby to his tent. Brown sugar and water sustained the infant, and Jackson sent him back to Tennessee for Rachel to care for. The Jacksons named him Lyncoya and raised him at the Hermitage as a son. Jackson wrote Rachel, "[H]e may have been given to me for some valuable purpose" (Remini, *Jackson*, 1977, 194; Griffith, 110).

As brutal as the Tallushatchee action was, it was only a portent of what was to come. Horrified by the killing, many Muscogees began to have serious second thoughts about supporting the Red Stick movement. For the Tennesseans, the engagement bolstered their resolve. Colonel William Carroll declared that Coffee's destruction of Tallushatchee set the pace of the campaign. "After Tallushatchee we had the measure of the Creeks," Carroll wrote. "All apprehension was dispelled. Every man in Jackson's army was serenely confident that contact with them meant victory for us, under any conditions." Coffee wrote his wife on November 4 that Tallushatchee was only "a small scirmish," and boasted, "Our men are in excellent spirits." "The die is now cast," he continued, "and I don't expect after this, the enemy will ever meet us, they have no kind of chance" (Moore and Foster, 346; Griffith, 119; Notes from Papers of Gen. John Coffee).

News of Coffee's victory spread quickly. Back at Camp Ross, on the Tennessee River, Cocke's foot soldiers received the news of Tallushatchee from some of White's advance troops. Captain Jacob Hartsell wrote in his journal on November 7, "[T]he hole army where we lay Shot and Drunck tell midnight for joy, which made much Noise" (McCown, vol. *11*, 101).

By November 8, Jackson's soldiers had built a stockade at Ten Islands. Called Fort Strother (after Jackson's topographical engineer, Captain John Strother), it was located on the west side of the Coosa, in present-day St. Clair County, Alabama. Fort Strother would be Old Hickory's forward supply base. It was here that word came in from Allied Creeks at Talladega that the town was under siege by a superior force of Red Sticks. The stage was set for the first major battle of the Creek War (Owsley, 65; Jenkins, 175; McCown, vol. 12, 127).

The Muscogee town of Talladega was east of the Coosa about thirty miles south of Fort Strother. As was the case in so many Muscogee communities, a mixed-blood trader had built a stockade and trading post there, called Leslie's (or Lashley's) Fort, located not far from the large spring at Talladega. It was here that some 160 friendly Creeks and their families had taken refuge. Surrounding the stockade were 1,100 Red Stick warriors—"the very choice of the Creek nation," according to David Crockett—under the command of William Weatherford. Red Eagle was anxious to prevent Muscogee towns from going over to the enemy, especially after what happened at Tallushatchee, and he intended to make a lesson of Talladega. The defenders were running out of food and water. Weatherford had granted them a three-day truce to make up their minds whether to support the Red Sticks, and they used that time to stall while they sent a runner to seek help from Jackson (Owsley, 66; Lossing, 764; McCown, vol. 11, 103; Faust, 210; L. Thompson, 433; Crockett, 62).

Like many of his soldiers, Jackson had come down with dysentery, the most serious of camp diseases, and he was still ailing from the bullet in his shoulder. He was not really well enough to ride out, but he insisted on going. Old Hickory left Fort Strother at midnight on November 8 at the head of 1,200 foot soldiers and 800 mounted troops. Meanwhile he sent orders to General White at Turkeytown, just twenty miles to the east, to march to Fort Strother and protect the post, where Jackson had left 200 of his sick and wounded soldiers and his supplies. Jackson's army moved forward in three columns, the standard formation on the march in hostile country. If attacked, the troops could more easily deploy into a "hollow square" for defense (Griffith, 121; Owsley, 65; Elting, 167; Moore and Foster, 347; Skeen, 52).

The Tennesseans crossed the Coosa, where the mounted soldiers expedited the process by doubling up with the infantrymen and carrying them across. After moving through the woods all day, Jackson halted his column about six miles from Talladega. It was late that night, after Jackson had just received his scouts' reports on the Red Sticks' location, that the allied chief, Chennabee, brought in an alarming dispatch from White. Major General Cocke had ordered White to abort his march to Fort Strother and to join him at Fort Armstrong instead. This put Old Hickory in a very difficult position. If he moved ahead with his plans to attack Talladega, Fort Strother with his sick and wounded would be vulnerable to attack from other Red Stick war parties. If he withdrew to his supply base, the allied Creeks at Talladega might be annihilated. Jackson decided to go ahead and risk an assault at Talladega (Owsley, 65–66; Remini, *Jackson,* 1977, 196; Lossing, 764; Clayton, 79; Elting, 167).

Without White's support, Jackson was gambling that he would be able to score a quick victory at Talladega and move his army back in sufficient time to cover Fort Strother. If he failed, the results could be disastrous, because Weatherford might destroy his army, move on Fort Strother, and then possibly overwhelm Cocke's force as well. The Tennesseans were back on the march at daybreak on November 9 and by 7 A.M. were within a mile of Talladega.

Jackson's army halted just above the big spring north of Talladega and deployed for battle. The scouts had judged the Red Stick encampment to be to their south, along the little creek that flowed from the hillside spring past Leslie's Fort where the allied Muscogees were gathered. It would be necessary to envelop both the fort and the hostile encampment, and the Tennesseans began fanning out in a crescent formation, the two points aimed toward either side of the creek (Jemison, 39; Reid and Eaton, Sketch of the Battle of Talladega).

Coffee and Jackson planned on using the same encircling tactic that proved so successful at Tallushatchee, but this time the foot soldiers formed part of the surrounding force. Coffee's troops divided into three components: Colonel Cannon's mounted riflemen to encircle the Red Sticks and the friendly fort on the left, Colonel Alcorn's cavalry to encircle on the right, both columns to meet on the other side of the fort, and a reserve force under Lieutenant Colonel Dyer to be held in the rear. Roberts's militia brigade would close up behind Cannon's mounted troops on the left, and Hall's volunteer brigade would follow Alcorn's cavalry on the right. Colonel William Carroll would lead an advance guard of four selected companies that included Captain Deaderick's Nashville artillerymen armed with muskets, two rifle companies, and John Gordon's mounted spy company. As at Tallushatchee, the advance detachment was expected to flush the Red Sticks into the open (Quimby, 409; Lossing, 764–765; Clayton, 79; Crockett, 62; Bassett, vol. 1, 348–349).

There was no sign of the enemy. Weatherford was far too resourceful to allow himself to be taken by surprise. His scouts had spotted the Tennesseans moving in the woods toward the town, and Red Eagle had set a trap of his own. Hidden by the thick bushes along the bank of the stream, the main party of Red Stick warriors was now poised to attack the white troops as soon as they came within range. When Jackson's advance detachment was within eighty yards of the creek bed, the Red Sticks opened fire, and the engagement began (Crockett, 62).

On the far side of the little stockade, the two columns of mounted volunteers had met and were in position. As William Russell's rangers rode forward in the cool of the early morning, they could see the defenders atop the stockade waving to them and shouting, but they paid no attention and nearly rode into the Red Stick ambush. Finally two of the Talladegas ran from the fort, seized the bridle of Russell's horse, and made him understand that he was headed straight into a trap. The Red Sticks rose from their hiding place and rushed at the Tennesseans "like a cloud of Egyptian locusts," according to Crockett, "and screaming like all the young devils had been turned loose." "They were all painted as red as scarlet," Davy wrote, "and were just as naked as they were born" (Crockett, 62–63).

The rangers whirled, and many stumbled from their horses in a mad dash for the safety of the fort. The horses stampeded toward the waiting lines of the Tennesseans drawn up in the woods. The warriors then saw Coffee's mounted troops and rushed toward them. As soon as they were within range, the Tennesseans opened fire. Many of the Red Sticks fell. "They then broke like a gang of steers," Crockett wrote, "and ran across to our other line, where they were again fired on" (Crockett, 62–63).

Carroll's advance detachment had returned fire on Weatherford's warriors, and now the Tennesseans rushed toward the creek. Dislodged from their hiding place, the Red Sticks charged yelling and firing toward the Tennessee foot militia, drawn up on the left of Old Hickory's battle formation. Several companies of Roberts's militia, frightened by the Red Sticks' boldness, took to the rear, and a dangerous gap yawned in Jackson's lines. Jackson ordered Colonel Edward Bradley of Hall's brigade to fill the gap with his regiment. Bradley was too slow. But quickly Lieutenant Colonel Dyer brought up the reserve cavalry, including Captain Eli Hammond's rangers and four other companies. The soldiers rode up and dismounted, plugged the opening, and drove back the Red Stick warriors. Roberts's militia was bolder now and joined the advance. Soon Jackson's army closed in for the kill (Quimby, 409; Lossing, 765; Clayton, 79; Bassett, vol. 1, 349).

The battle lasted about twenty minutes. Volley after volley blanketed the Alabama woods with smoke, as the shouts of the officers mingled with the bloodcurdling cries of the warriors. Although the Red Sticks fought fiercely, with muskets and with bows and arrows, it was clear that they were surrounded and outnumbered. At one point, a Red Stick warrior urged Weatherford to surrender; Red Eagle simply dropped him with his tomahawk. The fighting continued. The Creeks sought desperately for a way out, and they found one. Old Hickory's ring of soldiers was not tight enough. The Red Sticks saw an opening and poured through, melting away into the woods (Owsley, 66; L. Thompson, 437).

The Allied Creeks' deliverance was assured now. The Talladegas, famished after days of siege, streamed from the stockade to drink at the spring nearby. Coffee's mounted troops pursued the Red Sticks and inflicted more casualties as they chased them for three or four miles (Quimby, 410; Remini, *Jackson*, 1977, 197).

A postbattle body count revealed that Jackson's soldiers killed 300 Red Sticks at Talladega. A Spanish flag discovered after the battle was convincing proof for Old Hickory that America's European enemies were clearly at the root of the Red Stick rebellion, and he was more eager than ever to see the war to a conclusion. In the fighting at Talladega, fifteen Tennesseans were killed and eighty-five were wounded. Two soldiers later died of their wounds. Before leaving Talladega, the troops buried the fifteen dead soldiers in a single grave (Holland, 15; Elting, 168; Quimby, 410; Faust, 210; Crockett, 64).

As many as 700 Red Sticks managed to get through the Tennesseans' lines to escape the net. Jackson's plans had gone well until part of Roberts's militia fell back, creating a temporary gap in the encircling lines. Alcorn's cavalry had left a gap too, between the rear of their column and Hall's brigade, and the Red Sticks had quickly exploited these openings to make their getaway. But for these mishaps, Talladega might have been the decisive battle of the Creek War. Jackson concluded, "Had I not been compelled by the *faux pas* of the militia in the onset of the battle, to dismount my reserves, I believe not a man of them would have escaped" (Holland, 16; Owsley, 66; Crockett, 64; Quimby, 410; Skeen, 165).

Jackson heaped high praise on Colonel Carroll's advance detachment and on Lieutenant Colonel Dyer's reserve. Overall, Old Hickory was well satisfied with his troops' performance at Talladega. Coffee was forced to acknowledge that the Red Sticks were tougher than he had first thought. Still, he wrote his wife optimistically predicting the conclusion of the war: "We only want supplies to enable us to finish the campaign in three weeks" (Moore and Foster, 347; Griffith, 122; Owsley, 66).

And indeed it was Jackson's continuing problem with supplies that crippled his first offensive against the Red Sticks. Had he been able to follow up his victory at Talladega, he probably would have brought the Creek War to a speedy conclusion. The Red Sticks had suffered staggering losses in just one week's time; probably 1,000 of their warriors were killed and wounded at Tallushatchee and Talladega. But Jackson was prevented from going further. Low on food and worried about the security of his base at Fort Strother—left unprotected because of Cocke's failure to cooperate with him—he reluctantly withdrew to the Coosa (Owsley, 66).

While Old Hickory understandably fumed about Cocke's upsetting his plans, the East Tennessee commander had problems of his own. His army was experiencing food shortages too; in fact they had never had more than five days' rations since leaving Knoxville. Cocke realized that Jackson expected him to have supplies for the West Tennesseans when he rendezvoused with him, and since he had none, it made sense to him to operate on his own, which he preferred to do anyway. "If we follow Genl. Jackson's army," he had written White, "we must suffer for supplies, nor can we expect to gain a victory." Cocke had put the question to his own officers: Should the East Tennessee army follow Jackson? Unanimously, the officers said no. But should the army advance, conduct a campaign of its own, and hit Red Stick towns on the Tallapoosa? The officers unanimously favored this independent course of action. Cocke decided to go with the consensus of his officers. "I wish you to unite with me," he wrote White. "I want the E. Tennessee troops together" (Quimby, 413–414).

White's mounted brigade and the Cherokees under Colonel Gideon Morgan had joined Cocke's army at his supply base—Fort Armstrong, at the junction of the Coosa and Chattooga Rivers. White's troops were nearly starving. Although the Cherokees were allies, the white soldiers thought nothing of plundering their nearby communities of food and livestock, but foraging parties sent out to the Cherokee towns failed to bring in much. Many of Cocke's foot soldiers reached Fort Armstrong on November 13. They had marched from Camp Ross, on the Tennessee, across country and had passed through several Cherokee villages. Captain Jacob Hartsell commented on the Cherokee women he saw there with their children, was amused by one young girl "with one amost as large as hurself" on her back sleeping soundly (Quimby, 413–414; Hoig, 117; McCown, vol. 11, 102).

Cocke prepared to move against Red Stick towns on the upper Tallapoosa, and he dispatched White's brigade—consisting of Colonel Samuel Bunch's mounted infantry regiment, Major James Porter's cavalry battalion, and Colonel Morgan's Cherokees—to begin the campaign. Sometime between November 11 and 17, they struck the towns of Odfuskudshi (Little Okfuskee) and Atchina-algi (Genalga), and captured five Red Sticks. Then they rode toward the Hillabee towns. The Hillabees had played a major role in the fighting at Talladega, and word came to Cocke that Billy Scott, one of the principal Red Stick chiefs who had fought at Talladega, was at the Hillabee towns, still threatening attacks against whites and friendly Creeks. Cocke instructed White to attack the Hillabees and informed Jackson of his plans on November 14 (Owsley, 66; Quimby, 415–416; Owen, 111–113).

White's soldiers were ignorant of developments three days later, when the chiefs of the Hillabee towns sent Robert Grierson (or Grayson), a Scottish trader and "Indian countryman," with a message to Jackson. These

Red Stick towns had had enough and wanted peace. The chiefs realized that the Hillabee towns would be the next target of the Tennesseans and that treatment of them would likely be harsh because of the role they had played at Talladega. Jackson agreed to suspend operations against the Hillabees on condition that they turn in any of the Red Stick leaders there and that they surrender property, particularly slaves, taken from white settlers. And he promptly sent a message to Cocke on November 18 informing him of the Hillabees' surrender (Quimby, 414–415).

But it was too late for news of these important events to reach White. Unaware of the truce, White's troops made a dawn attack on the unsuspecting Hillabee town on November 18.

The town targeted by the East Tennesseans was on Hillabee Creek, a tributary of the Tallapoosa. Its main occupants—sixty-five wounded warriors who had escaped the bloody Talladega encounter, plus their women and children—thought they were under Jackson's protection and were not expecting to be attacked. White's troops and Cherokees dismounted and surrounded the town during the predawn darkness and then attacked at sunrise. The Cherokees were the first in and did their work very effectively; many of the white troops didn't even have time to take part in the killing. The slaughter took less than fifteen minutes. White's soldiers shot or bayoneted the occupants of the cabins, took 256 prisoners—including Billy Scott—put the town to the torch, and withdrew to Fort Armstrong. They left sixty Hillabees dead (Quimby, 415–416; Owsley, 66–67; Owen, 111–113).

Most of the prisoners were women and children who were sent on to the Hiwassee garrison in the Cherokee nation. Ridge sent one Muscogee girl and several black slaves back home to his wife. Like Lyncoya in the Jackson household, the young girl was treated like a member of the Ridge family. Some of the male captives were not so fortunate. Hartsell witnessed the killing of two prisoners by the Cherokees—shot and then tomahawked "in a crewal maner," he wrote. The Cherokees took one of the captive's scalps. The other they took three scalp locks from, because they said he had killed three white men (Quimby, 415; Ehle, 111; Wilkins, 71; McCown, vol. 11, 107–108).

The tragic Hillabee massacre dashed any hopes of bringing the Creek War to an immediate end. The Hillabees blamed Jackson for a cruel betrayal of their trust. They resolved to fight to the end and were among the last die-hard Red Sticks to give up. Had the massacre not taken place, other Red Stick towns probably would have followed the lead of the Hillabees and surrendered to Jackson. Now it was not to be (Faust, 210–211; Griffith, 123; Owsley, 67).

The Hillabee affair also strained relations between Jackson and Cocke. Jackson eventually preferred charges against Cocke, who was court-martialed but acquitted. Cocke had actually informed Jackson of his intentions to send an expedition against the Hillabee towns on November 14, and Jackson was aware of it. Yet when Old Hickory wrote Cocke four days later telling him of the Hillabees' offer of surrender, he made no mention of the proposed operation. His mind may have been occupied by more pressing problems in camp—problems that threatened to sabotage the entire campaign (Owsley, 67; Quimby, 416; Skeen, 165).

CHAPTER 8

The Mutineers

Jackson had marched back to Fort Strother on November 10 only to find that his army's meager rations had finally given out. His soldiers had eaten less than two meals in five days. Now they faced starvation. Nights were much colder now as well, and many of the Tennessee troops had not brought proper clothing for winter. Fighting Red Sticks was one thing; that they could handle. Starving in the cold while waiting for supplies that never came was something else entirely. Jackson's troops began to talk of going home.

Conditions were no better for Jackson and his officers. Earlier, Jackson had vowed to live off acorns if he had to. Now, when a Tennessee soldier complained to the general that he was starving, Old Hickory offered to share what food he had with him. He drew out a handful of acorns from his pocket and offered them to the young man (Remini, *Jackson*, 1977, 197).

Jackson wrangled with contractors over their failure to provide supplies, and he fumed at General Cocke for failing to back up his strike against Talladega. He even wrote Major General Flournoy at Mobile— who had supply problems of his own—asking if provisions could be sent up the Alabama. Flournoy was astonished that Jackson was not already at the Hickory Ground and wrote that he could not help him until Brigadier General Claiborne was able to march up the Alabama. Jackson was in almost constant pain—from diarrhea and from the troublesome bullet he still carried in his shoulder. Unable even to stand without support, he braced himself on a horizontal pole sometimes for hours at a time. One thing kept him going. Seeing the war to its end had become a personal obsession, and he would let nothing stand in his way (Remini, *Jackson*, 1977, 197; Quimby, 411, 416).

It was an obsession that his weary soldiers did not share. A number of officers presented Jackson with a petition politely requesting leave to return to Fort Deposit, where at least the troops could be properly fed. Jackson responded with characteristic stubbornness and bristled that his men should even think of abandoning the campaign. There should be ample supplies at Fort Deposit by now; they would arrive at Fort Strother at any time. Besides, it was too dangerous to try to move the wounded over such rugged country, he said. The general counseled patience. His troops had fought well. Why spoil things now by dishonorable conduct (Owsley, 68; Quimby, 411; Remini, *Jackson*, 1977, 197)?

But the soldiers had had enough and were resolved to take matters into their own hands. General Roberts's militia brigade was the first to act. Still Jackson felt he could surely depend on Hall's volunteer brigade, the veterans who had gone with him to Natchez. When the militia tried to leave, Jackson deployed the volunteers across the road with orders to stop them. The militia backed down and returned to camp. But in hashing over the day's events, the volunteers began to have second thoughts, concluded that the militia was right to try to leave, and planned on trying it themselves. The next day, Hall's volunteers attempted to march out of Fort Strother. This time Jackson had the militia—the same men who had tried to leave on the previous day—formed up to block the path of the volunteers, who backed down. But it was obvious that these "divide and conquer" tactics would not work indefinitely (Owsley, 68; Quimby, 411).

Old Hickory asked the troops to give him two more days. If supplies had still not arrived from Fort Deposit by then, he would not try to stop them from leaving. He again praised them for their conduct so far, told them he realized that conditions were intolerable, and promised that things would get better. Many of the soldiers just laughed at him. The three brigades each took a vote. Coffee's men chose to remain with Jackson for as long as he needed them. Roberts's militia would stay for two more days. Hall's volunteers refused to wait any longer, and Old Hickory watched in frustration as the disgruntled soldiers marched out of camp. He did get them to agree to return from Fort Deposit as soon as they could, and to bring supplies with them (Owsley, 68–69; Remini, *Jackson*, 1977, 198; Reid and Eaton, 67).

Two days passed, and Jackson's time was up. No supplies were to be seen at Fort Strother. The general was forced to keep his promise to the remainder of the army, and the soldiers prepared to leave for Fort Deposit. Jackson begged for volunteers to remain a while longer to garrison Fort Strother. "If only two men will remain with me," he coaxed, "I will never abandon this post." John Gordon, the old ranger captain, stepped forward. "You have one, general," he vowed—and quickly added, "Let us look if we can't find another." Jackson was finally able to cajole 109 reluctant men into agreeing to remain, while he marched north to Fort Deposit with the troops (Remini, *Jackson*, 1977, 198).

On November 17, Old Hickory and his starving soldiers left Fort Strother and began trudging north over the same rough country they had crossed three and a half weeks earlier. After marching twelve miles, they met what Jackson was hoping they would encounter and what the soldiers probably dreaded to find at this point—a supply convoy coming down from Fort Deposit with a herd of 150 cattle and nine wagons of flour. Jackson halted the column, and soldiers slaughtered the cattle on the spot. The army was finally able to quell its hunger (Remini, *Jackson*, 1977, 198; Elting, 168; Owsley, 69).

Even after they had eaten, the soldiers were still reluctant to march back to Fort Strother, where they knew that conditions would probably not improve. One company quietly ambled out of camp and started north. Jackson rode after them, accompanied by a few of Coffee's troops, who deployed across the road ahead. The furious Jackson faced down the mutineers, threatening to fire on them if they refused to halt. The soldiers finally turned around and marched back to camp (Owsley, 69; Quimby, 198–199).

The confrontation was still not over. Now a whole brigade prepared to desert. Jackson again rode to the front of the troops. Using his good right arm—his left still in a sling—he grabbed a musket from one of his soldiers, propped it on the pommel of his saddle and leveled it at the rebellious troops, threatening to send a musket ball into the first man who moved. "You say you will march," he declared. "I say by the Eternal God you shall not march while a cartridge can sound fire." And there he remained, a lone rigid figure defying an entire brigade of sullen, angry men. Moments passed, and no one moved. Coffee and Major Reid rode up to Jackson's side. Minutes ticked by. Now loyal soldiers, their muskets at the ready, began to assemble behind the three officers. The mutineers finally murmured among themselves and returned to camp. The soldiers did not know that the musket that Jackson had used was so old that it could not even be fired (Owsley, 69; Remini, *Jackson*, 1977, 199).

Jackson had refused to be intimidated. Despite his own health problems—and the fallout from the tragic developments in the Hillabee towns that were unfolding at this same time—he was able to focus on the predicament at hand and force the mutineers to back down. The food crisis was over and the first threat of mutiny and desertion as well. The army marched back to Fort Strother, where—from then on—a barely adequate flow of supplies continued to come in. Jackson agreed to release Coffee's mounted brigade temporarily to Huntsville in order to seek forage for their exhausted horses; they were to return, however, as soon as possible (Remini, *Jackson*, 1977, 199; Owsley, 69–70; Quimby, 413).

Old Hickory's soldiers were far from satisfied, however. Jackson held out hope that things would improve when Cocke's army finally arrived at Fort Strother, but Cocke apparently was still having problems as well. Jackson wrote the East Tennessee commander on December 6 and expressed surprise and concern over Cocke's failure to receive supplies from Knoxville. He was unhappy with the contractors, too. "Every letter I receive from the governor," he wrote, "assures me I am to receive plentiful supplies from him.... it is wholly unaccountable that not a pound of it has ever arrived" (Bassett, vol. 1, 374).

The next crisis to rear its head came as the short-term enlistments of the troops expired, and this proved to be an even thornier issue than the supply problem. Hall's soldiers contended that their time was up on December 10, the end of their year's enlistment for the Natchez expedition. Jackson had released them in April 1813, and when they had been recalled in September they argued that the five months they had spent at home counted as part of their time in service. Most of their officers agreed. Would Old Hickory allow them to go in peace? The general interpreted things differently and left no misunderstandings about it. The volunteers had five more months to serve and were bound to remain until they had completed their mission. Besides, he had sent Colonel William Carroll on to Tennessee to raise troops to be their replacements, and they should be content to wait until these soldiers arrived. But after the Natchez fiasco, an unwelcome recall in September, and the hardships of the Creek campaign, Hall's men were fed up and declared that they would leave anyway—on December 10 (Owsley, 69–70; Quimby, 420–421; Remini, *Jackson*, 1977, 199–200).

"There is much sickness in camps," a volunteer wrote his wife on November 25, "and one or more dies every day." It had been snowing nearly all day off and on; Jackson's freezing soldiers huddled around campfires and grumbled about the injustice of army life. "There is grate talk about the 10th of December," the soldier wrote. "I do not think that Genl. Jackson intends to discharge us on that day tho still I think we shall go home" (Bains, 405).

The showdown took place on the night of December 9. After Hall alerted Jackson that his brigade planned to march out that night, Old Hickory swung into action. He ordered Hall's brigade to fall in outside the walls of the fort and posted Roberts's brigade of militia athwart the road to Fort Deposit. Facing Hall's brigade was Captain Deaderick's company of Nashville artillery, their two small cannons ready, the lighted fuses in the hands of the gunners. And squarely in front of the mutineers was "Old Hickory-face," as Davy Crockett called him, mounted on his horse. At first Jackson was calm, deliberate, and persuasive, again spoke in praise of how well the volunteers had performed. But he made it clear they were not leaving. "I have done with entreaty," he concluded. "It has been used long enough—I will attempt it no more. You must now determine whether you will go or peaceably remain. If you still persist in your determination to move forcibly off, the point between us shall soon be decided" (Remini, *Jackson*, 1977, 200–201; Quimby, 422; Crockett, 64–65).

Again the crisis unfolded. The men stirred restlessly, grumbling among themselves but hesitating to move against the general. "I demand an explicit answer," Jackson thundered. Still no one moved, unwilling to risk Andy Jackson's wrath. The officers realized they must make the next move, and they still refused to concede that the general had any legal right to keep the troops. There was a heated exchange between Jackson and Colonel William Martin, commander of one of the volunteer regiments, who had never given Jackson any reason to doubt his loyalty until now. Finally, after talking things over with the men, some of the officers walked forward and told Jackson that the soldiers agreed to stay until reinforcements arrived or until their arguments were resolved by higher authorities (Quimby, 422; Clayton, 80).

Jackson blamed the whole affair on a conspiracy by disloyal officers of the volunteer brigade, especially Colonel Martin. Martin later denied that a mutiny took place; he claimed that Jackson had overreacted to the situation. "It is hardly supposable," he wrote, "that if they had been in a state of mutiny, as charged, they would, with such promptitude have obeyed the order to parade for the purpose of being disarmed, *deep in the enemy's country.*" Ultimately, Governor Blount felt the controversy was not worth pursuing politically. He wrote Jackson on December 15 to go ahead and discharge the volunteers, because Colonel Carroll would soon be raising another brigade of equal strength (Bassett, vol. 1, 383; McCown, vol. 12, 131).

But the damage was done. Jackson could never depend on these troops again. He wrote to Rachel of his bitter disappointment, his volunteers of whom he had been so proud after the Natchez expedition now reduced to "Mere, wining, complaining...mutineers." "This was a grating moment of my life," he confessed. Lieutenant Richard Keith Call visited the general's tent that night. He found Old Hickory in a gloomy mood. Call volunteered to give up his commission and reenlist as a private to serve as Jackson's personal bodyguard. The old general brightened and thanked Call for his offer but turned him down, saying, "If I had 500 such men I would put an end to the mutiny before the sun sets" (Remini, *Jackson*, 1977, 201).

Jackson could at least take heart in one consolation. General Cocke's troops from East Tennessee were finally due at Fort Strother, and Hall's soldiers had agreed to hold off leaving until Cocke arrived. After posting a small garrison to man his supply base at Fort Armstrong, Cocke marched in on December 12 with 1,450 troops. With his soldiers drawn up in review, Old Hickory had his artillery company fire off their two small cannons as a salute to the East Tennesseans. Captain Jacob Hartsell had never heard cannon fire before. He gazed at Jackson's ragged, cheerless troops and later recorded in his journal, "[T]he men Loocked verey bad In general" (Owsley, 70; McCown, vol. 12, 123, 125).

Hartsell learned from an officer in Hall's demoralized brigade that Jackson's soldiers had been eating cowhides and guts and that some had even dug around in the manure and dirt of the horse pens to retrieve half-chewed corncobs that they parched and ate. Grumbling and discontent was everywhere in camp. Hartsell wrote, "[T]her was more Confution than I ever Saw in my Life at one plase." Many of the soldiers were sick and disillusioned; they just wanted to go home. Even the simplest camp utensils were hard to find. Hartsell had only one tin bucket to cook with for his entire company (McCown, vol. 12, 126).

Inactivity was almost as hard for Jackson's troops to deal with as the cold and hunger. Old Hickory had hoped that with Cocke's reinforcements he just might be able to resume the campaign against the Red Sticks. But this was not to be. The East Tennessee troops' enlistment period was about up as well. Old Hickory discovered that Cocke's soldiers were as deficient in clothing and equipment as the West Tennesseans. A thoroughly disgusted Jackson finally ordered Cocke to lead one of his regiments, whose time was up on December 23, back to Fort Armstrong and discharge them. Meanwhile, Hall's brigade was finally marching back to Tennessee (Quimby, 422–423; Elting, 168; Owsley, 70; Remini, *Jackson*, 1977, 202).

The next setback for Old Hickory was the desertion of John Coffee's brigade, which had performed so well at Tallushatchee and Talladega. Jackson had sent the mounted troops north of the Tennessee River temporarily to locate feed for their horses. Half of them never returned to Fort Deposit, and what remained of the brigade quickly disintegrated as well. What Hall's resentful soldiers told them as they straggled back through Huntsville convinced the mounted troopers that they might as well leave for home, too. The ever-loyal Coffee was ashamed of them and wrote to Jackson, "They are now lying encamped with that holy body of Infantry that deserted you and their country in the hour and moment of danger" (Quimby, 423; Remini, *Jackson*, 1977, 202).

Recovering from an illness, Coffee was not his usual energetic self just now. He had seen this action coming for a while, though; he knew that his troops were unhappy and anxious to go home. He wrote his father-in-law on December 22 that "each man seems to keep his calendar before him." Even though he was ailing, the big man took to horse and rode to talk with his soldiers, but even by appealing to them in person he was unable to persuade them to stay. Coffee was embarrassed and disappointed. "I cannot bring myself to believe," he wrote his wife on December 27, "the friends of those who return in disgrace will receive them friendly and will rather condemn their conduct" (Remini, *Jackson*, 1977, 202; Notes from Papers of Gen. John Coffee).

Of the major components of Jackson's West Tennessee army that had marched with him into the Muscogee nation, only Roberts's militia brigade was left. Now a difference of interpretation over their period of service took place. Roberts's soldiers insisted their term of enlistment was for three months. Jackson argued that it was for six months, because this was the prescribed term of service for U.S. troops (Remini, *Jackson,* 1977, 202–203).

Roberts and Jackson argued over the status of the militia, Roberts insisting they were enlisted for only three months, that most of them were poor farmers, and that they needed to get back to their families. Old Hickory railed that it made no difference, that this was war, and that soldiers should stay on for six months and do their duty to their country. On December 28, the argument became hot, and the two officers—drawing their swords—nearly came to blows until other officers separated them. The two generals spent the night writing angry letters back and forth to each other (McCown, vol. 12, 135).

But Governor Blount agreed with the men. Since the virtual disintegration of Old Hickory's army left little to fight the Red Sticks with, the governor suggested that Jackson evacuate Fort Strother and abandon the campaign, fall back to Fort Deposit or even to Huntsville and mark time, at least for the present. It was a bitter pill for Jackson to swallow (Owsley, 70; Remini, *Jackson,* 1977, 203).

Old Hickory composed a sharp, lengthy letter to Blount late in the night on December 29. He urged the governor not to give in to political pressure and to maintain an army in the Creek country. Jackson pleaded with Blount to raise more troops immediately. "And are you my Dear friend," Jackson wrote, "sitting with yr. arms folded under the present situation of the campaign recommending me to retrograde to please the whims of the populace and waiting for further orders from the Secy war. Let me tell you it imperiously lies upon both you and me to do our duty regardless of consequences or the opinions of these fireside patriots" (Remini, *Jackson,* 1977, 203–204).

On January 4, the day that the militia brigade's enlistment expired, there was another confrontation at Fort Strother. Lieutenant William M. Kirby, the officer of the guard, had dismissed his men to their camp and was marching away, when Jackson appeared with Gordon's ranger company, which by now had evolved into the embattled commander's personal guard. Jackson ordered the lieutenant to halt, and he refused. Jackson drew his pistol, and the lieutenant drew his sword. Men on both sides cocked their weapons. Old Hickory ordered the lieutenant to surrender his sword. The young officer refused, explaining that he would need a weapon on his trip to the Tennessee River. Other officers intervened, separated the two men, and persuaded the lieutenant to give up his sword. Kirby was arrested, but he later apologized and Jackson pardoned him (McCown, vol. 12, 138).

Jackson made one more appeal to Roberts's brigade. If the militia soldiers would agree to stay just six more weeks, he would give them all an honorable discharge. They would have no part of it. Roberts's brigade marched out that afternoon. Old Hickory fumed, "I wish they and they volunteers had a smoke tail in their teeth, with a Peticoat as a coat of mail to hand down to their offspring" (McCown, vol. 12, 137–138, 141).

Now Colonel William Lillard's regiment was due to leave—the last of the East Tennessee troops. Jackson tried to convince them to remain, but they just laughed at him. "Some Swore that before they wold Stay three monthes," Jacob Hartsell wrote, "they wold kill General Jackson." On January 10, the mountaineers left Fort Strother—having never fired a shot at the Red Sticks and glad to be going home. The bitter Jackson was glad to see them go. "I think of all damned Rascals I ever saw," he wrote, "is some of the Holston soldiers, nothing can excape them" (Holland, 17; McCown, vol. 12, 131, 141).

Jackson's army had melted away before his eyes. He was left with his faithful Nashville artillery company and Gordon's and Russell's two companies of scouts, only 130 soldiers to man Fort Strother. "I was abandoned by all the forces ordered on the field," he wrote, "& left with my brave guards & fifty men to keep possession of this post and defend the frontier" (Owsley, 70; Stephen, 126; Holland, 17; Clayton, 80).

With the campaign against the Red Sticks hopelessly stalled, even the Cherokees, left by Cocke to garrison Fort Armstrong, became restless. On December 18, Colonel Gideon Morgan dismissed them "for the present." He added, "Fifty nights shall not pass ere your swords, your lances, and your knives shall drink the blood of your enemy." Many of the warriors were shocked at what they found when they reached their homes. In spite of complaints by Cherokee families to agent Return J. Meigs, the East Tennessean soldiers had pillaged their homesteads of livestock and corn from Camp Ross to Turkeytown. While their warriors served in Jackson's army in the war against the Red Sticks, Cherokee families were starving (Ehle, 112; Wilkins, 71; McCown, vol. 12, 142).

Because of the nation's dependence on the militia and volunteers, almost all of the American armies in the War of 1812 experienced problems with short-term enlistments. On the northern frontier in April 1813, Virginia militiamen refused to stay one day past their end of enlistment, even though their garrison at Fort Meigs was left vulnerable to an impending attack. At Fort George on the Niagara peninsula, Brigadier General George McClure faced the same kind of dilemma as Jackson when his militia troops' term of enlistment expired in December 1813. The militia marched home, leaving McClure only a hundred soldiers to hold the fort (Owsley, 70–71; Skeen, 59–60).

Supply also was a universal concern for American armies in the War of 1812. Congress encouraged the use of private contractors even though they generally proved unreliable, as with the Tennessee forces. The Georgia and Mississippi armies shared the same difficulties with supply that plagued Jackson. And, on the northern frontier, General William Henry Harrison coped with these same problems in his campaign against the British and Tecumseh's confederacy. More methodical and patient than Old Hickory, Harrison constructed a chain of fortified supply bases through hostile country. Unlike Jackson, he was not embroiled in a civil war among Native American tribes, and concern for the safety of the friendly faction was not a problem. He could take his time (Quimby, 472–473; Skeen, 52–53).

Acts of desertion and insurrection by state militias were not unique to Jackson's army. The northern frontier witnessed similar cases. In the autumn of 1812, a company of Kentucky militia in Harrison's army simply marched back home because they did not approve of an order given by the commanding general. In November 1812, a New York militia brigade staged a mutiny after a dispute over inadequate quarters, and at least one hundred men deserted. Four soldiers were shot for desertion and another for mutiny. Two more New York militia regiments mutinied just a few days later in protest at not being paid, and more than 1,500 Pennsylvania militia refused to cross the border into Canada (Skeen, 44, 102–104).

The Tennesseans' continuing supply problem was welcome news for William Weatherford, who had suffered two serious defeats at Tallushatchee and Talladega. Jackson's problems with supply and the short-term enlistments of his troops left his army idle for ten weeks. Red Eagle used this time to regroup and reorganize his forces. He continued to wrestle with the problem of keeping a reliable large army in the field long enough to deliver a serious defeat to the white forces. Red Eagle was attempting to concentrate his warriors at Eccanachaca (Holy Ground), the Red Sticks' stronghold on the Alabama River. With the cooperation of Menawa and other Red Stick leaders, he would also form a heavy concentration of warriors at Tohopeka on the Tallapoosa, because he knew that Sharp Knife would be back (Griffith, 123; L. Thompson, 441).

CHAPTER 9

"They Are Killing Everything"

As they had threatened to do, the Red Sticks struck back at the Allied Creeks. While Jackson had his hands full quelling mutiny among his troops and John Cocke's raiders were needlessly burning the Hillabee towns, the rebels moved against Coweta and surrounded the Lower Creek capital. On November 18, the Allied Creek chiefs—Big Warrior, Little Prince, William McIntosh, and Alexander Cornells—sent a compelling appeal for help to Brigadier General John Floyd, commander of the Georgia army preparing to invade the Muscogee nation. The chiefs informed Floyd that the Red Stick army, outnumbering their own warriors more than two to one, had Coweta under siege. "They are killing everything," the chiefs reported, "and burning all the houses." The Red Stick move against Coweta was probably retaliation for William McIntosh's October attack on a war party of 150 Uchees intercepted in Georgia on their way to join the rebels. McIntosh had also burned several Red Stick villages and destroyed their crops (Griffith, 118; Southerland and Brown, 42; Owsley, 52).

Floyd, a forty-four-year-old planter and former shipbuilder, was already aware of the problem. Runners from Coweta had reached him earlier with news of the Red Stick threat, and Floyd had reported to the Georgia governor on November 16 that Coweta was in a "state of great alarm." The general suspected that Peter McQueen was behind all this, and that the Red Sticks—low on supplies like the Americans—intended to seize what the Cowetas had (Griffith, 124).

For two months Floyd's army—2,364 men enlisted in late August and September—had languished at Fort Hawkins on the Ocmulgee waiting for enough rations to be collected to allow him to begin a campaign. Arms and ammunition also were in short supply. In fact, Governor David Mitchell admitted that the Georgia militia was "destitute of all supplies." "Nothing detains the army here but the want of provisions," Floyd wrote on November 8. "The contractors and Quartermaster Department are badly managed. They have been a dead weight on the movements of the army." Camp sickness was a problem as well (Owsley, 52; Skeen, 162–163; Coleman and Gurr, 315; Floyd, 233).

Most of Floyd's soldiers were volunteers and were regarded as the best troops in the Georgia Militia. There were two regiments of infantry, a battalion of riflemen, and one company of artillery. Unlike Jackson, who had Coffee's large brigade of mounted troops, Floyd had only a small detachment of light dragoons. There were not enough supplies and no corn for the horses (Owsley, 56; White, 290).

Floyd's soldiers were men such as twenty-two-year-old Private James A. Tait from Elbert County in the hill country of northeastern Georgia. Tait mustered with his company at the county courthouse and began a long seven-day march to the Ocmulgee. "I walked 20 miles the second day," he wrote in his journal. "The farthest I ever walked in one day on a journey." The Elbert County men reached their camp on the Ocmulgee in a pouring rain in the steaming south Georgia summer heat. Tait and his comrades soon became accustomed to camp life and exposure to the heat and rain, with few adequate shelters and little food and supplies. "This little army has been badly provisioned with victuals since it encamped," he wrote. "Much and just complaint has arisen" (Brannon, "Journal," 230–231).

At least the delay gave Floyd more time to train his little army, and training was something his men badly needed. With drums and fifes playing, Floyd reviewed his two militia regiments of infantry. Scruffy in their hunting shirts and homespun garb, the men presented arms as Floyd, dressed in his blue uniform coat with gold epaulets and lace, looked on, possibly wondering just how to go about whipping these men into shape for the coming campaign. Tait described Floyd as "about the middle size, of a dark complexion and formed for strength." Colonel Daniel Newnan, veteran of the campaign against the Seminoles the previous year, commanded one of Floyd's infantry regiments. To Tait, Newnan was "the most able, or skillful, commander in the southern country" (Brannon, "Journal," 231).

Also in Floyd's army was the Baldwin Volunteer Artillery, Captain Jett Thomas's company from Milledgeville, the Georgia state capital. A capable junior officer, the thirty-seven-year-old Thomas, a former carpenter and now a well-to-do contractor, had built the statehouse at Milledgeville. Although the self-made Thomas had no military experience, his natural ability as an officer soon became evident to his men as he drilled them, first at the state capital and then at Fort Hawkins. Thomas's expertise as a builder soon made him invaluable as Floyd's chief engineer officer. Floyd would be in need of Thomas's men and their guns when he finally met the Red Sticks in battle (Howard, 378–379).

Public criticism had set in quickly as Floyd's army sat idle, waiting on rations, drilling and training, but not advancing against the dreaded Red Sticks. Lack of support from the Georgia governor's office also frustrated Floyd. While the general felt that available military forces should be consolidated under his command for the proposed offensive, David Mitchell—and Peter Early, who succeeded him as governor—believed that Georgia's long frontier was too vulnerable to attack, and they held back numbers of militia along the Ocmulgee. Major General David Adams still maintained a separate command of 500 militia north of Floyd's army (Owsley, 52; Heidler and Heidler, *Encyclopedia,* 206).

Finally Floyd managed to collect twenty days' rations of flour and a small supply of beef. Although these supplies were skimpy, still he felt he should risk an advance into Red Stick country. His tiny army finally marched out of Fort Hawkins—"Took a joyful farewell of the sweet waters of boggy branch," James Tait wrote—on October 29. Floyd's troops followed the Federal Road, crossed the Flint River on November 2, and made camp at Fort Lawrence near Hawkins's Creek agency. Floyd left for Coweta on November 18. "The men are eager for battle," he wrote his sister, "and I am equally desirous of having them tried." He added, "[T]he means and risk of regular supplies is my greatest dread." Floyd had only 950 soldiers who were fit to march. Camp sicknesses, coupled with the cold and rain, had thinned his ranks, and Floyd himself suffered from a bad cold (Brannon, "Journal," 233; Floyd, 234; Owsley, 52; Quimby, 427–428).

The Georgians reached the Chattahoochee, crossed the river, and rendezvoused with the allied Muscogee chiefs at Coweta. Floyd was relieved to learn that the Red Sticks had lifted the siege of Coweta and had withdrawn. Alexander Cornells wrote to Hawkins from Coweta on November 20, "[T]he hostile Indians have retreated, they were nearly naked and not well armed." Two miles from Coweta, Floyd began construction of his forward supply base, Fort Mitchell, in present-day Russell County, Alabama (Owsley, 52, 54; Brannon, "Journal," 233; Quimby, 427; Grant, 676).

At Fort Mitchell, 300 to 400 Allied Creeks under William McIntosh augmented Floyd's forces. William McIntosh (Tustunnuggee Hutkee, or White Warrior) was becoming the most important chief of the Lower Creeks. The thirty-eight-year-old McIntosh—like his Red Stick adversary William Weatherford—was the son of a Scottish father and a Muscogee mother. And like Red Eagle, McIntosh benefited from his father's ties to the white world and his mother's connections via the politically powerful Wind clan. McIntosh's cousin, George M. Troup, was a prominent state political personality and a future state governor. Raised in Coweta, White Warrior had become the speaker for Little Prince, raising his political power in the Muscogee nation. He was also the head of the Muscogees' police force (Owsley, 54; Heidler and Heidler, *Encyclopedia*, 334).

Although the Georgians welcomed their help, the friendly Muscogees created an additional burden for Floyd's little army, already weakened by supply shortages. The Red Sticks had burned the crops of the Cowetas, and the population faced starvation. Although he naturally had earmarked what supplies he had for his own troops, Floyd felt responsible for feeding the Muscogee families. Floyd was fearful of what they would do if he did not feed them—possibly go over to the side of the Red Sticks (Owsley, 55–56).

Considering his shortage of rations, Floyd's next move was a daring one. He struck out with his entire command on a raid sixty miles into the heart of Red Stick territory. The Georgia army's objective was Autossee, a major Red Stick town on the eastern bank of the Tallapoosa, not far from Tuckabatchee, the Upper Creek capital, and Tallassee, the town of Hopoithle Miko and Peter McQueen. Autossee was located in a swampy area at the mouth of Calabee Creek, just northwest of present-day Shorter, Alabama. Its name meant War Club, and it was the town of High-Head Jim, sworn enemy of William McIntosh and the peace party. According to the Red Stick prophets, Autossee was sanctified ground where no white man could enter and live (Owsley, 54; Bassett, vol. 1, 398; Lossing, 768; L. Thompson, 262; Brannon, "Journal," 234).

Besides its importance as a major economic center, Autossee was also a prime military target. Floyd had reliable intelligence that McQueen was at Autossee with about 1,000 warriors, many of them survivors of Jackson's campaign driven from the north. Farther south of Autossee was Othlewallee, one of the Red Sticks' three main strongholds or camps, where prophet leader Paddy Walsh was encamped with more than 500 warriors. The Georgia army's attack on Autossee would represent the first allied strike at a major Red Stick concentration (Quimby, 427; Owen, 94; L. Thompson, 262; Stiggins, 123).

Floyd's troops left Fort Mitchell on November 24 with only five days' rations in their knapsacks. Their guide was Abram Mordecai, a Jewish trader who was very familiar with this part of the Muscogee country since he had lived in Autossee. Mordecai had once built a cotton gin near Charles Weatherford's racetrack on the Alabama River, but an affair with an attractive married Muscogee woman had raised the ire of her townsmen, who destroyed the gin. The Georgia troops made good progress on their march through the Muscogee nation. Mordecai was a skilled guide, knew the country well, and was able to lead Floyd's soldiers through the woods even at night. The little army arrived before their objective just before dawn on November 29. They were actually ahead of schedule (Elting, 168; White, 291; Griffith, 124).

Using the same tactics employed by Jackson and Coffee, Floyd had planned to divide his army into two columns that would encircle the town while securing his right flank on Calabee Creek and his left on the Tallapoosa below Autossee. Lieutenant Colonel David S. Booth's battalion of infantry formed the right column, with Captain William E. Adams's rifle company as the flank company. Captain Thomas's artillery company took its place in front of the right column. Lieutenant Colonel James C. Watson's battalion of infantry would comprise the left column, with Captain James Meriwether's rifle company, led by Lieutenant Hendon, on flank. Floyd's mounted dragoons under Major Frederick Freeman would be held in reserve. The Allied Creeks, led by McIntosh and their own chiefs, were to cross the Tallapoosa and occupy the far bank so as to block any Red Stick retreat from Autossee (Griffith, 125; Owsley, 54; Quimby, 428; Lossing, 768; Brannon, "Journal," 234).

Floyd's plans did not go as he had intended. His scouts discovered what he described as a second Red Stick town about 500 yards below Autossee. The name of this settlement is unknown. Whether it was an extension of Autossee or a smaller Red Stick encampment, it still posed a dilemma to Floyd, who could not afford to have a concentration of enemy warriors behind his left flank. The only alternative to Floyd was to destroy both towns, so he had to overextend his left column to encircle the lower town as well. He detached three companies of infantry from his left column under Colonel Watson, the left flank rifle company under Lieutenant Hendon, and two troops of mounted dragoons under Captains John Irwin and Samuel S. Steele with orders to attack the lower town (Owsley, 54; Griffith, 125; Quimby, 428; Lossing, 768).

Another disruption to Floyd's tactical plan was his inability to block the Red Sticks' escape route. The Allied Creeks failed to cross the river. Due to the recent heavy rains, the Tallapoosa was too deep and the weather was too cold. Floyd ordered them to cross Calabee Creek instead and prevent the Red Sticks from escaping in that direction (Owsley, 54; Griffith, 125).

Some time before dawn, the Georgians were spotted by a Muscogee who was out in the woods hunting wild turkeys. He quickly ran to the lodge of Coosa Miko, commander of the warriors at Autossee, and found him in conference with the prophet Tewasubbukle. The news of Floyd's approach gave the chiefs time to evacuate their women, old men, children, and slaves. Apparently, they sought to avoid the tragedies of Tallushatchee and Hillabee by segregating their noncombatants, who were sent downriver to Othlewallee (Owsley, 55; Stiggins, 125; Martin, 159).

Weatherford and Josiah Francis were at Eccanachaca on the Alabama River. Apparently, Peter McQueen held nominal command at Autossee, but George Stiggins identified Coosa Miko as being in charge there, with the prophet Tewasubbukle leading the Red Sticks at the lower town. Also present was the venerable former speaker Hopoithle Miko, who led warriors from his own town, Tallassee. Coosa Miko also sent a runner to Othlewallee with an appeal for reinforcements from Paddy Walsh (Quimby, 428; Stiggins, 127; Floyd, 235; L. Thompson, 468).

Floyd's troops launched their attack before daybreak. The morning was bitterly cold. Frost blanketed the fields around Autossee so thick that it looked like snow in the morning sun. To the beat of their drums and the shouts of their officers, the foot soldiers quickly formed into lines of battle. Anxious soldiers, many of whom had never tasted combat before, readied their muskets and rifles. Thomas's artillery company went about its business efficiently, just as they had trained for, placing their two small fieldpieces in range of the Red Stick town. The gunners began loading (Floyd, 235; L. Thompson, 466).

Coosa Miko deployed his warriors and watched as the white army approached. The crackle of twigs and tree limbs told them the white troops were closing in near the edge of town. Soon their buckskin hunting shirts and hats were visible through the trees, and the woods erupted in a volley of gunfire, blanketing Autossee in smoke. The Red Sticks were eager for combat, and Coosa Miko faced them with pride. "He encouraged his men to fight bravely and calmly," Stiggins wrote, "without shrinking back and not to waste their fire in fear." The warriors saluted him, and he returned the honor. Then the warriors gave their war cry, shattering the chill early morning air (Stiggins, 126).

The Red Sticks fought with ferocious tenacity, opening fire as soon as the Georgians were in range. They boldly charged toward Floyd's infantry, but a frightening salvo from Captain Thomas's artillery quickly drove them back. "The Indians presented themselves at every point," Floyd related, "and fought with the desperate bravery of real fanatics." The Georgia gunners fired a barrage at the town that demoralized the Red Sticks and set their houses ablaze. Booth's infantry then lowered bayonets and charged into the town. The Red Sticks retreated to the shelter of the thick underbrush behind the town near the river (Griffith, 125; Brannon, "Fort Mitchell," 11).

Apparently the Red Sticks used their firearms to good advantage at Autossee. "The balls whistled as thick as hail," Floyd wrote. Early in the engagement, a bullet slammed into the general's knee. His kneecap was shattered, and he was in great pain. Other officers urged him to leave the field, but he would have none of it. Both his aides lost their horses, shot from under them. Colonel Daniel Newnan received a minor wound in the leg (Floyd, 236; Griffith, 125; Brannon, "Journal," 234; Quimby, 429).

The Georgia troops fired volley after volley at the Red Sticks hiding in the underbrush. As the white formations reached the bluffs, they were greeted by an intense fire. The rebels resisted furiously, and heavy firing continued for some time. The warriors hauled their dead down to the river, and "the water of the river near the shore was crimsoned with their blood," according to Floyd. Some even tried to swim the frigid Tallapoosa and were shot by the soldiers. "They were as thick below the bank as fiddlers," Floyd observed, "of all sizes, perfectly naked, scampering, and screeching, in every direction" (Floyd, 236).

The Georgia artillery proved a key element at Autossee, and Floyd was especially complimentary of Thomas's gunners. "Captain Thomas and his company killed a great many Indians," the general wrote, "and deserve particular praise." James Tait recalled eighteen cannon rounds being fired during the engagement. Many of the Red Sticks had been barricaded in their houses firing at the white troops through gunports. "When the big guns let loose," Tait wrote, "they left their huts and scampered like so many wild ants." Even with their world collapsing around them, some of the diehards preferred to perish in the flames. Tait recalled, "[S]everal of them remained in their houses quite passive during the battle, suffering themselves to be slain without resistance" (Owsley, 54; Howard, 378; Brannon, "Journal," 234–235).

At the lower town, the Red Sticks met with equal disaster. Swinging their sabers, Floyd's mounted troops led by Major Freeman came crashing out of the woods and threw themselves against Tewasubbukle's defenders. The dragoons' charge was so sudden and so violent that the Red Sticks panicked, broke, and ran. Tewasubbukle was killed in the fighting. Coosa Miko rode from Autossee in a desperate attempt to rally the warriors there and push back Floyd's left flank, but he soon realized the hopelessness of the effort. Shot twice and slashed across the cheek by a dragoon's saber, Coosa Miko was losing blood rapidly. The chief abandoned his wounded mount and retreated into the swamp (Quimby, 428; Stiggins, 126–127).

Hopoithle Miko became a casualty of the fighting at Autossee. The elderly Red Stick chief—identified by Floyd as the Tallassee King, "the greatest conjurer of all the fanatics"—ascended his warhorse and galloped among his warriors waving his red war club, rallying his men, and firing his rifle at the white soldiers. He caught the attention of Captain Thomas. The Georgia artillerists leveled a charge of grapeshot straight at him, and the old chief—hit in the neck—was blown off his horse. He died on the battlefield, and Floyd later sent his pipe to Governor Early. "The friendly chiefs observes," the general wrote, "that it was the pipe of the greates man in their nation, and for many years their king, but he was grown old, and foolish, had forsaken them" (Floyd, 235; Brannon, "Journal," 235; Griffith, 125; L. Thompson, 468; Brannon, "Fort Mitchell," 3).

Sporadic fighting raged in the woods and fields around Autossee for two or three hours. Soon the frost-covered fields were littered with the bodies of Red Stick warriors. By 9 A.M., the Red Sticks had been driven off, and both towns were in flames. The Georgians claimed to have killed 200 warriors, and Hopoithle Miko's death was a great bonus. Eleven of Floyd's men were killed and fifty-three wounded. The heaviest casualties were in Captain Willoughby Barton's infantry company from Augusta— four killed and five wounded. In Captain Irwin's mounted company, three dragoons lay dead and two were wounded. Several of the Allied Creeks also were casualties. The Allied Creeks had fought well, especially the Cowetas led by William McIntosh and the Tuckabatchees led by a chief called Mad Dog's Son. Although they failed to cut off the Red Sticks' retreat across the Tallapoosa, they did block the escape path across Calabee Creek, and had joined in the assault on Autossee as soon as the white troops had the Red Sticks on the run (Brannon, "Journal," 234; Quimby, 429; Owsley, 54–55; Griffith, 125; Eaton).

As a decisive victory eluded Old Hickory at Talladega, so Floyd was also frustrated at Autossee. The Georgia commander was not able to complete the encirclement of both Red Stick towns. There was too much of an area to cover. So most of the enemy warriors escaped. Red Stick survivors were holed up in the caves along the bluffs of the Tallapoosa dug earlier for hiding from the white troops. Short on rations now, Floyd's troops hadn't the time to root them out. "Had we got possession of the lower banks of the river," Floyd declared, "all their women and children would have fallen into our hands, and what to have done with them would have been a question, as we could not have fed them, and I had placed restraints on the friendly Indians from destroying them" (Owsley, 54–55; Griffith, 125–126; Quimby, 428; Floyd, 235).

Still, the Georgians' raid had destroyed one of the largest Red Stick towns. As the foot soldiers pillaged through the ruins of Autossee, flames licked around them and black clouds obscured the sun. Floyd noted the carnage, wrote that "dogs, cats, and some of the savage tenants fell victims to the devouring flames." Floyd's soldiers discovered some of Peter McQueen's "effects" at Autossee, so they knew he had been there, but if he was present at all during the battle, he escaped with the refugees from the town in the bluffs below. The Georgians also found literally piles of scalps that they were convinced came from Fort Mims. They believed the Red Sticks here were likely the very warriors that had wiped out the unlucky stockade (Floyd, 235; Griffith, 126).

Seriously short of food, Floyd's army was compelled to withdraw to his base on the Chattahoochee. Floyd had his men form up for the march back to Fort Mitchell. Most of the Allied Creeks stayed behind to plunder Autossee. Meanwhile, another force of Red Stick warriors from Othlewallee—led by Paddy Walsh—had arrived too late to save their comrades at Autossee but just in time to fall on the Allied Creeks who were looting the town. The Allied Creeks retreated, losing several of their warriors killed, including Mad Dog's Son.

Walsh's war party then began to track Floyd's retreating Georgians. The white troops had halted to bury their dead a mile from Autossee when Walsh's Red Sticks attacked their rear guard. Taken by surprise at first, the Georgians repelled the assault, losing four or five soldiers killed. They then continued their withdrawal to Fort Mitchell (Floyd, 235; Quimby, 429; Griffith, 126).

Still in severe pain from his knee wound, Floyd was discouraged to find no provisions waiting for his soldiers at Fort Mitchell, and adequate supplies would not reach his starving troops until December 29. Morale was low, and Floyd now faced many of the same difficulties that had undermined Andrew Jackson's campaign. Floyd's army had only two months before its term of enlistment ran out, and he wondered whether he would be able to launch another campaign against the rebels. Brigadier General David Blackshear assumed command of Floyd's army while he recovered from his wound (Owsley, 55; Quimby, 429).

The Red Sticks reacted to their defeat at Autossee by consolidating their forces around their three major strongholds at Eccanachaca, Othlewallee, and Tohopeka. The warriors had used up their limited supply of gunpowder now, and some of them made their way south to Spanish Pensacola or took refuge in the swamps (Owsley, 55, 56; Bassett, vol. 1, 399; Stiggins, 127).

Meanwhile, Major General Thomas Pinckney had arrived at Fort Hawkins to personally direct the war against the Red Sticks. His appearance on the frontier was welcome to agent Benjamin Hawkins, who rather distrusted the Georgia militia, although he had cooperated with Floyd so far (Pound, 109).

With Floyd's army stuck at Fort Mitchell, Pinckney sent Major General David Adams's independent command of Georgia militia to strike at Red Stick towns on the upper Tallapoosa. Adams, a forty-seven-year-old veteran militia officer and former scout, rode out from Monticello, Georgia, with 530 mounted troops on December 9. The expedition was intended as a diversionary operation to disrupt the Red Sticks' food supply. Pinckney had wanted Jackson to send out a similar raid from Fort Strother, but Old Hickory was unable to move farther south. By then, he had released Coffee's mounted brigade to north of the Tennessee (White, 501; Quimby, 429; Owsley, 51).

When Adams's mounted troops reached the Chattahoochee, they found that heavy rains had swollen the river, and they were unable to cross until December 15. Their main target, an Upper Creek town called Nuyaka (after the 1790 Treaty of New York) was thirty miles west. Adams had planned to attack it the next day, but rain and darkness delayed him and robbed him of the element of surprise by the time he reached his objective (Quimby, 429).

Adams deployed his forces. He had planned carefully and applied the typical tactic of three attacking columns. The troops dismounted after reaching half a mile from the town. A small detachment remained mounted as a reserve. When the three columns surrounded Nuyaka, the Georgians discovered that the town had been evacuated. They burned the town of about eighty-five houses and moved out. The Tallapoosa River also was high due to recent rains, so Adams was unable to cross it to strike other towns. The Georgians withdrew the same way they had come, and it was probably fortunate for Adams that he did not cross the river, since his relatively small force was insufficient to engage the strong Red Stick concentration at Tohopeka anyway (Quimby, 430).

In December, Old Hickory's Tennessee army had gotten no farther than Fort Strother, and Floyd's Georgians seemed stalled at Fort Mitchell. The action now shifted back to the 'Bigbee settlements, where the war had begun. General Ferdinand L. Claiborne's army was on the eve of a major engagement with the Red Sticks that would shatter one of the three key strongholds of the Muscogee nation—and the prophets' dubious claim of invincibility.

CHAPTER 10

"Untrodden Wilderness"

The commander of the Mississippi territorial militia was anxious to strike back at the Red Sticks. A forty-year-old Natchez planter and Virginia native, Brigadier General Ferdinand L. Claiborne had fought red men on the Ohio frontier, serving under General "Mad Anthony" Wayne in his 1794 victory at Fallen Timbers, an engagement in which a young Tecumseh fought on the opposing side. Claiborne realized that he was desperately short of men and supplies, and he actually mortgaged his own land to raise cash for the Creek campaign. He was in the saddle every day riding from one outpost to another, running down fresh rumors of Red Stick attacks, coordinating his scattered garrisons, and worrying about possible British moves against Mobile in his rear. But he still hoped that, with reinforcements from Major General Flournoy, the district commander, he could go on the attack soon. What he really wanted was to get in one good blow at the Spanish, whom he considered the source of the Red Stick uprising. "I would advise a stroke at the root of all present distress," he wrote, "—Pensacola" (E. Rowland, 13, 41, 52–54; McLemore, 230).

Claiborne's hard-pressed little brigade of about 400 men was spread dangerously thin among the dozen small forts erected by the panicky settlers in the forks of the Tombigbee and Alabama Rivers. On duty—in addition to the local militia—was Colonel Joseph Carson's First Regiment of Mississippi Infantry, enlisted for one year in January 1813. Carson was one of the 'Bigbee settlers, an attorney like Major Daniel Beasley, the ill-fated commander at Fort Mims, where two companies of the First Mississippi (William Jack's and Hatton Middleton's) had been annihilated. It was Carson's soldiers in the relief detachment led by Major Joseph P. Kennedy who had viewed the mutilated bodies of the Fort Mims victims. They had shared the grim news of what they had seen with their comrades, and the First Mississippi was filled with soldiers eager for revenge. But they were not ready to strike back, defending undermanned isolated stockades like Fort Sinquefield from attack, alert for ambushes by Red Stick war parties rampaging through the forks during the dark days of September 1813 (D. Rowland, 5–6; E. Rowland, 54- 55).

Like Claiborne, the Mississippi Territory's governor, David Holmes, was concerned about Spanish activity on the Gulf coast and possible British moves against New Orleans. And like Governor Mitchell of Georgia, he was unable to provide his militia with adequate supplies for a campaign. "The Territory has not the funds," Holmes had written General Flournoy in August 1813, "requisite to furnish camp equipage, forage, and ammunition without which troops cannot be marched to a distant part of the country." But Fort Mims convinced the governor that haste was essential. On September 22, Holmes dispatched more soldiers to Fort Stoddert, trusting that the federal government would take up the financial slack. Receiving no cooperation from the inflexible Flournoy, who would not be responsible for paying the troops, Holmes wrote, "I am confident the President will consider them as in the service of the United States" (Skeen, 160; McLemore, 230).

First to arrive were the Mississippi Dragoons—the territory's entire force of cavalry—led by Major Thomas Hinds, a dark-eyed young Virginian who was an acquaintance of Andrew Jackson and a rising political favorite in the territory. They were the best that the territory had to offer, aristocratic sons of frontier planters anxious to prove themselves in action against the Red Sticks. The dragoons made up a battalion of four troops mostly from the area near Natchez, about 200 men in all. They were volunteers, and in their dragoon caps and dark blue jackets with scarlet facings, armed with muskets and sabers dangling from their white belts, they must have been a dashing sight compared to the drab foot militia. "The arrival of these troops," a confident Holmes wrote, "rendered the entire force on the eastern frontier efficient and reputable" (Chartrand, 71; D. Rowland, 9, 14, 16).

The departure of Hinds's troopers from Natchez alarmed frontier families in the western part of the Mississippi Territory, fearful that their settlements would be left open to attack by the Choctaws, whom many of them believed to be in league with the Red Sticks. Holmes took aggressive measures to persuade settlers not to abandon the frontier. He cautioned them not to provoke the red men and not to believe reckless rumors. He ordered more blockhouses built to secure the frontier settlements. In October, he mobilized more militia companies, two of mounted riflemen and five of infantry. Indian agents were active among the Choctaws, dissuading them from joining the Red Sticks. These efforts made little impact on jittery families who virtually deserted the frontier, fleeing to the safety of Natchez and Mobile (McLemore, 230–231).

Claiborne encountered the same kind of supply and logistical problems that plagued General Floyd in Georgia and General Jackson in his indecisive autumn campaign against the Red Sticks. In addition, he had the difficulty of dealing with Flournoy, who made no secret of his contempt for Claiborne's untrained militia and distrust of his Choctaw allies. Flournoy seemed especially peeved with Hinds's dragoons. Having signed up to fight Red Sticks, the young aristocrats were restless at being assigned dull garrison duty in the local stockades, and Hinds pestered the commander with requests to be sent into action. Fed up, Flournoy accused Hinds of insubordination; his militia soldiers were undisciplined and of no use to him. The general's attitude was perplexing to Claiborne, who saw no sense in Flournoy's testiness (Owsley, 46).

Finally ready for an offensive, Claiborne's army—about 800 strong now, along with Pushmataha and his Choctaw allies—had marched out of St. Stephens on October 12, crossed the Tombigbee, and moved across the forks toward the Alabama. Flournoy had instructed Claiborne to drive the Red Sticks back and take their towns, to "kill, burn and destroy all their negroes, horses, cattle, and other property that cannot conveniently be brought to the depots." The Mississippians made a deliberate and cautious advance, fighting isolated skirmishes with small war parties of Red Sticks. Weatherford's main Red Stick army had long since withdrawn up the Alabama River to a more secure area (Owsley, 45; Pickett, 560; Skeen, 161; T. Woodward, 87).

Claiborne's objective was Weatherford's Bluff on the Alabama. Weatherford's Bluff was named for Red Eagle's father, Scottish trader Charles Weatherford. Corn and cattle were plentiful in this area, providing the Red Sticks with much of their supplies. Now the area would furnish the white armies with needed foodstuffs. The Mississippians were to construct a fort and supply depot and wait for General Flournoy to come up from Mobile with his two regiments of regulars (Griffith, 127; Pickett, 573; Bassett, vol. 1, 361–362; Owsley, 45).

Claiborne rode at the head of the Mississippi dragoons. Hinds's troopers had gained valuable experience in the forks of the Tombigbee and Alabama in the previous weeks, and Claiborne's confidence in them had grown. Their youthful enthusiasm and bravado impressed the general, and he felt they would be reliable troops. Speaking with Sam Dale, Claiborne advised the tough frontiersman to count on the dragoons if he needed good men on a mission. "When you see danger ahead," he told him, "take Hinds with you" (Pickett, 560; E. Rowland, 58, 63, 66).

Claiborne's troops encountered a grim reminder that the Red Sticks were still a dangerous threat. On October 16, they reached Bashi Creek, where a mounted patrol had been ambushed less than two weeks earlier.

The dragoons discovered the bodies of Colonel William McGrew, "a much-esteemed militia officer," according to George Gaines, and a veteran of the Burnt Corn Creek skirmish, along with three other soldiers. Hinds's dragoons buried the four victims, and several skirmishes followed as they searched in vain for the marauders (Gaines, 167; Owen, 95; Pickett, 560–561; E. Rowland, 42, 63).

In a reconnaissance of the area across the Alabama from Weatherford's Bluff, the Mississippi horsemen encountered a Red Stick war party. Bullets flew, and in a short skirmish the dragoons killed ten of the rebels before they returned to Claiborne's camp. Hinds's young troopers had scored a "handsome little victory," Claiborne wrote, and he informed General Jackson that "My Partizans have not been inactive" (Pickett, 572; Quimby, 430; Bassett, vol. 1, 362).

Just when Claiborne seemed to be making some headway, new difficulties with Flournoy cropped up. Flournoy received orders on November 6 informing him that General Pinckney had been given overall command of the military operations against the Red Sticks, and ordering him to turn over the Third U.S. Infantry to Pinckney. "It concerns me," the indignant Flournoy snorted, "that I am not to be among the conquerors of the Creek Indians, but this seems to be determined otherwise by a power beyond my control." Furious, he left the Third U.S. Infantry at Mobile and marched his remaining regulars back to New Orleans, depriving Claiborne of badly needed reinforcements (Skeen, 161).

Also, on November 8—in a final gesture of pettiness—Flournoy dismissed Major Hinds's dragoons and ordered them back to Natchez. Claiborne objected, but to no avail. Flournoy contended that Hinds's troops had been mobilized on Governor Holmes's authority and that he was not responsible for them. He directed the Mississippi brigadier to "have nothing to do with them." When Claiborne protested, it only earned him a reprimand from the commanding general. Although Claiborne wanted to press the campaign, Flournoy—still disdainful of the frontier militia—advised him to stay on the defensive. "You had better never fight a battle," he cautioned, "than run the risk of defeat." Without his dragoons and Flournoy's regulars, Claiborne had no choice but to fall back to Pine Level, near present-day Jackson, Alabama, just ten miles east of St. Stephens (Skeen, 161; Owsley, 46).

Meanwhile, Claiborne had sent out Captain Sam Dale—armed with his long rifle ("good for a hundred yards")—and a detachment of volunteers and militia on a reconnaissance up the Alabama River. On November 12, just south of Weatherford's Bluff, Dale's party was surprised by a group of Red Stick warriors sailing ominously downstream in a large flat-bottomed boat. After an exchange of gunfire, Dale, determined to bring the big enemy boat to bay, leaped into the smaller of his two canoes, followed by nineteen-year-old Jeremiah Austill, twenty-five-year-old Georgian James

Smith, and a free African American named Caesar. Dale managed to board the Red Stick boat, and the four men—using their rifles as clubs—engaged the warriors in a bloody hand-to-hand combat. When the brief fight was finished, the Red Sticks had been killed or tossed overboard, leaving the boat strewn with blood and brains. The "Canoe Fight," as it came to be known, was only a minor skirmish, but it helped to raise the morale of the 'Bigbee settlers, and it made a frontier hero of Big Sam Dale (Pickett, 563–566; E. Rowland, 63–65; Claiborne, 130–131; Owsley, 45–46).

Claiborne's hopes revived—and the spirits of his men brightened—when new orders from Flournoy instructed him to proceed to Weatherford's Bluff. He left Pine Level on November 13, and the Mississippians reached the Alabama River on November 16 and pitched camp. At daybreak they began crossing the river in rafts, and by noon the whole army was landed at Weatherford's Bluff, at the site of present-day Claiborne, Alabama (Halbert and Ball, 241; Pickett, 572).

It took about ten days for the Mississippians to complete Fort Claiborne, a 200-foot-square stockade with three blockhouses and a half-moon battery overlooking the river. "From this position," Claiborne reported to Governor Holmes, "we cut the savages off from the river, and from their growing crops. We likewise render their communication with Pensacola more hazardous." Fort Claiborne was to be a supply base, for use by Jackson's Tennessee army as well as the Mississippians. Claiborne was concerned about British activity in Pensacola—"that sink of iniquity," he called it—and expected that once Jackson's Tennesseans joined him, their forces would unite for an attack (Halbert and Ball, 241–243; E. Rowland, 70).

Although Claiborne regretted the loss of Major Hinds and his dragoons, he did get the benefit of the regular troops that Flournoy had released at Mobile, for now these troops were coming to join him. Lieutenant Colonel Gilbert C. Russell with the Third U.S. Infantry Regiment, its ranks filled mainly with volunteers from the Mississippi Territory, arrived at Fort Claiborne on November 26. Set loose by Flournoy, Russell—an enterprising, aggressive officer—had already communicated with General Floyd of the Georgia army and told him that he would join him at the Hickory Ground. He let a highly pleased Claiborne know that his troops would also cooperate with him for a push up the Alabama. This was an officer whom Claiborne could work with. The energetic Russell was anxious to pursue the campaign "and even force our way into the towns over the Tallapoosa without support or co-operation from any quarter" (Halbert and Ball, 243; E. Rowland, 56; Quimby, 431).

Claiborne had about 1,200 troops now. Besides Colonel Russell's regulars, there was Colonel Carson's First Mississippi volunteers. Also on hand was Major Benjamin Smoot, a veteran of the Burnt Corn Creek action, with the local militia battalion of which Sam Dale was an officer, as well as Major

Henry Cassel's battalion of mounted riflemen. And there were 150 Choctaw warriors led by Pushmataha (Owsley, 47; Pickett, 573–574).

Choctaw war parties traveled light, each warrior carrying his weapons and a *bota kapossa*, or rations bag. Moving through the woods in single file, trailers marched in the lead, followed by the war chief and the other warriors, each taking care to walk in the footsteps of the warrior who preceded him—the last in the file covering the tracks. When camped, the warriors slept in a circle, with their feet to the campfire in the center. Each warrior placed his musket propped against a forked stick in the ground next to his head as he slept (Halbert, 3–8).

Although they had received twenty new rifles at Fort Madison, only about fifty of Pushmataha's warriors were adequately armed. Like the white soldiers of the Mississippi army, the Choctaws were poorly fed and poorly clothed. Still they were eager to participate in the war against their old enemies, the Muscogees. John McKee spoke with one war chief who informed the agent that "he had left home to kill Creeks and that he would not return till he had done it." While the white troops were busy building Fort Claiborne, Pushmataha and fifty of his warriors conducted a strike at the Red Sticks' supply line to Pensacola. In a night attack, they surprised a Red Stick camp at Burnt Corn Creek. The Choctaws killed several of the rebels and brought their scalps back to Fort Claiborne (Halbert and Ball, 241, 242–243; DeRosier, 36; McKee Journal, 3).

Claiborne had made Pushmataha a gift of a handsome U.S. army officer's blue uniform, complete with gold epaulets, sword, silver spurs, and feathered chapeau, bought in Mobile for three hundred dollars. The Choctaw war chief became a familiar figure at Fort Claiborne. He made it clear that he would associate only with the American officers of higher rank, as befitted his station, and he seemed completely at home in the general's tent (Claiborne, 133; Griffith, 127; L. Thompson, 419).

The time was rapidly approaching when the white volunteers' enlistments would be up, and Claiborne desperately wanted to strike a blow at one of the major Red Stick towns while he still had an army. What he had in mind was an attack on the rebels' encampment at Eccanachaca (Holy Ground), 120 miles up the Alabama. Although Flournoy finally approved the expedition, twenty-two officers in the Mississippi Volunteers signed a petition opposing the action and presented it to Claiborne. They cited the isolation of Eccanachaca, without even a path leading to the sacred town. Serious obstacles stood in the way of a white attack—the lack of adequate transportation to get there, the severity of the weather that had settled into rain and cold, and the scarcity of supplies. Their soldiers were without proper winter clothing, shoes, and blankets. The enlistment period of 218 volunteers was up on December 17. Although they wanted Claiborne to reconsider the timing of the campaign, they promised to "cheerfully obey your orders and carry out your plans" if he chose to go through with it (Halbert and Ball, 244–245; Pickett, 574; Quimby, 430).

When Claiborne still insisted on a march to the Holy Ground, the volunteers accepted his decision. "Their patience was equal to their courage," the general noted. "Not a murmur was heard; not a complaint was made." These were the men who had first felt the impact of the Fort Mims massacre. Although they had not been paid for months, were ragged, hungry, and poorly equipped, and many were beyond their end of enlistment, they were anxious for revenge and had already waited more than three months. Sam Dale recalled that the general was moved to tears and took each soldier by the hand as they marched out of Fort Claiborne. Stepping off to the tune of "Over the Hills and Far Away," the little army moved out on December 13 (Claiborne, 139–140; Quimby, 432; Halbert and Ball, 246).

Soon Claiborne's column struck the lower leg of the Federal Road and followed it northward. South of Letohatchee Creek, the soldiers halted and built an earthwork fort called Fort Deposit, in present-day Lowndes County. Now they would leave the road. Holy Ground was thirty miles north, beyond the "untrodden wilderness" (Southerland and Brown, 41; Halbert and Ball, 244, 246).

The soldiers moved out again on the morning of December 22 with only three days' rations of flour. Claiborne left behind at Fort Deposit his sick soldiers, his cannon, baggage, and a guard of one hundred men. On the march to the Holy Ground, Claiborne's troops were guided by Sam Moniac, Red Eagle's brother-in-law—who had spurned the Red Sticks the previous summer—and by an African American slave. By nightfall the army was within ten miles of the Holy Ground (Halbert and Ball, 246; Pickett, 574; L. Thompson, 475).

Like some sinister enchanted citadel of the forest, Eccanachaca sat on an isolated neck of land on the south bank of the Alabama River just two miles north of present-day Whitehall, Alabama. Surrounded by marshes and forests, in one of the most beautiful parts of the Muscogee nation, the forbidding Holy Ground was the command center of William Weatherford and the prophet Josiah Francis. The settlement had been built in the summer of 1813, at the height of the Red Stick movement, and was intended as a special holy refuge for the rebel warriors and their families. The prophets contended that an invisible boundary encircled Eccanachaca and that the ground was consecrated. "It was never to be sullied," George Stiggins wrote, "by the footsteps of the white man." Any white man who attempted to cross the barrier would be swallowed up by the sacred earth. The town contained 200 homes, and many of the Red Sticks' women and children were here. The chiefs had also stored their war materials and provisions here (Halbert and Ball, 246–247; Martin, 159–160; Stiggins, 116; Griffith, 126; L. Thompson, 472, 475).

Eccanachaca also occupied a good defensive position, and Weatherford undoubtedly favored it for this reason. The town was located on a bluff on the western side of present-day Cypress Creek just south of the point where it empties into the Alabama. The creek and river created a kind of peninsula where the town sat, surrounded by water on three sides. On the western or land side of the town, two wooded ravines—each about 200 yards long—ran north to the river, and Weatherford had erected a stockade wall running from the river above the two ravines to the creek. The fortified stronghold enclosed about fifty acres (Halbert and Ball, 247–248).

Besides the Muscogees, another group of rebels had much riding on the defense of Holy Ground. Numbers of runaway slaves had taken up the cause of the Red Sticks, and these African Americans were resolved to hold on to their freedom or die trying. They played a prominent role in the defense of the Holy Ground. Some 240 slaves taken as captives from Fort Mims and from neighboring plantations also were at Eccanachaca. Eccanachaca also held a number of the white and mixed-blood captives taken by the Red Sticks—as well as much of the plunder from Fort Mims and abandoned white farms. Weatherford's aunt, the elderly Sophia Durant, was one of the prisoners, and the prophets may have used her as a hostage to insure Red Eagle's continued loyalty to the Red Stick cause (Braund, 633; Stiggins, 119; Saunt, 269–270; L. Thompson, 476–477; Claiborne, 137; E. Rowland, 72).

The discordant views of Red Eagle and Josiah Francis on military strategy clashed at Eccanachaca. While the prophets relied on the supernatural power of the Holy Ground to make the Red Sticks invincible, Weatherford chose more conventional approaches. When he received news early in the morning of December 23 that the white army was on the outskirts of the town, Weatherford sent the women—including his wife, the beautiful Sofath Kaney, who had just learned that she was expecting a baby—and children across the Alabama to safety in the forest. The prophets' reaction to the enemy's approach was to order their mixed-blood captives, including Weatherford's Aunt Sophia, taken to the central square to prepare them for burning at the stake (Halbert and Ball, 249; T. Woodward, 87; L. Thompson, 476–477, 482–483; Pickett, 574–575; E. Rowland, 73).

In spite of Weatherford's better judgment as a military man, the Holy Ground was not heavily guarded. Weatherford had only about 200 warriors—including the blacks—with which to make any kind of defense. Red Eagle stationed a large number of his riflemen in a low hollow or dry branch emptying into the creek just south of the town. Another body of riflemen crouched behind a stout log breastwork next to the hollow where the white troops would probably approach. Behind this thin defensive line was a second formation of Red Sticks armed with bows and arrows (Stiggins, 119; Halbert and Ball, 250–251).

At 11 A.M. on December 23, Claiborne's army was deploying for battle two miles south of Eccanachaca. Claiborne used the standard American formation of three assault columns. Colonel Carson and the First Mississippi Volunteers would form the right column, Major Smoot and the territorial militia—along with Pushmataha and the Choctaw warriors—the left. Each would encircle the enemy town like the horns of a crescent, while Claiborne with the center column—Lieutenant Colonel Russell's regulars and some mounted riflemen—would go in for the kill. Two troops of mounted soldiers were held in reserve. Major Cassel's battalion of mounted riflemen was to circle to the west and make for the Alabama River to cut off the Red Sticks' escape route (Halbert and Ball, 249–250).

The white soldiers began moving forward through the forest, stumbling through the dense tangles of vines and brush. The Muscogees' scouts could hear them coming—hundreds of feet treading through the damp leaves of winter, equipment clanking, limbs and branches crackling, horses moving cautiously through the underbrush, men brandishing their muskets and rifles carefully. "[T]he weather was very wet and bitter cold," Sam Dale recalled. "[W]e had neither meat, coffee, nor spirits" (Claiborne, 140).

Carson's troops were having difficulty moving through the marshy terrain east of Holy Ground along present-day Cypress Creek. Claiborne had wanted the Mississippi volunteers to advance up the eastern side of the creek and secure the river bank to prevent the Red Sticks from escaping—or, if necessary, turn west, ford the creek, and hit the town from above. But Carson's soldiers soon found the east bank of the creek to be so rain-sogged and swampy that they could make no headway. So they stuck to the western side of the creek. The terrain was bad enough here, as the soldiers slogged their way for a mile through the marsh, wading through water standing two feet deep. The damp and bitter cold, plus the soldiers' hunger and fatigue, added to the misery (Halbert and Ball, 250).

Carson's men could hear the steady pounding of the Red Sticks' drums and the bloodcurdling war cries of their warriors in Eccanachaca just ahead through the trees. It was about noon. The enemy was there, waiting for them, and they wondered if this was what their friends at Fort Mims had heard before they were slaughtered. The Mississippians were turning from the creek now and were moving on more solid ground. They deployed into a line of battle (Halbert and Ball, 250).

The volunteers had reached the hollow where the Red Sticks under Weatherford had taken up a defensive position. They were startled by a furious volley of musket fire from the Red Stick barricades. The soldiers took cover and returned fire. Carson's troops moved in, firing from behind trees and stumps as they advanced closer to the enemy. The Muscogees refused to give ground and continued firing from the woods ahead. The bowmen to their rear loosed a shower of arrows, but the warriors aimed too high and the missiles fell without harm behind the soldiers' battle line (Halbert and Ball, 250–251).

Suddenly the soldiers spotted a Red Stick prophet—decked out in war paint and feathers—dancing in front of the Creek bowmen and brandishing a red cow tail in each hand. The holy man kept up a continuing war chant as he ran here and there among the Muscogee warriors. He made an inviting target, and one of Carson's soldiers—propping his musket against the trunk of a tree—finally dropped the prophet with one carefully aimed shot. The shaman fell—struck in the chest and through the arm. He was probably Sikaboo, the Shawnee prophet who had remained with the Muscogees after Tecumseh's visit in 1811 (Halbert and Ball, 251–252, 258; Quimby, 446 n. 234).

A party of Mississippians finally worked their way around the log barricade and opened up on Weatherford's warriors with enfilade fire. Several of the Red Sticks went down. The warriors fired back and wounded several soldiers before they fell back from the barricade, and Red Eagle's defenders retreated across the hollow. There they took up new positions behind fallen logs and tree trunks, firing intermittently at the troops as they continued to advance. The fighting had gone on for about half an hour (Halbert and Ball, 251).

Cassel's mounted riflemen found the going too difficult in the swamp west of the town. They were unable to reach the Alabama River in time to prevent the Red Stick warriors from escaping and scattering into the marsh. Cassel placed the blame on Sam Moniac, who was to have guided the mounted troopers to the river. Perhaps Moniac intentionally misled Cassel so as to allow Weatherford and his men a chance to escape. The horsemen altered their planned movement and fell back to support Carson. Claiborne's left column—the territorial militia under Major Smoot along with Pushmataha and the Choctaws—had reached the town and now started to press the warriors who began to retreat (Halbert and Ball, 251–252; Pickett, 576; L. Thompson, 486).

The warriors were giving ground rapidly now, and Carson was unable to contain his soldiers any longer. He had hoped to fix the Red Sticks' line until the other columns were all up and the town was encircled, but that was not about to happen. The colonel saw that his men were impatient to close in. "Boys," he shouted, "you seem keen! Go ahead and drive them!" (Halbert and Ball, 252).

The First Mississippi surged ahead with bayonets lowered, the furious yell sounding from hundreds of throats that had waited for this moment since Fort Mims. Revenge was at hand. The white troops poured into Eccanachaca, as the Red Sticks broke and ran. Russell's Third Infantry came up quickly on the heels of Carson's regiment and also went in with the bayonet. The Red Sticks had had enough. Many of the warriors tossed their weapons aside and scattered for cover. Still they managed to carry their wounded with them as they fell back to the Alabama River (Halbert and Ball, 252; Owsley, 47).

The warriors under Josiah Francis fired one volley at the white troops, then turned and made for the river. Francis, who had shown little anxiety at the sudden appearance of Claiborne's army, had placed absolute faith in the mystical barrier. When it failed, he had no backup tactical plan. But he did

Muscogee Village on the Apalachicola. English settlers called these Native Americans Creeks because their settlements were usually located on streams. (Florida State Archives)

Tecumseh's Death at Battle of the Thames, October 5, 1813. The Shawnee chief's call for an Indian confederacy helped incite the Creek War. (Library of Congress)

British Camp on Dauphin Island, February 1815. The threat of foreign military intervention on the Gulf Coast was a major concern to U.S. leaders. (Alabama Department of Archives and History)

Benjamin Hawkins, agent to the Creeks. His ambitious acculturation program provoked resentment from many Muscogees. (Florida State Archives)

William McIntosh, prominent mixed-blood chief, led Allied Creek forces against the Red Sticks. (Florida State Archives)

Sam Dale. A well-known settler in the 'Bigbee country, his Creek War exploits made him a frontier hero. (Alabama Department of Archives and History)

Major General Andrew Jackson. The Creek and Seminole conflicts catapulted him to national fame. (Library of Congress)

Fort Mims, August 30, 1813. Norman Price's painting captures the terror of the worst frontier massacre in American history, the event that triggered the Creek War. (Courtesy of The Museum of Mobile)

Jackson faces down a mutiny in his Tennessee militia, November 1813. Old Hickory's iron will was often the only thing that held his army together. (Library of Congress)

General John Floyd's Georgia Militia attacks Autossee, November 29, 1813, striking the first blow at a major enemy concentration in the Creek War. (Courtesy of Hargrett Rare Book and Manuscript Library/ University of Georgia Libraries)

Pushmataha and his Choctaw warriors allied themselves with the American armies. (Alabama Department of Archives and History)

John Coffee. Jackson's close friend, he commanded the Tennessee mounted arm in the Creek War. (Alabama Department of Archives and History)

Major Ridge led Cherokee warriors fighting against the Red Sticks. (Library of Congress)

David Crockett. The famous Tennessee frontiersman served as a scout in Jackson's army. (Library of Congress)

Tennessee troops at New Orleans, 1814–1815, as depicted by Peter Copeland. Old Hickory's veterans earned their tough reputation in campaigns against the Red Sticks. (Courtesy of the Company of Military Historians)

American artillery crew. Artillery often proved to be a key element in the American armies' campaigns against the Creeks. (Courtesy of the Company of Military Historians, *Military Uniforms in America,* vol. 2, *Years of Growth*)

U.S. regulars building a fort on the Western Frontier, as depicted by David P. Geister. Disciplined regulars formed the backbone of American armies fighting the Red Sticks and Seminoles. (Courtesy of the Company of Military Historians)

Opothleyaholo. As a teenager, he fought at Horseshoe Bend. In his later life this Muscogee leader witnessed the loss of the tribe's last lands east of the Mississippi. (Alabama Department of Archives and History)

Site of Eccanachaca, on the Alabama River. General Ferdinand Claiborne's Mississippi army destroyed the Red Stick stronghold here on December 23, 1813. (Author's photo)

Aerial view of Horseshoe Bend shows the terrain in which opposing forces fought on March 27, 1814 (Alabama Department of Archives and History)

Storming the barricade. Jackson's troops overwhelm Red Sticks at Horseshoe Bend in the decisive battle of the Creek War. (Photo Courtesy of Horseshoe Bend National Military Park)

Weatherford surrenders to Jackson. Red Eagle's meeting with Old Hickory ended major Red Stick resistance. (Library of Congress)

Jackson's army defeats the British at New Orleans, January 7, 1815. Veterans of the Creek War helped win Old Hickory's greatest victory. (Library of Congress)

Seminoles attack an army blockhouse. Refugee Red Sticks joined with their Seminole brethren to continue their war against the Americans. (Library of Congress)

Jackson reviews his troops, preparing to campaign against the Seminoles in 1818. (Florida State Archives)

John Ross. A veteran of the Creek War, the Cherokees' principal chief waged an obstinate but futile battle to prevent his tribe's removal west. (Library of Congress)

Menawa led Red Stick defenders at Horseshoe Bend. (Library of Congress)

have a prearranged escape route, and the prophet immediately fell back to it, with his followers close on his heels. The shock of the white soldiers penetrating the sacred barrier so demoralized them that they did not even make a final stand. They likewise abandoned the idea of executing their hostages, and Sophia Durant was freed (Stiggins, 117–118; Owsley, 47).

Only the small force of warriors and blacks under Red Eagle continued to offer any resistance, fighting from tree to tree and falling back toward the rear of Eccanachaca, delaying the advance of the soldiers until the rebels could evacuate their wounded and a few of their possessions from the town. When a runner breathlessly bore word that Claiborne's regulars and mounted rifles were closing in on the western side of Eccanachaca—sealing off exit—Weatherford's men at last gave up the fight and fled to save themselves. The most desperate of Red Eagle's men—the African Americans—especially regretted having to abandon the town. The "negroes were the last to quit the ground," one American officer reported (Stiggins, 119; Saunt, 270).

The rebels reached the bluff near the mouth of the creek, with Carson's soldiers in hot pursuit, and scattered into the canebrakes and marshes, some swimming the Alabama to reach safety on the opposite shore where their women and children were waiting, others fleeing in canoes. Many others fled through the swamp west of the town, which Cassel's horsemen had been unable to seal off. Soldiers fired at the fugitives as they made their escape. One warrior, struck by a white bullet, toppled forward, tossed in anguish for a few seconds, and then rolled down the bluff, where he lay dead (Halbert and Ball, 252–253).

Red Eagle was one of the last to leave Eccanachaca, holding off until his own warriors had evacuated the town. He almost waited too long. With the soldiers closing in above and below the town, there was only one escape route open to him—to swim the river. Mounted on his splendid warhorse, Arrow, Weatherford rode down one of the ravines leading to the river, ascended a twelve-foot-high bluff, then—taking a great gamble—spurred his charger into the river below. The war chief never lost his seat as he plunged into the chilly water. Holding his rifle above his head, he urged Arrow toward the opposite bank. Musket balls splashed into the water around him as the soldiers on shore—members of Cassel's mounted rifles—began firing, but Red Eagle reached the safety of the far bank without injury. Out of range on the opposite bank, Weatherford calmly dismounted, unsaddled Arrow and checked to see if the horse had been wounded, and found that he had been nicked slightly in his mane but otherwise was unhurt. Red Eagle then wrung the water out of his blanket, saddled up again, mounted, and—in a final gesture of bravado—gave one fierce war cry at the white soldiers watching on the southern bank before he rode away into the forest (Halbert and Ball, 253–256; Stiggins, 120; Pickett, 576).

The entire action at Eccanachaca had taken about an hour. The white army lost one man killed—a young ensign—and twenty soldiers wounded. Had the Red Sticks been better armed with a greater supply of ammunition, the Mississippians' losses would probably have been much heavier. The soldiers discovered thirty-three dead Red Sticks—twenty-one Muscogees and twelve African Americans. Probably many more rebels were wounded. Claiborne might have succeeded in trapping the warriors at Holy Ground—and slaughtering many more of them—if Cassel's mounted troops had managed to reach the river below the town in time to seal it off. As with Jackson at Talladega and Floyd at Autossee, flawed execution of orders robbed Claiborne of a decisive victory (Owen, 114; Halbert and Ball, 256, 258).

All that remained for Claiborne's troops was to mop up. His left and center columns—Smoot's militia and Russell's regulars—now were in Eccanachaca. Claiborne had given orders to his men not to plunder the fallen Red Stick stronghold. But he made no attempt to restrain his Choctaw allies, who rampaged through the houses in Eccanachaca, looting the homes of clothing and personal belongings left behind by the rebel families. Claiborne's soldiers surmised that much of the loot probably belonged to the slaughtered families at Fort Mims. Famished after their long march to the Holy Ground, the soldiers were relieved to find a large supply of badly needed food—1,200 to 1,500 bushels of corn—at Eccanachaca. What they could not consume, they burned (Halbert and Ball, 256).

Prowling through Red Eagle's quarters, the Mississippi soldiers were excited to turn up the very letter written to Weatherford by Spanish governor Gonzalez Manrique, complimenting the Red Stick chief for his victory at Fort Mims. But the most startling discovery at Holy Ground was a tall pine pole sitting at a sixty-degree angle in the town square. Hundreds of grisly scalps hung from the pole. A surgeon with the Mississippi militia wrote that there were "scalps of every description from the infant to the grayhead," presumably taken from the unlucky victims at Fort Mims (Halbert and Ball, 257; Fredriksen, 116).

One of Colonel Carson's soldiers, searching through a Red Stick cabin, discovered a Muscogee woman who had managed to hide from the Choctaws. The terrified woman—in sign language—begged the soldier not to hurt her. The man took her to Claiborne, and the general ordered the troops to give her something to eat and not to harm her. The looting over, Claiborne ordered his men to put the town to the torch. As the buildings began to blaze, a door to one of the cabins suddenly burst open and a heavyset black man—who had managed to stay hidden—ran out. He did not get far, as a dozen musket balls brought him down. The dead Red Sticks fell victim to the Choctaws' scalping knives. The delighted warriors carried the Muscogees' scalps back to their towns in triumph, but the scalps of the black men they flung aside in contempt (Halbert and Ball, 257–258).

Claiborne's troops made camp for the night not far from the burning embers of Eccanachaca. The next day—December 24—they fanned out to raid and destroy the Holy Ground's satellite villages and farms. Jeremiah Austill accompanied Pushmataha and a party of Choctaw warriors on a raid across the Alabama River. After crossing the river in a canoe, the detachment surprised a Red Stick camp. "Shoot! Shoot!" the excited Pushmataha commanded. "Kill all! Kill all!" In a brief skirmish, the Choctaws killed three Red Sticks, and the rebels fled, leaving behind their supplies (Halbert and Ball, 259–260).

Sam Dale rode with Cassel's mounted troops, who moved a few miles upriver and destroyed another Red Stick village at the mouth of Pintlala Creek. The soldiers pitched camp that night in one of William Weatherford's abandoned farms as a chill downpour set in. "On Christmas eve," Dale recalled, "we lay shivering in our old blankets in Weatherford's cornfield, and General Claiborne, his officers and men, dined next day on boiled acorns and parched corn." Christmas Day found the soldiers burning several other Muscogee villages and farms in the neighborhood. The weary troops then began their withdrawal to Fort Deposit, and from that outpost they started down the Federal Road on their return march to Fort Claiborne (Halbert and Ball, 260–261; Griffith, 132; Claiborne, 141).

A new year was dawning, but January 1814 marked the end of Claiborne's army. The First Mississippi volunteers' twelve-month enlistment had expired, as well as that of the mounted troops. There was no alternative for Claiborne but to disband his army. Only Colonel Russell's 600 regulars—and about sixty soldiers whose own term would be up in January—were left to garrison Fort Claiborne. Pushmataha's Choctaws headed for home. Claiborne's volunteers left with eight months' pay still coming to them. "They have served the last three months of inclement winter weather," Claiborne wrote, "without shoes or blankets, almost without shirts, but are still devoted to their country" (Halbert and Ball, 261; Pickett, 576; E. Rowland, 77).

Claiborne himself set off for Natchez. He never fought another campaign. The rigors of the previous months had taken their toll physically, and the general returned home a broken man. A wound that failed to heal continued to trouble him. In just another year he was dead. Although Claiborne lived to see the end of the war and Jackson's spectacular victory at New Orleans, the conflict had cost him his wealth, his health, and finally his life (McLemore, 232).

But for now, the Tensaw-Tombigbee region breathed much easier. At St. Stephens, the settlers celebrated the welcome news of Claiborne's victory with a torchlight parade on the night of December 30. Claiborne's troops had struck further into the heart of the Muscogee nation than any white army. Eccanachaca did not completely destroy the rebels' faith in the prophets, but the battle had a damaging effect on Red Stick morale. George Stiggins wrote, "[I]t finally closed the hostile operations of the lower-town Indians." Josiah Francis and Paddy Walsh moved their headquarters back to Othlewallee, where they planned to regroup to receive the next white attack. "It taught the savages that they were neither inaccessible nor invulnerable," Sam Dale wrote, "…and it proved what volunteers, even without shoes, clothing, blankets, or provisions would do for their country" (Halbert and Ball, 262; Martin, 161; Quimby, 434; Stiggins, 121; Claiborne, 141–142).

But the Red Sticks were not destroyed. Claiborne had struck a damaging blow at a major rebel stronghold, as had Floyd at Autossee, and Jackson at Talladega, and Cocke at the Hillabees. But after five months of hostilities, logistical weaknesses and manpower shortages still robbed the white armies of a decisive victory. And the Red Sticks still had much fight in them.

CHAPTER 11

Red Stick Resurgence

Restless and impatient as ever, Andy Jackson crossed the Coosa on January 15 on his second campaign into Muscogee territory. He had received word that the Red Sticks were concentrating their warriors at Tohopeka, their stronghold on the upper Tallapoosa, and that they were planning an attack on Fort Armstrong, garrisoned by a small force of Allied Creeks and Cherokees and a handful of whites. Old Hickory intended to strike the enemy encampment at Tohopeka and destroy it. General Pinckney had also written him that Floyd's Georgia army was moving into the field again, planning to hit Othlewallee, the rebels' other major encampment on the Tallapoosa. In the first attempt at a coordinated offensive by the allied armies, Jackson's troops would divert the Red Sticks away from Floyd and prevent them from concentrating their forces (Bassett, vol. 1, 443–444, 448; Elting, 170; Owen, 100).

It was a different army that Jackson led into Creek country. At Fort Strother, he still had his faithful Nashville Artillery Company, which Major John Reid called "the General's life-guard," armed with one six-pounder. And there were the two companies of scouts—John Gordon's and William Russell's—who had stood by him during the trying days of November and December of the previous year. Loyal John Coffee, deserted by his own mounted brigade, now commanded a company made up of volunteer officers who had been left without commands after the evaporation of Jackson's first army. There was also an infantry company of forty-eight soldiers under Captain Ferrell. But the bulk of Old Hickory's army—about 800 men—were two mounted regiments of fresh volunteers from Tennessee, inexperienced and untrained, led by Colonels

Nicholas T. Perkins and William Higgins. They arrived at Fort Strother on January 14, raising Jackson's force to 930 men, and Jackson had ordered them into the field the very next day (Bassett, vol. 1, 447–448; Reid and Eaton, 120–122; Heiskell, 407).

Old Hickory explained the reason for his haste in a report to General Pinckney. The new troops were anxious to see combat, but their term of enlistment was desperately short—just sixty days. Remembering his problems with the mutinous Tennessee troops in the fall of 1813, Jackson wrote, "The ill effects of keeping soldiers of this description long stationary and idle, I had been made to feel too sensibly already." Jackson wanted to get these new recruits into action as soon as possible. They could not be expected to conduct a lengthy campaign, but he was gambling that if they moved quickly enough they could strike a damaging blow at the Red Sticks' base and then withdraw (Bassett, vol. 1, 448).

The old problem of insubordination had raised its ugly head again. Coffee, with the rank of brigadier general, should have commanded the two mounted regiments, but both Perkins and Higgins refused to accept his authority, arguing that all officers should be elected by the soldiers. Coffee was flabbergasted. Jackson hesitated to begin a campaign by placing the commanders of his two untested regiments under arrest. But he wanted Coffee to be given the respect he was entitled to, and Coffee insisted that the two officers be disciplined. Higgins and Perkins finally came forward and apologized to Coffee, who agreed to drop charges (Heiskell, 122–123; Quimby, 450).

By January 18, the Tennessee army had reached Talladega, site of the major battle the previous November—a battle in which total victory had eluded Jackson when the bulk of the Red Stick warriors escaped his enveloping columns. The troops camped at Leslie's fort, where 200 red allies, poorly armed and rather lukewarm to the idea of joining Jackson's puny army, also fell in. Most were Allied Creeks led by local mixed-blood chief Jim Fife, but sixty-five were Cherokees. The bulk of Gideon Morgan's Cherokees, discharged at the end of the previous campaign, had no advance warning of Jackson's raid, so they could not join his army at this time (Bassett, vol. 1, 448; Wilkins, 72).

Jackson pushed his troops southward, and by January 20 his army was camped at Enitachopco, one of the Hillabee villages. Despite the efforts of his scouts, Jackson quickly became aware of how sketchy his intelligence had been about the nature of the Red Stick country, the distances involved, and the strength of the enemy. The troops were getting restless, their officers' inexperience becoming more evident. Jackson's small army probably was the only American army in the Creek War to take the offensive against a Red Stick force of near equal size. Still he continued toward Tohopeka (also called Cholocco Litabixee or Horseshoe Bend), the Red Stick encampment on the Tallapoosa. The Tennesseans made camp at Emuckfau Creek, three miles from the rebel stronghold (Bassett, vol. 1, 448–449; Owsley, 75).

Peter McQueen and Josiah Francis, according to British accounts, commanded the Red Sticks at Tohopeka, numbering between 800 and 1,000. They already knew of Jackson's approach. The warriors were moving their women and children away from their encampment and were dancing the war dance. Jackson's scouts interpreted this as the prelude to one of two things: the Red Sticks were preparing either to retreat or to launch an attack on the Tennesseans' camp. Old Hickory ordered his men to encamp in a hollow square, doubled the guards, and sent out his scouts to watch for enemy movement. He cautioned his soldiers to be ready for a night attack (Bassett, vol. 1, 449; Griffith, 138; Parton, 497).

The blow fell at six o'clock on the morning of January 22. With a ferocious war cry, the Red Sticks swarmed out of the woods on Jackson's left flank and hit Colonel Higgins's Tennesseans hard, but the inexperienced militia held firm. Jackson had ordered them to light fires outside the perimeter of the camp, so the troops could pick off the shadowy figures of the Red Sticks as they ran past the fires and made for the battle line. The soldiers also were able to fire at the flashes of light that marked the muzzles of the warriors' muskets in the dark (Bassett, vol. 1, 444, 449; Heiskell, 127; Mahon, *War of 1812,* 241).

Coffee and Colonel William Carroll were in their saddles at the first sound of gunfire, and they galloped to the scene of action. They joined Colonel Higgins, quickly took in the situation, and encouraged the recruits to stand firm. The firing continued for about half an hour, and the militia held on.

By now, the dim light of dawn was beginning to peek through, and the white troops could make out the dark forms of the Red Sticks in the woods. Coffee, Carroll, and Higgins could also determine the extent of damage that the Tennesseans had suffered. Many soldiers appeared to be wounded. Jackson dispatched Captain Ferrell's company of "about forty raw infantry"—all that he had in the way of a reserve—to scurry to the weakest part of the line, where Coffee took command and ordered them to charge. The foot soldiers plunged forward with a shout, and the Red Sticks began to fall back, giving way at the point of the bayonet. Higgins's troops and the Allied Creeks fell in with the pursuers, chasing the Red Sticks about two miles through the woods (Bassett, vol. 1, 444–445, 449).

The crisis was over, at least for now. Jackson's officers counted up their losses. Five soldiers had been killed in the assault, and twenty were wounded, but the Red Stick dead totaled twenty-four (Bassett, vol. 1, 445; Heiskell, 127).

While he collected his wounded, Jackson sent Coffee with 400 mounted troops and Allied Creeks to probe the Red Stick defenses at Horseshoe Bend. Old Hickory was particularly anxious to find out if rumors were true that the rebels had built fortifications around the town. If he found the town unfortified, Coffee was to overrun the settlement and burn it. But if the rebels had fortified, he was to fall back to Jackson's camp. Coffee did as he was instructed, and his horsemen moved forward through the woods (Bassett, vol. 1, 445, 449–450).

What Coffee's men saw at Horseshoe Bend quickly convinced them that this was not the time for an attack on Tohopeka. The Red Sticks had indeed erected fortifications—a stout barricade of earth and logs across the wooded neck of the peninsula formed by the bend in the Tallapoosa. Coffee returned to camp, where he advised Old Hickory of the situation and prepared to order up the Nashville artillerists with their six-pounder to blast the barricade apart. But he had not been back more than thirty minutes before McQueen launched another surprise attack, this time on Jackson's right flank (Bassett, vol. 1, 445, 450).

The second engagement of the day began when some of Gordon's mounted scouts—searching the nearby woods for a Muscogee they had spotted and fired on the previous night—suddenly drew fire from the trees ahead. Once again the war cry was raised. Coffee asked Jackson to let him take 200 men and attack the Red Sticks' left flank, and Old Hickory nodded agreement. Coffee was on his way when he discovered—to his dismay—that no more than fifty soldiers, mainly his own company and some of the scouts, were behind him. Still he plowed ahead and launched a spirited attack on the rebels' left, where the Red Sticks were firing from the shelter of a pine-topped ridge. Coffee ordered his soldiers to dismount and take the ridge. Jackson meanwhile ordered the Allied Creeks to support Coffee by swinging around to the right of the Red Stick party. The red allies were following his orders when it occurred to Jackson that the attack on his right appeared somewhat feeble and might be a feint designed to divert his attention away from another assault on his weakened left flank (Bassett, vol. 1, 445, 450; Heiskell, 128).

Jackson's suspicions soon proved correct, as the Red Sticks came out of the woods on Old Hickory's left and opened fire. But the Tennesseans were ready for them. At the first gunshot, Jackson galloped to his left, taking Captain Ferrell's foot soldiers with him. There were several volleys of musket fire. The Red Sticks, who seemed to be fairly well armed in this engagement, fired from cover—using fallen logs, trees, and tangled brush for concealment—firing, falling down to reload, and rising to shoot again. Higgins's regiment stood their ground for the second time that day, and again they drove the Red Sticks back. With Colonel Carroll in the lead, the Tennessee boys set out after the rebels with bayonets lowered. They pursued the Red Sticks for about a mile and a half, killing twenty-three warriors. On Jackson's right flank, Coffee's Tennesseans and Jim Fife's Allied Creeks charged the Red Sticks and scattered them (Bassett, vol. 1, 445, 450; Heiskell, 128).

McQueen, skillfully striking at two separate flanks of Old Hickory's line, had come close to destroying the Tennessee army. The warriors had also planned to launch a third assault—against the front of Jackson's army—but canceled the operation when one of the tribes earmarked to take part in the assault simply decided to go home instead. Considering his own experience with undisciplined troops, it was a development that Jackson would have appreciated (Remini, *Jackson*, 1977, 207–208).

The Red Sticks had withdrawn. But the Tennesseans' victory was not without cost. Coffee was wounded in the side in the engagement, and his aide-de-camp (and also his brother-in-law and Jackson's nephew) Major Alexander "Sandy" Donelson was killed, shot through the head. Three other soldiers were dead as well (Bassett, vol. 1, 445, 450; Parton, 496).

And Jackson's victory was a Pyrrhic victory. He had come here to destroy the Red Stick stronghold at Tohopeka, but Coffee had found it too strong to attack. Instead, his Tennesseans had to beat off two stiff Red Stick attacks. Old Hickory took in the situation. Many of his men were wounded, and the inexperienced militia—although they had performed well so far—appeared to be getting edgy. Their horses had not been fed for forty-eight hours, and rations for the men were low. Jackson decided to withdraw to Fort Strother, and if they accomplished nothing else they might draw the Red Sticks away from Floyd's army approaching from the southeast. He ordered his troops to throw up a breastwork of fallen logs around the camp and prepare for another possible Red Stick attack that night. They would move out in the morning. All night, the sentinels were jittery, firing at anything that moved or at any noise in the darkness (Bassett, vol. 1, 445, 450–451; Heiskell, 130).

McQueen and Francis would have preferred another attack, but their forces were not concentrated. Many warriors were with Weatherford on the other side of the Tallapoosa. Others were working on the fortifications at Horseshoe Bend. They did not attack again that night (L. Thompson, 511).

On January 23, Jackson began a slow and cautious withdrawal north. Twenty-three wounded soldiers carried in litters—including Coffee—made the going more difficult. His troops watched for another surprise attack, but none came. At sunset the soldiers made camp at Enitachopco Creek, again threw up a hasty breastwork, and remained alert throughout the night as a cold rain set in (Bassett, vol. 1, 445, 451; Heiskell, 131,135).

The following morning, McQueen's Red Sticks attacked Jackson's column again, falling on the Tennesseans' rear guard as it was crossing Enitachopco Creek, with the bulk of the army already on the other side. The Nashville Artillery Company with its six-pounder was caught just as they were entering the stream. The Red Sticks opened fire on Russell's scouts, in the extreme rear of the column, and the fight was on. Russell estimated the size of the Red Stick force at 500 warriors (Bassett, vol. 1, 446, 447, 451; L. Thompson, 513).

Jackson saw a chance to fall back on the Red Sticks, envelop them, and destroy them completely. His army was moving through the woods in the standard battle order of three columns, with an advance guard and a rear guard—designed so that the army could respond if attacked in front, in the rear, or on the flanks. He was confident that the rear guard—with Carroll in command of the center element and Colonel Perkins and Lieutenant Colonel John Stump commanding the right and left detachments, respectively—would hold their ground, while he wheeled his right and left columns back across Enitachopco Creek to pin the Red Stick force between them. "I knew," Jackson wrote, "if the men would stand and fight I would destroy every nine out of ten of the enemy" (Bassett, vol. 1, 446, 451; Heiskell, 406).

But things went disastrously wrong. As soon as firing began, Perkins and Stump and their men gave way and bolted into the woods or the creek, and most of Carroll's column panicked and followed suit. Jackson galloped to the bank to try to intercept and stop Stump and his men as they stumbled down into the creek, but they only rushed past him. Old Hickory, struggling to draw his sword, shouted furiously to them to halt and form up, but he was unable to stop them. This dangerous turn of events left Jackson's army in dire peril, as Carroll, with about twenty-five men—plus the artillery company and Russell's scouts—were all that stood to meet the Red Stick assault (Bassett, vol. 1, 446, 451–452).

The Nashville gunners' moment was at hand. With Captain David Deaderick absent due to sickness, Lieutenant Robert Armstrong commanded the small company, "my little Spartan band," Jackson called them. Armstrong ordered his men to form up, unharness the cannon, and prepare to fire. The artillerists, armed with muskets, scrambled back up to the top of the creek bank to form a ragged firing line, while Armstrong and five or six of his gunners strained to pull the cannon out of the water (Bassett, vol. 1, 446, 452).

Armstrong and his gunners managed to manhandle the fieldpiece to the top of the hill where the rest of his company were already under fire, only to discover to their horror that they had left the rammer and picker for the cannon lashed to the limber. It was too late to retrieve them, and the Red Sticks were almost upon them now. Dodging a hail of bullets, Private Craven Jackson yanked the iron ramrod from the end of his musket and quickly made an improvised picker to prime and fire the piece, while Private Constantine Perkins used his musket as a rammer to drive home the load. The little cannon belched forth a charge of grapeshot at the advancing Red Sticks (Bassett, vol. 1, 452).

The rebels returned fire. Captain William Hamilton, whose enlistment had expired but who had volunteered to remain with Jackson's artillery, fell dead. Lieutenant Armstrong was hit, wounded in the groin, along with several other soldiers, but as he fell he cried out, "Save the cannon!"

The foot soldiers loosed a volley of musket fire, and Jackson and Perkins reloaded and fired a second time (Bassett, vol. 1, 446, 452; Lossing, 775).

Carroll's small band of soldiers and Russell's scouts were holding firm, and by now Gordon's scouts had recrossed the creek and were joining in the action, along with the Allied Creeks. Gordon's men were partly able to turn the rebels' left flank. Higgins's regiment came back across the creek too. Seeing support at hand now, the Nashville artillerists leveled bayonets and charged the Red Sticks, driving them back. Coffee, although still feeble from his wound, was also back in the saddle, rallying the troops and directing them (Bassett, vol. 1, 446, 452; Clayton, 81; Heiskell, 135).

Perhaps the Red Sticks did not fight as aggressively as usual at Enitachopco. They should have been able to overwhelm Jackson's rear guard had it not been for the courage of Armstrong's artillerists. It is possible that Jackson's officers overestimated their numbers. In any event, once the Tennesseans reclaimed the offensive, the rebel resistance crumbled. Old Hickory's boys were too eager for blood now even to take cover behind trees. "They ran right on," Major Reid wrote, "and wanted only the sight of the enemy, then fired upon him, or charged him with the bayonet; in less than half an hour the Indians gave way and fled in every direction." In their haste, the rebels discarded blankets and other items that could have slowed down their flight (Quimby, 454; Heiskell, 407; Reid and Eaton, 135).

Led by Carroll, Gordon, and Higgins, the Tennesseans pursued the Red Sticks for two and a half miles. Twenty-six rebel corpses lay in the woods, but the Red Sticks managed to carry off most of their dead and wounded. Jackson estimated their total dead in the fighting at Emuckfau and Enitachopco at probably 200, while twenty-four soldiers had been killed and seventy-one wounded. "Our great loss," Coffee wrote, "has been occasioned by our troops being raw and undisciplined, commanded by officers of the same description. Had I had my old regiment of cavalry, I could have driven the enemy wherever I met them without loss" (Bassett, vol. 1, 447, 452, 453; Parton, 497).

As for Perkins and Stump, the colonels who had fled from the field with their men, Old Hickory wrote his wife, "[T]hey ought to be shot." But for their cowardly action, Jackson claimed, he would have killed many more Red Sticks and several of his good men would still be alive. He lamented, "[R]aw troops with officers at their head seeking for popularity will not do." Perkins and Stump later answered Old Hickory's charges before a court-martial. Perkins argued that he had ordered his soldiers to dismount and form a battle line, which only a few actually did. He stayed with this small detachment, then he crossed the creek to try to rally his troops. The court acquitted Perkins but found Stump guilty and dismissed him from the service (Bassett, vol. 1, 447, 452; Quimby, 454–455).

After Enitachopco, the little Tennessee army continued its withdrawal north to Fort Strother without any further brushes with the enemy. With the short enlistment of his troops about to expire, Jackson discharged them and waited for fresh reinforcements to arrive.

In spite of his close escape at Enitachopco, Jackson saw his raid as a success. He had accomplished what he had set out to do. If Floyd was moving toward the Tallapoosa from the east, then Jackson's raid must have helped decoy away some of the Red Stick warriors. And if the rumored Red Stick attack on Fort Armstrong was a real threat, then he had prevented that from happening. He felt his militia volunteers had fought well, considering the hazards they had experienced, and placed the blame for the panic of the troops at Enitachopco Creek on their officers (Quimby, 453; Bassett, vol. 1, 453).

The engagements at Emuckfau and Enitachopco, while tactical victories for the Americans, were close calls. They could have resulted in catastrophe for Jackson's army. But American morale was low at this point in the War of 1812—the British had captured Fort Niagara on the northern frontier and burned Buffalo, New York, late in December—and the Madison administration in Washington welcomed any positive news from the front. Accounts of the fighting in Alabama actually stimulated recruiting in Tennessee. Folks back home sensed the war was coming to an end, and young men wanted to be in on the final blow that would destroy the Red Sticks. General Pinckney, watching the progress of the campaign, marked Old Hickory as a man destined for promotion. Were it not for Jackson, he wrote, "[T]he Indian war, on the part of Tennessee, would have been abandoned at least for a time" (Remini, *Jackson*, 1977, 209; Owsley, 76).

While McQueen and Francis were holding Jackson's Tennessee army at bay, William Weatherford focused on another invasion by the Georgia army. After his defeat at Eccanachaca, Weatherford's strategy was to use his armed force—located in the Muscogee heartland between the advancing Tennessee and Georgia armies—to hit each white army separately and defeat them piecemeal. If his warriors suffered defeat, he could more easily combine them for continued resistance (Heidler and Heidler, *Encyclopedia*, 548).

The continuing problem of lack of firearms and ammunition plagued the Red Sticks. Weatherford and a small party had traveled to Pensacola to seek more gunpowder from the Spanish. Gonzalez Manrique still was without adequate supplies and could not provide the Muscogees with anything. Weatherford had better success with British agents and private merchants in Pensacola, but still he returned with only three horseloads of ammunition. But even this small amount was enough to keep Red Stick hopes alive (Owsley, 56).

By the middle of January, General John Floyd was ready to make his second foray into Red Stick territory with his Georgia army. Floyd had recovered somewhat from his wound sustained at Autossee, and sufficient rations for his troops had arrived at Fort Mitchell on the Chattahoochee. On January 18, the Georgia commander advanced into the field again. Floyd's objective was the Red Stick camp at Othlewallee on the Tallapoosa, where Weatherford's forces were waiting. Floyd had 1,200 Georgia volunteers whose term of enlistment was to expire shortly, a company of cavalry, and McIntosh's 400 Allied Creeks (Owsley, 56; Quimby, 455–456).

About forty miles west of Fort Mitchell, the Georgians—under the direction of Captain Jett Thomas, Floyd's engineer officer and artillery commander—built a forward supply base, Fort Hull, four miles southwest of present-day Tuskegee, Alabama. After making the post as secure as they could, Floyd's troops pushed off on January 25 toward the Tallapoosa and the old Muscogee capital at Tuckabatchee just beyond (Owsley, 56; Brannon, "Journal," 236; Howard, 379).

Floyd expected an attack. After marching three miles, the troops formed a line of battle in the swamp. The Allied Creeks prepared for combat with their old enemies and—crouching around several burnt tree stumps—began daubing their faces and bodies with black war paint. But no attack came. The Georgians moved on the following morning and marched only a couple of miles before a drenching rain set in. The baggage wagons, constantly bogging down in the mud, slowed the column down, and Floyd finally sent most of them back to Fort Hull before pushing on to the northwest. Under Thomas's supervision, the Georgians began constructing a fortified camp, called Camp Defiance, on Calabee Creek, not far from Autossee, the Red Stick town that they had destroyed two months earlier (Brannon, "Journal," 236; White, 291; Howard, 379).

Floyd's troops were unaware that the Red Sticks already were planning a surprise attack on Camp Defiance. The rebel leaders hoped to smash the Georgians before they had time to complete work on their fortifications. Thomas Woodward, who served in Floyd's army at Calabee Creek, speculated that the Red Sticks also hoped to seize ammunition from the whites. At their Othlewallee stronghold, the prophets—Paddy Walsh and Cusseta Hadjo (Jim Boy or High-Head Jim)—conferred with the military men—Weatherford and mixed-blood chief William McGillivray—to iron out details in the plan of attack (Stiggins, 128–129; T. Woodward, 89).

Paddy Walsh—"small, ugly, and a diminutive man in personal appearance," according to George Stiggins—directed the attack. He knew that the whites had the advantage in firearms and artillery. The tactical advantage of the poorly armed Red Sticks lay in surprise attacks, when they could use their tomahawks and war clubs to the utmost. Walsh's plan was to creep up on the Georgians' camp in the morning darkness, overcome the sentries, and attack the soldiers, killing as many of them as they could, then withdraw at daylight. Also, the Creeks would try to capture the Georgians' two pieces of artillery. Cusseta Hadjo concurred with Walsh's plan (Stiggins, 129, 136).

As on other occasions, the prophets and the military men disagreed on tactics. Weatherford suggested that a force of 300 warriors first rush upon the officers' tents and kill them before the general attack. Without their leaders, the soldiers would be confused and helpless. This idea struck the prophets as near suicidal, and since he was to lead the assault, Walsh suspected that Weatherford might be trying to get him killed. Weatherford promptly volunteered to lead the attempt himself, but few warriors seemed willing to follow him. The prophets ruled out Red Eagle's plan as too risky. Disgusted, Weatherford stormed off and refused to take part in the battle (Stiggins, 129–131).

On January 27, the silence of the chilly Alabama predawn was shattered as 1,300 painted warriors streamed out of the nearby swamp to overrun the Georgians' camp. It was the best-planned Creek attack of the war, and it almost worked. Floyd described the surprise attack in his report of the engagement: "They stole upon the sentinels, fired on them, and with great impetuosity rushed upon our line." Within minutes the camp was in confusion and panic as soldiers, half asleep and disoriented, stumbled to their feet uncertain of the source of the enemy attack. Officers rushed about, trying to rally their men. Colonel Daniel Newnan was an early casualty of the engagement, wounded three times. The abruptness of the assault in the morning darkness came close to routing Floyd's army. Part of the camp was overrun, enabling the Red Sticks to get close to the two field-pieces (Owsley, 57; Palmer, 273–274).

As Jackson's Tennesseans had done at Emuckfau, the Georgians had built campfires beyond their perimeter to provide light in case they were attacked. But Georgia infantryman James Tait recalled that when the soldiers withdrew behind the fires, they had little room to maneuver. "The camp was too small," Tait wrote, "the men being too deep in line when drawn up to our camp" (Brannon, "Journal," 237).

Floyd quickly regained his composure. "Cheer up, boys," he yelled. "We will give them hell when daylight comes." Fortunately for the Georgians, some of the veteran companies already were rallying. Especially, Captain Thomas's Baldwin Volunteer Artillery from Milledgeville held steady and kept up a consistent fire against the enemy. Captain William E. Adams's rifle company also remained steadfast. Captain John Broadnax's small picket guard had a close call when they were cut off from the camp by the Red Stick attackers. With the help of the Allied Creeks—a party of friendly Uchees led by Timpoochy Barnard—they fought their way back to their own lines (Griffith, 135; Palmer, 273).

A desperate struggle raged for control of the cannon. Thomas's artillerists spotted a large number of Red Stick warriors within mere yards of the fieldpieces. Ezekiel M. Attaway, one of only three men left at one of the guns, urged his comrades to hold fast. "We must not give up the gun, boys," he cried. "Seize the first weapon you can lay your hands upon, and stick to your posts until the last." As with Jackson's army at Enitachopco, the small artillery company played a decisive role in the battle. The cannoneers quickly depressed the guns and discharged several rounds of grapeshot directly into the attacking warriors at close range. The resulting carnage broke the spirit of the attackers, who began to fall back (Howard, 379; Owsley, 58).

Fortunately for the whites, it was now becoming light enough to see the enemy in the dawn, and the Red Stick attack was faltering. The warriors apparently were not well armed, most of them having only war clubs and bows and arrows, and those who did have muskets were low on ammunition. Thomas Woodward reported hearing some of the Red Sticks asking each other to "give me some bullets—give me powder" (T. Woodward, 89).

Floyd ordered his infantry to counterattack. Captain Duke Hamilton's mounted dragoons—who had joined Floyd only the previous day—took their position in the rear. The foot soldiers went in with the bayonet, and the Red Sticks "fled in every direction." Then the mounted troops galloped forward, using their sabers and cutting down more than a dozen of the rebels. Floyd ordered a vigorous pursuit by two of his rifle companies and McIntosh's Allied Creeks, most of whom (with the exception of Timpoochy Barnard and his Uchees) had taken little part in the fighting. Hamilton's mounted company joined in the pursuit. The troops tracked the rebels by their blood trails through the swamp but with little success (Palmer, 273).

The Calabee Creek fight lasted nearly an hour. It had been a near disaster for the little Georgia army, but determination and quick reflexes saved the day. The actions of Thomas's gunners in saving the cannon may have been the most critical phase of the battle. The Red Sticks left forty-nine warriors killed. Jim Boy lay dead, and Paddy Walsh was seriously wounded. The Georgians lost seventeen men killed and 132 wounded (Owsley, 58; Griffith, 137; Stiggins, 132).

The Allied Creeks, who lost five warriors killed and fifteen wounded, took a gruesome revenge, mutilating and dismembering the Red Stick corpses. James Tait wrote that the warriors "riped them open, cut their heads to pieces, took out the heart of one, . . . cut off the private parts of others." After lifting one body onto a dead horse, they laughed and yelled, "Whiskey too much," as the corpse fell off (Owsley, 58; Brannon, "Journal," 237–238).

The Georgia troops remained at Camp Defiance for six days, and the Red Sticks did not attack again. Floyd withdrew to Fort Hull, where he was thankful to find rations for his exhausted troops. Floyd began to hear ominous talk about mutiny if the troops were not allowed to go home. Their time was up on February 22. Morale was low after the close call at Calabee Creek. Out of his army of nearly 1,500 men, 352 were sick or wounded.

Although Fort Hull was deep in Muscogee territory, and Floyd feared being cut off from his supply base at Fort Mitchell, he desperately wanted to hold the little outpost. Floyd knew that General Pinckney—back at his command center at Fort Hawkins—had ordered a fresh force of militia from South Carolina to the frontier to relieve Floyd's Georgians. These troops were already on the march, and Floyd wanted to hold the fort until the South Carolinians arrived (Brannon, "Journal," 237; Owsley, 59).

By February 16, the Carolinians had not shown up, and—although none of his men had deserted yet—Floyd's troops were threatening to march back to Georgia with or without him. Floyd relinquished command of Fort Hull to Colonel Homer V. Milton, a regular army officer from the Third U.S. Infantry. Milton had a small detachment of regulars to garrison the fort, and 140 Georgians—including Thomas's artillerists—volunteered to remain until the replacements from South Carolina arrived. Floyd took the bulk of his Georgia army and marched them back to the Ocmulgee and from there to Milledgeville, where his men were discharged. There would be no more battles for the Georgia army in the Muscogee nation (Owsley, 59; Quimby, 458; Griffith, 138; Howard, 380).

Ill supplied and more poorly organized than the white army, the Red Sticks had made remarkable tactical achievements on the battlefield in January 1814. They had turned back both white offensives and fought four engagements in five days. For some of the warriors, these accomplishments gave them a false sense of security, and they boasted that they had "whipped" Jackson and "drove him to the Coosa River." But their losses were heavy, and they now reverted to the defensive for the remainder of the war (Pickett, 584; Quimby, 458–459).

At least the Red Sticks did not have to face yet a third white army in January 1814. Since their defeat at Eccanachaca, the rebels had virtually abandoned any active operations on the Alabama River. But Claiborne's Mississippi army had gone home, and Lieutenant Colonel Gilbert Russell, with his Third U.S. Infantry at Fort Claiborne, lacked the manpower and supplies to launch an offensive up the Alabama. Russell was not idle, though. In January he undertook an ambitious series of raids to clear out isolated pockets of Red Sticks and to sever the rebel supply line to Pensacola. The regular officer also received welcome reinforcements of Choctaw and Chickasaw warriors enlisted by Colonel John McKee (Owsley, 49).

On January 22, McKee and 400 Choctaws crossed the Black Warrior to raid Red Stick towns. McKee again struck Black Warrior Town, which Coffee's troops had burned the previous October. During the next several days, McKee's warriors ravaged the countryside, destroying corn and livestock—effectively withholding food supplies from the enemy, who lacked the manpower to prevent the destruction. McKee hoped that his raids would help to put more pressure on the Red Sticks, as Jackson's army advanced southward. Complaining of great pain from rheumatism in his wrist, he wrote Jackson on February 26, "I hope however we will be able to do something towards convincing the muscogees that they are surrounded by a ring of fire and crush their warring spirit" (McKee Journal, 3–4; McKee Letters; L. Thompson, 529).

CHAPTER 12

"He *Makes* Them Do Their Duty"

While Jackson and Floyd battled Red Sticks in January 1814, Lieutenant Colonel Gilbert Russell yearned for a more active role in the Creek campaign. With only his 600-man Third U.S. Infantry at Fort Claiborne, Russell could not launch an offensive campaign, so his main function would have to be to support Jackson's Tennessee army. General Pinckney instructed Russell to obtain boats, load supplies aboard them, and sail them up the Alabama River to the Hickory Ground—the proposed rendezvous point for the allied armies at the junction of the Coosa and Tallapoosa. Itching for action, Russell decided to conduct an expedition against Red Stick towns on the Cahaba River, a major tributary of the Alabama. Russell led his regulars, joined by Sam Dale (now a major) with a company of territorial militia and a company of mounted troops. A separate detachment under Captain James E. Dinkins was to take two armed keelboats loaded with provisions upriver and rendezvous with the main column near the targeted Cahaba towns (Owsley, 49; Claiborne, 143).

Seven days of forced marches brought Russell's troops to the Cahaba towns, only to find—as McKee and his Choctaw raiders had discovered on the Black Warrior two weeks earlier—that the Red Sticks had abandoned them. Russell ordered the towns burned. But now Russell's supplies had given out, and Dinkins had not appeared with the barges. Twenty-two-year-old Lieutenant James M. Wilcox, a West Point graduate, volunteered to take three soldiers and set out to search for Dinkins. Russell would take his column south and try to make it back to Fort Claiborne (Owsley, 50; Claiborne, 143; Owen, 153).

Wilcox and his party set out in a small pirogue, but when they reached the mouth of the Cahaba, the boat capsized. Although the men were able to right the boat and continue on their journey, most of their powder was wet. They had not gotten far when a Red Stick war party in a canoe spotted them and zoomed in for the kill. Wilcox bashed in the skull of one warrior with his paddle, but the Red Sticks quickly overpowered the bluecoats. One soldier escaped into the cane. The others were not so lucky. The Red Sticks tomahawked and scalped the ill-fated lieutenant, who met his end just as the supply barges appeared in the river. Dinkins had missed the mouth of the Cahaba and had continued up the Alabama when he realized his mistake. He was now on his way back to Fort Claiborne, but he reached the scene of the Wilcox ambush too late to save the young officer (Claiborne, 144–145; Pickett, 578).

The main detachment was having problems of its own. Russell's starving troops were now eating horse meat, rats, and acorns to stay alive. "Colonel Russell was in a tight place," Sam Dale wrote. "I saw a soldier offer two dollars for a rat, and the offer was rejected; the owner demanded ten dollars." Russell finally reached Fort Claiborne, happy to be back in more comfortable surroundings and disappointed that his expedition had accomplished so little (Claiborne, 145).

Although he fought no major battles after Eccanachaca, Russell still made an important contribution to the war effort. Without the supplies that he eventually collected and carried up the Alabama, Old Hickory's Tennesseans would have been unable to operate in the Muscogee nation for long. Russell also effectively disrupted the Red Sticks' supply line to Pensacola. Still, the lack of cooperation from Flournoy delayed Russell's movement up the Alabama for many weeks (Owsley, 50).

East of the Tallapoosa, Russell's fellow officer in the Third U.S. Infantry, Colonel Homer V. Milton, dealt with a similar situation. Left in command of Fort Hull after Floyd's Georgians marched back to the Chattahoochee, Milton had only twelve days' worth of rations. But in just a few days the relief column of 1,000 South Carolina militia soldiers ordered out by Pinckney arrived. Milton quickly put them to work building a new stockade, Fort Bainbridge, during a heavy snowstorm. The new fort—just sixteen miles east of Fort Hull—would help to protect the precarious supply line from Fort Mitchell, and now wagons could make the distance between the forts in a journey of one day. The methodical Milton continued to strengthen his supply line during February and March 1814. Moving most of his troops back to Fort Mitchell, he garrisoned Forts Bainbridge and Hull with small detachments of soldiers. By March he had moved an ample amount of supplies to Fort Hull, where he had gradually assembled 600 troops, mostly regulars, and Allied Creeks (Owsley, 59–60).

As with Russell at Fort Claiborne, Pinckney saw Milton's role as one of support for Jackson's army. Milton was to stockpile enough supplies at Fort Hull to furnish the Tennesseans when they arrived at the rendezvous point at the Hickory Ground. Still Milton sought a more aggressive role, and by early April, when large numbers of militia from North Carolina arrived to augment his force, the regular army officer had moved from Fort Hull to the Tallapoosa. His army occupied the bank of the river opposite Tuckabatchee, and they soon built yet another outpost—Fort Decatur—to serve as a supply base (Owsley, 59–60).

On the Georgia frontier, the string of defensive forts along the Ocmulgee thrown up by nervous whites earlier in the conflict now seemed unnecessary. It was becoming fairly obvious that the Ocmulgee settlers were in no real danger of attack by the Red Sticks. In November 1813, Georgia troops had constructed an even more northerly outpost, Fort Daniel, in present-day Gwinnett County, to protect settlers against a possible attack by the Cherokees. By January 1814, the Georgians could see that they had overreacted to these concerns as well. But the Georgia forts could still play a useful role in communication and supply (Barnard and Schwartzman, "Tecumseh," 501–502).

Late in January 1814, Pinckney conceived an idea to use the Chattahoochee River as a highway for supplying Floyd's and Jackson's armies in the Muscogee country. The linchpin in this plan was a fort to be built at Standing Peach Tree, a Cherokee village on the future site of Atlanta, Georgia. Supplies would be floated down the Chattahoochee from that point 150 miles south to Fort Mitchell. In a trial run, one boat made the trip successfully. With twenty-two soldiers, the Georgia militia's Lieutenant George R. Gilmer, later to become a governor of Georgia and an architect of Indian removal, took charge of the project. James M. Montgomery, a veteran of the battle of Autossee, supervised the artisans. Work did not get under way on the new fort until March 14. Fort Peachtree was located at the point where Peachtree Creek empties into the Chattahoochee. But Pinckney's plan to supply the white armies by floating boats down the Chattahoochee really came to nothing, and the war ended before it could be implemented (Barnard and Schwartzman, "Tecumseh," 502–504).

But one issue had been settled. Pinckney was confident now that Jackson was the most capable commander in the field. Claiborne and Floyd were gone. Pinckney determined to entrust the final offensive to Old Hickory, and he planned to promote him as soon as the opportunity arose. He assigned Russell and Milton, his two regular army commanders, a support role for the Tennessee army. Now it was all up to Sharp Knife (Owsley, 76).

Pinckney also intended to strengthen the Tennessee army by providing it with a stable core of regulars. Although Colonel John Williams's Thirty-ninth U.S. Infantry had been earmarked for service at New Orleans, Pinckney assigned the regiment to Jackson. Recruited in East Tennessee for one year in the summer of 1813, the Thirty-ninth had not seen combat, and as late as January 23 only a third of the regiment had arms. But its officers were well qualified and the men well disciplined. On February 6, to the delight of Old Hickory, the blue-coated Thirty-ninth Infantry—600 men strong—marched into Fort Strother (Elting, 171; Quimby, 459–460).

At last Jackson had a regiment of troops he could rely on, and this made all the difference in enforcing discipline on the rest of his army. With the memory of mutiny still fresh in his mind, Sharp Knife relished the presence of regulars to keep the unsteady militia in line. At first he feared that Williams might be sent on to New Orleans. "[I]f he is taken from me," he wrote, "my main prop is gone, and I will have to risk my character and the public service with raw, inexperienced troops, commanded, perhaps, by raw, inexperienced officers." When it became evident that the colonel would remain, Jackson was elated. "His regiment will give strength to my arm," he declared, "and quell mutiny" (Heiskell, 358).

The thirty-six-year-old Williams, a North Carolina native who now practiced law in Knoxville, had led East Tennessee mounted volunteers in the Florida campaign against the Seminoles in 1812. His capable young officers included Major Lemuel P. Montgomery, a twenty-eight-year-old Nashville attorney whose grandfather had fought in the Revolutionary War. Also marching with the Thirty-ninth was Third Lieutenant Sam Houston, the son of a Revolutionary War soldier. A restless young man, the twenty-one-year-old Houston had tried his hand at farming, clerking in a general store, and for a brief time operating a small school. But what he really preferred was the outdoor life. He spoke fluent Cherokee, because he had lived off and on for three years with the tribe near Hiwassee during his late teens. The Cherokees called him Raven. When he enlisted in the Thirty-ninth Regiment, his mother sent him off with the gift of a ring inscribed "honor" (Heiskell, 355; Quimby, 459; Ratner, 99–101).

The Thirty-ninth U.S. Infantry joined the largest army that Jackson had yet assembled. Governor Blount had called up 5,000 militia, about half of them from West Tennessee under Brigadier General Thomas Johnson and half from East Tennessee under General John Cocke. And John Coffee was resurrecting his old mounted command. Two companies of his veterans were assembling at Huntsville. With the addition of 700 more mounted troops under Colonel Robert Dyer, they would be organized into a brigade as soon as the campaign began. Captain David Deaderick's Nashville Artillery Company—which had served Old Hickory so faithfully—faced the expiration of their enlistment at the end of March. But a new company of artillerists was on the way—recruited by Captain Joel Parish, a veteran of Deaderick's company, with Lieutenants John and William Allen, former NCOs (Quimby, 459–460, 466; Stephen, 130).

The Cherokees were back, too. Ridge, now a major—he would adopt the rank as his first name from now on—arrived at Fort Strother on February 26 with John Lowrey and John Walker and 200 recruits. The Cherokee detachment soon swelled to 500 mounted warriors, armed with rifles, muskets, lances, and tomahawks, again wearing white feathers and deer

tails to distinguish them from the enemy. Colonel Gideon Morgan commanded once again, with Lowrey and Richard Brown as lieutenant
colonels. Young John Ross, a second lieutenant, served as adjutant
(Wilkins, 73).

At Fort Strother, Ridge was getting to know Sharp Knife on a personal
basis. Ridge's friend Charles Hicks, influenced by Moravian missionaries
and considering converting to Christianity, spent much of his time in
camp discussing religion and studying the Bible. The Cherokee warriors
prepared themselves for the coming campaign, dancing their war dance
and listening to the chants of their shamans (Wilkins, 73; Ehle, 114–125).

Jackson's troops now were well supplied, with rations issued regularly.
The old starvation days of November and December were behind them.
The difficulty now was accumulating enough rations to feed a large army
on an extended campaign into the Muscogee nation. As usual, the problem of supply held up the beginning of the offensive for several weeks.
When many of the militia showed up without arms, this also delayed the
campaign in that weapons had to be obtained. While waiting for his old
sixty-day volunteers' enlistments to expire, Jackson put these troops to
work building boats to carry supplies downriver. Jackson needed more
wagons to haul supplies overland from Fort Deposit to Fort Strother, and
the road was poor. He could not hope for help from the Georgia army, but
Pinckney expected that Colonel Milton with his regulars and Carolina
militia from Fort Hull could join Jackson if he made it as far as Tuckabatchee (Owen, 117; Owsley, 77; Quimby, 460–462).

Old Hickory still wrestled with a problem that would not go away. Isaac
Roberts, who had clashed with Jackson over troop enlistments in December, was back at the head of one of the West Tennessee brigades. Apprehensive, General Roberts brought his column to a halt just short of Fort
Strother and rode in to confer with Jackson. At issue once again was the
enlistment period of the new recruits. Jackson had instructed his recruiters
to sign up all the new volunteers for six months. But the West Tennessee
recruits had been enlisted for only three months, and Roberts insisted that
Jackson agree that the men would serve no longer. Jackson flatly refused.
The troops then turned around and started for home. But Old Hickory
acted quickly. He had Roberts placed under arrest and declared the troops
to be mutineers, but he offered to pardon any of the soldiers who would
return to Fort Strother. In the end, he agreed not to hold them more than
three months, and most of them returned (Owsley, 77).

Meanwhile, Jackson's old nemesis General John Cocke, who had
enlisted the East Tennessee troops for six months, felt it unfair that West
Tennesseans should serve only for three and said so to his men. He
warned them that Jackson would use force to keep them in, that if they
wanted to avoid it, then they might as well go home now. When word of
this got back to Jackson, he ordered General George Doherty, one of

Cocke's brigade commanders, to arrest him, but Cocke had already left camp. Back in Tennessee, Cocke was eventually arrested and court-martialed but was acquitted of the charges (Owsley, 78).

Despite all the delays caused by bad weather, poor roads, and insubordination, Jackson's new troops—including the West Tennessee brigade under Johnson, the East Tennessee brigade under Doherty, and the mounted troops under Colonel Robert Dyer—had arrived at Fort Strother by March 12. Old Hickory was ready to begin his final campaign against the Red Sticks (Quimby, 464).

Jackson's scouts—the old ranger companies under John Gordon, William Russell, and Eli Hammond—had not been inactive during February and early March. They had been busy reconnoitering the Red Sticks' stronghold on the Tallapoosa that Jackson had been unable to assault in January. Sharp Knife would have more reliable intelligence about the location and strength of the enemy this time. He chose Tohopeka as his next objective (Owsley, 77).

The Red Sticks had now congregated the flower of their military forces at Tohopeka, the "hot bed of the war party," Jackson called it. The town of Tohopeka (fenced-off place or fort) lay in a sharp bend in the Tallapoosa called Cholocco Litabixee (horse's flat foot), or Horseshoe Bend. A thousand die-hard warriors were there, drawn from the Nuyaka, Hillabee, Okfuskee, Eufaula (not the Lower Creek town on the Chattahoochee, but an Upper Creek town on the Tallapoosa), and Fish Pond towns. Also there were about 300 women and children. The principal war chief was Menawa, with the prophet Monahoe wielding considerable spiritual clout. Other major Red Stick leaders were present, too—Peter McQueen and his Tallassee warriors, Josiah Francis, and William Weatherford (Bassett, vol. 1, 462; Owen, 116–117; Owsley, 79; Quimby, 466; L. Thompson, 534, 536).

Coffee and his mounted men had gotten a disquieting glimpse of the rebel defenses at Tohopeka when they had scouted them back in late January. The bend in the Tallapoosa enclosed about a hundred acres of woodland, a peninsula with water on three sides. All the way across the neck of the peninsula—about 350 yards long—the Red Sticks had constructed a stout European-style breastwork. The barricade, five to eight feet high, was made of earth and large pine logs, with firing steps and two rows of portholes through which the defenders could shoot. An attacker would have been unable to use enfilade fire against the breastwork even if he managed to capture one flank, because the wall curved inward and ran in a zigzag pattern, so the white troops would have to face a cross fire. The Red Sticks had also erected a formidable abatis of felled trees and brush behind the barricade, and between them and the village were a number of ravines covered in thick underbrush where they could take cover if the barricade was breached and they had to fall back (Reid and Eaton, 149;

Heidler and Heidler, *Encyclopedia,* 244; Owen, 118; Owsley, 79; Quimby, 466; Remini, *Jackson,* 1977, 213).

Weatherford was familiar with the Spanish defenses at Pensacola, and he may have designed the Muscogee barricade at Horseshoe Bend. The Red Sticks also could have constructed the breastwork with the direct aid of Spanish agents. One thing was sure—this was no ordinary Native American work and was "really astonishing," Jackson reported. The rebels were obviously placing great confidence in these defenses. They had only one backup plan. The Red Sticks' canoes lined the riverbank at the edge of the town. This would be their escape route across the Tallapoosa in case the barricade failed and the white army broke through. The Tennesseans would face a hard fight at Horseshoe Bend with the threat of many casualties (Bassett, vol. 1, 488–489; L. Thompson, 535; Quimby, 466).

But the attackers at Tohopeka would be prepared for a hard fight if Old Hickory had his way. In the weeks prior to the spring campaign, Jackson instilled tougher training in his army, with the Thirty-ninth Infantry as its backbone. The Tennessee volunteers began to learn obedience and discipline. Jackson even forbade the transportation of whiskey. "He *makes* them do their duty," one young officer wrote (Remini, *Jackson,* 1977, 211).

Old Hickory's obsession with discipline claimed a casualty in John Woods, an eighteen-year-old private in one of Roberts's West Tennessee companies whose men had deserted and then returned to Fort Strother after Jackson had offered them a pardon. Woods had not been with the company during the incident; he had offered to serve as a substitute for a soldier who was not willing to return to duty, and he joined the company before it returned to Fort Strother. Jackson was unaware of this, and no one told him (Quimby, 465).

Woods's problems began on sentry duty one cold and rainy February morning. The shivering private received permission from an officer to leave his post to retrieve a blanket from his tent. When Woods found that his pals had left him some breakfast in the tent, he sat down to eat it. Minutes passed, and the young soldier's meal was interrupted by another officer who stalked into the tent and—apparently angered by the sight of Woods eating—ordered the private in abusive language to get back to his post. Woods replied that a different officer had given him permission to leave his post, and he refused to move. Tempers escalated, more angry words were exchanged, and the officer ordered Woods placed under arrest (Remini, *Jackson,* 1977, 211).

Finally Woods seized up his musket and threatened to shoot anyone who tried to lay a hand on him. The heated argument soon got the attention of others in the camp, and the incident went from bad to worse when someone ran to Jackson with word that a mutiny was in progress. This was like waving a red flag in front of the embattled commander, and Old Hickory—exhausted from tension and lack of sleep in the fevered preparations for the campaign and angry through and through—rushed to the scene of the trouble. "Shoot him!" he thundered. "Shoot him!" (Remini, *Jackson*, 1977, 211; L. Thompson, 531).

The young private was placed under arrest, charged with mutiny, and tried by a court-martial that convened in the woods between two tents, with the prisoner sitting on a nearby log. To the surprise of many, the court found Woods guilty and sentenced him to be shot by a firing squad. Officers pleaded with Jackson to show leniency, especially since Woods was the main support for two elderly parents. Old Hickory sternly refused, intending to make an example of the unruly private. The prisoner was brought out on March 14 and the entire army called to assembly to witness the execution. A firing squad of regulars fell in to carry out the sentence. The muskets roared, and the bewildered Woods fell dead (Parton, 509; Quimby, 465; Remini, *Jackson*, 1977, 212).

No one had believed that Jackson would actually go through with it. To carry out a death sentence on a militia soldier was practically unheard of, and Woods was the first since the Revolutionary War to be executed by the army. But there was no more disobedience in Jackson's camp. And there was a price to pay. The Woods incident haunted Jackson for the rest of his life and was often used by his political enemies on the road to the White House (Mahon, *War of 1812*, 243; Quimby, 465; Remini, *Jackson*, 1977, 212).

On the same day that Private Woods was executed, Jackson's army moved out of Fort Strother and launched the spring campaign against the Red Sticks. About thirty miles downriver was the mouth of Cedar Creek, where the general planned to build a new forward supply base. Flatboats manned by Williams's regulars carried the supplies down the Coosa while Jackson with the bulk of the army crossed the river and moved south. Because of low water levels, the supply boats grounded a mile and a half short of Cedar Creek. This delayed the offensive for three days while the soldiers transported the supplies overland to the rendezvous point, but it gave the Tennesseans time to construct Fort Williams, the new supply base. Coffee's mounted troops—including the Cherokees—spent the time raiding enemy settlements downriver, burning two deserted Muscogee towns, and then returning to Fort Williams (Griffith, 144; Owsley, 77–78; Quimby, 467; Remini, *Jackson*, 1977, 213; Wilkins, 75).

Leaving a strong garrison of 450 West Tennesseans at Fort Williams, with Brigadier General Johnson in command, Jackson moved out on March 24 with his main force and eight days' rations. From Fort Williams it would be an overland march of just forty miles to the Red Stick stronghold at Horseshoe Bend. Riding with Jackson now were 100 Allied Creeks under William McIntosh. These Coweta warriors had already served with Floyd's Georgia army, and their knowledge of the Muscogee country and of the strength and disposition of the enemy forces proved invaluable to Jackson (Owen, 117; Owsley, 78–79; Quimby, 464; L. Thompson, 533).

With the addition of his red allies, Jackson now had a striking force of over 3,000 troops for his assault on the Horseshoe. Marching on Tohopeka were 2,000 foot soldiers, including Williams's Thirty-ninth U.S. Infantry and Doherty's infantry brigade from East Tennessee. There were 700 horsemen in Coffee's mounted brigade, plus the ranger companies, the Cherokees, and the Allied Creeks. Captain Parish's artillery company was hauling two cannon through the woods, the old six-pounder that had seen such rough service at Enitachopco and a new three-pounder. It was night-fall on March 26 when the Tennessee army made camp about five miles from Horseshoe Bend near the site of the encampment at Emuckfau two months earlier (Owsley, 79; Quimby, 467).

The following day would bring what Jackson hoped would be the decisive battle of the Creek War. Sharp Knife had already issued his general orders in which he made it clear that "any officer or soldier who flies before the enemy without being compelled to do so by superior force and actual necessity—shall suffer death." With the fate of Private John Woods fresh in their minds, the Tennessee soldiers knew that he meant business (Bassett, vol. 1, 488).

The showdown at Horseshoe Bend would not find the Red Sticks' most capable general there to face Old Hickory. Weatherford left Tohopeka on March 25 and headed downriver to the encampment at Othlewallee. The exact reason for Red Eagle's decision is unknown. He may have believed that Jackson was not ready to launch an attack at that time. It is also possible that he meant to take his wife, Sofath, four months pregnant, to a place of safety. Or Weatherford may have intended to make contact with British agents said to be at Othlewallee. In his absence, all hell would fall on Horseshoe Bend (L. Thompson, 536–537).

CHAPTER 13

"The River of Blood"

On March 27, 1814, Jackson's army broke camp at Emuckfau at 6:30 A.M. and began the march to Horseshoe Bend. Old Hickory's plan was to lead his infantry straight to the Red Stick barricade, while Coffee with his 700 mounted troops and 600 red allies would cross the Tallapoosa downriver and deploy along the bank opposite Tohopeka to block the rebels' escape route (Bassett, vol. 1, 489; Holland, 22–23).

Coffee's command crossed the river at a ford three miles below the bend. The horsemen moved back upriver, keeping away from the cliffs. About half a mile from the village, they heard the sound of Red Stick war cries and feared that rebel scouts had spotted them. There was a chance that the Red Sticks might be about to cross the river to attack, so Coffee deployed his troops for battle in the hilly woodland and moved forward toward the sound of the yelling. He also suspected a possible move from Okfuskee, the Red Stick town farther down the Tallapoosa, so he had his mounted Tennesseans form up on the higher ground about a quarter mile from the river in case they were attacked. This precaution would prove to be unnecessary, since the Okfuskees were already in Tohopeka (Holland, 23, 25; Quimby, 467; Ghioto, Spier, and Johnson, 19).

Coffee had already detached the Cherokees, Allied Creeks, and Captain William Russell's scouts with orders to move on toward the bend to take up a position opposite the town. Soon the red allies, eager to strike a blow against their enemies, fanned out all along the bank around Horseshoe Bend. From the cover of the trees, they quietly watched the activities in the Red Stick town across the Tallapoosa (Holland, 23; Quimby, 467).

While Coffee's forces were cutting off the rebels' only route of retreat, Sharp Knife's infantry detachments made their way slowly toward the

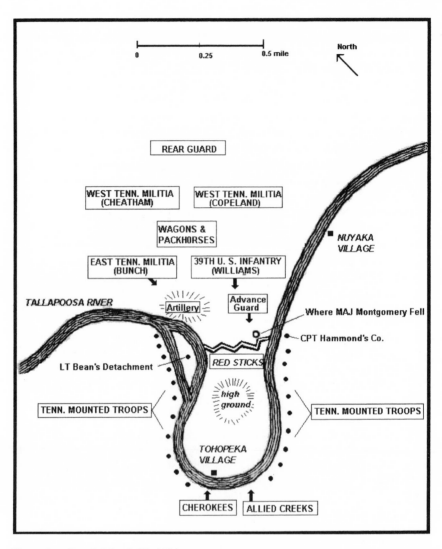

Horseshoe Bend, March 27, 1814

Red Stick breastwork, where they methodically deployed into a line of battle. Colonel James Sitler, formerly a lieutenant in the old Nashville Artillery Company and now Jackson's adjutant, led the advance guard that included Captain John Gordon's rangers and a detachment of West Tennessee troops under Captain McMurry. Just behind them, forming the left wing of Jackson's main assault line, the regulars were drawn up, with Colonel Samuel Bunch's East Tennessee regiment over to their right. Two more regiments of West Tennessee militia under Colonels Stephen

Copeland and Archer Cheatham formed a reserve line behind the regulars and East Tennesseans. While the white soldiers shuffled into line in the chilly morning air, the rebels gave their defiant war cry and challenged the Tennesseans to fight (Bassett, vol. 1, 489; Holland, 25).

The soldiers had ample opportunity now to study the Red Sticks' impressive fortifications. "You can scarcely imagine a situation stronger by nature," Major John Reid wrote his father, "or rendered more secure by art." The thick log and earth barricade, with its two rows of portholes through which Red Stick eyes peered and muskets protruded, looked formidable indeed. The thing stood six to eight feet high, constructed of large logs piled atop each other. Many a young Tennessee soldier felt a sense of dread at the thought of storming such strong defenses. But to Old Hickory, this obstacle was only another barrier to overcome by will and determination. The Red Stick works, stout as they were, had their disadvantages. The rebels had backed themselves into a corner. With their retreat across the river blocked, there was no way out. "They have penned themselves up for slaughter!" Jackson gloated (Reid to his father, April 5, 1814, "Horseshoe Bend First Hand Accounts"; Quimby, 466–467; E. Rowland, 80).

Now Jackson would see how well the Red Sticks had built their breastwork. He placed Captain Joel Parish's artillery company with their two fieldpieces on a rise less than a hundred yards from the barricade. At 10:30 the gunners opened up, concentrating their fire on the center of the earthworks. Captain William Bradford, an infantry officer attached to Jackson's army for temporary duty as chief engineer, directed the fire from the little three-pounder and the six-pounder. From their works, the Red Sticks attempted to pick off the cannoneers, but Jackson's infantry poured on a stubborn musket fire whenever a Muscogee head appeared above the ramparts. The soldiers also fired at Red Stick warriors coming up from the village to reinforce the wall (Bassett, vol. 1, 489–490, 492–493; Quimby, 467).

The bombardment continued for two hours, with the cannoneers firing about seventy rounds. The cannon fire did kill and wound a number of Red Sticks inside the works, but—even with Bradford's skillful direction—it did little real damage to the barricade itself. The Red Sticks obviously had done their work well. Breaching these works would require a costly frontal assault (Quimby, 467; Owen, 119).

Behind the barricade, the rebels defied the white army by shouting and occasionally showing themselves. Faces black, feathers decorating their heads and shoulders, dancing and waving their red cow tails, jingling their bells, the prophets moved among the warriors, encouraging them and assuring them of victory. Despite the Tennessee infantry's covering fire, a number of Red Stick bullets and arrows found their marks. Several artillerymen, including Lieutenant John Allen, were hit (Owen, 119; Quimby, 467; Remini, *Jackson*, 1977, 214; Reid to his father, April 5, 1814, "Horseshoe Bend First Hand Accounts").

Coffee's soldiers and red allies could hear the gunfire to their north. Watching the Red Stick women and children plus about a hundred warriors running to and fro in the village, the Cherokees and Allied Creeks were especially eager to get into the fight. According to legend, Shoeboots, an old Cherokee chief, thumped his chest, hopped up on a tree stump, flapped his arms and crowed like a rooster. "No chicking heart me," he declared (Holland, 27; Ghioto, Spier, and Johnson, 19–20; Hoig, 118).

Finally the Cherokees could contain themselves no longer. Impulsively, three of their zealous warriors—Charles Reese, The Whale, and one other man (possibly either White Path, John Ross, or George Guess)—threw themselves into the cold Tallapoosa and began swimming the 120 yards toward the opposite bank, while Ridge and others provided covering fire. No one knew it then, but this would be the decisive moment of the battle, and Congress would later reward these three Cherokees with silver-mounted rifles for their part in it (Ghioto, Spier, and Johnson, 19–20; Hoig, 119).

With their attention focused on the barricade, the rebels had left few warriors in the village. Their canoes were unguarded, and the Red Sticks did not see the three swimmers until too late. Then they opened fire. Although Whale was wounded, his comrades reached the boats. Reese seized one of the canoes and offered it to Whale, but he was too weak to follow. Whale waited for them to return while the others made off with their prizes and carried them back across to the opposite bank (Ghioto, Spier, and Johnson, 19–20; Ehle, 117).

Now more of the Cherokees and a few of Russell's rangers as well plunged into the river, while the gun battle along the banks of the Tallapoosa intensified. Aware of their danger now, the Red Sticks laid down a determined fire at their enemies in the stream, but they were unable to prevent the Cherokees from crossing and making off with several more canoes. The captured boats presented the Cherokees with a golden opportunity to ferry more warriors back across the river for an attack on the Red Stick town, pinning the rebels between Jackson's and Coffee's forces. Colonel Gideon Morgan, the Cherokees' commander, circled back upstream along the Tallapoosa and rode with great speed to Jackson's battle line, where he spotted Major Lemuel P. Montgomery at the head of the left wing of the Thirty-ninth Regiment. Morgan reined in his horse and breathlessly reported the developments on the river, to the delight of the regular officer (Reid and Eaton, 152; Quimby, 468; Ghioto, Spier, and Johnson, 14–15).

Morgan had no sooner ridden back from his meeting with Montgomery than he learned that Ridge and about 150 to 200 more Cherokees had already crossed the river in the captured boats and were fighting for control of the village. The Allied Creeks led by William McIntosh also crossed the Tallapoosa just above the Cherokees. Morgan, John Walker, and thirty more warriors crossed the river, along with Russell and his rangers, and found that the Cherokees had already taken the high ground behind the town. The Red Sticks had put up a stubborn fight, but most of their warriors were at the barricade. Although outnumbered by the rebels at first, the red allies soon gained the upper hand as they continued crossing the river. They captured the village easily (Ghioto, Spier, and Johnson, 15, 20; Griffith, 147, 289 n. 34; Wilkins, 76).

Within minutes, the red allies were pushing north through the wooded high ground, leaving the cabins in Tohopeka in flames. From there they began to advance toward the rear of the Red Sticks' barricade. But the stubborn enemy made them pay dearly for every foot of ground they gained. Concealed by logs and underbrush behind the barricade, the Red Sticks poured a determined fire into the Cherokees and rangers as their juggernaut ground to a halt. A rebel musket ball grazed Morgan in the side of his head, and he fell to the ground unconscious. Richard Brown was also wounded, along with many other warriors. But although they were not strong enough to dislodge the rebels from their earthworks, the Cherokees had made the Red Sticks' position much more precarious, with Jackson attacking them in front (Bassett, vol. 1, 489–491; Ghioto, Spier, and Johnson, 15; Quimby, 468; Moulton, 20; Owsley, 80).

The attack by the Cherokees and Allied Creeks left the bank of the river across from the village unoccupied. Coffee wanted none of the enemy to escape the trap this time, and he quickly remedied this situation by shifting his mounted troops to fill the gap. He sent about a third of his soldiers to take up a position at the bend. The rest held fast, still thinking that the Okfuskees might attack their rear (Holland, 27).

There were two potential river crossings that Coffee especially wanted guarded. One was the bank of the Tallapoosa across from the eastern end of the Red Stick barricade. Captain Eli Hammond's rangers quickly took up a position there, prepared to shoot any Red Sticks attempting to swim to safety. The other weak spot was a small island in the Tallapoosa just across from the western end of the barricade. Coffee dispatched Lieutenant Jesse Bean and forty rangers to that spot. The riflemen would be able to pick off any Red Sticks attempting to swim the river and make for the island. The rebels would meet the same fate everywhere along the river bank—to be shot the moment they showed themselves (Holland, 27; Bassett, vol. 1, 491; Quimby, 468).

North of the Red Stick barricade, Jackson's soldiers could see the smoke from Tohopeka rising in the distance behind the earthworks, and they could hear the sound of gunfire coming from the direction of the burning village. But the gunfire was weakening. The red allies had pushed the rebels back south of the barricade, but they could push them no farther (Lossing, 770).

Old Hickory's attention was on the barricade. The Cherokees and rangers were not numerous enough to eject the Red Sticks from behind,

and Jackson feared the Red Sticks might overwhelm them. Determined
that this was the time for a frontal assault, he gave the order for his troops
to storm the barricade, and at 12:30 the long drum roll began. The Tennesseans appeared ready. "Never were men more eager to be led to a
charge than both regulars and militia," Jackson reported. "They had been
waiting with impatience to receve the order, and hailed it with acclama-
tion" (Bassett, vol. 1, 489, 493; Quimby, 468–469; Holland, 29; Ghioto,
Spier, and Johnson, 4).

There was little conversation amid the rattle of drums, shouts of officers, snorting of horses, and clanking of equipment—while behind their
earthworks the Red Sticks looked on and defied the enemy to come. Jackson's Tennesseans had waited a long time to deliver the death blow to the
Muscogees. Now each soldier looked into his own soul and found a quiet
resolve—that sense of apprehension mixed with excitement—as he prepared for close combat. Major Reid expressed it this way:

It was a moment of feeling and not of reflection. I never had such emotions as
while the long roll was beating, and the troops in motion. It was not fear, it was not
anxiety or concern of the fate of those who were so soon to fall but it was a kind of
enthusiasm that thrilled through every nerve and animated me with the belief that
the day was ours without adverting to what it must cost us. (Reid to his wife, April
1, 1814, "Horseshoe Bend First Hand Accounts")

The spectacle of the whites' line of battle moving forward must have
been an awesome sight to the Red Sticks crouching and peering over the
barricade. The Thirty-ninth Infantry stepped off briskly, looking sharp in
their dark blue coats, dark pants with gray gaiters, and tall leather "tomb-
stone" military caps, their muskets and bayonets gleaming. Their blue silk
regimental colors—with an American eagle, the eighteen stars of the
Union, and the motto "By Obedience, Unanimity, Coolness and Bravery,
the Soldier Ensures Safety to his Standard"—flapped in the cool March air.
The militia—more plainly dressed in their slouch hats, dark blue or brown
hunting shirts, or civilian clothing—looked equally determined (Chartrand, 38–39, 43–44; J. A. Reid, 35–37; Parton, 367).

Greeted by a volley of arrows and musket fire, the regulars lowered bayonets and surged forward with a shout, Colonel Williams and Major Montgomery in the lead. Colonel Samuel Bunch's East Tennesseans also made
for the barricade. On the left, Colonel James Sitler's advance guard led by
Gordon's rangers and Captain McMurry's West Tennesseans joined in. The
air was black with Red Stick arrows. Despite the cold, the soldiers were
sweating by the time they reached the barricade. The Red Sticks' war cries
reached a crescendo (Bassett, vol. 1, 489, 491; Owsley, 80; Quimby, 469).

There was a fierce struggle at the barricade as the soldiers shoved muskets into the portholes to shoot the Red Stick marksmen on the other side.

The contest was literally muzzle to muzzle. In the frenzy, Red Stick musket balls welded themselves to American bayonets and muzzles, as the contest at the portholes unfolded. At the same time, soldiers scrambled up the rampart (Bassett, vol. 1, 489, 491; Remini, *Jackson*, 1977, 215; Quimby, 469).

First on the parapet was Major Montgomery. The young officer had just discharged his pistol through a porthole, killing a Red Stick. Atop the barricade now, Montgomery turned, waved his hat, and called for his troops to follow him over. Just at that moment a Red Stick bullet struck him in the head, killing him instantly (Cutrer, 38; Reid and Eaton, 150; Remini, *Jackson*, 1977, 215; Quimby, 469).

Close behind Montgomery came Lieutenant Sam Houston. Houston fell with a barbed Red Stick arrow buried in his thigh. But he was inside the Red Stick breastwork now, and other soldiers followed. Blue-coated troops poured into the rebel works (Remini, *Jackson*, 1977, 215; Quimby, 469).

Atop the barricade, there was frantic hand-to-hand combat. Outnumbered and outgunned, the Red Sticks put up a furious resistance and fought to the end—"with all of the fury of desperation," Major Reid recalled. In the end, Red Stick courage was not sufficient. The assault carried the works, but it was costly. Besides Montgomery, Second Lieutenant Michael C. Moulton and First Lieutenant Robert M. Somerville died in the charge on the barricade. "The carnage was dreadful," Jackson recorded (Bassett, vol. 1, 491–492; Reid to his father, April 5, 1814, "Horseshoe Bend First Hand Accounts"; Remini, *Jackson*, 1977, 215).

Seriously wounded, Lieutenant Houston ordered a soldier to pull out the barbed arrow that had buried itself in his thigh. The man grabbed hold but was unable to budge it. Houston screamed at him to pull it out or he would kill him. Finally, they removed it, as Houston's blood gushed out. Riding by, Jackson noticed the young officer, told him he had done enough fighting that day, and ordered him to retire from the field (Heiskell, 473; Quimby, 469).

The rebels fell back, taking cover among the brush and fallen trees behind the barricade, continuing to fire at the advancing troops—resisting all the way, falling back, asking no quarter. They remembered the Hillabee massacre. With their only route of retreat cut off by the Cherokee capture of the town, the warriors fled down the banks of the Tallapoosa and took cover in the cliffs. From concealment, they continued to fire at the soldiers and had to be rooted out pocket by pocket (Reid and Eaton, 151; Quimby, 469; Remini, *Jackson*, 1977, 215).

One group of die-hard Red Sticks occupied a particularly strong position, under the bluff and concealed by part of the barricade. Jackson sent out several staff officers and Allied Creek interpreters with an offer of protection and pardon if the rebels would lay down their arms. The Red

Sticks answered with a volley of arrows and musket balls, killing or wounding several in the party (Coffee to Houston, April 25, 1828, "Horseshoe Bend First Hand Accounts"; Reid and Eaton, 151; Quimby, 469).

Jackson ordered up Captain Parish with the artillery company. The cannoneers positioned their two small cannon and opened fire on the rebel pocket. The rebels would not budge. Jackson called for volunteers to root the rebels out. Sam Houston, back into the fight again despite the wound to his thigh, grabbed a musket and offered to lead an assault, but no one was willing to follow him. Houston went ahead, but he soon fell with a bullet in his right arm and another in his right shoulder. The Raven finally left the battlefield. The Tennesseans ultimately lit torches and tossed them down the bank, setting fire to the brush and trees, forcing the Red Sticks from their hiding places to be shot one by one as they emerged (Reid and Eaton, 151; Quimby, 469; Heiskell, 476).

Gleefully, Jackson's red allies had witnessed the collapse of the rebel defense at the barricade. Gideon Morgan was conscious again, happy to hear of the assault and capture of the breastwork. The Cherokees and Allied Creeks had already thwarted the Red Sticks' escape plan. Now they joined the white soldiers in the pursuit of the rebel warriors fleeing across the peninsula (Ghioto, Spier, and Johnson, 15).

Ridge and the Cherokees were hot on the heels of the Red Sticks who made for the river. Ridge plunged into the water, slashing at one rebel with his sword, as the Red Stick turned and grappled with him in a desperate struggle. Ridge was able to get his antagonist's knife from his belt and stab him. But the wound failed to kill him, and the rebel fought on with determination. At that moment another Cherokee stabbed the Red Stick with his spear, and Ridge finished him off. In all, he killed six Red Sticks in the river (Wilkins, 78).

Desperate, the Red Sticks tossed tree trunks and large limbs into the river in an effort to climb aboard and escape in the stream. They made easy targets for Coffee's riflemen on the opposite shore—who picked them off one by one. Across the river from the eastern end of the barricade, Hammond's scouts did their work thoroughly, shooting any of the warriors who tried to swim the river. On the small island across from the western end of the breastwork, Lieutenant Bean's riflemen did the same, littering the banks of the Tallapoosa with Red Stick dead (Bassett, vol. 1, 491; Ghioto, Spier, and Johnson, 25).

One rebel dove into the water and submerged, coming to the surface only once for air—just long enough for a flurry of shots to splatter the water around him. Wounded in the shoulder, he made it to the opposite bank, only to be taken prisoner by the Cherokees. They took him to Coffee for interrogation, and one warrior raised a tomahawk to make him talk. The Red Stick remained defiant and thrust his head forward to receive the blow (Ghioto, Spier, and Johnson, 25).

One of Coffee's young soldiers caught sight of an officer behind a tree nearby rubbing his eyes. A shot from a Red Stick musket had hit the tree and scattered bark into his eyes. He asked him what was wrong; was he crying? "No," the officer replied. "I want you to kill an Indian for me." The young soldier spotted an old Muscogee, obviously too old to be a warrior, calmly seated on the ground in the village, seemingly oblivious to the carnage going on around him, pounding corn. Unable to resist the temptation to kill a red man, he deliberately took careful aim and shot him dead (Ghioto, Spier, and Johnson, 25; L. Thompson, 546).

It was no longer much of a battle on the peninsula—just relentless killing, as Jackson's army ferreted out the rebels from their hiding places. Acting on their own now, and not in a regular battle line, the Tennesseans killed warriors and noncombatants alike. One soldier clubbed a small Muscogee boy to death with the butt of his musket. When an officer sought to reprimand him, the man replied that the child would have grown up to become a Red Stick warrior one day. Jackson acknowledged that at least two or three women and children were killed—accidentally, he insisted. The soldiers slaughtered Red Sticks until it was too dark to find them. Even after nightfall, gunshots continued to echo along the Tallapoosa as the Tennesseans caught up with stray Red Sticks attempting to swim across the river (Bassett, vol. 1, 492.; Faust, 213; Cutrer, 38).

A few Red Sticks managed to escape in the night. Jackson and Coffee—who had crossed the river and joined Jackson's army at 7:00 p.m.—thought no more than twenty warriors could have made it to safety. Some of the Allied Creeks later insisted that they knew of no more than ten rebels who had managed to escape. But a Hillabee warrior named Talwatustunnugge, who had been wounded nine times at Horseshoe Bend, later stated that many more Red Sticks escaped during the night, possibly as many as 200 (Ghioto, Spier, and Johnson, 21; Bassett, vol. 1, 493; Owsley, 81; Martin, 162).

The Red Sticks' commander, Menawa, had fought with his warriors to the last. Wounded seven times, one of them a serious wound in the face, he fell near sundown and lay unconscious until dark, when he awoke to find himself under a pile of dead warriors. Under the cover of night, he dragged himself to the river, managed to find a canoe, climbed in, and floated downriver to safety (Owen, 47; Griffith, 148).

Monahoe was not so lucky. Jackson's troops found the prophet's body among the Red Stick dead. He had been shot in the mouth by grapeshot — "an appropriate punishment," Old Hickory commented. Soldiers also found the bodies of two other prophets. Jackson was displeased to learn that William Weatherford was not among the dead or captured (Bassett, vol. 1, 491; Holland, 31; Quimby, 470).

The next morning, Jackson's soldiers discovered a final pocket of resistance, a band of sixteen warriors who had taken refuge in a cave in the riverbank. Defiant to the end, they refused to surrender, and the soldiers were unable to get close enough to force them out of their stronghold. Finally the Tennesseans drove sharpened stakes into the ground on the bluff above the caves, pried loose the earth, and caused it to slide down and bury the rebels alive (Bassett, vol. 1, 492; Owen, 122).

Many white soldiers mutilated the dead Muscogees, cutting off long bands of skin from the bodies to make into belts and bridle reins for their horses. They started near the heel and cut two parallel slits with a knife up the leg all the way to the shoulder blade, then across to the other shoulder and down the other leg. Then they skinned out the flesh between the slits (Remini, *Jackson*, 1977, 216; Faust, 212–213; Wilkins, 78–79).

Seeking a body count from the previous day's slaughter, Jackson's soldiers moved among the dead and sliced off the nose of each Red Stick corpse to keep an accurate number. Old Hickory's officers counted 557 enemy dead—and estimated 250 to 300 more warriors killed in the river, raising the total close to 850. Jackson's victory was complete and devastating. The Tennesseans had annihilated the Red Stick army. "The sun was going down," Sam Houston observed, "and it set on the ruin of the Creek nation." The Muscogees had fought fiercely with bows and arrows, spears, and war clubs, only about one in four armed with a musket. There had never been any real doubt of the outcome (Remini, *Jackson*, 1977, 216; Quimby, 470; Owsley, 81–82; Day and Ullom, 12).

Victory had not come without cost to Old Hickory's army. Twenty-six Tennessee soldiers lay dead, and 106 were wounded. Among the white troops, the Thirty-ninth Regiment suffered the greatest with seventeen killed and fifty-five wounded. In the East Tennessee militia, seven men died and eighteen more were wounded, while casualties among the West Tennesseans were light. Coffee lost two of his mounted volunteers killed and ten wounded. Eleven artillerists were wounded, including Lieutenants John Allen and Henry Ridley. Colonel William Carroll received a wound in the side (Quimby, 470; Bassett, vol. 1, 492; Ghioto, Spier, and Johnson, 13, 21).

But it was the Cherokees who had the highest number killed at Horseshoe Bend, and they were proud of the part they had played in the battle. The Cherokees lost eighteen warriors killed and thirty-six wounded, while the Allied Creeks lost five killed and eleven wounded. Total losses in Jackson's army were forty-nine killed, 153 wounded (Bassett, vol. 1, 492; Ghioto, Spier, and Johnson, 21; Hoig, 218; Owsley, 81; Quimby, 470).

Some of Jackson's officers reported that many of the Red Sticks had been wearing clothing taken off the dead soldiers buried at Emuckfau two months earlier. Jackson ordered his dead at Horseshoe Bend weighted and buried in the river to prevent the Red Sticks from returning and scalping them. There was only one exception—Major Montgomery, the first white soldier to be killed at the breastwork. Montgomery had been a close friend of Jackson's, and the news of his death disturbed Old Hickory deeply. A small burial detail laid the young major in a grave just fifty yards from the barricade and carefully camouflaged it with brush to prevent its being discovered by the enemy (Griffith, 149; Remini, *Jackson,* 1977, 216–217; Owsley, 81; L. Thompson, 548–549).

The decisive battle of the Creek War (and a major engagement in the War of 1812), Horseshoe Bend shattered the strength of the Red Sticks. Major Reid called it "the most signal victory that has ever been obtained over Indians." Coffee agreed. "[W]e may have one battle more," he wrote his wife, "…but they cannot hold out, they are already nearly starved to death, having eat up all their provisions." And Jackson was superbly proud of his Tennesseans and the victory they had won. "The fiends of the Tallapoosa," he crowed in a proclamation to his troops, "will no longer murder our Women and Children, or disturb the quiet of our borders" (Owsley, 81; Remini, *Jackson,* 1977, 216; Reid to his wife, April 1, 1814, "Horseshoe Bend First Hand Accounts"; Coffee, 283; Ghioto, Spier, and Johnson, 16).

The Tennesseans' triumph at Tohopeka claimed the highest number of deaths ever in a battle between Americans and Native Americans. Major Alexander McCulloch, an aide to Coffee, declared, "[T]he Red Sticks paid severely for their folly in waging war against the whites." McCulloch commented, "The Tallapoosa might truly be called the River of blood for the water was so stained that at 10 Oclock at night it was very perceptibly bloody so much so that it could not be used." "I had thought that the numbers killed in former battles had been exagerated," Captain William Bradford wrote, "but I cannot be mistaken in what passes before my own eyes—that 557 indians were found dead on the ground is a fact and that the river ran red with blood from the number that were killed in it is equally true—I never witnessed such carnage" (Martin, 162; Cutrer, 37–38; Ghioto, Spier, and Johnson, Bradford to Harrison, April 5, 1814).

Although he had devastated the Red Stick army, still Old Hickory could show compassion. Jackson's soldiers discovered the hiding place of two young Red Stick warriors and took the prisoners to the general's tent. Jackson observed that one of them, an eighteen-year-old, was seriously wounded in the leg. He directed the surgeon to treat the wound. While the surgeon was dressing his wound, the rebel faced Sharp Knife and demanded, "Cure 'im, kill 'im again?" No, Jackson promised, he would not allow him to be killed. Old Hickory kept his word. The two Muscogees remained with him on the march back to Fort Williams. Jackson sent the young men on to Nashville, where they later learned a trade and went into business for themselves (Coffee to Houston, April 25, 1828, "Horseshoe Bend First Hand Accounts"; Remini, *Jackson,* 1977, 216).

The Tennesseans had more than 300 prisoners, largely women and children. Some they turned over to the Cherokees, some to the Allied Creeks, to be taken to Huntsville. The remainder were to be escorted to the Black Warrior. Jackson ordered that they be "humanely treated." Most probably became slaves of their red captors (Bassett, vol. 1, 492–493; Faust, 212; L. Thompson, 549).

Now the Tennesseans yearned to be heading for home. Jackson looked forward to seeing Rachel again, wrote her that he was bringing home to young Andrew a Red Stick warrior's bow and quiver. "I wish the war was at an end," Major Reid wrote his father, "as I long anxiously to be at home, and in peace" (Bassett, vol. 1, 493; Reid to his father, April 5, 1814, "Horseshoe Bend First Hand Accounts").

CHAPTER 14

"My Warriors Can No Longer Hear My Voice"

Old Hickory and his victorious troops arrived back at Fort Williams on April 1. The next few days were consumed by correspondence as Jackson reported to General Pinckney, Governor Blount, and others on his triumph at Horseshoe Bend. Jackson needed more rations for his army before he could march again. Then he would be ready for the final campaign to destroy the Muscogee nation.

At Fort Williams, Jackson released his Cherokee allies to return to their homes. On their way back to the mountains, the Cherokees again were dismayed to find that East Tennessee troops had passed through their nation plundering the land. Although some of their officers attempted to stop them, the white soldiers had taken out their hatred of all red men on the Cherokees. They shot cattle and hogs and left them to rot, terrorized Cherokee families, made off with horses and even what little clothing the families possessed. "These depredations may at first sight seem incredible," Return J. Meigs complained to Secretary of War Armstrong, "but I have no doubt of the justice of the statements." Meigs declared that the white troops had done more damage to the Cherokees than the Red Sticks could ever have done, that it would take years for some parts of the Cherokee nation to recover. Although Meigs backed up his charges with testimony by white militia officers and by Cherokee officers as well, Jackson denied that this ill treatment had taken place, insisting that the reports were overblown or distorted (Quimby, 470; Wilkins, 80; Ehle, 121).

The Cherokees were proud of their service in the Creek War and were astonished at the shabby treatment their nation received at the hands of the United States once the Red Stick threat was ended. "Father," they later wrote President Madison, "your officers treated us as friends embarked in a common cause with them, acting against a common enemy, and we felt honored...but we have now to state to our father that a great many white young Warriors...destroyed our Cattle, sheep, and hogs, and in some instances our horses, for mere sport or prejudice." But not only did the government fail to address their complaints, Washington also dragged its feet on the issue of equal pay for the Cherokee volunteers and balked at providing pensions for the Cherokee wounded or for widows of Cherokee dead. It was a sad indication of the future handling of the United States' red allies (McLoughlin, 194–197).

But for the present, there was joy over the Red Sticks' defeat. Just days after their discharge at Fort Williams, one band of Cherokee warriors reached their village at Standing Peach Tree on the Chattahoochee. The Georgia militia soldiers working on their outpost at Fort Peachtree were startled to hear gunshots from the village, and Lieutenant George R. Gilmer ordered his men to deploy for battle. The Georgians were relieved to learn that the Cherokees were only celebrating their recent victory at Horseshoe Bend. The warriors had brought back eighteen scalps (Barnard and Schwartzman, "Tecumseh," 504).

The war was really over, since the Red Sticks never recovered from the blow dealt them at Horseshoe Bend. But William Weatherford was still on the loose, and there still remained the last Red Stick stronghold at Othlewallee. Jackson suspected the rebels might make a final stand there. One more campaign, he felt, probably would finish them off.

Old Hickory proposed to march his army back down the Tallapoosa to its junction with the Coosa at the Hickory Ground—the original objective in the American strategic plan—and to link up with Colonel Homer Milton. Jackson had only eight days' rations for his troops, but he had General Pinckney's assurances that he could get more from Milton, who had been storing supplies at Fort Hull and the recently constructed Fort Decatur on the Tallapoosa. Milton's small contingent of regulars had just been reinforced by Brigadier General Joseph Graham with his North Carolina militia (Quimby, 470; Owsley, 59–60).

At the head of an army of about 3,000 men, Jackson started for the Hickory Ground on April 7, moving first down the Coosa, then down the western bank of the Tallapoosa. With him were his regulars, the Thirty-ninth U.S. Infantry, plus 663 mounted volunteers in Coffee's brigade, 930 troops of Doherty's East Tennessee militia, and 911 soldiers from Johnson's West Tennessee militia. Heavy rains made the going difficult, and the Tennesseans made slow progress. As he approached Othlewallee, Jackson was forty-eight hours behind schedule (Owsley, 82; Quimby, 470–471; Holland, 33, 35).

By April 13, the Tennesseans had reached Fushatchee, a Creek town near Othlewallee, and found it empty. They soon learned that Othlewallee was abandoned too, and they burned both towns. Jackson's advance was turning into a triumphal march. There were reports that most of the Red Sticks had fled across the river and were heading toward Pensacola, that their army was completely broken up. The rebels who still remained in the area seemed merely to be waiting for an opportunity to come in and surrender. By now Old Hickory was in contact with Milton. The two armies would coordinate their movements from this point, moving down both banks of the Tallapoosa toward the Hickory Ground, about twenty miles away, clearing out the Red Sticks before them (Bassett, vol. 1, 500; Griffith, 150; Owsley, 82–83; Quimby, 470–471).

Jackson's soldiers reached the Hickory Ground on April 17. Milton's troops were already there. By the end of the month, Graham's North Carolina militia joined them. The American troops began constructing a new fort, to be named Fort Jackson, on the site of old Fort Toulouse, a former French outpost, at the junction of the Coosa and Tallapoosa Rivers. The Carolinians and the regulars finished the fort by June (Owsley, 83; Quimby, 471; Parker, 121–123).

The rebellion was crushed, its leaders scattered. Menawa, still mending from wounds received at Horseshoe Bend, was in hiding with his people on the Cahaba. William Weatherford and his people had taken refuge on an island in the Alabama River west of present-day Montgomery. Peter McQueen's warriors were south of the Tallapoosa along Line Creek, while those of Josiah Francis waited on Catoma Creek near the Federal Road crossing. Amazingly, both McQueen and Francis briefly fell into the hands of Milton's troops but then managed to escape. They and as many as 2,000 Muscogees fled to Spanish Florida, along with numbers of African Americans who had fought on the side of the Red Sticks. There they joined the Seminoles in their ongoing struggle against the Americans (Holland, 35, 47 n. 129; T. Woodward, 38–39; Bassett, vol. 1, 503; Grant, 683; Martin, 163).

The war had cost the Red Sticks 1,800 warriors killed plus several hundred women and children. White armies had burned some fifty Creek towns and villages and had destroyed their food crops. The survivors were literally starving, "mere skeletons," according to a Georgia newspaper reporter. "Look to the towns," Benjamin Hawkins wrote, "not a living thing in them; the inhabitants scattered through the woods, dying with hunger, or fed by Americans." Besides the rebel faction, the Allied Creeks had suffered as well. Coweta and Cusseta, the main Lower Creek settlements, had taken in and fed hundreds of refugees from Tuckabatchee and other towns. Now their food supplies were giving out, and they turned to the Americans for help (Martin, 163–164).

Realizing that they had no other choice now, many of the rebel Muscogees began coming in to Fort Jackson to surrender. A number of the slaves who had been taken at Fort Mims also turned up now, as well as white captive Polly Jones and her three children. Sharp Knife's terms to the

defeated Red Sticks were rigid: They must move north of Fort Williams
where Jackson could be sure that they would have no further contact with
the Spanish and British at Pensacola. Only then would he make peace
with them. The Muscogees had no choice but to comply. Jackson also
ordered the chiefs to prove their goodwill to him by bringing in William
Weatherford, his most deadly adversary, who was still at large (Remini,
Jackson, 1977, 217–218; Quimby, 471).

No one seemed to notice when a lone Muscogee on horseback arrived at
the Tennesseans' camp, rode confidently up to the general's tent, and
waited patiently until he attracted Jackson's attention.

"I am Bill Weatherford," the stranger announced calmly.

Old Hickory was thunderstruck. "How dare you," he sputtered (Griffith, 151; Pickett, 594).

Weatherford dismounted, and the two men went into the general's tent.
Inside was Major John Reid, who described Red Eagle as "the greatest of
the barbarian world," a warrior with "all the heroism of soul, all the comprehension of intellect calculated to make an able commander." Weatherford's speech would be reported many times, but what particularly
impressed the young officer was the chief's manner, "his looks & gestures—the modesty & yet the firmness that were in them" (Griffith, 151).

"I am in your power," Red Eagle continued. "Do with me as you please.
I am a soldier. I have done the white people all the harm I could; I have
fought them, and fought them bravely: if I had an army, I would yet fight,
and contend to the last: but I have none; my people are all gone" (Reid and
Eaton, 165).

Choking with emotion, the Red Stick chieftain explained that he had
come voluntarily to give himself up, hoping that Jackson in turn would
have pity on the Muscogee women and children starving in the woods. He
also insisted that he had done his best to stop the massacre at Fort Mims.
Jackson listened attentively. Then he stated to him his conditions for
peace—the same that he had offered to the other renegades who had come
in to surrender—and promised to protect Red Eagle if he would abide by
them. Weatherford gave careful thought to his reply, then responded:

There was a time when I had a choice, and could have answered you: I have none
now,—even hope has ended. Once I could animate my warriors to battle; but I cannot animate the dead. My warriors can no longer hear my voice: their bones are at
Talladega, Tallushatchee, Emuckfau, and Tohopeka. I have not surrendered myself
thoughtlessly. Whilst there were chances of success, I never left my post, nor supplicated peace. But my people are gone, and I now ask it for my nation, and for
myself.

"You are a brave man," Red Eagle concluded. "I rely upon your generosity.... You have told us where we might go, and be safe. Yours is a good talk, and my nation ought to listen to it. They shall listen to it" (Reid and Eaton, 166–167).

Weatherford's dramatic talk made a deep impact on the stern Jackson. Clearly he admired the courage and sincerity of the Red Stick war chief. In the end, Old Hickory believed he could trust Red Eagle to persuade his warriors and their families to surrender. Jackson and Weatherford then drank brandy together, something neither would have conceived of doing months earlier (Remini, *Jackson*, 1977, 218–219; Quimby, 471; Griffith, 153–154).

By now word had spread throughout the camp that Weatherford had come in. There was a growing crowd gathering around the general's tent, many of the spectators to this drama shouting, "Kill him! Kill him!" Jackson called for quiet and addressed the crowd. "Any man who would kill as brave a man as this," he declared, "would rob the dead!" (Pickett, 594–595).

Old Hickory's words had little impact on the Allied Creeks in the camp, who now included Big Warrior and other sworn enemies of Weatherford. Big Warrior lunged toward Red Eagle, but Jackson's soldiers checked him. "You damned traitor," Weatherford snarled. "If you give me any insolence, I will blow a ball through your cowardly heart" (Pickett, 594–595).

The extraordinary affinity that Jackson seemed to acquire for Red Eagle, a man he had sworn to hang, was one of the most moving developments of the Creek War. From a practical angle, Weatherford was much more useful to Old Hickory alive than dead. Jackson may even have held out the olive branch of peace—and a promise of amnesty—if Red Eagle would turn himself in. But he allowed Weatherford to go free. And he and Red Eagle became friends (Faust, 213; Owsley, 84–85; Remini, *Jackson*, 1977, 219).

Weatherford kept his agreement with Jackson. After spending a few days at Fort Jackson, while Old Hickory refereed in talks between Red Eagle and the Allied Creek chiefs, he began traveling to the various refugee bands hiding in the woods, and he convinced most of them to come in and surrender on Jackson's terms. According to some reports, he also guided troops in operations against rebel parties near Pensacola in June 1814 (Saunt, 277; Griffith, 154).

William Weatherford never took up the war club again. He made for the Alabama River country, where he tried to resume his life as a planter. But his frontier neighbors remembered his part in the Fort Mims massacre. After threats against his life, Weatherford rode into Fort Claiborne and surrendered to Colonel Gilbert Russell, who promptly assigned a guard of soldiers to keep him under protection. One of the guards turned out to be James Cornells, who had an old score to settle with the Red Sticks who had kidnapped his wife and carried her off to Pensacola. Cornells blamed Weatherford, even though Peter McQueen had been responsible, and he threatened to kill Red Eagle as soon as he had the chance. Finally Weatherford asked Cornells straight out if he intended to kill him while he was guarding him. Cornells replied no, that he was assigned to guard Weatherford and that he would do his duty. "But when this time is over," he warned him, "I intend to kill you." Red Eagle replied that if Cornells was as good as his word, then he would entrust himself to his protection for the time being. Cornells's temper cooled, and as he learned that Weatherford had not actually been a part of the war party that had abducted his wife, he made no more threats and in fact developed a fondness for the chief (Griffith, 154–155).

But there still were others in the Tensaw settlements who would not forgive, and Colonel Russell remained concerned about Weatherford's safety. He finally decided to send the chief back to Fort Jackson, providing him with a horse and arranging for him to escape at midnight (Griffith, 155).

In spite of the disintegration of the war faction of the Muscogees—and the efforts of Weatherford to restore peace—there were still some small bands of hostile Red Sticks about. One war party descended upon the home of Gerald Byrne in April. Assuming that the war was over, Byrne—who had fled to Mobile with his family after the Fort Mims massacre—returned to his farm with several black slaves to begin spring planting. The Red Sticks surprised and killed Byrne and two men who were visiting him; they also killed one of the slaves and took the others captive (Littlefield, 66).

Jackson sent out detachments to search the Coosa and Tallapoosa river basins and destroy any hostile Muscogees that they found. He also let it be known in the Muscogee settlements that any who were ready to give up must surrender unconditionally. As he had explained to Weatherford, the Red Sticks must agree to abandon their contact with Pensacola and must migrate north of Fort Williams. If they failed to do so, he would consider them as enemies and treat them as such (Remini, *Jackson*, 1977, 219; Bassett, vol. 1, 502, 507).

On April 20, General Pinckney reached the Hickory Ground and took command of all the forces gathered there. Just in time, too, for friction was already growing between Jackson and Colonel Milton. Jackson accused Milton of allowing the Red Stick refugees to escape across the Tallapoosa when he could have intercepted and destroyed them. Milton cooperated in providing supplies to the Tennesseans, but as a regular army officer he balked at taking orders from Old Hickory, a militia general. As far as Pinckney was concerned, the war was over, and he and Benjamin Hawkins were authorized to negotiate a peace treaty with the defeated Creeks (Owsley, 83; Quimby, 471; Holland, 35).

The crisis on the frontier apparently over, Pinckney wasted no time in relieving the Tennessee troops. On April 21, he dismissed them. Glad to comply, Old Hickory marched his army out of Fort Jackson that same day—just two hours after receiving Pinckney's orders. The Tennesseans were back at Fort Williams three days later (Holland, 35; Quimby, 471; Remini, *Jackson*, 1977, 220).

It was necessary to leave some troops on duty to man the forts Jackson had built to serve as a communications and supply line into the Muscogee country. Old Hickory had promised the West Tennessee militia not to keep them longer than three months, so he turned to Doherty's East Tennessee regiments, which had been enlisted for six months. A few detachments, commanded by Colonel Bunch, remained in the Muscogee country, 250 at Fort Strother, 50 at Fort Armstrong, and 400 at Fort Williams. Captain Hammond's rangers garrisoned Fort Deposit. From Fort Jackson, Graham's Carolina troops conducted mopping-up operations in the upper Alabama River valley in May and June and received the surrender of remnants of the Red Stick bands from Okfuskee and the Alabamas. The Carolinians' enlistments would expire at the end of July and they would return to Fort Hawkins (Quimby, 471–472; Grant, 688–689).

Early in May, Colonel Milton and his regulars moved down the Alabama to Fort Claiborne, where they rejoined Russell and the rest of the Third U.S. Infantry. Pushmataha and Colonel John McKee with 661 Choctaws and Chickasaws were there, but the red allies now seemed anxious to return to their homes since the war was over. Milton, anticipating a possible move on Pensacola, urged McKee to hold on to his warriors as long as possible, but by the end of the month they had all melted away. Pushmataha, Milton mused, "appears to be a restless kind of a being." Meanwhile, Jackson's old nemesis Lieutenant Colonel Thomas H. Benton brought the Thirty-ninth U.S. Infantry down to Fort Claiborne, while Colonel Williams returned to Tennessee to recruit more soldiers. The Thirty-ninth Infantry, aided by Colonel George H. Nixon's regiment of Mississippi Territory volunteers, conducted operations against Red Stick refugees along the Escambia River in July (Quimby, 480 n. 79; McKee Journal, 5; Milton to McKee, May 16, 1814, Williams to Flournoy, May 2, 1814, "Third U.S. Infantry"; D. Rowland, 7).

While the regulars ran down scattered bands of Red Sticks in the Alabama valley, Old Hickory was being welcomed as a conqueror back in Tennessee. Considering his problems with mutiny and insubordination, Jackson seemed unusually accommodating to the West Tennessee militia. In his farewell message to his troops, soon to be mustered out at Fayetteville, he complimented them for their role at Horseshoe Bend. "The conduct of the militia on this occasion," he wrote, "has gone far towards redeeming the character of that discription of troops. They have been as orderly in their encampments and on the line of march, as they have been signally brave in the day of battle." "Accept the expression of your General's thanks," he told them, "& of his admiration, within a *few weeks*, you have annihilated the power of a nation that had for *twenty years* been the disturber of our peace" (Holland, 36, 47 n. 121).

A hero's reception greeted Jackson when he reached Huntsville on May 7. Conducted to the town square by a grateful citizenry, the victorious warrior was presented with a stand of colors. He was also reunited with Lyncoya, the Muscogee infant orphaned at Tallushatchee, who had been kept temporarily by a woman in town. That night there was a grand dinner and ball in Jackson's honor. Then it was on to Nashville, where admiring mobs of people crowded the streets, eager to get a peek at the victor of Horseshoe Bend. Throughout the state, Jackson received acclaim, even among his former enemies. There was talk of a run for governor (Holland, 36; Remini, *Jackson,* 1977, 222).

The war with Britain had produced few real military heroes, and the crushing of the Red Sticks at Horseshoe Bend came as glorious news to the Madison administration. On May 22, Secretary of War Armstrong offered Jackson a commission as a brigadier general in the United States Army. Four days later, Major General William Henry Harrison, the hero of Tippecanoe and the Thames, turned in his resignation from the army after a running series of disagreements with Armstrong and Madison. Since this created a vacancy, Jackson received the rank of major general, to command the Seventh Military District, Flournoy's old command, with headquarters at Mobile. Flournoy turned in his resignation on September 13 (Remini, *Jackson,* 1977, 222–223; Holland, 37; Heidler and Heidler, *Encyclopedia,* 190).

These rapid and favorable developments put Old Hickory in a position to negotiate a much harsher peace treaty with the Muscogees. Like most Westerners, Jackson feared that Pinckney and Hawkins would offer lenient terms to the defeated Red Sticks, and this proved to be the case. In fact, the Secretary of War had instructed them to offer such terms. The Creeks must surrender their prophets and war instigators, must sever their communications with the British and Spanish, must compensate the United States for damages done in the war and return property taken. But nothing was said about the cession of Muscogee territory, and this was really what Jackson and most white Westerners demanded (Remini, *Jackson,* 1977, 224; Owsley, 87).

It was clear to Old Hickory that the danger of another Red Stick uprising was still present. Already he had received dispatches informing him that Peter McQueen and Josiah Francis commanded a large number of Red Sticks at Pensacola and Apalachicola. He had sent his loyal scout John Gordon with a letter to Gonzalez Manrique at Pensacola to complain of this and to demand that the rebel leaders be arrested, but the Spanish governor had denied that the chiefs were there. To complicate matters, Jackson learned that the British were providing the refugees with extensive amounts of arms and gunpowder and had landed a detachment of Royal Marines to act as military advisors to the rebels. If the beaten Red Stick chiefs had been inclined to lay down the war club after Horseshoe Bend, the British had given them new hope to renew the struggle. With the right conditions, even the Allied Creeks and the other southern tribes might be drawn in, renewing and escalating the war with the red men on an even greater scale (Owsley, 87–88; Bassett, vol. 2, 20–21; Clayton, 81–82).

As long as the Muscogees had contact with the British and Spanish, there would continue to be trouble. Jackson wanted to create a buffer between the Muscogees and Tennessee and Georgia. Like most white frontiersmen, he believed that the Native Americans claimed too much land, land that could be better used for planting. The sooner the red man surrendered his large land holdings, the sooner that land would be made available to white settlers and properly developed—and the sooner the red man would become settled and learn to farm the land like the whites (Faust, 215; Remini, *Jackson*, 1977, 226–227).

By July 10, Sharp Knife was back at Fort Jackson. His first act as the new district commander was to let Hawkins know that he was summoning the Muscogee chiefs to a general conference on August 1. Hawkins had been sick for much of the year and had turned in his resignation as agent to the Creeks in April. But no replacement had arrived, so he continued in his duties. Jackson wanted the agent present at the August 1 conference to help placate the chiefs, but he made it very clear that they must attend, and he notified John Coffee to be ready to use force if necessary. If the chiefs failed to comply, he wrote Coffee, "a sudden and well directed stroke may be made, that will at once reduce them to unconditional submission" (Remini, *Jackson*, 1977, 225; Grant, 677).

On August 1, the Creek chiefs met with the general at Fort Jackson. The stage had been carefully prepared to include an intimidating military presence, provided by the Third U.S. Infantry. A large canopy had been set up for the meeting, with one side reserved for the visiting chiefs—friendly as well as hostile—and the other for Jackson, Hawkins, and their staffs. Big Warrior, William McIntosh, Little Prince, and Timpoochee Barnard were among the Allied Creek dignitaries. There was also a sixty-man delegation of Cherokee observers that included Richard Brown, Major Ridge, and agent Return J. Meigs. But none of the prominent Red Stick leaders were present (Remini, *Jackson*, 1977, 226; Griffith, 158; Owen, 11; Hood, 51; Wilkins, 81; Bassett, vol. 2, 23).

Old Hickory came straight to the point—the terms of the proposed peace treaty between the United States and the Muscogee nation. The chiefs listened with growing alarm as the general enumerated, and the interpreters translated, the points one by one: The Muscogees must surrender twenty-two million acres of land—all their land west of the Coosa and south of the Alabama—all the way eastward to the Ocmulgee in Georgia. The land cession itself amounted to three-fifths of present-day Alabama and one-fifth of Georgia. Jackson later confided to John Coffee that this enormous land grab "will secure to the U.S. a free settlement from

Georgia to Mobile and cuts off (as soon as settled) all foreign influence from the Indians and gives to the U.S. perfect security" (Owsley, 88; Remini, *Jackson*, 1977, 226; Holland, 38).

The treaty pledged to the Muscogees autonomy in the territory that remained to them, but the United States claimed the right to build roads, trading posts, and forts there. The Muscogees were to sever all communications with the Spanish and British and must surrender their prophets and hostile chiefs. They must also restore persons and property taken earlier in the war. There was to be a permanent peace between the Muscogees and their neighbors—Cherokees, Choctaws, and Chickasaws. Recognizing the destitute situation of the Creek towns, the United States agreed to provide food until the Muscogees could harvest their corn crop (Remini, *Jackson*, 1977, 227; Holland, 38).

The Cherokee observers were disappointed to learn that the treaty failed to define the boundary between Muscogee and Cherokee lands, leaving unresolved the Cherokee claims of land south of the Tennessee River—land that was included in the Creek land cession to the United States. The Muscogee chiefs feared that Sharp Knife would demand additional territory from them if they acceded to the Cherokee claims (McLoughlin, 198).

For the Muscogees, the biggest blow was the forced land cession. The chiefs were astonished. The Allied Creeks had expected to be rewarded for their aid in defeating the rebels. At the very least, if land was to be given up it should be the rebel faction that would be affected, not the loyal Creeks. Instead, the treaty proposed that the Muscogee nation surrender more than half its total territory (Owsley, 88; Remini, *Jackson*, 1977, 226).

There was no immediate reply from the stunned chiefs. Instead, they convened a private conference to discuss the terms offered by Jackson. The next day they gave their response. First to speak was Big Warrior. Old Hickory's demands would ruin the Muscogee nation, he argued, and he reminded his listeners that the Creeks had struggled faithfully on their part to adhere to the 1790 Treaty of New York. "I made this war," the speaker continued, "which has proved so fatal to my country, that the treaty entered into, a long time ago, with father Washington, might not be broken. To his friendly arm I hold fast. I will never break that chain of friendship we made together, and which bound us to stand to the United States." Big Warrior reminded Jackson of the devastation that the Red Sticks had brought upon Muscogee. "Hard is our situation," he said, "and you ought to consider it" (Reid and Eaton, 187–188).

Another chief, Shelocta, explained that he understood Jackson's reasoning in his demand that the Muscogees surrender their lands on the Alabama; that would indeed cut their nation off from the British and Spanish, the enemies of the United States. But at least, he argued, let us keep our lands west of the Coosa. Shelocta, who had served with the

American army throughout the Creek campaign, implored Jackson to remember the loyalty of the Allied Creeks during the war (Remini, *Jackson*, 1977, 228).

Jackson refused to budge an inch. Pushing his demands as a representative of western interests—without authorization from Washington—he listened calmly as the chiefs unanimously voiced their objections. Then he told them that the Muscogee nation as a whole must pay for the Red Stick uprising. The loyal Muscogees should have taken Tecumseh prisoner when he came fomenting rebellion; they did not, and now they must suffer the consequences. As to the land west of the Coosa, he reminded the chiefs that it was this path that had led Tecumseh into the Muscogee nation. "That path must be stopped," he declared grimly. "Until this is done your nation cannot expect happiness, mine security." The chiefs could either accept his terms, Sharp Knife concluded, or they could join the rebels in Florida. If they chose to go, he would provide them with food and ammunition for their journey. But soon he would follow with an army and destroy them (Remini, *Jackson*, 1977, 229; Owsley, 89; Faust, 216).

The chiefs resorted to one last argument. Earlier, Pinckney had written Hawkins promising to compensate the friendly chiefs for their losses in the war with the Red Sticks. The Muscogee nation, Pinckney wrote, was to surrender "as much of the conquered territory as may appear to the government to be a just indemnity for the expenses of the war; and as a retribution for the injuries sustained by its citizens and by the friendly Creek Indians." Pinckney pledged that the chiefs would be fully rewarded for their service against the Red Sticks, that "the United States will not forget their fidelity" (Grant, 680; Martin, 164–165).

Sharp Knife replied—truthfully—that Pinckney's promises had not been authorized by the secretary of war. The letters sent to Pinckney by Armstrong, and which Jackson had been directed to follow as well, made no mention of compensating the Allied Creeks. Ironically, Jackson himself had written the secretary of war back on April 25 suggesting the new boundaries for the Muscogee nation that the treaty now called for. At that time he had proposed that "[p]rovision might be made for the Big Warrior" and other friendly chiefs. But that was months earlier. Perhaps he now felt that he was in a much stronger negotiating position and could conveniently forget his prior comments about recompense for the allied chiefs (Remini, *Jackson*, 1977, 229; Bassett, vol. 1, 508).

The chiefs hammered home their argument, though. Jackson, they insisted, should honor the pledges that Pinckney had made to Hawkins, and that Hawkins had passed on to the chiefs. Jackson finally agreed to put the decision in the hands of President Madison. But for now, he insisted, the chiefs must either sign the treaty as he had written it, or reject it. They would show by their action which of them was friend or foe. "Consult," he told them, "and this evening let me know who will sign it, and who will not. I do not wish, nor will I attempt, to force any of you;—act as you think proper" (Reid and Eaton, 191).

Sharp Knife clashed with Hawkins, who insisted the terms of the treaty were too harsh and might incite the Allied Creeks to join the rebels. At one point during the peace talks, Hawkins wrote to the secretary of war asking that he remove Jackson as negotiator, but Old Hickory's popularity at this stage in the war made this a very unlikely action. The chiefs sent a desperate message to their agent on August 7. "We are again in trouble," they wrote him, "and need your advise." It was a last-ditch effort to win support against the terms of Jackson's treaty. The terms were so unfair, they complained to Hawkins, that Sharp Knife was punishing them—the friendly Muscogees—more than the Red Sticks! Hawkins agreed, but there was nothing he could do. Reluctantly, he advised the chiefs to sign the treaty (Owsley, 88, 91; Pound, 110).

On August 9, the chiefs signed the treaty. Of the thirty-five names to appear on the document, only one was a Red Stick. As historian Robert Remini observes, Jackson had concluded a peace treaty with his own allies and used it as an excuse to dismember the Muscogee nation (Remini, *Jackson*, 1977, 231).

The chiefs also drafted a letter complaining of the harsh terms of the treaty, stating that they signed it only under protest. They asked that this statement be included with the treaty when Jackson forwarded the document to Washington, and Old Hickory agreed to this. However, when the treaty reached Washington, the attachment was gone (Martin, 166).

In an ironic gesture, the chiefs also made Old Hickory a present of three square miles of Muscogee land. Jackson agreed to accept it, if the president approved, on the condition that he be permitted to sell the land and use the proceeds to feed and clothe destitute Muscogee women and children. For all his harshness toward the Muscogee nation, the iron general was the same man who wrote home to his wife, "Could you only see the misery and wretchedness of these creatures, perishing from want of food and picking up the grains of corn scattered from the mouths of horses...I know your humanity would feel for them." The chiefs would not hear of this; they insisted that the land was a gift, that they wanted Jackson to use the land to live on and pass on to his children. It was not intended to be something used for charity. The Muscogees wished to show that, despite the humiliating terms of the treaty, their land was still theirs to give (Martin, 166; Remini, *Jackson*, 1977, 230–231; Faust, 217).

CHAPTER 15

Red Coats and Red Allies

With the Treaty of Fort Jackson concluded, Old Hickory's focus shifted toward Pensacola, which had always been his real objective, the Creek campaign merely a prelude to the conquest of Spanish Florida. But Secretary of War John Armstrong did not share Jackson's concerns about British activity on the Gulf Coast and did not believe the enemy was actually readying an invasion there. And even if it turned out to be true, surely no offensive would be forthcoming in the late summer and early fall of 1814. The redcoats would probably wait until the following spring, he felt. Armstrong believed Jackson's regular detachments would be sufficient to defend the district, and he declined to authorize additional troops. But in fact, the British were planning an offensive for late fall or early winter, and their Seminole and Red Stick allies were to be an important part of the operation (McAlister, 315–316; Owsley, 88).

The conflict between Britain and America was taking a new and dangerous turn. In May 1814, the war in Europe had ended with a British victory over France. Napoleon abdicated his throne and sailed off to exile on the island of Elba—only to stage an escape and a startling return to power in March 1815, leading to a final showdown at Waterloo. But for now, the British were free to turn their undivided attention to the war in America and were planning to go on the offensive in the summer of 1814.

The northern frontier first felt Britain's wrath. A red-coated army of 14,000 veterans of the European war marched south from Canada into New York. But a surprising American naval victory at Lake Champlain on September 12 thwarted the invasion plan, and the British army returned to Canada.

A British thrust into the Chesapeake Bay had more grim consequences. After thrashing the hastily organized defenders—mostly poorly trained militia—at Bladensburg, Maryland, on August 24, the redcoat veterans marched unopposed into Washington, D.C. Finding that President Madison and the U.S. government had evacuated the capital, the British proceeded to burn the White House and the Capitol, retaliation for the U.S. burning of public buildings in York (present-day Toronto) the previous year. But their attempt to capture Baltimore failed due to unexpectedly strong resistance at Fort McHenry.

Political shakeups followed in the embarrassing wake of Washington's capture. Secretary of War Armstrong was out of a job, to be replaced by James Monroe. The late summer of 1814 was a dark time for the United States.

But it was at the Gulf Coast where the redcoats aimed their most potentially dangerous military operation. Vice Admiral Sir Alexander Cochrane proposed an armed lunge up the Mississippi to link up with British forces in Canada. Cochrane expected that the Spanish and the renegade red men would aid the British troops, and it would take few soldiers to accomplish his objective. The United States would be isolated from the trans-Mississippi and hemmed in by British possessions on three sides. From the very start of the war, British strategists had urged an invasion of the Gulf Coast, as a diversion to take pressure off the redcoats in Canada. Now, with British regulars free of the European war and with southeastern Native American tribes hostile to the United States after the Red Stick defeat and the signing of the hated Treaty of Fort Jackson, it seemed like an excellent time to implement the plan (Remini, *Jackson*, 1977, 235; Mahon, "British Strategy," 285).

As news of the Fort Jackson treaty filtered down into the Lower Creek towns on the Chattahoochee and Flint Rivers, many of the red men whom Jackson and Benjamin Hawkins had regarded as loyal began to have second thoughts about staying neutral. Land along the southern Chattahoochee and Flint was part of the treaty cession—even though none of the towns had sent representatives to the peace talks. The Lower Muscogees had always had the closest ties with the British, and now many of them were actually waiting for their red-coated friends to provide military aid. They did not make the mistake of the Red Sticks in taking up the war club prematurely. And across the border in Spanish Florida, the Seminoles appeared eager to accept British arms and renew the struggle that they had begun in 1812 (Owsley, 92, 188; Heidler and Heidler, "Between," 269–270, 276).

Also in Florida were the desperate red warriors of Peter McQueen and Josiah Francis, who were still willing to take up the war club again. The refugee Red Sticks had never accepted the defeat at Horseshoe Bend; they had viewed the conflict only as moving southward into Florida. Especially after the Treaty of Fort Jackson, they were more determined than ever to resist American expansion. In the summer of 1814, Red Sticks from eight different Upper Creek towns were in exile in Florida, about 200 of them in Pensacola and another 1,500 scattered in camps along the Escambia River (Heidler and Heidler, *Old Hickory's War,* 32; Mahon, "British Strategy," 287; Sugden, 278).

The British had already been active on the Gulf Coast. On May 10, the warship *Orpheus,* under command of Captain Hugh Pigot, dropped anchor at the mouth of the Apalachicola River. Pigot quickly made contact with ten local chiefs, the same group of Lower Muscogee and Seminole leaders who had been seeking aid from the British as early as September 1813. Included was interpreter Alexander Durant, Peter McQueen's brother-in-law who had fled with him to Florida. On May 20, the rebel chiefs came aboard the *Orpheus* and met with Pigot and his interpreters. They asked for British military assistance and assured Pigot that the refugee Red Sticks were prepared to furnish some 3,000 warriors to back an invasion of the Gulf Coast (Remini, *Jackson,* 1977, 235; Owsley, 99; Owen, 36; Mahon, "British Strategy," 287).

Pigot was quick to oblige the chiefs with 2,000 muskets and plenty of ammunition. He also requested a supply of carbines to be issued to the younger boys, who he felt were too little to use the muskets. The British commander assigned Brevet Captain George Woodbine, a white Jamaican sent by Governor Charles Cameron of Nassau, and two enlisted marines, Sergeant Samuel Smith and Corporal James Denny, as military advisors to the Creeks to train them and provide them with food and supplies (Owsley, 99–100; Grant, 677, 682; Remini, *Jackson,* 1977, 301; Sugden, 281).

An experienced trader who knew most of the local chiefs, Woodbine established a British base at the Forbes Company store at Ackaikwheithle, or Prospect Bluff, sixteen miles up the Apalachicola. At the end of May, the British and their Seminole allies began constructing a storehouse and fort there with a powder magazine. By early June 1814, Pigot left Woodbine in command at Prospect Bluff and returned to Nassau to report to Admiral Cochrane (Saunt, 276; Owsley, 99–100).

At Prospect Bluff, Seminole chief Kinache (Thomas Perryman) was quick to extend a warm reception to Woodbine. Now elderly and bitter, Perryman was William Augustus Bowles's father-in-law and had supported the British adventurer in his unsuccessful attempt to establish an independent state of Muscogee more than a decade earlier. He had migrated from his original settlement, Perrymans (or Old Fowltown), on the lower Chattahoochee, and was now the leader of Mikasuki, the largest of the Seminole towns, located near present-day Tallahassee, Florida. Perryman had been receptive to Tecumseh's message in 1811, had attended his famous talk at Tuckabatchee, and had attempted to dispatch warriors up the Chattahoochee to join the Red Sticks. The Allied Creeks had blocked their path (Heidler and Heidler, *Old Hickory's War*, 39; Covington, 34–35).

Woodbine also courted support from another Florida group known to be hostile to the Americans. The African Americans, or Maroons, eagerly digested a British declaration promising aid "to all those who may be disposed to emigrate from the United States." Woodbine offered runaway slaves the opportunity to enlist in the British military, to remain with their families as free permanent settlers in Florida, or to settle in the West Indies (Saunt, 275).

By early June, word of the new British base at Prospect Bluff had reached Josiah Francis and Peter McQueen at Pensacola. The Seminole chiefs had informed Pigot of the Red Stick defeat at Horseshoe Bend. The survivors of this bloody encounter, despite their willingness to continue the fight, were dying of hunger in their refugee camps near Pensacola. The Red Stick leaders immediately appealed to the redcoats for aid, drafting a letter to the British on June 9. "Our Case is really miserable and lamentable," they wrote, "driven from House and Home without Food and Clothes to cover our Bodies by disasters and an Enemy, who has sworn our ruin, and hovering about Pensacola and its Vicinity, where We can get now [sic] Assistance, as the Spanish Government tells Us that it is scarsely [sic] able to support its Own Troops." Anxious to present their case, McQueen led twenty-five of his warriors to Apalachicola by boat, followed shortly by Francis and interpreter Henry Durgen with twenty more warriors (Owsley, 92, 98, 99; Saunt, 276–277; Sugden, 280, 282).

After hearing how desperate the rebels at Pensacola really were, Woodbine left a small detachment at Prospect Bluff and set sail for Pensacola on the sloop *Sophie* with supplies. He reached there on July 28, and hundreds of hungry Muscogees soon flocked into the town. Thomas and Benjamin Perryman, with Sergeant Smith (now an acting lieutenant), were to take 300 Seminole warriors and march overland to rendezvous with Woodbine at Pensacola (Saunt, 276–277; Sugden, 287).

The shortage of food in the area, both at Prospect Bluff and at Pensacola, came to be Woodbine's most difficult obstacle. It was far easier to arm the red men than to feed them. The shallowness of the Apalachicola made it necessary for the British to use small boats and canoes to transport supplies to Prospect Bluff. But hunger had its positive side, too, Woodbine reasoned. He expected that some of the Allied Creek chiefs, heretofore loyal to the Americans, would join the British in return for food. Even Big Warrior, who seemed to be awaiting the outcome of the proposed British offensive, was rumored to be leaning toward joining the Red Sticks if they could receive adequate aid from the British. The Choctaws, Woodbine felt, would desert the Americans too—once the British captured Mobile (Owsley, 92–93, 99–100; Heidler and Heidler, *Encyclopedia*, 53).

British aid was welcome, but it came too late to change the outcome of the Creek War. If Pigot and Woodbine had arrived a few months earlier, or even before Horseshoe Bend, the Red Sticks would have actually been better armed than the white armies. The Red Sticks would have been more effective allies for the British, and a stronger British offensive in the Gulf Coast region could have resulted in the taking of Mobile and New Orleans—and a completely different end to the War of 1812. But now it was too late. Woodbine also failed to appreciate the deep division that still separated the Upper Creeks from the Lower Creeks, or the Red Stick faction from the Allied Creeks. Too much bad blood existed between these two groups for them to effectively cooperate now, even though both groups sought a British alliance (Owsley, 92, 99; Remini, *Jackson*, 1977, 300, 305; Heidler and Heidler, "Between," 274).

Still, the British were encouraged at their reception on the Gulf Coast. With strong concentrations of pro-British red men at Pensacola, Mikasuki, Fowltown (not far from the junction of the Flint and the Chattahoochee), and other settlements along the Apalachicola, Woodbine felt he could indeed muster 3,000 warriors. If adequate supplies could be had, Woodbine envisioned an offensive up the Chattahoochee to capture Fort Mitchell. Perryman and the rebel chiefs pledged that their warriors would "spare the lives of all the prisoners taken, whether man, woman or child" (Sugden, 282, 284; Heidler and Heidler, "Between," 276; Covington, 35).

Woodbine's efforts seemed so promising that Cochrane decided to expand the operation by sending a capable, battle-hardened Irish officer, Major Edward Nicholls, with 100 Royal Marines to establish a more permanent military presence among the Creeks. With the help of the red allies at Pensacola and Apalachicola, Cochrane expected Nicholls to orchestrate an attack on Mobile, which would become the launchpad for an invasion of the Mississippi Valley. From Mobile, British forces could march on Natchez and cut off New Orleans. It was what American strategists had feared from the beginning of conflict with Britain—that the British would turn Pensacola into an enemy base (Remini, *Jackson*, 1977, 235–236; Owsley, 103; Heidler and Heidler, *Encyclopedia*, 388).

Nicholls first conferred with Governor Cameron in Nassau, where he obtained supplies for the Gulf Coast operation—two fieldpieces (24-pounders); 2,000 more muskets; as well as launches and flatboats, belts, flints and powder flasks, sabers, jackets, epaulets, and assorted gifts for the red men. Then he sailed for Cuba on HMS *Hermes*, captained by Sir William Percy, to meet with Juan Ruiz Apodaca. Nicholls extended the Spanish captain general a letter from Cameron pledging that British intentions in Florida were peaceful—and that Britain would aid Spain if the United States attacked. According to Nicholls, Ruiz Apodaca was "extremely civil and extremely jealous." He insisted that no British troops be landed in Pensacola, St. Marks, or St. Augustine. The rest of Florida was open to the British (Owsley, 104–105; Sugden, 286).

The *Hermes* and her companion ship, HMS *Carron*, reached Apalachicola on August 10, and Nicholls found that the food shortage was still a serious problem. He wrote of one group of refugee Red Sticks, "[S]uch objects I never saw the like of, absolute skin and bone, but cheerfull [sic] and resolved to do their utmost against the common enemy." When he asked one old warrior how far away the enemy was and if he could lead troops back there, he replied that "he could not miss the way for it was marked with the graves of his five children" (Owsley, 105; Sugden, 285, 287).

Woodbine was still with the refugee Creeks at Pensacola, where the food situation was even worse than at Apalachicola, and where an uneasy Governor Don Mateo Gonzalez Manrique expected an attack at any time by the Americans. Woodbine had dispatched Captain Nicholas Lockyer back to Apalachicola with orders to return with all the arms and men he could bring. With Woodbine and most of his red allies already at Pensacola, it made sense to Nicholls to consolidate his forces there. He set sail for Pensacola and reached the town on August 14 (Owsley, 105).

Alarmed by the fear of Jackson, Gonzalez Manrique made a desperate decision. Despite Ruiz Apodaca's warning to the British to steer clear of Pensacola, he invited Nicholls to land his troops there, and the redcoats promptly took control of the port. Nicholls garrisoned his 100 marines in Fort San Miguel, near the town square, where he had both the Spanish and British flags flying. In the town itself, he stationed about 500 armed Red Stick warriors, uniformed in red coats. Much to the chagrin of the Spanish governor, Nicholls and his officers restricted travel, posting Seminole war parties at the edge of town to check passports, and they confiscated private property. Nicholls recruited practically all of the local slaves, and when these recruits began looting and intimidating local townspeople, Gonzalez Manrique began to regret his decision to bring in the British (Remini, *Jackson*, 1977, 237; Saunt, 278; Owsley, 105–107).

Nicholls was dismayed to find that the Spanish seemed to have no stomach for the coming encounter with the Americans. He feared that a number of the townspeople and some of the Spanish officers as well appeared ready and willing to surrender the town as soon as Jackson's army arrived. The redcoats' heavy-handed methods aroused the anger of John Innerarity of the Forbes Company, as well as other local residents, who acted as informants and passed on reports of the British activities to Jackson. Taking advantage of Pensacola's status as a neutral port, Old Hickory had already sent Captain John Jones to secretly observe Pensacola's defenses, giving him a good idea of how things stood (Remini, *Jackson*, 1977, 236–237, 243; Owsley, 93, 107).

Gonzalez Manrique may have had second thoughts about inviting Nicholls—the "impatient blustering Irishman" whom a friend in Havana had written him about—and his marines into Pensacola, but to the Musco-gees, the British arrival was a godsend. Happy to see the redcoats in charge instead of their "weak, frail friends" the Spanish, rebel leaders Francis, McQueen, and Kinache wrote Cochrane on September 1, "[S]ince your sons came here...we walk like men in their streets." The Red Sticks were determined to "live or die free of which we have given hard proof by choosing to abandon our Country rather than live in it as slaves" (Heidler and Heidler, *Old Hickory's War*, 41; Sugden, 288).

Nicholls was especially anxious to cement an alliance between the red men and his black recruits. Cochrane had given him authority to raise a regiment of blacks and red men led by British officers. Nicholls had as many as 100 Maroons on duty in Fort San Miguel. He urged the Red Stick leaders, Francis and McQueen, to do all they could to bolster black recruit-ment, and the chiefs responded very favorably, promising to "get all the black men we can to join your warriors." Nicholls was excited about the possibilities of all this. "Indians and blacks are very good friends," he wrote, "and cooperate bravely together." The British enticements to run-away slaves to cross the border from Georgia seemed to be bearing fruit. Nicholls reported that "several of Colonel Hawkins' negroes" were at Prospect Bluff. Reports of frontier raids by Red Stick–black bands alarmed Georgians as well as Allied Creeks (Saunt, 278–279; Owsley, 103, 107).

Nicholls even tried to recruit Jean Lafitte and his Baratarians of Louisi-ana. He sent Captain John McWilliams on the *Sophie* with a letter to Lafitte offering him a commission as a captain in the British navy—and rank and lands to his men as well—in return for an alliance and the use of Barataria as a base against the United States. Instead, Lafitte turned the letter over to Governor W.C.C. Claiborne of Louisiana and offered to fight for the Americans in return for a pardon for smuggling and unlawful use of American territory (Owsley, 107–109).

While Nicholls had been strengthening his hold on Pensacola, Old Hickory had not been idle. After concluding the peace treaty with the Creeks, he left Fort Jackson on August 11 with his regulars of the Third U.S. Infantry, moved down the Alabama to Mobile, and arrived there on August 22. Jackson quickly dispatched Major William Lawrence to strengthen Fort Bowyer at the entrance to Mobile Bay and then turned his attention to Pensacola (Grant, 693; Remini, *Jackson*, 1977, 236).

On August 24, Jackson wrote a blistering letter to Gonzalez Manrique, accusing him of harboring "refugee banditti from the Creek nation" and of allowing British officers to train and equip them. Old Hickory charged the Spanish governor to arrest Peter McQueen, Josiah Francis, and other rebel leaders, and to jail them as criminals. True to his usual aggressive style, he threatened to exact vengeance in an eye-for-an-eye manner if the Spanish failed to comply with his demands. Jackson was even more disturbed at reports that the rebels were going about the streets of Pensacola in British uniforms and brandishing British arms, that the redcoats had promised them a bounty of ten dollars for every scalp they took (Griffith, 163; Grant, 692; E. Rowland, 88).

Meanwhile, Nicholls planned an offensive operation of his own. He felt that a first strike by the British could win a victory and boost morale among his red allies. Captain Percy, the naval commander, suggested an attack on Fort Bowyer, the gateway to Mobile Bay. A successful occupation of Fort Bowyer would open the door to Mobile, would encourage the Creeks and Seminoles, and would open up dialogue with the Choctaws. Although reluctant at first because of lack of manpower, Nicholls finally agreed (Owsley, 109).

Word of Nicholls's decision to assault Fort Bowyer leaked out to John Innerarity, who—worried about the potential danger to his company's property in Mobile—sent off a messenger on horseback to warn the American garrison. Nicholls learned of this and soon had marines and red allies galloping in pursuit, but they failed to catch up with Innerarity's rider, who reached Fort Bowyer in time to deliver the warning. Nicholls still felt confident he could take the fort (Coker, 49–50).

American troops had occupied Fort Bowyer since their takeover of Mobile more than a year earlier. It was a small wooden outpost with probably no more than fourteen small guns, of which only eleven were actually mounted. The commander, Major Lawrence, had only 158 regulars to defend the fort (Remini, *Jackson,* 1977, 238; Owsley, 110–111; Sugden, 291).

On September 12, a flotilla of four British ships—the *Hermes, Carron, Sophie,* and *Childers*—all under Percy's command and carrying 600 men and seventy-eight guns, appeared before Fort Bowyer. On board were Major Nicholls and his marines, along with nearly 200 red warriors, including Francis and McQueen with their Red Sticks and Thomas Perryman with a detachment of Seminoles. While the four British ships bombarded the small fort by sea, Nicholls and his marines and red allies would attack the fort by land. But Nicholls fell ill and was unable to lead the attack. The duty fell to Captain Robert Henry, who landed his seventy-two marines and 180 warriors on the narrow peninsula about six miles east of the fort and began moving toward their objective (Owsley, 109; Remini, *Jackson,* 1977, 237–238; Covington, 35; Sugden, 291; Coker, 50).

Fighting began on September 14. After marching to within 800 yards of Fort Bowyer, Henry's small land force, dragging along a small howitzer, waited until the ships opened fire, then they attempted to storm the fort. They didn't get very far. The defenders of Fort Bowyer stubbornly held their ground, and the marines retreated, losing one man killed. The next day, the redcoats tried again but were forced to withdraw when their ammunition gave out. The defenders were able to keep Henry's small invasion force at bay, since their artillery dominated the approaches to the fort. But could they hold out against the British naval vessels, out-gunning them more than three to one (Owsley, 110; G. A. Smith, 17; Sugden, 291)?

Now Fate dealt the Americans a favorable hand. Because the wind died down and the water near Fort Bowyer was shallow, only two of the four British ships were able to get in position to open fire. On the afternoon of September 15, the *Hermes* and *Sophie* engaged in a hard-fought gun battle with the little American fort. Furious volleys from the ships and the fort blanketed the area with smoke. There was considerable damage to the fort, and several guns were destroyed. But the sailors found that they had to elevate their guns as high as they could just to strike the fort. After an American shell tore loose the *Hermes's* anchor cable, the badly damaged ship was pulled toward shore by the current and eventually grounded. Percy abandoned his vessel, transferred his men to the other ships, and set fire to the disabled *Hermes*, which later exploded in a fiery finale (Remini, *Jackson*, 1977, 238; Owsley, 111).

Percy collected his men and sailed back to Pensacola, while Henry and his troops marched overland. The redcoats had lost thirty-two sailors killed and thirty-seven wounded. On board the *Hermes*, Nicholls had sustained wounds to his head and his leg and had lost the sight in his right eye. Percy was also wounded. American losses were four killed and five wounded. The British attempt to capture Mobile was over (Remini, *Jackson*, 1977, 238; Owsley, 110–111; Griffith, 169; Sugden, 291).

The redcoats' repulse at Fort Bowyer may have been a minor engagement, but it marked a significant turning point in the Anglo American struggle for control of the Gulf Coast. British commanders, stung by their defeat at Fort Bowyer, now began to back off from their plan to occupy Mobile, reasoning that if they could not overcome the little fort at the entrance to Mobile Bay, then they could hardly expect to take the Gulf City, which surely must be more heavily defended. In reality, Fort Bowyer was extremely vulnerable and could have easily been taken. The British had failed to commit a large enough force to do the job. Instead, they began to focus on a strike at New Orleans (Owsley, 112; Remini, *Jackson*, 1977, 238).

At the same time, the clash at Fort Bowyer also deceived Jackson into concentrating too heavily on the defense of Mobile. Old Hickory immediately sent reinforcements to Fort Bowyer and ordered the walls repaired and strengthened. He also dispatched Joseph P. Kennedy and a force of Choctaws with orders to go after Henry's marines and Creek allies and cut them off before they could return by land to Pensacola. Kennedy was not quick enough, and the redcoats made it back safely to Pensacola (Owsley, 112).

On a more strategic level, Jackson—satisfied that Mobile probably was Britain's objective on the Gulf—began to concentrate all available troops for defending that city. He called up all of the militia he could get for duty. Had he continued to consolidate his forces in the Mobile area, he would have been totally unprepared to defend New Orleans. Fortunately for the Americans, later intelligence caused him to change his plans (Owsley, 112; Remini, *Jackson*, 1977, 238–239).

CHAPTER 16

"Hot Bed of the Indian War"

As the fall of 1814 deepened, the British turned their invasion plans from Mobile to New Orleans. But Jackson did not know this. Even after Secretary of War James Monroe warned him on October 10 that a British invasion force was aimed at New Orleans, he remained convinced that Mobile was the likely target and that his primary objective should be a preemptive strike at Pensacola, the staging area for Major Nicholls's recent attack on Fort Bowyer (Owsley, 112–113; Remini, *Jackson*, 1977, 238–239).

As he had done so many times before, Old Hickory began assembling a frontier army from scratch. The rendezvous point was Fort Montgomery on the Alabama River—a new post near the ruins of old Fort Mims. Jackson already had his regulars in the Third, Thirty-ninth, and Forty-fourth U.S. Infantry Regiments, but he needed more men. On August 27, he wrote to his adjutant, Colonel Robert Butler, in Tennessee and appealed for volunteers. By October 1, faithful John Coffee was on the way with 2,000 Tennessee mounted troops. Remembering his Nashville artillerists who had saved the day for him at Enitachopco, Jackson called on veteran officers David Deaderick and Joel Parish to raise an artillery battalion and to bring along the old "favorite six pounder." But Deaderick and Parish weren't available this time, so Jackson detailed Captain James E. Dinkins's company of the Third U.S. Infantry to serve as artillerists (Bassett, vol. 2, 32, 98, 128; Remini, *Jackson*, 1977, 239–240; Clayton, 82).

On September 14, Jackson recalled Thomas Hinds and his Mississippi Dragoons to service. Governor David Holmes also dispatched 500 Mississippi territorial infantry to augment Jackson's forces in the Tensaw country. Holmes reminded Old Hickory that none of his men had received any pay since Fort Mims and that shortages of equipment were also a problem. He wrote Jackson that Hinds's troopers would be "partly armed with muskets, and as well furnished in other respects as our means would permit" (D. Rowland, 9; Skeen, 167).

As usual, Jackson needed red warriors to augment his forces. Surprisingly, considering their treatment at the treaty signing at Fort Jackson, the Allied Creeks still showed willingness to serve with the Americans. They had received no pay either, and agent Benjamin Hawkins wrote, "Our Chiefs complain much against us." But about 1,000 warriors responded to Jackson's call to arms. Hawkins still insisted that most of the Muscogees were loyal to the United States, but he regarded the Red Stick refugees as obstinate. "They were still haughty, brave and moved by fanaticism," he wrote (Grant, 677, 679, 696).

Hawkins had been aware of British activity at Apalachicola for some time. By June 14, he was in possession of information from Folappo Hadjo, chief of the Eufaula town on the Chattahoochee, information he passed on to the secretary of war. Folappo Hadjo had spoken with a young man from his town who had been to Prospect Bluff and had witnessed British marines issuing arms and ammunition to the refugees from the Tallapoosa. Another informant, Wolf Warrior, also verified rumors of the British activities, that they were arming the Seminoles. "It is not for war they say," he reported, "but it looks very suspicious in my eye" (Grant, 683–684).

Hawkins moved to neutralize the British threat among the Lower Creeks. On September 23 William McIntosh, at the head of some 200 Allied Creek warriors, marched down the Chattahoochee with orders to seize all arms and ammunition being stored up and to use force if necessary. On reaching Eufaula, McIntosh learned that the British had moved from Prospect Bluff to Pensacola. After marching farther into Seminole country, McIntosh also met with Thomas Perryman, who assured him that the Seminoles wanted only to remain at peace. Still suspicious, but finding no concrete signs of British activity, McIntosh returned to Coweta empty-handed (Grant, 694, 696; Griffith, 164; Heidler and Heidler, *Old Hickory's War*, 43).

Despite Perryman's assurances, Hawkins was worried about the Seminole threat against the Georgia frontier. Mikasuki, the main Seminole town in Spanish Florida, was definitely hostile. On November 3, an alarmed Hawkins alerted local military commanders that "a large party of hostile Seminole Indians" from Perrymans (or Old Fowltown, on the eastern bank of the Chattahoochee twenty-two miles above its junction with the Flint) was massing to attack the Georgia frontier. And on November 6, Hawkins received word that at least twenty-eight hostiles—"half red, half black"—were headed toward the frontier town of Hartford on the Ocmulgee River. "I cease to have any reliance on the pacific promises of the Seminoles," Hawkins wrote. "They have taken part against us and must be chastised or they will begin to destroy our frontiers, if not in a body, in their small predatory parties" (Grant, 699–702, 704, 705, 707).

Also disturbing were reports that the redcoats had agents as far north as Fort Decatur on the Tallapoosa mingling among the Muscogees and recruiting warriors for their force at Pensacola. Fort Mitchell, Fort Hull, Fort Bainbridge, and Fort Decatur were all being garrisoned by Allied Creek warriors, since the white militia soldiers had marched for home that summer (Heidler and Heidler, *Old Hickory's War*, 29, 43).

Hawkins called on Big Warrior and Little Prince to assemble their warriors to meet the Seminole threat. Hawkins would meet them at Coweta to take command. Along the Flint River, Hawkins planned to post Timpoochee Barnard and some 100 of his Uchee warriors about twenty miles south of the Creek agency and a force under the chiefs of Aumucullee (a friendly Lower Creek town farther down the Flint) thirty miles below the Uchees "to reconnoiter the movements of the enemy." Hawkins called on Governor Peter Early for mounted militia. "It will never do to act defensively against Indians on a frontier as extensive as yours," he wrote. "On the appearance of hostility they must be traced up to their Towns and crushed." Early agreed and offered to furnish 200 to 300 more mounted troops provided that they could be fed. On November 10, an advance detachment of 100 Georgia militia was on its way from the Creek agency to rendezvous with Barnard and his Uchees (Grant, 700–705).

In the Tensaw country, agent John McKee got the word that Jackson would probably need his Choctaw warriors again. "I have not received a cent," he complained to Jackson, "either to reward the Choctaws for their service last winter or even to pay for the provisions furnished to them." Without at least the promise of payment, it would be difficult to raise a force of warriors from the Choctaws. "A reasonable encouragement," he went on, "will bring out a considerable number of naked badly armed brave fellows, who seem as heartily engaged in the cause as you could wish…but they must eat" (McKee to Jackson, August 8, 1814, McKee Letters).

But like the Creeks, the Choctaws were still willing to follow Sharp Knife, and 700 warriors under Pushmataha joined up. McKee wrote on August 27:

We may count pretty well on our Choctaws and they say they are prepared to fight our *red* enemies. I have never yet asked them to fight any other. And perhaps it is best not to ask them to fight the whites. When they have joined the army they will fight along side of your soldiers against *white* or *red* foes—of this I have no doubt. P.S. Money, money. (Sugden, 292; McKee to Jackson, August 27, 1814, McKee Letters)

Finally there were the Cherokees, who had been steadfast during the Creek campaign. From Fort Deposit, Richard Brown wrote Jackson that

Cherokee families in his area were suffering for lack of food. His warriors had received no pay, and their families needed them at home. But if Jackson was in desperate need, he would raise a company and start out anyway. Although Brown, Ridge, Gideon Morgan, and John Walker were still willing, promising Jackson as many as 500 warriors, Sharp Knife would receive no help from the Cherokees this time. When Meigs appealed to the Cherokee council, he found them less than enthusiastic. Ridge and Walker did offer to serve and even tried to recruit volunteers. But the poor response found them unable to raise a sufficient force until December. The war was over before they could join Jackson's army, so they broke up and returned home (Hood, 56; Wilkins, 83–84).

Jackson had determined to plow ahead with an attack on Pensacola. "I act without any orders from the Government," he boasted. Although President Madison and Secretary of War Monroe never came out officially in support of his action, they secretly approved, and Jackson was convinced that he had an implied go-ahead. Old Hickory was adamant that the young republic's troubles with the red man on the southern frontier would continue as long as Spain and Britain maintained a presence there. Most southerners and westerners supported acquisition of Florida, and if Jackson could carry off such a coup, so much the better (Owsley, 112; Remini, *Jackson*, 1977, 240–241).

Old Hickory marched his troops out of Fort Montgomery on October 25. Coffee's horsemen from Tennessee soon joined him. Including 520 regulars, 750 Choctaw and Chickasaw allies, and his militia volunteers from Tennessee and the Mississippi Territory, Jackson commanded an army of over 4,000 troops. Hawkins and McIntosh with their Allied Creeks were still in the Muscogee country and would coordinate their operations for a lunge against the British base at Prospect Bluff. By November 6, Jackson's invasion force had reached Pensacola (Skeen, 167; Remini, *Jackson*, 1977, 239–241; Owsley, 112–113).

The iron general sent a surrender demand to Governor Gonzalez Manrique under a flag of truce, but British marines from Fort San Miguel opened fire on the party and sent them scurrying back to the American lines. Jackson tried again. His men had captured a Spanish corporal, whom he sent with a second surrender demand to Gonzalez Manrique. Old Hickory called for an immediate British evacuation of Pensacola. The Spanish governor flatly refused. Sharp Knife ordered his officers to pass the word on to their troops to prepare for a predawn attack for the following day (Owsley, 113; Remini, *Jackson*, 1977, 241).

Pensacola's Spanish garrison of 500 poorly armed, hungry soldiers—commanded by what one American visitor called "an old set of lazy pot-gutted officers"—included 272 black militia sent from Cuba after the American occupation of Mobile in 1813. A number of forts and blockhouses protected the town and could have formed a strong defense if properly manned. But the Spanish simply did not have the manpower. If any real resistance was to be offered, it would have to be from Nicholls's British marines and their red and black allies, aided by the British naval squadron in Pensacola Bay (Owsley, 113–114).

Relations between Gonzalez Manrique and Nicholls had deteriorated after the British repulse at Fort Bowyer. The Spanish governor now had far less confidence that the redcoats could defend Pensacola against an American attack. On their withdrawal from Fort Bowyer, Captain Robert Henry's marines and Indians had stopped long enough to loot the Innerarity–Forbes Company stores at Bon Secour. There was still bitterness over the redcoats' recruitment of over 100 black slaves in Pensacola. Torn between fear of the British and fear of the Americans, Gonzalez Manrique wavered, unsure whether to request aid or not. In the end, he simply vacillated helplessly, leaving the redcoats confounded while the American army prepared to attack (Owsley, 115–116).

Captain James Gordon of HMS *Sea Horse* now commanded the British naval squadron in the harbor of Pensacola, replacing Captain William Percy. Appalled by Gonzalez Manrique's indecision, he washed his hands of the whole affair. But Nicholls and his force of marines and red men prepared to make a last-ditch defense of the town. Nicholls had transported the Seminole and Red Stick women and children across Pensacola Bay where they would be more secure (Owsley, 116; Sudgen, 296).

Before dawn on November 7, Jackson circled through the woods to the north of Pensacola and launched his attack from its eastern approaches, while a column of 500 mounted troops made a diversionary feint on the western side. The feint worked. Believing that the American attack would come from the west, the British naval commanders had the guns of their ships aimed in that direction; before they could swirl around eastward it was too late. Jackson's soldiers—three columns of American troops and one of Choctaw warriors, with the Third U.S. Infantry in the lead—were swarming into the town. Nicholls's marines abandoned Fort San Miguel and moved to the more secure Fort Barrancas, west of Pensacola (Owsley, 116–117; Bassett, vol. 2, 96–97; Remini, *Jackson*, 1977, 242).

A handful of die-hard Spanish soldiers, using two cannon left by Nicholls's men, made a brief stand. Placing the guns in one of the two streets leading into Pensacola's main square, they concentrated their fire on the attacking Americans. But Captain William Laval's advance company of bayonet-wielding regulars quickly overcame the batteries. The attack was over in a matter of minutes, and Spanish resistance crumbled. Gonzalez Manrique hoisted a white flag and surrendered the town. Jackson wrote that his seasoned regulars, Tennessee riflemen, and Mississippi dragoons had all acted with "steady firmness." Old Hickory especially praised the Choctaws for their part in the fighting (Owsley, 117; Bassett, vol. 2, 96–97; Fredriksen, 22).

The Americans had taken the town, but the harbor forts still remained; and whoever held them really controlled Pensacola, because they guarded the entrance to Pensacola Bay. Jackson readied his troops to storm them the next morning. Old Hickory expected a hard assault on Fort Barrancas, the stronghold fourteen miles west of Pensacola. But before Jackson could attack, Nicholls embarked his troops and red allies, along with the small Spanish garrison, onto the British ships and then blew up the fort. The British also destroyed the battery at Point Siguenza (Fort Santa Rosa) on the western tip of Santa Rosa Island across from Fort Barrancas. The taking of Pensacola had cost Jackson seven men killed and eleven wounded. The Spanish had lost fourteen killed and six wounded, while British and Native American casualties are unknown (Owsley, 117–118; Remini, *Jackson*, 1977, 242).

Jackson had little time to enjoy his long-awaited victory. He probably would have left an American garrison to occupy Pensacola, but the destruction of the key harbor forts left the town open to a future British attack. Besides, word had just reached Jackson at Pensacola that the enemy was definitely planning an offensive at New Orleans. So Sharp Knife set out for Mobile. Fully satisfied that he had accomplished his objective in Pensacola, Jackson wrote Monroe that he had "broken up the hot bed of the Indian war." He had delivered a forceful reminder to the Spanish that the United States would act to protect the southern frontier. He had thwarted a very good invasion plan by the British. And he had driven a wedge between the British and their Spanish allies. Jackson wisely forbade his troops from plundering in Pensacola and insisted that the townspeople be treated with respect. This went a long way toward soothing Spanish pride, especially since their British friends now seemed unable to protect them. Most of all, the Red Sticks' confidence in their British allies had been shaken. Admiral Cochrane had to concede that the British had been stung at Fort Bowyer and at Pensacola and that their offensive in the Gulf had been weakened (Remini, *Jackson*, 1977, 242–243; Owsley, 118).

The British were not entirely through in the Muscogee country, however. Nicholls intended to use Prospect Bluff—he called it Fort Apalachicola, while others dubbed it British Post—as a base of operations for raids on the Georgia frontier. Francis, McQueen, Perryman, and other rebel chiefs were still in close contact with the British, who offered them the hospitality of their ships anchored in Apalachicola Bay. More rebel warriors were arriving at Prospect Bluff, and runaway slaves were coming in as well. Nicholls formed four companies of black colonial marines at Apalachicola in December (Remini, *Jackson*, 1977, 244; Covington, 36; Sudgen, 297; Heidler and Heidler, *Encyclopedia*, 389, 434).

Jackson wanted to eliminate the British base at Apalachicola, and he contrived a coordinated operation by two separate columns to do it. First, before leaving Pensacola with the bulk of his army, he detached 1,000 troops under Major Uriah Blue of the Thirty-ninth U.S. Infantry to neutralize the rebel pockets along the Escambia River, plunder their camps, and destroy their crops. At the same time, Hawkins's Allied Creeks, with help from the Georgia militia, would move down the Chattahoochee and—if possible—join up with Blue's column for an attack on Prospect Bluff (Owsley, 174–175; Remini, *Jackson,* 1977, 244; Rucker, 328).

A fifteen-year veteran of the army, Blue had commanded the Choctaw column in the attack on Pensacola. A large number of warriors accompanied him still, along with a detachment of Chickasaws led by William Colbert. Blue had veteran white soldiers with him, too. Just arrived in Pensacola was William Russell, one of Jackson's best scout leaders in the Creek campaign, now a major leading a battalion of mounted Tennessee riflemen. Major John Child led a battalion of East Tennessee riflemen. And Davy Crockett was back, now a sergeant serving as a scout in Russell's command and succinctly summing up the real object of Blue's mission— to "kill up the Indians on the Scamby river." Sam Moniac, Red Eagle's brother-in-law, was to ride along as a guide (Rucker, 327; D. Rowland, 13; Gibson, 98; Heidler and Heidler, *Old Hickory's War,* 48).

But Blue's expedition had trouble from the start. The same old problems that had confounded Jackson's army so many times before—lack of food and bad weather—raised their heads again. Blue had to return to Fort Montgomery to wait for supplies, and early December found him still there waiting, while heavy rains flooded roads and streams in the area. Blue finally tired of the delay and set out on December 8 with twenty days' rations for his troops. With the roads too poor for wagons to use, Blue dismounted half of his column and used the horses to carry the rations. The weather soon turned bitterly cold, and the paths through the Florida swamps turned to mud (Rucker, 328; Owsley, 174).

Russell, Crockett, and about eighty Choctaws and Chickasaws preceded the main column and crossed the Escambia about twenty-four miles north of Pensacola. Applying their war paint, the Choctaws encouraged Russell to do likewise, and he did. Two Choctaw scouts, pretending to be deserters from Jackson's army, came upon a pair of Red Stick refugees, who gave them directions to a large hostile camp, which Blue's column captured the next day. As they were leaving, the Choctaws turned on the Muscogees and shot them, then beheaded them. That night in their camp Crockett found them in ritual—striking the severed heads with their war clubs. Crockett joined in, taking up a club and imitating the warriors. After Crockett whacked one of the heads, the Choctaws congratulated him, slapping him on the back and chanting, "Warrior—warrior" (Rucker, 326–329; Hauck, 27).

During mid-December, Blue's soldiers moved eastward and made several separate raids on enemy camps along the Escambia, Blackwater, and

Yellow Rivers. They penetrated as far east as the Choctawhatchee River, where—desperate for food supplies—they expected to capture a large rebel town. The column arrived at Choctawhatchee (or Holmes Town), near present-day Vernon, Florida, on December 26, deployed for battle, and moved in. To his disappointment, Blue found that the Red Sticks had abandoned the town, and he put it to the torch (Rucker, 329–332; Owsley, 174–175).

Out of supplies now, Blue never got any closer to Apalachicola. By January 9, the expedition was back at Fort Montgomery. Old Hickory's mopping-up operation failed to eliminate the Red Sticks, and he would have to deal with these refugees at a later date. But although he had not reached the Apalachicola, Blue had destroyed several enemy camps, killed some fifty Red Sticks, and taken some 200 captive—all while traveling 100 miles into enemy country in the most primitive and exhausting conditions. And although his men were nearly starved, he had not had any killed (Rucker, 325, 336–337).

The other component of Jackson's proposed thrust against Prospect Bluff, Hawkins's Allied Creeks, got off to an even slower start than Blue's expedition. By January 7, Hawkins and his forces were still camped near Coweta, waiting for transports to carry their supplies down the river. Morale was poor, and Hawkins reported that his Allied Creeks were cold, hungry, and poorly clothed. "The Indians under me have rec'd neither clothing or money for three years," he complained. "I am taking them to seek the enemy without one dollar." At the same time, Brigadier General David Blackshear's Georgia militia had finally reached the Flint River, where they began building Fort Early, to be used as a supply base as they advanced downriver. After struggling for weeks with delays, Blackshear's troops were plagued by hunger, cold, and sickness. They were forty miles west of Hartford, the closest white settlement (Grant, 709–710, 714–715; Owsley, 175; Chalker, 108–112).

Suddenly, Blackshear received orders to march back to Georgia, where British forces were raiding the state's Atlantic coast. Near the end of January, the Allied Creeks, about 1,000 strong, headed south to the junction of the Flint and Chattahoochee. Hawkins served as commander, although his age and ill health caused him to relinquish command in the field to William McIntosh. Without the support of Blackshear's militia, Hawkins hesitated to advance on Apalachicola. The Allied Creeks launched several raids across the border against the rebel Muscogees and Seminoles in Spanish Florida, but they did not feel strong enough to risk an attack on Prospect Bluff (Owsley, 175; Grant, 677, 713, 714; Chalker, 113–115).

Secure in their new stronghold, Nicholls's forces never carried out any serious raids against the Georgia frontier, but they did keep 3,500 American troops—Blue's expedition, Georgia militia, and Allied Creeks—engaged, preventing them from aiding Jackson. Nicholls also was able to interrupt communications between the Georgia frontier and Mobile, and Old Hickory did not learn until much later that the Allied Creeks and Georgia militia had failed to neutralize the British base on the Apalachicola (Owsley, 135, 174).

What Jackson did know was that the British definitely were poised to strike New Orleans. It still made more sense to him for the enemy to invade through Mobile, so as a precaution he strengthened his defenses there and at Fort Bowyer, leaving them under the command of Brigadier General James Winchester. The rest of his forces were headed for New Orleans. Old Hickory dispatched Coffee and his mounted brigade to Baton Rouge to rendezvous with recently raised volunteer troops coming down the Mississippi from Tennessee and Kentucky. Jackson himself, exhausted and sick but as indomitable as ever, arrived in the Crescent City on December 1 (Remini, *Jackson*, 1977, 244–245).

The British expedition of 7,500 veterans under Major General Sir Edward Packenham got under way from Jamaica on November 26, headed for New Orleans. The redcoats landed on December 13, and after two weeks of preliminary probing and maneuvering, Packenham prepared to assault Jackson's main position along the Rodriguez canal. To defend the city, Jackson had only 3,100 men, but they included many veterans who had seen hard service with him fighting the Red Sticks in the Alabama swamps. John Coffee was there with his rugged Tennessee mounted riflemen, dubbed the "dirty shirts" by the British. Another Jackson crony, William Carroll, commanded a brigade of Tennessee militia. Thomas Hinds's blue-jacketed Mississippi dragoons earned a reputation for boldness and skill in scouting and harassing the enemy. Pushmataha and his Choctaw warriors, particularly effective as snipers, were posted on the swampy American left flank and fought back a British attack. Sam Dale served as a dispatch rider for Jackson during the fighting (Owsley, 156–164; Chartrand, 81; DeRosier, 36; Heidler and Heidler, *Encyclopedia*, 104, 142).

In the key January 8 assault, 291 British soldiers died in the cypress swamps in a futile attempt to storm the American defenses, while 1,262 were wounded, and 484 more were captured or missing. Major Edward Nicholls had accompanied Packenham, bringing along Josiah Francis and other Red Stick and Seminole chiefs to watch Old Hickory get beaten. Instead, they witnessed the destruction of Packenham's army, and one of the chiefs, Ecumchat Emaultau of Hickory Ground, reported that "[t]he ground appeared to him covered with dead, wounded." Packenham died during the assault, along with his two subcommanders. In an incredibly lopsided American victory, the greatest triumph of the war, Jackson lost only seven men killed and six wounded. And neither side was aware that American and British negotiators had signed a peace agreement in Europe on December 24 (Remini, *Jackson*, 1977, 285; Owsley, 134, 170; Grant, 718, 722; Sudgen, 300).

But the redcoats were not ready to quit. Admiral Cochrane decided to fall back on his original plan for an offensive against Mobile. Major General John Lambert would land troops south of the town, while Cochrane provided naval support in Mobile Bay. Nicholls and his red allies would strike from Apalachicola, capturing Fort Stoddert and cutting Mobile off from communications with the north; then they would attack the town. Cochrane wanted to act swiftly before Jackson could move his army from New Orleans. First he would neutralize Fort Bowyer (Owsley, 170–171; Heidler and Heidler, *Old Hickory's War*, 49).

The redcoats made their second attack on Fort Bowyer on February 8, and this time they did not repeat their mistakes of five months earlier. Lambert disembarked the bulk of his army on Dauphin Island, across the bay from Fort Bowyer. He landed 1,400 soldiers, with ample artillery support, three miles east of Fort Bowyer, and the assault column moved on the fort. During the next three days, the British tightened the knot around Fort Bowyer and had sixteen siege guns in place. Seeing no hope of resisting and no chance of reinforcement, Colonel William Lawrence surrendered on the afternoon of February 11. The British captured the 375-man U.S. garrison, at the cost of thirteen men killed and twenty-six wounded (Coker, 55; Owsley, 171).

Now Mobile itself seemed in jeopardy. Jackson had withdrawn the Third U.S. Infantry from Mobile, anticipating that the Georgia militia—he did not know that they had in fact marched back into Georgia—would arrive in time to defend the Gulf City, where General Winchester now had fewer than 3,000 poorly armed soldiers. The Gulf City was spared almost certain disaster when news arrived that British and American diplomats had signed the Treaty of Ghent, ending the fighting. Old Hickory got the word on February 13. The war was over. News of treaty reached Hawkins and his Allied Creek warriors still at the junction of the Flint and Chattahoochee later in the month. Hawkins ordered his warriors discharged on March 20 so that the red men could return home in time to prepare their fields for spring planting (Owsley, 172–175; Coker, 60; Grant, 724).

Although peace had been restored between the United States and Britain, the British base at Apalachicola remained, with Major Nicholls commanding at least 100 marines and Captain Woodbine acting as Indian agent. Francis and McQueen were still there—and in British uniforms. Renegade Muscogees and Seminoles continued to drift in, as well as runaway slaves, and by the beginning of 1815 there were close to 3,000 red people at Prospect Bluff, including women and children. Of these, there were at least 1,600 warriors and 250 armed blacks. Hawkins reported that the fort had "an abundant supply of clothing, arms and ammunition." Shortages of food still remained a serious problem, even though the British fleet was able to furnish some supplies. The fort at Prospect Bluff continued to take shape as Red Sticks, Seminoles, and blacks worked to complete the fortifications. By the opening of 1815, a ten-foot-wide moat surrounded the post. A log-and-earthen parapet with several mounted guns would soon follow. It was clear that the British were in no hurry to leave (Owsley, 175; Covington, 36; Saunt, 279–280; Grant, 717–718.).

Things might have gone much differently in America's war with Britain if the redcoats' military mission to the southern red men had dovetailed with the onset of the Red Stick rebellion. Had the British committed more men and supplies to aiding the Red Sticks and Seminoles, they could have established an Indian buffer state that would have effectively blocked American westward expansion. The British might have secured New Orleans as well. It was the folly of the Red Sticks in taking up the war club too soon—and the delay of the British in providing full-scale military aid until after Horseshoe Bend—that thwarted this plan. Had the Creek War not erupted, the United States would not have moved troops into the southwest. There would have been no American forces—no regulars, no battle-hardened Tennessee volunteers—to resist a British invasion. And no Jackson (Remini, *Jackson*, 1977, 300, 305; Owsley, 97, 190).

CHAPTER 17

A Troubled Peace

The end of the war between the United States and Britain did little to bring real peace to the southwestern frontier. The Red Sticks, in exile in Spanish Florida, never had accepted that the fighting was over. The Allied Creeks, angry over the loss of half of their nation's territory in the Treaty of Fort Jackson, were confused and uncertain about their future. British marines still occupied Prospect Bluff, and the Spanish flag still flew over Florida. The Seminoles remained defiant and ready to take up the war club if provoked. And a tide of restless, impatient white frontier settlers waited to be unleashed.

"When they told me they would assist me," Big Warrior lamented, "they never told me they would take away my land." The Allied Creeks had more to worry about than the loss of lands. No pay had arrived for their warriors for their services during the war. Neither had the food that the government had promised. When it finally would arrive, the red men would find much of it rotten and crawling with maggots. Families were hungry, and the threat of famine was a grim reality. Besides this, the government had held back the yearly annuity payments. The Muscogees must have wondered if things could possibly get any worse (Grant, 757; Griffith, 166; Heidler and Heidler, "Between," 279).

Conditions were no better in the Seminole country. So many Red Stick refugees had migrated to Florida that they soon outnumbered "native" Seminoles by two to one. The inrush of these refugees was straining the scant food supplies at Prospect Bluff, "nearly in a state of starvation and wretchedness," according to one British officer. A visitor reported in April 1815, "[T]he Indians in the country are living altogether on alligators. I have heard for a certainty an Indian woman ate her own child." The Red Sticks and Seminoles also had good reason to be disturbed about the Fort Jackson treaty, since neither had sent representatives to the peace conference (Griffith, 168–169; Heidler and Heidler, *Old Hickory's War,* 32; Saunt, 282; Grant, 724).

In spite of the hardships, one group's resolve remained undeterred. The Maroons, or African American Seminoles, were becoming more entrenched in Spanish Florida. In addition to groups of runaway slaves in established Seminole towns, several independent, well-armed black settlements had sprung up, the largest one north of Mikasuki. There was also a large colony of Maroons at Bowlegs' Town on the Suwannee River and another one at Tampa Bay. Many Maroons remained at Prospect Bluff, where Colonel Edward Nicholls's black marines kept watch. Nicholls gave his black troops the option of migrating to British colonies to receive land and a chance to live free. Numbers of black families took him up on his offer and made their homes in the West Indies, and some settled as far north as Halifax, Nova Scotia (Braund, 633–634; Owsley, 183; Littlefield, 72–73; Covington, 37; Saunt, 282–283; Wright, 190).

Although the British defeat at New Orleans had largely convinced Francis, McQueen, Kinache, and the black leaders that they could no longer count on the redcoats for military support, they still had one last card to play—the possibility that Britain, through diplomatic negotiation, could manage to restore the lost Muscogee lands. To cement their alliance, thirty Seminole and Red Stick leaders signed an agreement on March 10, 1815, asking the British to establish a permanent trade presence in Florida (Littlefield, 72; Covington, 36).

The Red Sticks hoped that their trump card would be article 9 of the Treaty of Ghent, which provided that the United States restore all land and property taken from Native American tribes during the war—actually nullifying the Treaty of Fort Jackson. Nicholls and his marines at Apalachicola were there to see that the United States honored its agreement. In ongoing correspondence with Benjamin Hawkins in the spring of 1815, Nicholls continued to insist that the American troops evacuate the Muscogee lands. Hawkins accused Nicholls of having "some speculative project of your own," in the manner of William Augustus Bowles. Still Nicholls assured his red allies that Britain would assist them in regaining their lands (Grant, 734; Remini, *Jackson,* 1977, 302).

But any actual redrawing of boundaries in the southwest would hinge on what Andrew Jackson would do, and he clearly had no intention of cooperating. Jackson argued that the Muscogees had already made a separate peace at Fort Jackson in 1814 and were technically at peace with the United States when the Treaty of Ghent was signed, so article 9 did not apply to them. The red men that Nicholls spoke for were Seminoles living in Spanish Florida who did not represent the Creek nation. Afraid to antagonize white westerners who looked on Jackson as a national hero, federal officials lacked the means to force him to comply and made no effort to do so (Remini, *Jackson*, 1977, 302–303; Owsley, 180).

Nor did Britain try to force the issue. Instead, they sacrificed their red allies in the south. The 1817 Rush-Bagot agreement would provide for a demilitarized border between the United States and Canada. The United States would make no more attempts to conquer Canada; in turn Britain would give the Americans a free hand to expand to the south and west. Britain's attempt to create a Native American buffer state between Spanish Florida and the southern United States was over (Remini, *Jackson*, 1977, 303–304; Owsley, 182–183).

Sad and discouraged, Nicholls gave in and evacuated Prospect Bluff in the summer of 1815, taking along the Red Stick prophet Josiah Francis. Back in London, Nicholls exerted all efforts to get the British government to honor its pledge to the red allies. He begged his superiors to create a permanent British presence in Florida and to formally recognize the Muscogees as an independent nation. But the matter had been settled, and London simply paid no heed to his appeals (Boyd, 72; Remini, *Jackson*, 1977, 304–305).

Francis, accompanied by his son, lingered in England for a year and a half. He met with Lord Bathurst and with the prince regent. Admirers showered him with presents and money. But British leaders feared that the Americans would go to war again if they attempted any more interference on the southern frontier, and after years of fighting, they were ready for peace. Francis left England on December 30, 1816, and whiled away the early months of 1817 in Nassau, still dreaming of his plans for Muscogee independence (Covington, 37).

With the redcoats gone, the continuing scarcity of food forced the Seminoles, Red Sticks, and Maroons at Prospect Bluff to part company. Peter McQueen, with most of his warriors and their families, moved eastward to a settlement on the Ecofina River. Other refugees moved south toward Tampa Bay, where they formed new settlements, and others moved into already-settled villages near Apalachee and Suwannee. By 1815–1816 it was becoming increasingly harder to distinguish between Seminoles, dissatisfied Lower Muscogees, and refugee Red Sticks. American accounts lumped all together under the label Seminole (Saunt, 282; Griffith, 189; Porter, 16; Covington, 37).

The African American allies were not so quick to leave Prospect Bluff. Several hundred black rebels, well armed and well fortified, lingered in what Americans now called the Negro Fort. A Spanish visitor wrote that the defenders "say they will die to a man rather than return" to slavery. So they stayed, much to the unease of the Spanish and the smoldering anger of the white settlers across the Georgia frontier (Remini, *Jackson*, 1977, 308; Saunt, 283).

The U.S. government began surveying the surrendered Muscogee lands in the summer of 1815. Especially along the Chattahoochee and Flint Rivers, red men who had either remained neutral during the Creek War or actually aided the white armies watched these developments with great alarm. It was a monstrous land grab. Thousands of squatters, mostly Georgians, flooded into the ceded lands like locusts. Along the Alabama River, descendants of Alexander McGillivray watched helplessly as the newcomers verbally abused the red people, beat them, and destroyed their livestock and property. The new secretary of war, William H. Crawford, wrote Benjamin Hawkins in October 1815, "The effect of these settlements is to place the very worst part of our citizens in the possession of the very best part of the public lands" (Griffith, 165–166; Martin, 166–167; Heidler and Heidler, "Between," 278).

And not only the Muscogees were upset. In January 1816, a delegation from the Cherokee nation—including Major Ridge, agent Return J. Meigs, John Walker, and young John Ross—made their way to Washington to meet with Crawford and President James Madison. They hoped to prevent Old Hickory from ceding—as part of the Treaty of Fort Jackson—over two million acres of Cherokee land south of the Tennessee River. The chiefs presented impressive evidence to support their claims, and Crawford ordered the Cherokees' lands returned to them along with $25,500 in damages and the back pay for their service during the Creek War. A livid Jackson fumed that the American people were being robbed of fertile land that would only be wasted by the red men, and his views were echoed by a flood of protests from westerners. By the summer of 1816, Crawford threw up his hands and gave in to the pressure. He told the Cherokees that they must surrender their lands south of the Tennessee—plus over a million acres of land north of the river. To soothe Cherokee feelings, there would be yearly payments, there would be bribes for individual chiefs, and the reparations and back pay would be paid (Griffith, 166–168; Remini, *Jackson*, 1977, 324–325; McLoughlin, 197–203).

The Cherokee National Council rejected the government's demands, refusing to give up the disputed lands. Meigs wrote Jackson that the Cherokees subscribed to a mistaken belief that theirs was a sovereign nation with inviolable boundaries. In reality the Cherokees were now dependent on the government to protect them from the flood of white settlers. They had no choice but to cede more lands whenever the government demanded it. Old Hickory thoroughly agreed. Meeting with Cherokee delegates in September 1816 and assuring them of friendship, he made them understand that he expected them to cede back the lands north and south of the Tennessee River that Crawford and Madison had agreed to return to them. Jackson was able to cajole, browbeat, and bribe enough of the Lower Towns chiefs—including Creek War veterans Richard Brown, John Lowery, and John Walker—who by now had become willing to emigrate west, as well as a few more on the National Council, and the result was a "treaty" signed by a minority of chiefs giving up the lands in Alabama (Remini, *Jackson*, 1977, 325–329; McLoughlin, 203–206, 209–211).

Jackson next dealt with the Chickasaws, resorting to secretly bribing individual chiefs to get what he wanted—cession of their lands in north-western Alabama. The Chickasaw chiefs signed the treaty on September 20. Guided by the powerful Colbert brothers, the Chickasaws yielded even more land two years later. Next were the Choctaws, who had fought so loyally for Jackson under Pushmataha. At Jackson's direction, a commission composed of John McKee, John Coffee, and John Rhea wrenched land east of the Tombigbee from the Choctaws in October 1816 (Remini, *Jackson*, 1977, 329–330, 337–340).

The land cessions coerced from the Cherokees, Chickasaws, and Choctaws, plus the enormous Muscogee cession of 1814, opened up vast western lands to white settlement and left the southeastern tribes weakened and isolated, now reduced to mere semi-autonomous fragments within Georgia and the new states of Alabama and Mississippi. All that remained of the old Muscogee nation was a chunk of east central Alabama and western Georgia. The Cherokee nation shrank to its core nucleus in mountainous north Georgia (and adjacent areas in Alabama, Tennessee, and North Carolina). The Choctaw domain was reduced to what is now central Mississippi, the Chickasaw lands to northern Mississippi. Cut off from all of these were the Seminoles in Florida.

While Jackson was busy tearing away more land from the southeastern tribes, clashes between whites and red men near the Florida border were escalating. White settlers moving into the ceded Muscogee lands often stole the red people's livestock, burned homes, and wantonly killed whoever got in their way. Muscogee raiders retaliated by stealing livestock from the whites, and sometimes they killed white settlers. Surveyors complained of intimidation by large groups of Muscogees who followed them (Covington, 38, 41).

Jackson's military successor in the southern district, thirty-nine-year-old Major General Edmund P. Gaines, was a career officer who had served in the army for seventeen years. Gaines built a chain of forts to protect the surveyors and keep the peace between the red men and the whites. Two of the new forts—Fort Gaines on the east bank of the Chattahoochee and Fort Scott near the junction of the Flint and Chattahoochee, southwest of present-day Bainbridge, Georgia—lay close to the border with Spanish Florida. Completed in June 1816, Fort Scott was to be an observation post for monitoring the Seminoles across the border and especially the Maroons at Negro Fort (Covington, 37–38; Boyd, 77).

Jackson's orders to Gaines instructed him that "until murderers are delivered and the stolen property is returned no Creeks can remain in ceded territory except friendly parties…all others to be treated as enemies." When Gaines saw how miserable and pathetic the red men were, he decided just to leave them alone. The commander at Fort Scott, Colonel Duncan L. Clinch, proposed a more aggressive approach. After two of his men were killed by Seminole raiders, Clinch asked permission to launch a retaliatory strike to destroy every village between Fort Gaines and Fort Scott. Jackson and Gaines preferred simply to beef up the defenses at Fort Scott (Covington, 38).

Jackson was more concerned about Negro Fort (or Fort Apalachicola), just sixty miles south of the border. He had written Governor Mauricio de Zuniga at Pensacola in April 1816 to complain about the fort and to demand that the Spanish do something about it. Old Hickory threatened that the United States would take action if the Spanish failed to do so. Zuniga replied that he had to wait for orders from the captain general in Cuba (Boyd, 76).

The Maroon fortress at Prospect Bluff had become the largest and most stoutly defended community of its kind ever seen in the southeastern United States. Protected by a high bluff in its front and swamps in its rear, Negro Fort lay 500 feet from the Apalachicola River bank. An eight-sided earthen fort with a larger rectangular stockade covering seven acres, it had bastions at the eastern corners with parapets fifteen feet high and eighteen feet thick. The walls bristled with an array of artillery—four heavy pieces (24-pounders) and six light pieces. The garrison of 250 to 300 black men was well armed with an arsenal of thousands of muskets and plenty of ammunition. The rebels also had at least one schooner, possibly more, armed with cannon and patrolling Apalachicola Bay for enemy vessels (Wright, 183; Boyd, 71–72, 80; Littlefield, 72–73; Patrick, 28; Griffith, 174; Porter, 16; Saunt, 284).

Three black leaders shared command of the Negro Fort community. The senior commander appears to have been a wiry, clever thirty-six-year-old Pensacolan named Garzon (or Garcia). The educated Cyrus, also from Pensacola, may have been the "Siras" who reportedly aided the Red Sticks in cutting down the picket walls at Fort Mims. And Prince, a master carpenter, was an experienced fighter who had led black Seminoles in combat with American troops in the summer of 1812; later, George Woodbine had recruited him and offered him a lieutenant's commission. Many of the black officers at Prospect Bluff wore British uniforms. Also in the fort were about twenty Choctaws, possibly a remnant of the group who had taken Tecumseh's talk in 1811 and joined the Red Sticks, and a few Seminoles from Bowlegs' Town (Saunt, 283–284; Griffith, 174; Porter, 16; Boyd, 76; Martin, 222–223 n. 41; Braund, 634).

Besides the armed black garrison, there were about 1,000 men, women, and children who had settled in the area around Negro Fort. By the summer of 1816 their cultivated fields of corn stretched some fifty miles up the river. The community at Prospect Bluff enjoyed regular trade and communication with the Maroons, refugee Red Sticks, and Seminoles in the Suwannee settlements, at Mikasuki, and on Tampa Bay. Their resolve was still strong. Kinache reported in June 1816 that the black defenders at Prospect Bluff "were determined to perish before surrendering" (Littlefield, 72–73; Saunt, 282–283, 285–286, 288).

The situation at Prospect Bluff absorbed much of Benjamin Hawkins's energies in the last months of his life. In the spring of 1816, the agent planned to send an Allied Creek party under Little Prince down the Apalachicola to gather intelligence on the fort, but he had to abandon this plan when the Muscogees—having gotten wind of American plans to build more forts on the river—backed out. The Maroons anticipated an American attack and remained defiant. Garzon sent word to Colonel Clinch at Fort Scott that "he was waiting for him and regretted the delay." The aging Kinache, concerned about what might happen if Hawkins unleashed the Allied Creeks, was able to secure a temporary truce. "I don't fear the Americans," the Seminole chief wrote from Mikasuki in May 1816, "but rather the many Indians who are coming with them" (Boyd, 76; Saunt, 287–288).

Hawkins died on June 6 at his agency on the Flint. He had coped with illness and frustration as he saw his plan for the Muscogees unraveling before his eyes. Brokenhearted over their plight and their future, he must have been galled greatly when an Augusta newspaper criticized him for his siding with the red men. Hawkins replied that if the president could find anyone else to do the job, then he was welcome to it. "This department," he wrote, "has always been strewed with thorns" (Pound, 112).

An American military operation into Spanish Florida was a delicate undertaking, but any attack on U.S. soldiers by the blacks at Negro Fort would open the door. Jackson and Gaines proposed to supply the new American post at Fort Scott by sending transports up the Apalachicola, and if the Maroons attempted to interfere with the convoy—as they were sure they would—it would justify a retaliation. Jackson and Gaines planned a joint army-navy operation against Prospect Bluff in July 1816. From New Orleans, the schooners *General Pike* and *Semilante,* accompanied by two gunboats, got under way under Sailing Master Jairus Loomis. At the same time, Colonel Duncan L. Clinch moved south along the Apalachicola from Fort Scott with a detachment of regulars from the Fourth U.S. Infantry (Patrick, 28; Owsley, 183).

When Loomis arrived at the mouth of the Apalachicola, he waited for word from Clinch before proceeding upriver. On July 15, Maroons in a small vessel emerged from the river, fired a volley at some of the American crewmen, then withdrew hastily. Two days later there was a deadly clash when Loomis sent a detachment of men ashore to fill water kegs. About forty Maroons ambushed them, killing three and taking one man prisoner. The following day near Negro Fort, Allied Creeks captured a

Maroon wearing a white scalp on his belt. As details of the incident emerged, the Americans learned that the blacks had covered the prisoner with tar and set him afire, burning him alive (Griffith, 174–175; Patrick, 30; Heidler and Heidler, *Old Hickory's War*, 71).

On July 17, Clinch's column of 116 regulars was just leaving Fort Scott and by dusk had rendezvoused with William McIntosh and 150 Allied Creek warriors from Coweta. The Red Sticks regarded McIntosh as an implacable enemy and traitor, and thirty rebel chiefs had signed a statement in March 1815 denouncing him and placing a price on his head. "He has caused much blood to be spilt," they declared. This did not seem to bother McIntosh, who—with Hawkins dead now and Big Warrior and Little Prince indecisive—was emerging as the strongman of the Muscogee nation (Patrick, 29; Boyd, 78; Griffith, 170).

The allied column reached the neighborhood of Negro Fort on July 20. Clinch directed McIntosh's warriors to surround the fort and to keep the black gunners busy. The Maroons fired back with their artillery with little effect. The fort was too strong to take by assault, so Clinch and McIntosh waited for Loomis and the gunboats to come upriver with their cannon (Griffith, 175; Patrick, 30).

Many of the blacks were not in the fort but had already moved farther inland on news of the approach of the enemy. Prince had accompanied one party, traveling by canoe and pirogue to settlements on the Suwannee and to Tampa Bay. Some went overland to Mikasuki, which had become a "refuge for those who don't belong elsewhere," according to the Spanish commandant at St. Marks. It is possible that no more than about sixty men remained in the fort, besides their women and children, under the command of Garzon (Saunt, 284–285, 287–288; Boyd, 81).

Clinch sent McIntosh and two other chiefs under a flag of truce to the fort on the evening of July 23, and the Allied Creeks called on the Maroons to surrender. Garzon showered them with abuse, chastising them for working with the Americans. The British had left him in command of the fort, he declared, and he had no intention of giving it up. He would sink any American ship that tried to sail past. As a further gesture of defiance, the black defenders quickly hoisted two flags—a British flag and the red flag of death (Patrick, 30–31).

By July 25, Loomis's naval convoy had prowled its way upriver, and the two commanders met to map out their plan of attack. Clinch wanted to erect a battery on the west bank of the Apalachicola across from Negro Fort. His regulars crossed the river, leaving a small detachment with McIntosh's Allied Creeks on the east bank, and waited for the transport *Similante* to land some eighteen-pounders that night. But first Loomis and Clinch decided to let the gunboats try to bombard the fort with their twelve-pounders. The two little vessels got into position at daybreak on July 27 (Boyd, 79; Patrick, 31).

A barrage of cannon fire from the fort's heavy guns greeted the two gunboats as they maneuvered into firing range. But the black gunners were inexperienced, and the shots fell short. Loomis's gunboats returned fire, and the naval cannonballs just bounced off the fort's walls. The exchange of gunfire lasted perhaps fifteen minutes. Loomis switched to a different tactic—heating the cannonballs red-hot and then firing them into the fort, hoping to set off a fire inside the stockade (Griffith, 175–176; Saunt, 288).

It was a lucky shot from one of the American gunboats that sealed the fate of Negro Fort. The first hot cannonball fired struck the fort's heavily stocked powder magazine. Someone had left its door open, and the cannonball sailed right through. The resulting explosion blew Negro Fort sky-high (Griffith, 176; Mahon, "First Seminole War," 63).

When the smoke cleared all that remained of Negro Fort was a smoldering wreck. The fortress had been completely leveled. Even the allies had not expected such total annihilation. As they cautiously approached the burning ruins, they saw what the explosion had done. It was "beyond description," Clinch reported. Mangled bodies of men, women, and children lay among the wreckage, buried in the sand, and even impaled upon or dangling from the pine trees. The survivors, many of them badly wounded, included Garzon, the black commander, and the chief of the Choctaw party that had remained with the fort to the end. Clinch at first ordered the captives treated humanely. It was then that he learned of the fate of the captive sailor whom the blacks had burned alive. Angered, he turned Garzon and the Choctaw chief over to the Allied Creeks, who executed them both (Griffith, 176).

Clinch had promised McIntosh free rein in looting the captured stronghold. The red allies plundered the fort, capturing clothing and supplies, as well as gunpowder. The quantity of arms that the blacks had hoarded at Prospect Bluff surprised even Clinch, who probably regretted his decision to turn the Allied Creeks loose. Some 2,500 muskets, fifty carbines, 400 pistols, and 500 swords all fell into their hands. The soldiers and Allied Creeks burned and plundered black settlements nearby. McIntosh and the Allied Creeks carried the black captives back up the Chattahoochee to Fort Mitchell (Boyd, 80–81; Mahon, "First Seminole War," 63; Griffith, 178; Littlefield, 74).

After transferring the cargo of the two transports to flatboats for easier passage, Clinch and his troops made their way back upriver. They had learned that Seminole war parties planned to ambush them along their route back. Peter McQueen had assembled a force of Red Stick warriors to engage the Allied Creeks, but when he learned that Negro Fort had already been destroyed, he reconsidered and withdrew. Perhaps the spectacular destruction of Negro Fort had the red men awed for the time being. Those Maroons who had escaped fled to the east and eventually joined the blacks and Seminoles on the Suwannee. Loomis destroyed the remains of the fort and village at Prospect Bluff on August 3 and set sail for New Orleans (Boyd, 81; Littlefield, 73–74).

The Americans were so pleased with the destruction of Negro Fort—and so confident that it would send a powerful warning to the Seminoles—that they evacuated Fort Scott in the fall of 1816, leaving George Perryman, one of Kinache's sons, as a caretaker at the post. But renegade Seminoles arrived at the fort, plundered it, and ordered Perryman to leave. Raids along the southern Georgia frontier began again, and the rebels murdered several settlers. Disturbing reports began coming in. In Fowltown, one informant reported, the rebels "speak in the most contemptuous manner of the Americans, and threaten to have satisfaction for what has been done—meaning the destruction of the negro fort." Another reported some 600 armed Maroons in the Suwannee towns, well disciplined and training under the command of Nero, one of Bowlegs's slaves. And there was an equal number of Seminoles under Bowlegs and McQueen, anxious to take on either the Americans or McIntosh's Allied Creeks, to "let them know they had something more to do than…at Appalachicola" (Boyd, 84; Littlefield, 74–75; Porter, 18).

In the fall of 1816, James Monroe won the U.S. presidency, defeating his closest rival, William H. Crawford (whom Jackson by now despised). Jackson already had a good working relationship with Monroe, especially since both were committed to acquiring Florida from the Spanish. Jackson advised Monroe that the sooner white families settled the Old Southwest, the sooner the security of the American frontier would be assured (Remini, *Jackson*, 1977, 331, 341).

Meanwhile, a new infusion of leadership breathed life into the refugee Muscogees' struggle. In January 1817, Alexander Arbuthnot, an elderly Scottish merchant from the Bahamas, had arrived at Ochlockonee Sound in his schooner *Chance*. Arbuthnot hoped to take advantage of the decline of the John Forbes Company, which had been tilting toward the Americans, and to set up a trading post of his own in the Apalachicola country. On a trip from Nassau in June 1817, he brought back the prophet Josiah Francis, returned from his sojourn in England and the Bahamas (Covington, 38–39).

The rebel leaders now turned to Arbuthnot as their final hope. He could supply them with arms and aid them in one more campaign against the Americans. Twelve of these leaders signed a document on June 17, 1817, giving Arbuthnot authority to act as their agent. Arbuthnot had now replaced Nicholls as the spokesman for the red men in Florida, and his name began to surface in correspondence with British officials in Washington and the Bahamas and American military officers on the southern frontier (Covington, 39).

Arbuthnot seemed to accept his newfound responsibility, as well as the lucrative opportunities it provided him, and—like Nicholls before him—

he came to respect and admire the red men. "These men," he wrote, "are children of nature; leave them in their forests to till their field and hunt the stag, and graze their cattle, their ideas will extend no further; and the honest trader in supplying their wants may make a handsome profit of them." He went on to allow that "They have been ill treated by the English and robbed by the Americans." Arbuthnot also cultivated a good relationship with the Spanish commander at St. Marks, who permitted him to operate in the area and to store his goods at the fort. The Scot did not urge the red men to make war on the Americans and sincerely believed that he could help them recover their lands through legal negotiation. But Arbuthnot failed to appreciate the seriousness of American military activities on the southern frontier (Covington, 39–40; Owsley, 185).

Returning from the Bahamas in October 1817, Arbuthnot now had with him two white men whose plans for Florida differed considerably from his own. George Woodbine and Robert C. Ambrister, both former officers who had served with Edward Nicholls, planned to use the Seminoles, Maroons, and assorted white adventurers to seize Florida from the Spanish. Woodbine viewed an independent Florida as a natural outgrowth of the wave of revolutions sweeping through Spain's Latin American colonies. Ambrister became especially active among the blacks on the Suwannee, drilling them and encouraging them to stand firm against the white men. It was Woodbine and Ambrister, the last of the Florida opportunists, who were the real instigators of violence against the Americans (Porter, 18; Covington, 40; Littlefield, 75; Owsley, 185).

Arbuthnot, Woodbine, and Ambrister planned to establish a trading post on the Suwannee. They made contact with Bowlegs and some of his black and Seminole warriors, who came aboard the *Chance* and discussed at some length Woodbine's plot to seize control of Florida. Arbuthnot also met with Peter McQueen and Kinache, who seemed to be operating together, although separately from Bowlegs. Arbuthnot promised to write to British minister Charles Bagot in Washington and articulate some of their grievances (Covington, 40–41).

Francis and his family settled three miles from the Spanish post at St. Marks, at a site along the Wakulla River. He may have mellowed in his attitude toward the Americans, and there is evidence that he was now a "moderate," ready to counsel peace and cooperation. The prophet had given thought to returning to Nassau, but Arbuthnot convinced him that he could do more good by remaining among the red men (Covington, 39; Owsley, 182).

Tensions continued to escalate along the southern frontier as red men and white men raided, stole from, and killed each other in the ceded lands. Gaines sent Major David E. Twiggs with regulars of the Seventh Infantry to reoccupy Fort Scott in July 1817, then increased the size of the garrison and came there himself in November. Gaines angrily communicated his concerns to Bowlegs and Kinache. "You have murdered many of my people," he charged, "and…you harbor a great many of my black people among you at Sahwannee" (Covington, 41; Boyd, 84).

Kinache fired back:

You charge me with killing your people, stealing your cattle and burning your houses; it is I that have cause to complain of the Americans. While one American has been justly killed while in act of stealing cattle, more than four Indians while hunting have been murdered by these lawless freebooters. I harbor no Negroes…I shall use force to stop any armed Americans from passing my towns or my lands. (Covington, 41)

Much of the new troubles centered around Fowltown (Tutalossee Talofa), east of the Flint fifteen miles from Fort Scott. For some time now, Fowltown warriors had been suspected of ambushing army supply wagons. This was the town of Neamathla, a Red Stick chief who had taken part in the capture of Fort Mims and had fled with Francis into Florida after the debacle at Horseshoe Bend. Soldiers from Fort Scott sometimes crossed the river to gather firewood. Neamathla made it clear that he considered this an intrusion, and he informed Gaines that he would not tolerate another such incident. "I warn you," he gave notice, "not to cross nor cut a stick of wood in the east side of the Flint. That land is mine. I am directed by the power above and below to protect and defend it. I shall do so" (Owen, 59; Mahon, "First Seminole War," 64; Heidler and Heidler, "Between," 277; Covington, 41; Boyd, 85).

Stung by what he saw as Indian insolence, Gaines issued an "invitation" to Neamathla to come to Fort Scott to discuss matters. When the chief failed to reply, Gaines ordered out Major Twiggs and 250 soldiers with orders to bring Neamathla in. Twiggs's troops made an all-night march and struck Fowltown at daybreak on November 21, but the rebels spotted them moving through the trees and gave the alarm. In the skirmish that followed, the soldiers killed four red men and one woman. Neamathla and the rest of the rebels escaped into the swamp. In a search of the village, Twiggs's soldiers found a British officer's uniform coat, along with a letter from Nicholls certifying that Neamathla had been a loyal ally. Several days later, American troops returned to Fowltown and put it to the torch. This time the soldiers lost one man killed and two wounded as they exchanged fire with the rebels (Covington, 41–42; Mahon, "First Seminole War," 64; Heidler and Heidler, *Old Hickory's War*, 104).

On November 30, Neamathla retaliated. His warriors waylaid an army keelboat commanded by Lieutenant Richard W. Scott on the Apalachicola. The transport—carrying forty soldiers along with their wives and children—was making its way upriver toward Fort Scott when a strong current forced the boat close to the shore. From cover of the bank, the

Seminoles opened fire, killing most of the soldiers in the first volley. The rebels boarded the boat, killed and scalped all of the women except one, and slaughtered the children by bashing their brains out, and they took one woman captive. Six soldiers were able to plunge into the river and escape, making their way to Fort Scott to report the horrifying details of the massacre (Mahon, "First Seminole War," 64; Covington, 42; Heidler and Heidler, *Old Hickory's War*, 107).

The peace on the southern frontier was deteriorating rapidly, and by late December white settlers were streaming into Fort Gaines for protection. A new war now seemed unavoidable. Gaines planned a retaliatory strike against the Seminoles, but before he could respond he received orders to head for Amelia Island, long a contested area between Spanish Florida and the United States. The new secretary of war, John C. Calhoun, ordered Jackson to the Florida border on December 26, giving him "full power to conduct the war as he may think best." Monroe and Calhoun expected Old Hickory to solve the Florida dilemma as only he could do it—by taking it from the Spanish by force. The leaders of the complex forces at work in Florida—Francis, McQueen, Neamathla, Kinache, Arbuthnot, Woodbine, and Ambrister—all would see their fates decided in one final confrontation with Sharp Knife (Boyd, 87; Covington, 42; Mahon, "First Seminole War," 64).

CHAPTER 18

The Return of Sharp Knife

As the year 1818 opened, terrifying rumors set nerves along the Ocmulgee on edge as virtually every outpost along the southern frontier was reported in danger of attack. Conditions were not quite that grim. On the Flint, Fort Scott's garrison had more to fear from starvation than from marauding Seminoles, because their food supplies were nearly exhausted. By January 13, the soldiers' meat rations were entirely used up, and the fort's new commander, Lieutenant Colonel Matthew Arbuckle, was desperate (Heidler and Heidler, *Old Hickory's War*, 112–113, 122, 126).

On the Ocmulgee, the Georgia militia was in no better shape. Hoping to head off a rebel attack, twenty-seven-year-old Brigadier General Thomas Glascock did his best to cope with the old twin dilemma of short-term enlistments and an inadequate supply system. So far his hungry soldiers, assembling at Fort Hawkins, had accomplished nothing. "There was little done," wrote Major Thomas S. Woodward, a veteran of Floyd's campaign against the Red Sticks, "except foot-racing, wrestling and drinking whisky, when we could get it" (G. B. Smith, 162, 294; T. Woodward, 135).

Glascock utilized the road (built by David Blackshear's Georgia militia three years earlier) from Hartford on the Ocmulgee to their forward supply base at Fort Early on the Flint. Delayed by heavy winter rains that turned the road into mud, Glascock's troops were forced to abandon their wagons and load their supplies on packhorses. Even more disturbing, they learned that a war party of rebel Fowltown Muscogees was in the area. Glascock sent a small detachment back to escort a pack train from Hartford, but some twenty or thirty rebels ambushed the column and killed two soldiers—an officer whom they decapitated and a private whom they scalped (G. B. Smith, 162; Chalker, 127).

Fort Gaines, on the east bank of the Chattahoochee, also was in desperate shape, as Glascock's soldiers learned from a runner arriving at Fort Early on January 14. Fort Gaines, he reported, was defenseless, packed with frightened settlers, while renegade Seminoles prowled about. Major Woodward led twenty-two soldiers on a relief expedition, making a forced march to Fort Gaines, where they arrived on the night of January 16 (T. Woodward, 137).

An eerie quiet met the relief column. "When we got within half a mile of the Fort," Woodward wrote, "we could see dogs trotting, and hear them howling in every direction." Woodward's men could make out only a dim light in one blockhouse—and no one in sight on the walls. The ominous stillness convinced them that the fort had been taken by the Seminoles. But when the Georgians approached the blockhouse, they breathed a sigh of relief. Inside were a couple of sentries playing cards and a young woman sitting with them singing. They invited Woodward in, and several days later a column of regulars arrived and relieved him (T. Woodward, 138–139).

Some men were still trying desperately to avoid a war with the Seminoles. Former Georgia governor David Mitchell, who had replaced Benjamin Hawkins as the new Indian agent, was in the midst of negotiations with the Muscogees for another land cession, and for him the timing was poor for another military clash. Mitchell had persuaded Big Warrior to send runners to Kinache at the Mikasuki towns. The Seminoles assured them that all they wanted was to remain at peace. But it was too late now. Andrew Jackson was already preparing his campaign, the last one he would ever lead against the red men. He fully intended that this war would deal the final blow to the rebel Muscogees and Seminoles—and win Florida in the process (Heidler and Heidler, *Old Hickory's War,* 123).

Still in Nashville, Old Hickory issued a call for 1,000 Tennessee volunteers. He would have two veteran regiments of regulars, the Fourth and Seventh U.S. Infantry, but he needed once again to fall back on the militia and volunteers for manpower. Remembering his troubles with militia in the Creek War, he questioned the dependability of Glascock's Georgians, whose term of service was nearing a January 31 expiration date. Georgia Governor William Rabun was raising more troops, to arrive at Fort Hawkins in mid-February, but Jackson doubted that many would make it into the field, confiding later to his wife that "Georgia at present does not display much Patriotism." "If I can get 1200 mounted gunmen from Tennessee," Jackson wrote John Coffee, "with my regular force, If the Georgians mutiny, I can put it down, and drive into the Gulf all the Indians and [their] adherents" (Heidler and Heidler, *Old Hickory's War,* 122–123, 126; Bassett, vol. 2, 347, 353; Suarez, 31).

For once, Coffee could not join his old friend for the campaign. He was busy handling an important land sale in the Tennessee Valley. Jackson turned to his inspector general, Colonel Arthur P. Hayne, a seasoned officer who had fought under him at New Orleans. Hayne had no trouble recruiting two full mounted regiments by early February—one under Colonel Robert H. Dyer and the other under Colonel Thomas Williamson, both veteran officers of the Creek War. Most of the volunteers had served under William Carroll at New Orleans (Suarez, 31; Bassett, vol. 2, 350, 353).

Old Hickory didn't wait for his volunteers, who were scheduled to join him later at Fort Scott. Accompanied by his mounted "Life Guard" company, under Captain Alexander Dunlap, he left Nashville on January 22, and by February 12 he was at Hartford on the Ocmulgee, where he met General Gaines and his regulars, back from Amelia Island. Also on hand was young Glascock with his Georgia militia—two regiments under Colonel John E. Little and Colonel Homer V. Milton (formerly of the Third U.S. Infantry) and a battalion under Major John Minton. Heavy rains hindered the movement of the little army of 1,100 blue-coated regulars and tattered militia as it moved overland to the Flint—streams swollen, roads so bad that Jackson (just as Glascock had done earlier) ordered his men to abandon the supply wagons and load everything on their horses (Suarez, 30; G. B. Smith, 162; Parton, 440–441; Remini, *Jackson,* 1977, 352).

By February 26, the army finally reached Fort Early—"without a barrel of flour or a bushel of corn," Jackson reported. And there was a dire message from Lieutenant Colonel Arbuckle at Fort Scott: The garrison's food was giving out, and the men would be forced to abandon the post unless relieved soon. Eager to be off, Gaines loaded himself and a dozen men aboard a small boat with a few meager supplies and sailed down the Flint ahead of the main column (Parton, 442–443; Chalker, 129–130).

Nine miles downriver from Fort Early, Jackson's regulars and militia reached Aumucculle (or Chehaw), a Lower Muscogee village with cattle, hogs, and horses and fields of corn, potatoes, and rice. The red men there provided Jackson's troops with food, and forty warriors joined Old Hickory's army and took up the march south. By March 9, Jackson had reached Fort Scott. But there were no Tennessee volunteers waiting there. And no General Gaines (Coulter, 369–371).

After a grueling twenty-two-day overland trip, Hayne and the Tennessee volunteers had reached Fort Mitchell on the Chattahoochee on March 2, disappointed to find no supplies waiting for them. Colonel David Brearly, commander of the post, explained the problem. The supply boats from New Orleans, which Jackson expected to be waiting in Apalachicola Bay, had been delayed by bad weather. Hayne had planned to lead his mounted volunteers down the Chattahoochee to Fort Gaines, but rumors of the bleak condition of that outpost caused him to choose another route to the Florida country. He decided to cross the Chattahoochee and follow the Federal Road east to Fort Hawkins—"the only point where I could feed and preserve the efficiency of my command" (Suarez, 30, 33, 34).

Hayne left the bulk of his command at Fort Hawkins and led an advance detachment of 350 men south to Hartford, where he expected to hear from Old Hickory. On March 19, word reached him from Jackson's aide-de-camp, Lieutenant James Gadsden. It was good news for a change. The supply convoy had reached Apalachicola Bay and was anchored there. Hayne determined to push on to Fort Scott, but before he could lead his troops southward, he came down with a critical case of measles and had to return to Tennessee. Colonel Williamson and Lieutenant Colonel George Elliott took command of the detachment and followed Jackson's path down the Flint. Colonel Dyer took charge of the larger part of the volunteers left behind at Fort Hawkins. Following Hayne's orders, he retraced their route along the Federal Road, then turned south and struck out on a long trek across country to Fort Gaines. He remained far behind the main army under Old Hickory (Suarez, 35–36, 41).

Jackson's army of regulars, militia, and volunteers was slowly coming together for the campaign against the Seminoles, but there was yet another group of fighting men that he had counted on many times in the past. On January 11, Gaines had instructed Colonel Brearly to admit up to 500 Allied Creek warriors into federal military service and provision them for the coming campaign in Florida. Brearly was surprised to find, once he began actively recruiting Muscogees, that practically the whole fighting-age male population in the starving Muscogee nation was willing to serve. In the end, Brearly mustered 1,500 Allied Creeks into service on February 24, forming them into a regiment at Fort Mitchell with William McIntosh, now a brigadier general, in command, and two other mixed-blood chiefs, George Lovett and Noble Kennard, as his subcommanders. Timpoochee Barnard, whose Uchee warriors had fought so well at Calabee Creek, was also back again (Griffith, 187; Heidler and Heidler, *Old Hickory's War,* 132).

While Jackson and his hastily assembled army marched to Fort Scott, McIntosh and his warriors had been prowling down the Chattahoochee. On March 13, the Allied Creeks fell on a contingent of Peter McQueen's Red Sticks at Red Ground, where they took fifty-three warriors prisoner, as well as 180 women and children. The prisoners got no mercy from McIntosh, the man they hated so much; he killed ten of them when they tried to escape (Griffith, 188–189; Heidler and Heidler, *Old Hickory's War,* 140–141; Parton, 446–447; Owen, 44).

The Seminoles and refugee Red Sticks were not prepared for this war. Although supplied with muskets by the British marines at Prospect Bluff, the Seminoles probably never had more than 500 warriors in the field during the war. Peter McQueen was still active as a war chief, but the prophet Josiah Francis now seemed to have taken a more subdued role. Still Jackson blamed Francis and McQueen—as well as British agents Arbuthnot,

Armbrister, and Woodbine—for inciting the Seminoles and the "outlaws of the old red stick party" (Littlefield, 75–76; Twyman, 103; Remini, *Jackson*, 1977, 351; Bassett, vol. 2, 365).

As Jackson had feared, there was little food at Fort Scott. There was no word of what had happened to Gaines either, and everyone dreaded the worst. On March 10, Old Hickory ordered the post's remaining livestock slaughtered, providing his hungry soldiers with three meat rations and one quart of corn apiece. He was anxious to begin the campaign, if only with his regulars and Georgia militia, and he spent most of the day getting his men across to the south bank of the Flint. Thomas Woodward came in with some Allied Creek recruits from the Georgia frontier. And from the Cherokee nation—surprising in view of Jackson's recent annexation of their western lands—a contingent of seventy-two warriors rode in, led by Creek War veteran Major Ridge. On March 12, the army crossed the border into Spanish Florida (Remini, *Jackson*, 1977, 252–353; Heidler and Heidler, *Old Hickory's War*, 133; T. Woodward, 139; Boyd, 90; Wilkins, 114).

The invaders' trek down the eastern side of the Apalachicola was uneventful. "We occasionally fired a few guns at straggling Indians," Woodward related, "and they in turn would fire upon us; now and then one was killed, and a prisoner or two taken." On March 13, Jackson's soldiers were delighted to spot a keelboat loaded with supplies heading upriver. After eating the first welcome meal in many days, the troops continued on down the Apalachicola to Prospect Bluff, where they reached the site of the old Negro Fort on March 16. So far, Woodward wrote, "There was nothing that could be called a fight" (Heidler and Heidler, *Old Hickory's War*, 137; Boyd, 90; T. Woodward, 139).

But Old Hickory expected a fight soon enough. Although a melancholy site, with its charred ruins and bones of the unlucky black defenders killed nearly two years earlier, Prospect Bluff offered such a favorable defensive position that he decided to follow the example of his British predecessors and build a supply base of his own there. He detailed Lieutenant Gadsden's engineers to build the new fort (Fort Gadsden) where the old Negro Fort had once stood. Jackson's army lingered there for nine days (Boyd, 90).

The mystery of what had happened to General Gaines became clear when Gaines himself wandered into camp—"nearly exhausted by hunger and cold, having lost his baggage and clothing," according to Jackson. After leaving Fort Early, Gaines's boat had capsized on the Flint, losing the provisions and drowning three men. The survivors had wandered for six days through the wilderness before finally locating Jackson's army at Prospect Bluff (Parton, 444–445).

McIntosh's Allied Creeks and the Tennessee volunteers were still far behind the main army, but Jackson's "Life Guard" had ridden with him to Fort Gadsden. Many there believed that Old Hickory showed favoritism to this company, composed mainly of young sons of Nashville's elite, assigning them only light duties while the regulars and Georgians did the hard work of constructing the new fort. "They performed no duty more than to ride along the trail on our march," Major Woodward wrote, "and when in camp strolled about when and where they pleased." Captain Dunlap was "a gentleman and a good officer," Woodward wrote. As for his volunteers, "[S]ome of them were very young, as well as very mischievous" (Heidler and Heidler, *Old Hickory's War,* 138; T. Woodward, 139–140).

Resentment of the Life Guard led to a near-blowup. Woodward was supervising a party of his red warriors, who were stripping bark from some pine trees to use as covering for the huts in the fort. Jackson, Gaines, Glascock, and other officers were watching them. When a group of the Nashville boys decided to have some sport at the expense of a bedraggled-looking Georgia militiaman, grabbing him and making ready to toss him into the river—and Jackson only smiled and made no effort to step in— Woodward intervened and stopped them. Sharp Knife, ailing from his ongoing health problems and still cavalier in his attitude toward the Georgia militia, was rankled. As Woodward walked away, Jackson called him an "Indian looking son-of-a-bitch" (T. Woodward, 140–141).

It was the wrong thing to say; Woodward was part Muscogee. "I turned and said to him," Woodward wrote, "that I had some of the blood, but neither boasted of, nor was ashamed of it." Jackson was furious. Later Woodward apologized and offered to leave the camp. Jackson said that he needed to curb his temper and be more respectful toward his superiors, but he wanted Woodward to stay, and that ended it (T. Woodward, 141).

During their stay at Fort Gadsden, Jackson's troops neither saw nor heard anything of the enemy. Things were too quiet. When a Georgia militiaman, Sergeant Duncan McKrimmon, wandered away from the fort to try his hand at a little fishing, a Red Stick war party fell on him and hauled him back to Josiah Francis's town on the Wakulla River. What awaited him there was not pleasant to think about (Heidler and Heidler, *Old Hickory's War,* 138).

The warriors quickly stripped McKrimmon and strung him up on a Red Stick torture rack. The fires were already being prepared for burning him, and the warriors had started their ritual dance. But Milly Francis, the prophet's beautiful sixteen-year-old daughter, felt compassion for the young white man and appealed to her father to spare him. The warriors reluctantly gave in to Milly's pleas and released the young Georgian, later exchanging him for seven and a half gallons of rum from the Spanish at St. Marks. McKrimmon never forgot Milly. After the war he brought her money that he had raised in Milledgeville to help her and her mother when they came in to surrender at Fort Gadsden. And he also asked Milly to marry him. But the gentle-hearted maiden declined. "I did not save you for that," she tenderly explained (Heidler and Heidler, *Old Hickory's War,* 139).

On March 25, a solitary transport finally made its way up the Apalachicola, to the delight of Jackson's troops. Convinced that rebel leaders and their warriors had congregated at St. Marks some fifty miles to the east and that haste was essential, Jackson was off the next day. He left instructions with Captain Isaac McKeever to head out into the Gulf with his naval vessels and prepare to enter the St. Marks River. Jackson did not intend for Francis and McQueen to escape by sea. But first he planned to deal with the Seminoles' largest town at Mikasuki, where old pro-British Kinache had defied the Americans for so long. Jackson's army crossed the rain-swollen Ochlockonee River on March 29. Sharp Knife sent Major David Twiggs and 200 Allied Creeks ahead of the main body to strike the town of Tallahassee. Twiggs found the town deserted and burned it (Heidler and Heidler, *Old Hickory's War*, 140–141).

On April 1, McIntosh and his Allied Creeks rendezvoused with Jackson's army, and finally Lieutenant Colonel Elliott with his mounted Tennessee volunteers caught up. After a rough overland journey, the Tennesseans' ranks were badly depleted by hunger and by sickness. Like Hayne, many had dropped out along the way. Jackson was disappointed to find that only three companies had made it (Bassett, vol. 2, 358; Heidler and Heidler, *Old Hickory's War*, 142).

The column wasted no time and continued their march to Mikasuki. Near nightfall, Jackson's "spy" companies caught sight of a small party of Seminoles herding cattle about two miles from Mikasuki, and Sharp Knife immediately stiffened this small vanguard with more companies of Allied Creeks. Jackson deployed the remainder of his army into two enveloping columns. The vanguard would push the rebel force toward the waiting arms of his right column, the Tennessee volunteers under Elliott, and crush them (Heidler and Heidler, *Old Hickory's War*, 142; T. Woodward, 141; Griffith, 189; Parton, 449).

The fight was short. The rebels occupied a piece of marshy land jutting out into a pond, and as Jackson's scout companies made contact with them, the Seminoles and Maroons poured on a heavy fire. But soon Old Hickory's flank columns were up, and the rebels could not hold. When they realized that Jackson's forces were carrying out an enveloping movement, they fell back. Jackson's plans unraveled as Elliott's Tennesseans spotted Allied Creeks on their left, mistook them for Seminoles, and opened fire on them. The resulting disorder gave the Seminoles just enough time to escape into the swamps, where Kinache and their families—already evacuated—waited for them (Bassett, vol. 2, 358; Heidler and Heidler, *Old Hickory's War*, 142; Griffith, 189; Parton, 449).

"There is nothing which is more exaggerated generally," Major Woodward observed, "than the official reports of fights, and particularly those little skirmishes with Indians." The rebels lost as many as a dozen killed at Mikasuki, but in the American army, Woodward quipped, "[E]very man along killed one of them." Jackson lost one regular soldier killed and four Tennessee volunteers wounded. The soldiers captured four Seminole women (Heidler and Heidler, *Old Hickory's War*, 142; T. Woodward, 141; Wright, 214).

The following day, detachments combed the Mikasuki villages. Burning and looting, the troops destroyed some 300 Seminole homes and confiscated large supplies of their cattle and corn. Old Hickory reported more than fifty fresh scalps found in Kinache's council house, as well as a red pole in the center of the town square—topped with the scalps of victims of the Scott massacre. At least one dead Seminole was wearing an American soldier's coat (Bassett, vol. 2, 358; Heidler and Heidler, *Old Hickory's War*, 143).

Jackson pushed on to the Spanish post at St. Marks, but he left McIntosh with the Allied Creeks to mop up in the Mikasuki towns. McIntosh's warriors spent several days in the area, terrorizing the refugees they could find and attempting to bring the rebels under the authority of Coweta, the new Creek capital—a goal that had been five years in coming (Bassett, vol. 2, 361; Wright, 204).

Sharp Knife wrote Secretary of War John C. Calhoun that he suspected many of the rebels had fled to St. Marks and that an immediate march on the Spanish outpost was justified. He wrote the commandant, Don Francisco Caso y Luengo, and explained that his invasion was necessary to "chastise a savage foe, who, combined with a lawless band of negro brigands, had been for some time past carrying on a cruel and unprovoked war against the citizens of the United States" (Bassett, vol. 2, 358; Mahon, "First Seminole War," 65; Parton, 450).

Jackson's occupation of St. Marks was almost ridiculously simple. Arriving there on April 6, he sent Lieutenant Gadsden with a letter calling on Caso y Luengo to turn over the fort. The Spanish had even left the gate to the fort open, so American officers could come and go at will. Brushing aside Caso y Luengo's assurances that the garrison was not furnishing aid to the rebels, Jackson proceeded to occupy the fort on April 7. Major Twiggs led two light companies of the Seventh Regiment and one of the Fourth to carry out the movement. The bluecoats advanced, entered the fort, lowered the Spanish colors, and ran up the American flag. None of the seventy Spanish soldiers offered any resistance (Heidler and Heidler, *Old Hickory's War*, 143–144).

And on this day Sharp Knife finally caught up with his old enemies. Alexander Arbuthnot—that "noted Scotch villain," as Jackson called him—fell into the hands of American troops when they occupied the fort. Meanwhile, Captain McKeever and his naval vessels had been waiting in St. Marks Bay, flying the British colors in an effort to deceive the Spanish and the red men. Under the impression that they were dealing with the British, Josiah Francis and Homathlemico—a Red Stick chief who had participated in the Scott massacre—came aboard McKeever's ship and were promptly taken into custody. So far Jackson's prosecution of the First Seminole War had been almost effortless (Heidler and Heidler, *Old Hickory's War*, 144–145; Boyd, 89; Remini, *Jackson*, 1977, 354; Bassett, vol. 2, 358; Covington, 44–45).

CHAPTER 19

"Every Principle Villain
...Killed or Taken"

On April 8, Jackson ordered both Josiah Francis and Homathlemico, who had accompanied him, executed immediately. The chiefs got no trial, no counsel to represent them. Francis requested execution by firing squad, but Jackson refused to meet with him and turned down his appeal. An American officer noted that Francis did not look at all like a murderous barbarian; in fact he seemed well cultured and mannerly. He was dressed in a fine gray frock coat, but the rest of his clothing was Muscogee. Homathlemico, on the other hand, was a "savage-looking man...taciturn and morose." The soldiers hanged the two chiefs in the courtyard of the fort at St. Marks, then hauled them by their heels from the fort, and tossed their bodies into an unmarked grave. Asked if they should be cast into the river, Old Hickory had replied no, that they should be given a decent burial (Heidler and Heidler, *Old Hickory's War*, 145; Remini, *Jackson*, 1977, 356; Covington, 44; Wright, 207; Parton, 457–458).

Jackson's army next set out on a hundred-mile trek eastward to attack Bowlegs' Town. Arbuthnot's trading post was there, as well as the large concentration of Maroon settlements and Bowlegs' rebel Seminoles. The remnants of Peter McQueen's Red Stick band could not be far off. And Sharp Knife hoped to bag them all and end the rebellion for good. Leaving 200 soldiers as a garrison, Jackson left St. Marks on April 9 with eight days' rations. On April 10, McIntosh and the Allied Creeks caught up with Jackson, and Robert Dyer with the last of the Tennessee volunteers finally arrived via Fort Gaines. For a welcome change, dry weather greeted the Americans as they marched toward the Suwanee, although the foot soldiers still had to wade through water that was often waist high (Mahon,

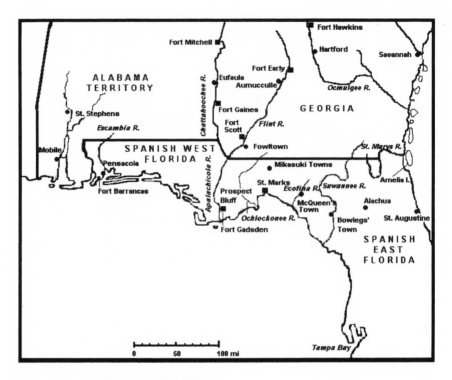

Scene of the First Seminole War, 1818

"First Seminole War," 65; Covington, 45; Heidler and Heidler, *Old Hickory's War*, 147; Bassett, vol. 2, 361).

Old Hickory's army now totaled 3,300. Included were 500 regulars of Colonel William King's Fourth Infantry and Colonel David Brearley's Seventh Infantry. There were 1,000 militia from Georgia and Tennessee and even a company of volunteers from Kentucky. The most recent arrivals were Dyer's depleted First Regiment of Tennessee Mounted Gunmen and Williamson's exhausted Second Regiment. Captain Dunlap's Life Guard was still on hand. And there were 1,800 Allied Creeks, plus Ridge's Cherokees, ready to do battle against their old foes (Mahon, "First Seminole War," 64; Covington, 43; T. Woodward, 139).

McQueen was the first to feel the blow. Moving closer to his town on the Ecofina River, in present-day Taylor County, Jackson's soldiers heard sounds of dogs barking and cattle lowing during the night of April 11. In the morning, McIntosh ordered out Noble Kennard and a small detachment of his warriors to explore what could be an enemy concentration. Not long after Kennard picked up the rebels' trail, he spotted McQueen's warriors concealed in a marshy area along the Ecofina. The Red Sticks made their final stand. Kennard's warriors, along with Timpoochee

Barnard's Uchees, soon forced them into the open. Although badly out-numbered, McQueen's 200 warriors managed to hold off the advance party until McIntosh arrived with the main body of the Allied Creeks (Griffith, 189–191; T. Woodward, 49; Covington, 46).

During breaks in the firing, McIntosh's warriors could make out the cry of a woman calling out for help in English. "Save the white woman!" McIntosh bellowed. "Save the Indian women and children." McIntosh sent in Kennard, Woodward, and some Allied Creeks to locate the woman and isolate her from the rebel warriors. They found her, along with a group of Muscogee women, hidden among the trees. There was an exchange of gunfire, but the small party managed to rescue the white woman and conduct her to the Allied Creek lines. She turned out to be Elizabeth Stuart, who had been taken prisoner by the warriors who had massacred the Scott party in November 1817. Apparently, she had not been mistreated by the Red Sticks (T. Woodward, 48–49; Parton, 460).

The fighting was over before white reinforcements—a company of fifty Tennessee mounted riflemen—arrived to aid McIntosh's warriors. McQueen's band evaporated into the swamp. The Allied Creeks had killed thirty-seven Red Sticks and had taken six warriors and ninety-seven of their women and children captive. McIntosh lost three men killed and four wounded (T. Woodward, 45–46; Bassett, vol. 2, 361; Covington, 46; Owen, 37, 39).

Jackson's troops moved faster now, hoping to cut Bowlegs' people off before they could cross the Suwanee. By now, Bowlegs knew that Sharp Knife was coming, and he was evacuating the town. A message from Arbuthnot had arrived, written before his capture, and Ambrister read it to the townspeople. "The main drift of the Americans," Arbuthnot warned, "is to destroy the black population of Suwany. Tell my friend, Boleck [Bowlegs], that it is throwing away his people to attempt to resist such a powerful force" (Mahon, "First Seminole War," 65; Porter, 21–22; Parton, 448).

While Bowlegs and his people put the Suwanee between them and the enemy, Nero, the leader of the Maroons, made preparations to stage a rear guard defense with 200 to 300 determined men. Ambrister had issued powder and lead to the Maroons, but although he had spent much time training them, he declined to take command and headed instead to Arbuthnot's schooner, the *Chance,* waiting at the mouth of the Suwanee (Porter, 21–22; Littlefield, 76).

By now, Bowlegs' Town had absorbed large numbers of black runaways and refugees from old Negro Fort, and it was the largest concentration of Maroons in the Southeast. The black settlements lay scattered for about three miles along the west bank of the Suwanee, while Bowlegs' Town lay directly to the south of these settlements away from the river. Really more like vassals to the Seminoles than slaves, some 300 to 400 Maroons had made their homes in these settlements, where they had erected wooden fences to protect their crops of corn, potatoes, beans, rice, peas, and fruit (Porter, 22; Wright, 204, 206; Heidler and Heidler, *Old Hickory's War*, 147; Covington, 45).

Meanwhile, Sharp Knife's army came on relentlessly, a juggernaut aimed at the total destruction of the Seminole-Maroon enclave. Jackson hoped to take the settlements by surprise, strike swiftly, and envelop them by 1 P.M. on April 16. But it was late in the afternoon when his slow-moving column arrived near the Suwanee. Jackson considered making camp and delaying the attack until the following morning. But his soldiers spotted half a dozen Seminole scouts, undoubtedly on their way to warn the towns of the army's approach. Besides wanting to trap the rebels, Jackson desperately needed the food supplies in those towns, so he hurriedly made ready for an attack (Bassett, vol. 2, 361).

Old Hickory organized his army into the old three-column assault formation that had worked so well in the past. McIntosh with part of his Allied Creeks and Colonel Dyer's First Tennessee Volunteers composed the right column. Its mission was to turn the rebels' left flank and cut them off from the river. The left column—Kennard's Allied Creeks and Colonel Williamson's Second Tennessee Volunteers—would strike the rebels' right flank. Old Hickory with the center column—his regulars, Georgia militia, Kentucky riflemen, and Tennessee guards—would advance straight in front of the rebels and crush them (Bassett, vol. 2, 360–362).

A small number of Bowlegs' warriors had joined the Maroons in their holding action, while the last of the women and children crossed the river to safety. The rebels held their ground firmly, but the outcome could never have been in any doubt. Badly outnumbered nearly four to one, they faced the setting sun and waited for the American army to close in on them. Their British muskets would be no real match for the Tennesseans' long rifles (Griffith, 192).

The attack came at sundown. The fight—"the severest brush that I was engaged in during that campaign," Woodward wrote—took only a few minutes. The Maroons fought obstinately, but they could not hold. One of their surviving warriors, years later, related that the Allied Creeks "came too hot upon them and they all ran to save their lives." The rebel resistance crumbled, and the rear guard fell back to the river. Nero was killed during the engagement (Griffith, 192; T. Woodward, 141; Covington, 46; Porter, 23, 26–27; Heidler and Heidler, *Old Hickory's War*, 150–151).

Kennard had already struck the Maroons' right flank before Jackson was up with his center column, and Old Hickory had to step up the pace to catch him. The Maroons and Seminoles streamed across the river, where many of them were picked off by Kennard's warriors. As at the Ecofina, most of the fighting was over by the time the white troops arrived. Jackson's soldiers counted nine Maroons and two Seminoles dead. The allies took nine Seminoles and seven Maroons prisoner. Thirteen Allied Creeks were wounded (Bassett, vol. 2, 360–362; Heidler and Heidler, *Old Hickory's War*, 150–151; Wright, 205; Porter, 23; Covington, 46).

But there was bitter disappointment for Old Hickory, who had hoped that this would be the decisive battle to finish the rebels for good. Instead, most of them had slipped away again. This was not another Horseshoe Bend. The failure to envelop the enemy towns once again came from lack of coordination between the American columns. Woodward blamed Colonel Williamson's left column, insisting that if Williamson had carried out Jackson's orders more strictly, "very few Indians and negroes could have escaped." According to another officer, the Allied Creeks failed to get behind the black villages—instead striking between the towns and the center—and left a way open for escape (Griffith, 192; T. Woodward, 141).

The next few days followed a familiar pattern as Sharp Knife's troops mopped up. Jackson sent General Gaines and William McIntosh on a pursuit of the rebels on April 18. They crossed the Suwanee and moved on for about six miles, but they were unable to capture any of the rebels who had dispersed into the swamps. A small supply of corn and fifty head of cattle were all that the troops could find (Griffith, 192; Mahon, "First Seminole War," 66; Heidler and Heidler, *Old Hickory's War*, 151).

Planning to sail the *Chance* to Tampa Bay, Robert Ambrister had returned to Bowlegs' Town to gather up more supplies—unaware that Jackson had already occupied it. On the night of April 18, the British adventurer, along with his aide and two Maroons, stumbled into an American camp—and into captivity. Searching one of the blacks, Jackson's soldiers found Arbuthnot's letter of warning to the Seminoles. Jackson ordered Ambrister held for trial, and he also dispatched Lieutenant Gadsden with a small detachment to seize the *Chance* and use it to carry their wounded back to St. Marks (Remini, *Jackson*, 1977, 356; Heidler and Heidler, *Old Hickory's War*, 11, 151–152; Covington, 46).

On April 20, Jackson discharged Glascock and his Georgia militia to march back to Hartford, where they would be mustered out. He also released McIntosh and his Allied Creeks. Meanwhile, Jackson and his regulars and Tennesseans marched back to St. Marks (Heidler and Heidler, *Old Hickory's War*, 152; Griffith, 192).

At St. Marks, both Arbuthnot and Ambrister faced a court-martial, with General Gaines presiding. Arbuthnot was charged with being a spy for the Seminoles and with inciting them to make war on the United States. The prosecution sought to show that he had furnished the rebels with ammunition, that he had acted as an agent for them in correspondence with British officials, and that he had supplied information on movements of the American army that allowed the rebels at Bowlegs' Town to escape (Remini, *Jackson*, 1977, 357).

Mild and courteous—not at all the monster that Jackson painted him to be—the seventy-year-old white-haired Arbuthnot defended himself to the court. As to the charge that he supplied ammunition to the Seminoles, he confessed to selling ten kegs of gunpowder to Bowlegs—to hunt with and kill game, not to kill American settlers. But despite the good impression he made, the court brought in a verdict of guilty and sentenced him to be hanged (Remini, *Jackson*, 1977, 358).

Arbuthnot and Ambrister disliked each other and testified against each other at their trial. Another witness also proved very harmful—Arbuthnot's bitter rival, William Hambly, of John Forbes Company. Hambly, whose trade with the Seminoles had suffered—ironically because Arbuthnot actually gave the red men fair prices for their goods—had a strong motive for eliminating his competition. Accused of aiding the Americans, Hambly had been taken prisoner by Fowltown warriors in December and had been under a death sentence until Nero had intervened and spared him, finally transferring him to custody of the Spanish at St. Marks. Hambly blamed Arbuthnot for his troubles (Remini, *Jackson*, 1977, 352; Boyd, 88–89; Owsley, 185; Wright, 206).

Ambrister also made a good impression on the court. The case against him was even stronger than that against Arbuthnot. He was accused not only of helping the rebels but also of actually commanding them in making war on the Americans. Caught red-handed, Ambrister did not have much of a defense to these charges, but he faced them like a soldier. The most damning evidence against him was a letter—in his own handwriting—in which he admitted dispatching a rebel war party to attack American troops. Ambrister was ordered to be shot by firing squad (Remini, *Jackson*, 1977, 358).

Jackson's soldiers executed the two British subjects on April 29. The sight of their bodies—Arbuthnot hanging from the yardarm of his own ship, the *Chance*, and Ambrister at the feet of a firing squad—horrified the red men filtering into the fort to surrender and not only enhanced Jackson's terrifying fame but in addition convinced them that their cause was indeed hopeless now. On the same day that the two men died, Jackson was already on his way back to Fort Gadsden with his army. The executions would bring international protest and would plague Jackson throughout his political career, but Old Hickory showed no sign of regret. Now, Jackson wrote his wife, "[E]very principle villain has been either killed or taken" (Remini, *Jackson*, 1977, 358–359; Bassett, vol. 2, 360).

While Old Hickory gathered more laurels with his army in Florida, other parts of the southern frontier were left virtually defenseless. One such area was the newly organized Alabama Territory. The first meeting of the territorial legislature convened at St. Stephens in January 1818, with Creek War veterans such as Sam Dale and Joseph P. Kennedy playing prominent roles. Governor William Wyatt Bibb objected to the withdrawal of regular troops to supplement Jackson's army in Florida, leaving only 100 soldiers to patrol the Escambia River area, where stray bands of refugee Red Sticks still roamed (Heidler and Heidler, *Old Hickory's War*, 136; Pickett, 615–617).

The Alabamians' concerns were mirrored by settlers on the Georgia frontier, especially in the Big Bend of the Ocmulgee, the most exposed part of the Georgia frontier. The Muscogee side of the Big Bend had long been a favored hunting ground for the Creeks, but by now whites were crossing the river in large numbers and taking up land illegally. In early March 1818, frontier families were horrified at the news of the rebel attack on squatters Joseph Burch and his son, both of whom were shot and scalped (Chalker, 131–132).

Major Josiah D. Cawthorn gathered thirty-four men, many of them veterans of the Creek War, and crossed the river in search of the raiders. They picked up their trail and caught up with them at Breakfast Branch on March 9. The woods blazed with gunfire, and the larger rebel party routed the Georgians, who fled in disorder, losing seven men killed and three wounded. News of Cawthorn's defeat generated even more hysteria on the Ocmulgee frontier. With Jackson's troops—including Glascock's Georgia brigade—busy engaging the Seminoles in Florida, Governor William Rabun took matters into his own hands and called up more militia on April 14. The Georgia troops were to assemble at Hartford and prepare for a campaign against two rebel chiefs whose towns lay south of Fort Early along the Flint River (Chalker, 133–135, 137–138; G. B. Smith, 163; Coulter, 371–372).

Rabun gave command of the retaliatory expedition to Captain Obed Wright, an officer with a reputation for reliability. Wright left Fort Early on April 21 with 270 men, militia troops from Jones and Twiggs Counties and from Fort Early. He decided to attack Aumucculle—the friendly town that had supplied Jackson with food and warriors less than a month earlier—instead of the two towns named in Rabun's orders. Wright had received information that one of the two rebel chiefs had taken over Aumucculle and was there with his warriors. Fort Early's commander, Captain Ebenezer Bothwell, refused to go with Wright, arguing that Aumucculle was a friendly village (Coulter, 372; G. B. Smith, 165).

The Georgia troops struck Aumucculle at noon on April 22. Exactly what happened in the little Muscogee town that day is unclear, but the events there sparked a controversy that flared for years and had political repercussions as well. Within two hours the town was in flames, and a number of people were dead, including an elderly chief—an uncle of William McIntosh—who reportedly waved a white flag as soldiers opened fire on him. The rest of the townspeople fled into the swamps. None of the Georgians were killed, and they marched back to Fort Early the same day (Coulter, 373–374; Heidler and Heidler, *Old Hickory's War*, 164).

Accounts of the number of Muscogees killed at Aumucculle conflicted. Wright initially reported between forty and fifty killed, including twenty-four warriors, and said that the chief of the town was also killed. But he probably exaggerated the figures. Other estimates of the casualties—given by Timothy Barnard, Thomas Glascock, Little Prince, and others—cite the numbers as between six and ten, including one woman and at least one child. Wright insisted that he gave his troops specific orders not to harm any women or children. He also claimed that his troops encountered resistance from the townspeople, that gunmen fired on his soldiers from barricaded houses, that the Georgians were forced to set fire to a number of the homes to bring things under control. Jacob Robinson, second in command, echoed Wright, insisting that the townspeople fired on the Georgians first and that the troops found British muskets and gunpowder in nearly every house in the village (Coulter, 373–374; Heidler and Heidler, *Old Hickory's War*, 164).

Brigadier General Glascock and his militia troops, returning from Florida, passed through Aumucculle just four days later and discovered evidence of the massacre. A furious Glascock passed on word of the atrocity to Jackson, still at St. Marks. Perhaps recalling the tragic Hillabee massacre in 1813, Old Hickory was enraged at the "base, cowardly, and inhuman attack on the old women and men of the Chehaw village, while the warriors of that village were fighting the battles of our country against the common enemy." He ordered the arrest of Wright (who was later scheduled for trial but escaped to Cuba) and fired off a scathing letter to Rabun accusing him of interfering with his authority. If the Georgians wanted to fight red men, he wrote, why did they not join him in his campaign against the Seminoles in Florida? The controversy set off a bitter exchange of words between Jackson and Rabun that went on for some time (Coulter, 378–379, 389–390; G. B. Smith, 166).

There was yet one more loose end to take care of in Florida. With Mikasuki and Bowlegs' Town destroyed, Jackson considered the campaign against the Seminoles over, and he returned to Fort Gadsden to discharge the remainder of his army. But there he changed his plans. William Hambly, who by now had ingratiated himself with Sharp Knife, passed on information that renegade Seminoles were near Pensacola. Even though he was sick again and anxious to get back to Nashville, Old Hickory left Fort Gadsden and set off on a 240-mile march west to Pensacola (Remini, *Jackson*, 1977, 359–360; Mahon, "First Seminole War," 66; Boyd, 91; Bassett, vol. 2, 362).

Since Old Hickory's occupation of Pensacola in November 1814, Governor Jose Masot had strengthened the city's defenses, enlisted all able-bodied men between sixteen and sixty into the local militia, and even recruited male slaves for military duty. Now came Sharp Knife once more, and—even though the American army was down to just the regulars and

Tennesseans—they still outnumbered the 175 Spanish defenders by more than four to one. Jackson occupied the town with no opposition on the evening of May 23. After a brief resistance at Fort Barrancas, which Old Hickory placed under siege, Masot raised the white flag and marched his garrison out (McAlister, 318–321).

Jackson placed Pensacola in the charge of Fourth Infantry's Colonel William King, with orders to supervise the discharge of the Tennessee volunteers. He sent out detachments of Alabamians to hunt down refugee rebel parties between Mobile and Apalachicola Bay—with orders to annihilate any who resisted. And he prepared to return to Nashville (McAlister, 321; Remini, *Jackson*, 1977, 364–365; Heidler and Heidler, *Old Hickory's War*, 174).

Jackson again had sacrificed his own health. Weak and gaunt, he wrote Monroe on June 2 that he was "worn down with fatigue and a bad cough...spitting blood." He was on his way home, but in the same letter he confidently guaranteed the president that if he would provide more troops, the Americans could take St. Augustine, Spain's last enclave in Florida. With an additional regiment and a frigate, he added, "I will insure you Cuba in a few days" (Mahon, "First Seminole War," 66).

The 1818 campaign destroyed the power of the Seminoles west of the Suwanee. Bowlegs died not long after the evacuation of Suwanee, and the Seminoles pulled back to central Florida and areas further south. The Maroons made their way to Tampa Bay, and many of the refugee blacks even traveled to the Bahamas, where they made a new home on Andros Island. Peter McQueen and the last of the Red Sticks made their way south to Tampa Bay, where they settled, and a few of these diehards may have accompanied McQueen as far south as present-day Miami. He died near there on one of the small offshore keys, not long after the conclusion of the war (Mahon, "First Seminole War," 66–67; Wright, 208–210; Covington, 47–48; Porter, 25–26).

In 1819, eighty-year-old Kinache and twenty-three other Seminoles sailed to the Bahamas with one last appeal to the Muscogees' former ally. They met with Governor William V. Munnings, who was sensitive to the red men's plight but unable to provide any help. The struggle was over. Shortly after his return to the mainland, Kinache died. Perhaps for him and McQueen, their last days were filled with wistful memories of the time so many years earlier when they listened to Tecumseh and dreamed of a strong and independent Muscogee nation (Covington, 47–48; Wright, 214).

Jackson's Florida campaign created an international incident, even as it enhanced Jackson's reputation as a military hero. The United States faced Spanish protests over the seizure of St. Marks and Pensacola, as well as British protests over the executions of Arbuthnot and Ambrister. Monroe and his cabinet, worried over the danger of a new British-Spanish alliance, finally agreed to return St. Marks and Pensacola to Spanish control. But the Spanish, convinced that they could no longer defend Florida, agreed to cede it to the United States. The two nations signed the agreement on February 22, 1819 (Mahon, "First Seminole War," 67; Remini, *Jackson*, 1977, 367–377).

Besides opening the door to the U.S. annexation of Florida, the war sealed the fate of the Seminoles, Red Sticks, and Maroons. Driven farther into the Florida peninsula, they faced a sad future—broken and destitute, their lands and property lost, their borders thrown open to American expansion and an ever-encroaching Cotton Kingdom. The outcome of Jackson's Florida campaign had convinced the rebels that no outside power would aid them, and it ended effective resistance for good (Littlefield, 76; Porter, 26).

CHAPTER 20

One Nation

The Indians are the subjects of the United States.
              —Andrew Jackson, 1817 (Remini, *Legacy*, 48)

Why cannot we be allowed to have land, and homes, and live like our white Brothers?
              —Opothleyaholo, Muscogee chief, 1825 (McBride, 59)

I see that the Indian fires are going out—they must soon be extinguished.
   —Yoholo Micco (Chief Eufaula), Muscogee chief, 1837 (Davis, 303)

In the decade before 1820, the population of the new state of Alabama increased by a startling 1,000 percent. New settlers, many of them veterans of the Creek War, poured into the fertile lands thrown open to them by the Treaty of Fort Jackson. The newcomers were men such as Williamson Hawkins, one of Old Hickory's Tennessee volunteers who liked what he had seen in the Muscogee land and returned in May 1815 with his cattle and "all the supplies he could pack on one horse." Hawkins cleared land in Jones Valley near present-day Birmingham and planted his first crop of corn before leaving a slave family in charge while he returned to Tennessee for his family (Rogers et al., 54, 58).

There were thousands more like Hawkins. Most of them made a good living out of their new lands. And a few became very successful planters. John Coffee's 1817 appointment as surveyor-general of the new Alabama Territory put him in a position to speculate in land and amass a fortune. Coffee was a key figure in the economic development of the Tennessee

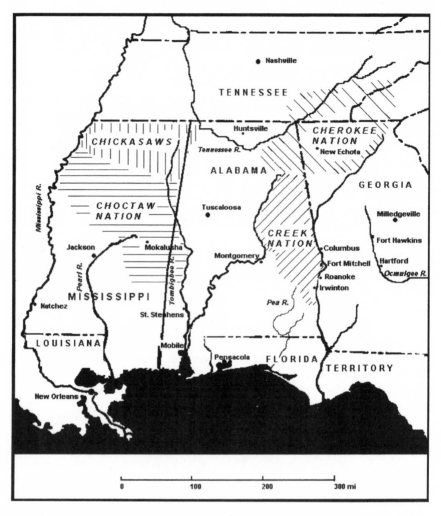

Southeastern Tribes, on the Eve of Removal, 1832

River Valley and became the richest planter in that area of north Alabama. The general's holdings included vineyards and orchards with fine apples, peaches, pears, and plums. But the primary crop, like that of all the planters, was cotton (Chappell, 24–45).

Mississippi, admitted to the union as a new state in 1817, became the nation's leading cotton producer by 1834. The new capital at Jackson—located on a site chosen by Creek War veteran officer Thomas Hinds—by 1823 boasted a brick statehouse, a newspaper office, three taverns, two stores, and a score of new frame homes as well as older log cabins. With the state's remarkably rapid economic growth came the birth of a planter oligarchy and the extension of an even deeper-rooted institution of slavery in the Old Southwest. In 1820, 44 percent of the state's population was slave. The transformation of white frontier society from a classless one to a class-dominated one was complete (Davis, 72–73, 105, 129–130).

The flow of new settlers into the eastern part of the old Mississippi Territory was so great that it led to the formation of two states instead of one. Just two years after Mississippi became a state, Alabama entered the union, its new capital at Huntsville pointing clearly to the direction in which its economic development would go. The Tensaw-Tombigbee settlements were quickly surpassed, and little frontier towns such as St. Stephens faded. Like John Coffee and Williamson Hawkins, Alabama's new settlers utilized the rich soil of north Alabama—and soon the rich Black Belt lands of central Alabama as well, giving birth to the heart of the Cotton Kingdom and to new cities like Tuscaloosa, Selma, and Montgomery (Davis, 232, 236).

The Georgia and Florida frontiers also experienced unparalleled growth in the 1820s. New cities such as Columbus sprang up along the Chattahoochee—and Atlanta further upriver—while steamboats carried their valuable cargoes of cotton down to Apalachicola. The rivers whose banks had once nourished Muscogee towns and villages now became conduits of commerce for Southern planters. In September 1823—in their first recognition of the Florida Seminoles as a tribe separate from the Muscogees—U.S. negotiators concluded the Treaty of Moultrie Creek. The Seminoles agreed to move to lands reserved to them in central Florida, leaving the white population clustered in the northern part of the territory in new towns such as Tallahassee and Quincy.

The white settlers of these frontier states overwhelmingly supported Andrew Jackson in the presidential elections of 1824 and 1828. And of all the policies that Old Hickory brought to the White House, the one that these westerners endorsed the loudest was Indian removal. After all, wasn't this what they had fought for in the Creek War, the freedom to settle the western lands? The two decades following the conclusion of the Creek and Seminole conflicts saw the steady erosion of southeastern Native American sovereignty—and ultimately their forced removal west of the Mississippi.

"The Indians are the subjects of the United States," Jackson proclaimed in 1817, "inhabiting its territory and acknowledging its sovereignty, then is it not absurd for the sovereign to negotiate by the treaty with the subject." Jackson believed that the red men now lived on conquered territory and that they would survive only if removed farther west, that removal was a "just and liberal policy." When he left office in 1837, he firmly believed that he had done what was best for both races (Remini, *Legacy*, 48, 50, 57, 59, 82).

"No man," a Jackson supporter asserted, "entertains kinder feelings toward the Indians than Andrew Jackson." Jackson's attitude toward

Native Americans was no different from his attitude toward virtually everyone—his soldiers, his family, even Congress. He rewarded loyalty and obedience, but he was a dangerous enemy when provoked. Although Jackson mirrored the racism of other white Americans in his view of the red men as an inferior people, his main motivation in pushing for Indian removal was national security. From his own bitter wartime experiences, Sharp Knife was convinced that the nation's southern frontier could never be free of the danger of foreign intervention until the red men were gone (Remini, *Legacy*, 46–47, 57, 64).

First to see the handwriting on the wall—and to face Old Hickory's unyielding iron will—were the Choctaws, who more than any other southeastern tribe had proven over and over their unwavering friendship for the whites. "They and my white children," Jackson decided, "are too near each other to live in harmony and peace." Jackson sat down with faithful Pushmataha and other Choctaw chiefs in October 1820 at Doak's Stand, a site on the Natchez Trace. Aided by Thomas Hinds, Pushmataha's former wartime ally, Sharp Knife demanded the cession of over five million acres of land—a third of the Choctaw nation—and promised to compensate the tribe with double the amount of land west of the Mississippi. Pushmataha, who had actually traveled west of the Mississippi, felt hurt and betrayed. The land out there, he protested, was different from the land in the east, nothing more than a barren wasteland. "If you refuse," Jackson threatened, "...[your] nation will be destroyed." The leaders reluctantly submitted. There was now little left of the old Choctaw nation in the east (Wallace, 74; Remini, *Jackson*, 1977, 394–397).

The Choctaws made a last-ditch appeal to President James Monroe. Now sixty years old and ailing, Pushmataha led a delegation to Washington in 1824, but the red men received few concessions. On Christmas Eve, the old warrior died in the capital city. Jackson had visited him at his sickbed and had asked if he could do anything for him. "When I am dead," the chief replied, "fire the big guns over me." Pushmataha was given full military honors at his burial. The Treaty of Doak's Stand provided white planters with the richest delta lands in west central Mississippi, and it became a model for Indian removal (Davis, 300; Remini, *Jackson*, 1977, 397; Owen, 69; Claiborne, 136).

Meanwhile, the Muscogee nation struggled to heal the bitter internal divisions that had led Red Sticks and Allied Creeks to kill each other. The spiritual, social, and political equilibrium that the Muscogees desperately sought for their nation was irrevocably shattered now. The Red Stick rebellion and tribal civil war had failed to restore balance. Plagued from without by demands for more land cessions and torn from within by political divisions, the once powerful Muscogee nation would soon cease to exist.

The greatest of the Red Stick military men, William Weatherford, turned from Muscogee politics to reinvent himself as a respectable planter in south Alabama. A bitter Red Eagle once told Sam Dale that he had suffered at the hands of just about every group. His former comrades, the Red Sticks, had slaughtered and eaten his cattle because they were starving. The Allied Creeks had killed and eaten them out of vengefulness. And the white squatters had eaten them simply because he was just a "damned Red-skin." "So," Red Eagle sardonically explained, "I have come to live among gentlemen" (Claiborne, 129).

Weatherford earned growing acceptance and admiration from Alabama's white society as he lived out the remaining years of his life in peace, content on his plantation along the Little River in Monroe County. The great war chief owned 300 slaves, and he maintained a stable of celebrated racehorses. Ironically, his large, comfortable home, enclosed by a grove of handsome oaks, lay not far from the site of Fort Mims (Griffith, 252; L. Thompson, 595).

Red Eagle died in March 1824, at the age of forty-four, following a deer hunt with friends. Someone in the party killed a white deer, and Red Eagle remarked that this was a sign that one of them would soon die. Weatherford became ill the next day and never recovered. While on his deathbed, he told onlookers that he had seen a vision: his beautiful wife, Sofath—who had died tragically after giving birth to their only child—patiently awaiting her warrior husband to go with her to the hunting grounds of the Muscogee spirit world (L. Thompson, 619–620; Griffith, 253–254).

Some of Weatherford's former comrades in arms—the few who had not been killed—managed to reintegrate themselves into Muscogee life. Menawa recovered from the ruinous defeat he suffered at Horseshoe Bend. Eventually his health returned, and once again he was a leader of the Okfuskee people and a prominent man in the Muscogee nation. And a rising star in his mid-twenties, Opothleyaholo was the new speaker to Big Warrior at Tuckabatchee. He had been only a teenager when he had fought at Horseshoe Bend (Owen, 48; McBride, 11, 25).

Although the aging Big Warrior and Little Prince were still renowned chiefs, it was William McIntosh, the speaker for the Lower Creeks, who wielded most of the power now. McIntosh basked in prosperity at Lockchau Talofau, his large two-story home on the banks of the Chattahoochee in present-day Carroll County, Georgia. The dwelling also functioned as a tavern, and whites called it Indian Springs. A planter and a slaveholder, McIntosh became an ally of David Mitchell, who retired in the midst of his second term as Georgia's governor to seek Benjamin Hawkins's former post as agent to the Creeks (Griffith, 195; Barnard and Schwartzman, "Trail," 705).

"McIntosh and Mitchell," Little Prince cynically observed, "used to steal all of our money, because they could write." Entirely dependent on the federal government now, the Muscogees relied on their yearly annuities to sustain the tribe. The government issued the money to the agent, and he in turn was to pass it on to the town headmen. But Mitchell and McIntosh persuaded the chiefs to accept payment not in cash but in highly overpriced goods from their trading post near Fort Mitchell. The devious partners then used the annuity money to buy more goods. Mitchell continued bilking the Muscogees until the discovery of his slave-smuggling operations out of Spanish Florida finally led to his dismissal in February 1821 (Griffith, 195; Barnard and Schwartzman, "Trail," 705–706).

Always ambitious, McIntosh had managed to walk a fine line between personal gain and loyalty to his nation. But he was about to go too far. In May 1824, the Muscogee National Council declared that no more land would be ceded. "We are Creeks," the leaders declared. "[W]e have a great many chiefs and head men but, be they ever so great, they must all abide [by] the laws. We have guns and ropes: and if any of our people should break these laws, those guns and ropes are to be their end" (Barnard and Schwartzman, "Trail," 709–711; McLoughlin, 372).

The new Creek agent, John Crowell, and U.S. commissioners Duncan Campbell and James Meriwether met with members of the Muscogee National Council—including Little Prince, McIntosh, and Opothleya- holo—at Broken Arrow, Little Prince's home near Fort Mitchell, in Decem- ber 1824. They offered to buy the Muscogees' entire territory left in Georgia and Alabama if the tribe would agree to move west of the Missis- sippi. The chiefs finally told them that removal was not an option. Little Prince insisted flatly that the Muscogees had "no land for sale." McIntosh emphasized to the commissioners that "we feel an affection for the land in which we were born, we wish our bones to rest by the side of our fathers." The ailing Big Warrior—through his speaker Opothleyaholo—"would not take a housefull of money" for his land, and the commissioners could con- sider this the final answer (McBride, 31–33).

Despite his eloquent talk against removal, McIntosh was shortly "bro- ken" as speaker. White Warrior's surprising and dramatic dismissal was an indication that the chiefs no longer trusted him and suspected him of carrying on private talks with the commissioners. When Campbell and Meriwether realized that the Upper Creeks were inflexible and were determined not to cede any more land, they focused on the Lower Creeks, whom they felt would be more likely to cooperate. They adjourned the meeting and agreed privately to reconvene in Georgia with the Lower Creek chiefs. McIntosh especially, Campbell wrote, would be "eminently useful" (Griffith, 227–230).

Because of his influence, his wealth, and his service during the Creek War, McIntosh still enjoyed prestige and power as a chief. A bodyguard of Coweta warriors clustered around him at Lockchau Talofau, while he began courting allies among the Lower Creeks. He may genuinely have come to the conclusion that removal was the best thing for his people. Or he may have expected to profit financially from the deal or to enhance his power as leader of the tribe once the move west was made. In any event, he chose to throw in his lot with the treaty negotiators (Griffith, 229–230).

When the talks convened again in February 1825—this time at McIntosh's home at Indian Springs—the bitter division in the Muscogee nation was painfully obvious. Big Warrior was dying, but 400 other chiefs gathered to hear the commissioners give the same arguments as before. This time the charismatic McIntosh gave a persuasive speech in favor of removal, but outside the tavern there was growing resentment as Opothleyaholo mounted a boulder and delivered a blistering indictment of the McIntosh party. McIntosh, he thundered, knew full well that Muscogee law was binding and that no one chief could sell land without the entire nation's approval. Opothleyaholo sent a clear signal, and a number of the Lower Creek chiefs left for home. The next day the commissioners had the proposed treaty read to the chiefs and ready for them to sign. As McIntosh prepared to do so, Opothleyaholo confronted him. "I have told you your fate if you sign that paper," he murmured. "I once more say, beware" (Griffith, 237–240; McBride, 38).

The Treaty of Indian Springs provided for the Muscogees to cede all of their lands left in Georgia. Of the minority who signed, only McIntosh was a chief of any rank. He was to receive at least $200,000 for his part, yet he insisted that he had acted "according to the dictates of my best judgment," and not out of personal ambition. The rival chiefs accused him of the basest form of treachery and denounced the treaty as a fraud. When McIntosh refused to answer Little Prince's summons to appear before the National Council to face the charges, they tried McIntosh in absentia in April 1825 and sentenced him to death (Griffith, 238–241, 246; Barnard and Schwartzman, "Trail," 716).

McIntosh's cousin, George M. Troup, who had been elected Georgia's governor in 1823, assured McIntosh that nothing would happen to him—that White Warrior was still revered in the Muscogee nation and that the state and federal government would protect him. McIntosh's guard was down when Menawa and 200 warriors—men from the Upper Creek towns of Tuckabatchee and Okfuskee—arrived at Lockchau Talofau on the night of April 29, 1825. Before dawn, they descended on the home, ordering the white guests and the Muscogee women and children to leave the building. Once the house was evacuated, Menawa's men set fire to it. McIntosh and Etome Tustunnuggee, an elderly Coweta chief, drew heavy gunfire when they came to the front door (Griffith, 248–250).

Etome Tustunnuggee fell dead, but McIntosh, wounded, retreated inside and exchanged fire with the attackers from an upstairs window. When the smoke and flames finally became too much for him, McIntosh made a run for it and was hit several times as he bolted from the home. White Warrior lifted himself up on one elbow and glared into the faces of his executioners one final time. One of them plunged a knife into his heart. Then the assailants fired at least fifty bullets into his body. Finally they scalped McIntosh and hauled his body to the river, where they cast it in. They spent the remainder of the morning plundering his plantation (Griffith, 250).

The Muscogees protested the Treaty of Indian Springs as bogus and appealed to President John Quincy Adams. Surprisingly—and to the chagrin of the Georgians—Adams agreed to investigate the matter. Opothleyaholo accepted the counsel of Cherokee chiefs Major Ridge, John Ridge, and David Vann. They met with General Edmund P. Gaines, who recommended that Adams revoke the treaty on the grounds that it was fraudulent. The outcry of anger from the Georgians was predictable, and for their own well-being the chiefs decided that they must placate them by renegotiating the treaty. The Muscogees agreed to cede the same amount of territory in Georgia provided the government pay them a fair price. This left them only their lands in eastern Alabama—about half of their former territory (McLoughlin, 373).

The Cherokees resisted removal with courage and dignity. In the decade after the Creek War, their nationalist movement progressed at a remarkable rate. In the summer of 1827, the Cherokees held a constitutional convention and drew up a document that was remarkably similar to the Constitution of the United States, even down to the wording of the preamble. Their new council met in October 1828, approved the new constitution, and chose John Ross as First Principal Chief. The Cherokee capital at New Echota, just a few miles from Major Ridge's home, boasted fine homes, a statehouse, a superior court building, and a newspaper office—in fact was fully as modern looking as any white settlement. Their national council met there with a president and thirty-two representatives, no longer appointed by chiefs but elected by the people of the Cherokee nation. This government began levying taxes for the first time in Cherokee history. There was also a court system of eight judicial districts with judges and marshals (Hoig, 121; McLoughlin, 396–407).

George Guess (Sequoyah), a combat veteran of the Creek War who had already moved west, introduced a Cherokee alphabet in 1821. Soon many Cherokee children as well as adults could read and write in their own language. The first edition of the Cherokee-language newspaper, *Tsa'lagi' Tsu'llehisanun'hi* (the *Cherokee Phoenix*) came off the presses in 1828. Major Ridge's nephew Elias Boudinot, the editor, was a well-educated young mixed-blood who had attended school in Connecticut. "These Indians," Sam Houston could declare proudly, "are not inferior to white men" (Hoig, 122–123; Wilkins, 6).

Many of the Cherokee nation's leaders were dying off now. Ailing from wounds received at Horseshoe Bend and suffering from illness, Richard Brown died in January 1818. Return J. Meigs died in 1823. The nation's principal and secondary chiefs, old Pathkiller and Charles Hicks (who had done much to advance Christianity in the Cherokee nation), both died in

January 1827. The literate Cherokee mixed-blood planters still formed the nation's elite, in contrast to the vast majority of the Cherokee people, who still worked their small farms in poverty. Some of the most respected leaders were Major Ridge, his son John, and George Lowrey. But the up-and-coming star of the Cherokee nation was John Ross, the First Principal Chief (Hoig, 121–124).

One of the most successful cotton planters in Georgia, Ross owned twenty slaves and 300 acres of land at the head of the Coosa River. His plantation included a spacious two-story house with a covered porch, a profitable ferry business, fruit orchards, a meeting house for visiting preachers, a blacksmith shop, barns, and stables. Ross—the successful self-made Cherokee entrepreneur—was really what white Georgians feared. Their biggest obstacle to acquiring the Cherokee lands was the cultivator's plow and overseer's whip—not the war club, bow, and scalping knife (Wallace, 9–11, 62).

Georgia began to put more and more pressure on the Cherokees, enacting a new law in December 1828 that extended state law over the Indian lands, which the state intended to survey and divide into counties. As of June 1, 1830, the Cherokee government and its laws would be null and void, and any Cherokees still living there would be subject to state laws—although still without the rights of whites. Alabama passed similar legislation in January 1829. These actions amounted to an ultimatum to the Cherokees to get out. Meanwhile, Andrew Jackson had been elected the new U.S. president in November 1828. The Cherokees sought his reaction to the new Georgia and Alabama laws. Would he uphold the federal treaty laws over state laws? He said that he would not (McLoughlin, 424–425; McBride, 69).

Jackson made it clear to the Cherokees that *only* the federal government could protect them from the states and the white settlers—that his removal plan would be better than the treatment they faced from the states. The Cherokees argued that Jackson was undermining the U.S. Constitution by supporting states' rights over the treaties so solemnly guaranteed by the federal government. But while many white Americans saw the justice of the Cherokees' case, most of them chose to believe that removal was for the best. After all, if white families could move west and start over, so could red men (McLoughlin, 428–429).

The discovery of gold on the Cherokee lands in the spring of 1829 aggravated the situation even further. The unexpected strike resulted in the first American gold rush, as white prospectors flooded into the Chestatee River area near present-day Dahlonega, Georgia. One can only speculate how the Cherokee nation might have evolved had it been allowed to develop its own mineral resources (McLoughlin, 430–431).

In a show of force in January 1830, Major Ridge and thirty members of his Light Horse rode into an area where white squatters had moved in and built cabins. Ridge was civil but adamant; he told the whites that they must get out. His men set fire to their cabins and burned their crops. The squatters left, but they came back in larger numbers after the Light Horse had departed. Surprising four of Ridge's men who were drinking whiskey in an abandoned cabin, they beat them so savagely that one man died. The marauders were never prosecuted (McLoughlin, 431–432).

The blow that the Cherokees, Muscogees, and Choctaws had all been dreading fell in May 1830. After weeks of debate—in which Creek War veterans Sam Houston and Davy Crockett spoke in support of the red men—Congress narrowly passed the Indian Removal bill. Jackson signed it into law on May 28. Just three days later, Georgia declared its sovereignty over all Cherokee lands, barred any further meetings of the Cherokee Council, shut down their courts, and nullified their laws. The Cherokee nation ceased to exist in Georgia. In the summer of 1830, Georgia formed its own security force for the Cherokee lands—the Georgia Guard, which soon earned a reputation for siding with white intruders and for harassing Cherokees. They arrested missionaries, shut down the Cherokee newspaper office, and held John Ross prisoner for a brief time (McLoughlin, 432–433, 436–437).

But, John Ridge protested, "You asked us to throw off the hunter and warrior state: We did so—you asked us to form a republican government: We did so—adopting your own as a model. You asked us to cultivate the earth, and learn the mechanic arts: We did so." Elias Boudinot responded to the depth of the betrayal in the *Cherokee Phoenix:* "Full license to our oppressors, and every avenue of justice closed to us." The Cherokees' anguish mirrored the plea of Opothleyaholo in the Muscogee nation: "Why cannot we be allowed to have land, and homes, and live like our white Brothers?" (Ehle, 235, 254; McBride, 59).

In September 1830, John Coffee and Jackson's secretary of war, John H. Eaton, went to the Choctaws to conclude the Treaty of Dancing Rabbit Creek. It was clear that this was a major event. Choctaw factor George Gaines was there, with enough food to feed 3,000 people for at least a week. Pushmataha's successor, Greenwood Le Flore, attended with other chiefs and their warriors. The opening days of the talks were friendly, almost festive, as whites looked on, some of them setting up temporary saloons and gambling tables on the outskirts of the Choctaw camps. But the atmosphere suddenly turned hostile when the government negotiators demanded that the Choctaws surrender all of their remaining lands east of the Mississippi and accept transportation west. A number of chiefs accused Le Flore of selling out, insisting that he did not speak for the entire Choctaw nation. Some of the chiefs angrily walked out of the council house, and others threatened privately to kill the negotiators. But in the end, they submitted. It was known that Le Flore had accepted sizable bribes and the government's pledge that he could stay on his own land.

"Which is worse," Le Flore shrugged, "for a great government to offer a bribe or a poor Indian to take one?" (Davis, 301–302).

The Choctaws—more than 12,000 of them—became the first of the southeastern tribes to leave their lands. Only 600 remained, bowing to the state government and agreeing to become citizens of Mississippi. As a steamship carried him across the Mississippi in February 1832, Choctaw chief George W. Harkins composed an open letter to the people of the United States. "We are hedged in by two evils," he wrote, "and we chose that which we thought the least." Sadly, Sharp Knife, who had promised he would "plant a stake and draw a line around us, that should never be passed, was the first to say that he could not guard the lines, and drew up the stake and wiped out all traces of the line" (Davis, 302; Ehle, 253; DeRosier, 5).

By 1832, the Muscogees in Alabama were feeling increasing pressure and harassment, with 1,500 white squatters already on their lands, besides a flood of destitute red refugees from their former country east of the Chattahoochee. The Alabama legislature enacted laws curtailing the rights of Muscogees; red men could not testify against whites in court. As in the Cherokee country, thieves and marauders victimized families, with no fear of prosecution. Muscogee leaders protested. "Murders have already taken place," they wrote, "both by reds and whites. We have caused the red men to be brought to justice, the whites go unpunished.... [T]hey daily rob us of our property; they bring white officers among us, and take our property from us for debts that were never contracted" (Willoughby, 58).

In March 1832 Muscogee leaders gave in and signed the Treaty of Cusseta, surrendering all of their lands east of the Mississippi—conceding that the Muscogee nation no longer existed. The treaty allotted to individual Muscogee families small plots of land that they could live on and farm, just as their white neighbors did. They were not required to move west—but they were strongly encouraged to do so. Land speculators quickly exploited the red men, selling them whiskey and other goods "on credit," inducing them to sign over their land titles as security. White squatters continued to pour into Muscogee lands in violation of the treaty provisions, and there were not enough federal soldiers to keep them out. In desperation, Opothleyaholo even tried to purchase land for the Muscogees to settle on in Texas, but the Mexican government turned him down. By 1838, the last of the Muscogees would be gone (Willoughby, 58–59; Wallace, 83–86; McBride, 78–81).

In central Florida, forced to relocate on swampland that proved far less useful for agriculture, the Seminoles seethed over years of unfair treatment. The problem was aggravated by the presence of the Maroon communities. Runaway slaves made use of a southeastern version of the "Underground Railroad," running not to the north but south through

Florida to the Bahamas and Cuba. Southern leaders continually complained to Washington to do something about the problem. In May 1832, they finally pressured Seminole leaders into accepting the Treaty of Payne's Landing, agreeing to surrender their Florida lands and emigrate to the west within three years (Wright, 249; Littlefield, 114).

In a last-ditch effort to avoid removal, the Cherokees carried their struggle to the U.S. Supreme Court. The Cherokees argued that they were a sovereign nation with the right to self-government, that the United States government had acknowledged them as such by virtue of the many past treaties made with them. They argued that the state of Georgia had no legal right to force them off their lands and asked for a federal restraining order. Georgia contended that the Cherokees were attempting to create an unlawful state within a state (Remini, *Legacy*, 68–69; McLoughlin, 438).

Chief Justice John Marshall heard arguments in the case of *Cherokee Nation v. Georgia* and released his decision on March 18, 1831. He rejected both the Cherokees' claim of independence as well as Jackson's claim that they were subject to state law. Instead, Marshall declared the Native Americans "domestic dependent nations," in effect wards of the federal government. They were not subject to any state law, but only to federal law. Ross felt that "domestic dependent nation" status at least was better than "tenants at will" (Remini, *Legacy*, 69; McLoughlin, 439).

The aged Marshall handed down a second opinion dealing with the Cherokees a year later in the case of *Worcester v. Georgia*. In an effort to curb the activities of white missionaries who encouraged the Cherokees to resist state law, Georgia had passed a law prohibiting white men from entering the Cherokee country unless they took an oath of allegiance to Georgia. Two missionaries, Samuel A. Worcester and Elizur Butler, chose to defy the law and were arrested. The Georgia Guard's cruel treatment of the two missionaries—jailed in shackles, cursed, and abused—provoked strong protests. The Cherokees felt that white Americans would finally become outraged enough to repudiate Jackson's removal plan. The two missionaries sued in court, challenging the Georgia law. Marshall agreed. On March 3, 1832, he declared all Georgia laws dealing with the Cherokees unconstitutional (Remini, *Legacy*, 69; McLoughlin, 441–444).

The Cherokees had won a great legal victory, but that was all. Reelected in November 1832, Jackson made it clear that he would not enforce the Supreme Court's decision. Had he tried to do so, he risked worsening a far more serious crisis that faced him that fall—the nullification crisis in South Carolina. In defiance of the federal government—foreshadowing events of 1861—South Carolina had just declared the new tariff null and void. Old Hickory preferred not to antagonize Georgia lest she fall in with South Carolina, and that might mean civil war. Jackson resolved the problem by inducing the Georgia governor to offer a pardon to the two imprisoned missionaries, who made things easy when they decided not to press for an appeal of their case. It was necessary to sacrifice the Cherokees to preserve the union (McLoughlin, 445–446).

As Cherokee hope turned to disillusionment, many prominent leaders—Major Ridge, John Ridge, Elias Boudinot, and others—reluctantly accepted that the struggle in the courts was over and that further resistance was useless. They were now resigned to accept removal. "I hope we shall attempt to establish [ourselves] somewhere else," John Ridge wrote, because "we can't be a nation here." Ross countered that if the Cherokees were not allowed to be a nation where they were, then they could not be a nation anywhere (McLoughlin, 449).

The split in the Cherokee political leadership caused a bitter power struggle, with Ross accusing John Ridge of making "one of the most consummate acts of treachery towards his country that the annals of any nation affords." As they had done with the Muscogees at Indian Springs, federal negotiators moved quickly to exploit the rift. They decided to deal with the Ridge faction, and in December 1835 they sat down with Major Ridge, John Ridge, and other leaders at Elias Boudinot's home in New Echota. They asked the Cherokees to surrender their lands east of the Mississippi in return for lands in the west, a payment of $4,500,000, and a yearly annuity (Ehle, 259).

With a heavy heart, old Major Ridge rose and addressed the group:

I am one of the native sons of these wild woods. I have hunted the deer and turkey here, more than fifty years. I have fought your battles, have defended your truth and honesty, and fair trading. I have always been the friend of honest white men.... We are few, they are many. We cannot remain here in safety and comfort.... Make a treaty of cession. Give up these lands and go over beyond the great Father of Waters. (Ehle, 294)

After carefully deliberating, the Cherokee chiefs sadly put their names to the treaty. Major Ridge shook his head as he made his mark. "I have signed my death warrant," he declared (Parins, 21).

John Ross—"a great villain," Jackson sneered—and the diehards still resisted. They gathered 16,000 Cherokee signatures on a petition branding the Treaty of New Echota a fraud. "We will not recognize, " Ross declared, "the forgery palmed off upon the world as a treaty by a knot of unauthorized individuals, nor stir one step with reference to that false paper." The majority of his nation supported him, but 2,000 Cherokees like Major Ridge simply threw in the towel and emigrated west (Remini, *Legacy*, 74, 78).

The Ross faction continued to draw a line of defiance in the sand, even after any hope of resistance was long gone. Ross lost his plantation—sold off in the Georgia land lottery—and saw his nation disintegrate before his very eyes. Once the deadline for voluntary removal had passed, federal troops entered the Cherokee nation and began rounding up the dissidents.

Squatters and looters descended upon Cherokee cabins to plunder anything the red people could not carry away. The suffering of the Cherokees, as troops herded them into stockades all across north Georgia, moved even some of the white soldiers to compassion. One was outspoken General John E. Wool, who—despite a personal reprimand from Jackson—wrote, "If I could, and I could not do them a greater kindness, *I would remove every Indian tomorrow, beyond the reach of the white men*" (Ehle, 302; Wallace, 92).

Thousands of Cherokees died of hunger and exposure on the Trail of Tears, the forced removal of 1838–1839. The removal of the Choctaws and Muscogees, while less publicized, was equally horrible. Some 1,000 Cherokees retreated to the mountains of western North Carolina, where they successfully hid out from the white troops. Their descendants still live there today.

Even in their new home west of the Mississippi, the bitter schism among the Cherokees continued to divide the nation. There were scores to settle. Some of Ross's followers ambushed and gunned down Major Ridge. The old warrior died instantly, riddled with bullets as he tumbled from his horse. The assassins also knifed and tomahawked John Ridge and Elias Boudinot to death in front of their families (Remini, *Legacy*, 79).

Epilogue:
"An Indiscriminate Slaughter"

Shivering in the chilly March wind, but moving as quietly as possible from tree to tree, the militia soldiers advanced cautiously through the murky water of the Pea River swamp in southeastern Alabama. Ahead was a camp of rebel Muscogees, doubtless the same party that the militia had tracked here by the smoking homes of white settlers left behind in their path. Suddenly gunfire shattered the morning stillness. Nineteen-year-old Buck Glenn, seeing movement in the bushes ahead, raised his flintlock musket and opened fire. As the piece discharged, the stiff wind caused powder to flash back into his face, singeing his eyelashes. The shot found its mark, as a red warrior toppled from behind the bush. Next to Glenn, young James Wellborn whooped, "Buck Glenn has killed an Indian!" Instantly a Muscogee bullet struck him in the head, and he fell back, screaming and flailing in agony (M. Thompson, 62–65).

By 1836 the Muscogee nation was in a tragic condition. Starving, their crops stolen by whites, their nation partitioned again and again, the remnant of the once-proud Creek confederacy was in despair and confusion, begging for food at Fort Mitchell. Having finally yielded to the bleak reality of removal to the west, Opothleyaholo struggled to maintain the last shred of Muscogee dignity in the face of overwhelming pressure. "I am endeavoring to keep my people together as much as possible," he moaned. "I talk to them but they have nothing to eat and what can I do? They must eat; they cannot live on air" (McBride, 88).

In a final grim irony, it was the Lower Creek towns of Eufaula, Hitchiti, and Uchee—who had so faithfully sent warriors to fight under Jackson,

Floyd, and other white commanders—that rose up now in desperation. White squatters—"roughnecks and hooligans" from the new Chatta- hoochee River settlement at Irwinton—burned Muscogee homes in old Eufaula town, took over the red men's cornfields, and drove them with their women and children into the woods nearby. The lesson was not lost on other towns in the Chattahoochee Valley. While Opothleyaholo and the Upper Creeks were resigned to removal, the Lower Creek towns under eighty-four-year-old Eneah Micco, Little Prince's successor, rebelled. One aged chief declared that he "would stay and die here, and the whites might have his skull for a water cup: they wanted everything, and when he was dead, they might have his skull, too" (McBride, 87; Willoughby, 54; Wright, 247–248).

Muscogee rage boiled over in May 1836. The Lower Creeks raided plan- tations, burned bridges, and ambushed mail stages on the Federal Road. They even fired at steamboats on the Chattahoochee. As violence esca- lated, rebel chiefs like Eneah Micco, Jim Henry, and Eneah Emarthla gath- ered hundreds of desperate followers into war parties. Marauders slaughtered a white family with seven children and cut off their heads, leaving the body of one child in the yard for hogs to feed on. Jim Henry, a twenty-year-old mixed-blood, led 300 warriors in a surprise attack on the Chattahoochee River town of Roanoke (present-day Florence, Georgia), killed fifteen white settlers and wounded twenty, and burned the village. Attacks bred terror throughout the Chattahoochee-Flint river valley and sent whites pouring into Columbus, Georgia, which braced for an attack (Willoughby, 61–62; McBride, 88–89; Wright, 265–267).

In June 1836, Major General Thomas S. Jesup took command of troops on the frontier. Fearful of white retaliation, Opothleyaholo and Menawa took the field with 1,150 warriors to aid in suppressing the rebellion. On June 15, the allied forces struck Eneah Emarthla's enclave on Hatch- echubbee Creek in present-day Russell County, Alabama, and destroyed it. By the end of the month they had taken hundreds of prisoners, includ- ing Eneah Micco and Eneah Emarthla, and Jesup reported the rebellion was over, although sporadic raids and bloody skirmishes continued into 1838 along the southern Georgia frontier (McBride, 92; Wright, 270–271).

As they had done in 1814, Muscogee warriors made for Florida to join their Seminole brethren, leaving a trail of death and destruction as they sliced their way through southwestern Georgia. Governor William Schley called out the state's militia, many of whom arrived at Columbus with no weapons. In June and July, the Georgians fought sharp, fierce skirmishes with the rebels at Boykin's Ferry (south of Columbus), at Shepherd's Plan- tation (near present-day Lumpkin), and at Chickasawachee Swamp (in present-day Baker County), where they smashed Jim Henry's band and took 150 prisoners, forcing the survivors to break up into small parties heading south (G. B. Smith, 200, 202–207).

In July, soldiers escorted the prisoners taken in the recent rebellion—1,600 men, women, and children—from Fort Mitchell to Montgomery on the Alabama River, a ninety-mile march, the warriors and their leaders in chains and handcuffs. When they reached the steamboats waiting to carry them downriver to Mobile and on to the west, one warrior cut his own throat (Willoughby, 62).

Jesup pressured Opothleyaholo and his warriors to serve two more months with the American army fighting the Seminoles in Florida. Opothleyaholo left Tuckabatchee with the first of the Muscogee removal parties in September 1836. Before departing, shamans doused the sacred fires in the town squares and removed the ashes, copper plates, and other holy relics, carrying them wrapped in deerskin—to be used again when they reestablished the Muscogee nation west of the Mississippi. Menawa, seeking to remain in Alabama as a citizen, reminded federal officials of his recent military service and their promise to exempt him from going. In the end, the promise was forgotten, and he was forced to march west with the rest of the tribe (McBride, 92–93; Wright, 296–297).

Thousands died en route. One survivor left this account:

Many fell by the wayside, too faint with hunger or too weak to keep up with the rest.... A crude bed was quickly prepared for these sick and weary people. Only a bowl of water was left within the[ir] reach, thus they were left to suffer and die alone. The little children piteously cried day after day.... Death stalked at all hours, but there was not time for proper burying or ceremonies. (Willoughby, 63)

Out of the 14,609 Muscogees who were removed west, probably only 2,495 had taken part in the rebellion. The people of seventy-seven Muscogee towns emigrated to the Indian Territory. When they reached their destination, only forty-four towns remained (McBride, 94).

And so it was that some 200 warriors and their families—cold, tired, and hungry—stood for the final time against the white militia in Pea River Swamp on March 25, 1837. Heading for Florida, the party under Ches-ke-Miko was camped on the high ground between the Pea River and Pea Creek just west of present-day Louisville, Alabama. But for several days they had been trailed by Colonel William Wellborn's mounted regiment, the Barbour Rangers.

Wellborn, a forty-five-year-old former brigadier general in the Georgia militia and now a prominent settler in Irwinton, was no newcomer to Indian fighting. On February 3, he had been wounded in a skirmish with Ches-ke-Miko's rebels. At Hobdy's Bridge on the Pea, Wellborn's Barbour Rangers, along with Lieutenant William Ash's company of mounted volunteers from Georgia, rendezvoused with Captain Jefferson Burford's Pike County militia company and fifty citizens from nearby communities. The white militia now totaled 250 men. Scouts had located the rebels on an island in the swamp cut off by high water. To reach their camp, the troops would have to wade through the swamp. But Wellborn was confident of his men. "I knew them," he wrote, "& could rely on them" (G. B. Smith, 207–208, 352; M. Thompson, 63; Walker, 48, 52–53; Beauchamp, 56).

The plan was for Burford's company to cross the Pea River from the western side, approach the rebels' camp from behind, engage them, and draw them out. Wellborn's troops, moving up on the east side of the river, would then attack them in the open. Burford's men crossed the river early on the morning of March 25 and dismounted not far from the rebel camp. They could hear the voices of the red men and the barking of their dogs. Burford left a few men in charge of the horses and moved forward with his command on foot. Progress was slow, with mud and water waist high. A volley of musket fire told them that they had been spotted. Burford and his men returned fire and began an orderly withdrawal. But panic set in as the red warriors overtook them, and Burford's men dispersed into the swamp in fear for their lives (Beauchamp, 56–57).

Wellborn arrived after Burford's company had been routed, too late to coordinate the attack. By now, the warriors were back in their camp. Wellborn ordered his men to dismount and form a line of battle. The line slogged forward through the swamp. At 200 yards of the enemy camp, the warriors loosed a furious volley of musket fire. Wellborn's company, under cover of trees, halted and fired back. The troops on the left and right kept moving forward, and soon the camp was nearly enveloped by a semicircle (Beauchamp, 57–58).

"As long as my firing was going on," Buck Glenn recalled, "I got along very well, but when there was a lull it was not very pleasant." James Wellborn, shot in the head, was still alive, and Glenn—unable to help him—could only stand by and watch as the youngster cried and rolled in agony. The firing continued until the white troops were nearly out of ammunition. Their officers decided that a charge on the rebels' camp would be less risky than a retreat, in which the whites might be overtaken by the rebels and killed. With a yell, the whites charged forward. Glenn's brother Mack fell as a rebel musket ball slammed into his knee. The Muscogees were making their last stand, and they fought with all their strength. Glenn acknowledged, "Some of the Indians stood their ground bravely" (Beauchamp, 57–58; M. Thompson, 64).

Suddenly the volunteers were stumbling into the enemy encampment. The rebels had used up all their lead, and campfires still burned where they had been melting down pewter plates and casting them into bullets. Perhaps this reminded the whites of a clash between a militia company from Louisville and a party of warriors in this same swamp six weeks earlier. Out of ammunition and desperate, the red warriors had loaded nails into the barrels of their rifles and opened fire. The eerie whirring sound had startled the whites for a few minutes, but they had charged again, and the rebels had dispersed (M. Thompson, 64; Beauchamp, 51–54).

The final struggle in Ches-ke-Miko's camp was a particularly brutal one. "The slaughter," Wellborn reported, "was unparalleled. A foot log, previously prepared by them across the river, was literally covered with blood." Even the Muscogee women fought, stabbing at the whites' horses and surrounding one volunteer who had to use his Bowie knife to cut his way out. But the militia overran the camp, then set fire to rebels' packs and provisions. Young Glenn would remember it for as long as he lived. "In coming out of the fight," Glenn recalled, "my pants were as bloody as if we had been killing hogs" (G. B. Smith, 207–208; Walker, 53; M. Thompson, 64).

Green Beauchamp, another of Wellborn's rangers, grimly summed it up:

For some time after the capture of the camp an indiscriminate slaughter of women, children, old men and warriors ensued. The killed were estimated at one hundred and fifty, though the number was never known accurately. Some were killed in the river and the bodies of others thrown in, so that no reliable count could be made. No warriors were made prisoners. The women and children were made slaves by the captors. (Beauchamp, 58)

When the last blow had been struck, Ches-ke-Miko was dead along with his wife and two children, and Wellborn had a young son lying dead in the mire. Wellborn reported four more men killed and ten wounded (Walker, 54).

The savage engagement at Pea River Swamp had taken nearly four hours. It was the last fight between whites and red men in Alabama. A quarter-century conflict that had started at Fort Mims on the Alabama River had ended now on the Pea River. Blood had been spilt along the Alabama, Tallapoosa, Chattahoochee, Flint, and Apalachicola. And the outcome had sealed the fate of white, red, and black people in the southeast.

But it would be in the Seminole country—so often the final refuge for fugitives and lost causes—that red resistance to removal would be the fiercest. Rebelling against the treaty of removal, the Seminoles—under the magnificent leadership of Peter McQueen's grandnephew Osceola—took up arms in December 1835. The Maroons furnished much manpower to the Seminole forces in Florida, and General Thomas Jesup, transferred from the Creek to the Seminole frontier in December 1836, wrote: "This, you may be assured, is a Negro, not an Indian war; and if it be not speedily put down, the South will feel the effects of it on their slave population before the end of next season." Until the conflict finally wound down in 1842, the Seminoles fought U.S. regulars and Southern volunteers in a bloody guerrilla war eerily reminiscent of the tactics and conditions that

American soldiers faced in Vietnam over 100 years later. The price tag to the U.S. government was ten million dollars and the deaths of 1,500 regular soldiers. It would become the most prolonged armed conflict ever waged by the United States against Native Americans (Wright, 275; Remini, *Legacy,* 80; Heidler and Heidler, *Old Hickory's War,* 232).

The Creek War of 1813–1814 and Seminole War of 1818 proved to be the most disastrous conflicts in Native American history. These conflicts shattered the power of the once mighty Muscogee nation forever and paved the way for the removal of all the southeastern tribes from their lands east of the Mississippi. The decisive battle at Horseshoe Bend alone claimed more Native American lives than any other battle ever fought between the United States and the red men. The American victory in the Creek War led to the surrender of the largest amount of land ever ceded by the southeastern tribes. No wonder that the red men never recovered from this devastating defeat (Remini, *Jackson,* 1977, 232; Owsley, 194; Martin, 1–2).

The conquered Muscogee lands quickly became the fertile Black Belt of the Cotton Kingdom. The removal of the southeastern tribes opened the door to millions of acres destined for cotton. By selling the land cheaply to settlers and speculators, the United States in effect financed the Cotton Kingdom and its expansion, and with it slavery. The Creek War secured for Andrew Jackson his reputation as a military hero, more greatly enhanced by his triumph over the British at New Orleans. Old Hickory's victories over the Muscogees in Alabama made his rise to the presidency a reality and indirectly contributed to the rise of western frontier democracy (Wallace, 11; Owsley, 194–195).

For the Muscogees, the war ensured the collapse of their civilization.

Bibliography

Abernethy, Thomas Perkins. *The Formative Period in Alabama, 1815–1828.* Tuscaloosa: University of Alabama Press, 1965.

Bains, Samuel. "Samuel Bains Letter." *Alabama Historical Quarterly* 19 (1957): 405–406.

Baird, W. David. *Peter Pitchlyn: Chief of the Choctaws.* Norman: University of Oklahoma Press, 1972.

Barber, Douglas. "Council Government and the Genesis of the Creek War." *Alabama Review* 38 (1985): 163–174.

Barnard, Susan K., and Grace M. Schwartzman. "Tecumseh and the Creek Indian War of 1813–1814 in North Georgia." *Georgia Historical Quarterly* 82 (1998): 489–506.

———. "A Trail of Broken Promises: Georgians and Muscogee/Creek Treaties, 1796–1826." *Georgia Historical Quarterly* 75 (1991): 697–718.

Bassett, John Spencer, ed. *Correspondence of Andrew Jackson.* 5 vols. Washington, DC: Carnegie Institute of Washington, 1926–1935.

Beauchamp, Green. "Some Early Chronicles of Barbour County." *Alabama Historical Quarterly* 33 (1971): 37–58.

Boyd, Mark F. "Events at Prospect Bluff on the Apalachicola River, 1808–1818." *Florida Historical Quarterly* 16 (October 1937): 55–96.

Brannon, Peter A., ed. "Fort Mitchell References." *Alabama Historical Quarterly* 21 (1959): 3–9.

———. "Journal of James A. Tait for the Year 1813." *Georgia Historical Quarterly* 8 (1924): 229–239.

Braund, Kathryn E. Holland. "The Creek Indians, Blacks, and Slavery." *Journal of Southern History* 57 (1991): 601–636.

Brown, Virginia Pounds, and Laurella Owens. *The World of the Southern Indians.* Leeds, AL: Beechwood Books, 1983.

Chalker, Fussell M. *Pioneer Days Along the Ocmulgee.* Carollton, GA: by author, 1970.

Chappell, Gordon T. "John Coffee: Land Speculator and Planter." *Alabama Review* 22 (1969): 24–43.

Chartrand, Rene. *Uniforms and Equipment of the United States Forces in the War of 1812.* Youngstown, NY: Old Fort Niagara Association, 1992.

Claiborne, John Francis Hamtramck. *Life and Times of General Sam Dale, the Mississippi Partisan.* New York, 1860.

Clayton, W. W. *History of Davidson County, Tennessee.* Philadelphia, 1880.

Coffee, John. Letters. *Tennessee Historical Magazine* 2 (1916).

Coker, William S. "The Last Battle of the War of 1812: New Orleans. No, Fort Bowyer!" *Alabama Historical Quarterly* 43 (1981): 43–63.

Coleman, Kenneth, and Charles Stephen Gurr, eds. *Dictionary of Georgia Biography.* Athens: University of Georgia Press, 1983.

Coulter, E. Merton. "The Chehaw Affair." *Georgia Historical Quarterly* 49 (1965): 369–395.

Covington, James W. *The Seminoles of Florida.* Gainesville: University Press of Florida, 1993.

Creek Letters, 1800–1816. Thomas Joseph Peddy Collection. Auburn University Archives. Auburn, AL (hereafter AU).

Crockett, David. *Autobiography of David Crockett.* New York: Scribners, 1923.

Cutrer, Thomas W. "Notes and Documents: 'The Tallapoosa Might Truly Be Called the River of Blood': Major Alexander McCulloch and the Battle of Horseshoe Bend, March 27, 1813." *Alabama Review* 43 (1990): 35–39.

Davis, William C. *A Way Through the Wilderness: The Natchez Trace and the Civilization of the Southern Frontier.* New York: Harper-Collins, 1995.

Day, Donald, and Harry H. Ullom. *Autobiography of Sam Houston.* Norman: University of Oklahoma Press, 1954.

Dean, Lewis S. "'Tecumseh's Prophecy': The Great New Madrid Earthquakes of 1811–1812 and 1843 in Alabama." *Alabama Review* 47 (1994): 163–171.

DeRosier, Arthur H. Jr. *The Removal of the Choctaw Indians.* Knoxville: University of Tennessee Press, 1970.

Doss, Chriss H. "Early Settlement of Bearmeat Cabin Frontier." *Alabama Review* 22 (1969): 270–283.

Doster, James F. "Early Settlements on the Tombigbee and Tensaw Rivers." *Alabama Review* 12 (1959): 83–94.

Dupre, Daniel. "Ambivalent Capitalists on the Cotton Frontier: Settlement and Development in the Tennessee Valley of Alabama." *Journal of Southern History* 56 (1990): 215–240.

Eaton, J. H. "Returns of the Killed and Wounded of American Troops in Battles or Engagements with the Indians." Miscellaneous Battles. War of 1812 / First Creek War. Alabama Department of Archives and History, Montgomery, AL (hereafter ADAH).

Edmunds, R. David. *Tecumseh and the Quest for Indian Leadership.* Boston: Little, Brown, & Co., 1984.

Ehle, John. *Trail of Tears: The Rise and Fall of the Cherokee Nation.* New York: Doubleday, 1988.

Elting, John R. *Amateurs, To Arms! A Military History of the War of 1812.* Chapel Hill: Algonquin Books of Chapel Hill, 1991.

Faust, Richard H. "Another Look at General Jackson and the Indians of the Mississippi Territory." *Alabama Review* 28 (1975): 202–217.

Floyd, John. "Letters of John Floyd, 1813–1838." *Georgia Historical Quarterly* 33 (1949): 228–269.

Fredriksen, John C. *War of 1812 Eyewitness Accounts, An Annotated Bibliography.* Westport, CT: Greenwood Press, 1997.

Freehoff, William Francis. "Tecumseh's Last Stand." *Military History* (October 1996): 30–36.

Gaines, George S. "Gaines' Reminiscences." *Alabama Historical Quarterly* 26 (1964): 133–230.

Ghioto, Paul A., Mark E. Spier, and Faye Johnson. *Facts, Legends, and Accounts of the Battle of Horseshoe Bend.* Daviston, AL: Horseshoe Bend National Military Park, 1979.

Gibson, Arrell M. *The Chickasaws.* Norman: University of Oklahoma Press, 1971.

Grant, C.L., ed. *Letters, Journals, and Writings of Benjamin Hawkins.* Vol. II, 1806–1816. Savannah: Beehive Press, 1980.

Griffith, Benjamin W. Jr. *McIntosh and Weatherford: Creek Indian Leaders.* Tuscaloosa: University of Alabama Press, 1988.

Guice, John D.W. "Face to Face in Mississippi Territory, 1798–1817." In *The Choctaw Before Removal,* ed. Carolyn Keller Reeves. Jackson: University Press of Mississippi, 1985. 157–180.

Halbert, Henry Sale. "Choctaw War Customs." Henry Sale Halbert Collection. ADAH.

Halbert, Henry Sale, and Timothy H. Ball. *The Creek War of 1813–1814.* Tuscaloosa: University of Alabama Press, 1969.

Harris, W. Stuart. "Rowdyism, Public Drunkenness, and Bloody Encounters in Early Perry County." *Alabama Review* 33 (1980): 15–24.

Hauck, Richard Boyd. *Davy Crockett: A Handbook.* Lincoln: University of Nebraska Press, 1982.

Hawkins, Benjamin. Papers. Frank L. Owsley Collection. AU.

Haynes, Robert V. "Early Washington County, Alabama." *Alabama Review* 18 (1965):183–200.

Heidler, David S., and Jeanne T. Heidler. "Between a Rock and a Hard Place: Allied Creeks and the United States, 1814–1818." *Alabama Review* 50 (1997): 267–289.

———. *Encyclopedia of the War of 1812.* Santa Barbara, CA: ABC-CLIO, 1997.

———. *Old Hickory's War: Andrew Jackson and the Quest for Empire.* Mechanicsburg, PA: Stackpole Books, 1996.

Heiskell, Samuel Gordon. *Andrew Jackson and Early Tennessee History.* Nashville: Ambrose Printing Co., 1918.

Hoig, Stanley W. *The Cherokees and Their Chiefs: In the Wake of Empire.* Fayetteville: University of Arkansas Press, 1998.

Holland, James W. *Andrew Jackson and the Creek War: Victory at the Horseshoe.* Tuscaloosa: University of Alabama Press, 1968.

Hood, Charlotte Adams. *Jackson's White Plumes: An Historical and Genealogical Account of Selected Cherokee Families Who Supported Andrew Jackson during the Creek Indian War of 1813–1814.* Bay Minette, AL: Lavender Publishing Co., 1995.

"Horseshoe Bend First Hand Accounts." War of 1812 / First Creek War. ADAH.

Howard, E. L. "Jett Thomas." In *Men of Mark in Georgia*, vol. 2, ed. William J. Northen. Atlanta: Caldwell Publishers, 1910. 378–380.

Hudson, Charles M. *The Southeastern Indians*. Knoxville: University of Tennessee Press, 1976.

Hunt, Robert C. "John Hunt." *Alabama Historical Quarterly* 22 (1960): 88–100.

Jemison, E. Grace. *Historic Tales of Talladega*. Montgomery, AL: Paragon Press, 1959.

Jenkins, William H. "Alabama Forts, 1700–1838." *Alabama Review* 12 (1959): 163–180.

Lengel, Leland L. "The Road to Fort Mims: Judge Harry Toulmin's Observations on the Creek War, 1811–1813." *Alabama Review* 29 (1976): 16–36.

Littlefield, Daniel F. Jr. *Africans and Creeks: From the Colonial Period to the Civil War*. Westport, CT: Greenwood Press, 1979.

Lossing, Benson J. *The Pictorial Field Book of the War of 1812*. Somersworth, NH: New Hampshire Publishing Co., 1976.

McAlister, L. N. "Pensacola During the Second Spanish Period." *Florida Historical Quarterly* 37 (January–April 1959): 312–322.

McBride, Lela J. *Opothleyaholo and the Loyal Muskogee: Their Flight to Kansas in the Civil War*. Jefferson, NC: McFarland and Co., 2000.

McCown, Mary Hardin, ed. "The 'J. Hartsell Memora': The Journal of a Tennessee Captain in the War of 1812." *East Tennessee Historical Society's Publications* 11 (1939): 93–113, 12 (1940): 118–145.

McDaniel, Mary Jane. "Tecumseh's Visits to the Creeks." *Alabama Review* 33 (1980): 3–14.

McKee, John. Journal. Choctaw / Chickasaw Indians. War of 1812 / First Creek War. ADAH.

———. Letters. Choctaw / Chickasaw Indians. War of 1812 / First Creek War. ADAH.

McLemore, Richard Aubrey, ed. *A History of Mississippi*, vol. 1. Hattiesburg: University and College Press of Mississippi, 1973.

McLoughlin, William G. *Cherokee Renascence in the New Republic*. Princeton, NJ: Princeton University Press, 1986.

Mahon, John K. "British Strategy and Southern Indians: War of 1812." *Florida Historical Quarterly* 44 (April 1966): 285–302.

———. "Daniel Newnan: A Neglected Figure in Florida History." *Florida Historical Quarterly* 74 (Fall 1995): 148–153.

———. "The First Seminole War, November 21, 1817–May 24, 1818." *Florida Historical Quarterly* 77 (Summer 1998): 62–67.

———. *The War of 1812*. Gainesville: University of Florida Press, 1972.

Martin, Joel W. *Sacred Revolt: The Muskogee's Struggle for a New World*. Boston: Beacon Press, 1991.

Matte, Jacqueline Anderson. *They Say the Wind Is Red: The Alabama Choctaw: Lost in Their Own Land*. Red Level, AL: Greenberry Publishing Co., 1999.

Moore, John Trotwood, and Austin P. Foster. *Tennessee, the Volunteer State, 1769–1923*, vol. 1. Chicago: S. J. Clarke Publishing Co., 1923.

Moulton, Gary E., ed. *The Papers of Chief John Ross*, vol. 1, 1807–1839. Norman: University of Oklahoma Press, 1985.

Notes from Papers of Gen. John Coffee. Frank L. Owsley Collection. AU.

Owen, Marie Bankhead, ed. "Alabama Indians." *Alabama Historical Quarterly* 13 (1951).

Owsley, Frank L. Jr. *Struggle for the Gulf Borderlands: The Creek War and the Battle of New Orleans, 1812–1815.* Gainesville: University Presses of Florida, 1981.

Palmer, T.H., ed. *Historical Register of the United States, Part II, For 1814,* vol. IV. Philadelphia, 1816.

Parins, James W. *John Rollin Ridge.* Lincoln: University of Nebraska Press, 1991.

Parker, James W. "Fort Jackson after the War of 1812." *Alabama Review* 38 (1985): 119–130.

Parton, James. *Life of Andrew Jackson.* 1860. Reprint. New York: Johnson Reprint Corp., 1967.

Patrick, Rembert W. *Aristocrat in Uniform: General Duncan L. Clinch.* Gainesville: University of Florida Press, 1963.

Pickett, Albert James. *History of Alabama, and Incidentally of Georgia and Mississippi, From the Earliest Period.* Birmingham: Birmingham Book and Magazine Co., 1962.

Porter, Kenneth W. *The Black Seminoles: History of a Freedom-Seeking People.* Gainesville: University Press of Florida, 1996.

Pound, Merritt B. "Benjamin Hawkins." In *Georgians in Profile: Historical Essays in Honor of Ellis Merton Coulter,* ed. Horace Montgomery. Athens: University of Georgia Press, 1958. 89–113.

Quimby, Robert S. *The U.S. Army in the War of 1812: An Operational and Command Study.* East Lansing: Michigan State University Press, 1997.

Ratner, Lorman A. *Andrew Jackson and His Tennessee Lieutenants: A Study in Political Culture.* Westport, CT: Greenwood Press, 1997.

Reid, John, and John Henry Eaton. *The Life of Andrew Jackson.* Tuscaloosa: University of Alabama Press, 1974.

Reid, John Alden. "The Silk Standards of the Thirty-Ninth U.S. Infantry, 1814." *Military Collector & Historian* 50 (1998): 35–37.

Remini, Robert. *Andrew Jackson and the Course of American Empire.* New York: Harper and Row, 1977.

———. *The Legacy of Andrew Jackson: Essays on Democracy, Indian Removal, and Slavery.* Baton Rouge: Louisiana State University Press, 1988.

Rogers, William Warren, Robert David Ward, Leah Rawls Atkins, and Wayne Flynt. *Alabama: The History of A Deep South State.* Tuscaloosa: University of Alabama Press, 1994.

Rowland, Dunbar. *Military History of Mississippi, 1803–1898.* Spartanburg, SC: Reprint Company, Publishers, 1978.

Rowland, Eron Opha Moore. *The Mississippi Territory in the War of 1812.* Baltimore: Genealogical Publishing Company, 1968.

Rucker, Brian R. "In the Shadow of Jackson: Uriah Blue's Expedition into West Florida." *Florida Historical Quarterly* 73 (January 1995): 325–338.

Saunt, Claudio. *A New Order of Things: Poverty, Power, and the Transformation of the Creek Indians, 1733–1816.* New York: Cambridge University Press, 1999.

Skeen, C. Edward. *Citizen Soldiers in the War of 1812.* Lexington: University Press of Kentucky, 1999.

Smith, Gene A. " 'Our Flag was display'd within their Works': The Treaty of Ghent and the Conquest of Mobile." *Alabama Review* 52 (1999): 3–20.

Smith, Gordon B. *History of the Georgia Militia, 1783–1861.* Vol. 1: Campaigns and Generals. Milledgeville, GA: Boyd Publishing, 2000.

Southerland, Henry DeLeon Jr. "The Federal Road, Gateway to Alabama, 1806–1836." *Alabama Review* 39 (1986): 96–109.

Southerland, Henry DeLeon Jr., and Jerry Elijah Brown. *The Federal Road through Georgia, the Creek Nation, and Alabama, 1806–1836.* Tuscaloosa: University of Alabama Press, 1989.

Stephen, Walter W. "Andrew Jackson's 'Forgotten Army.'" *Alabama Review* 12 (1959): 126–131.

Stiggins, George. *Creek Indian History: A Historical Narrative of the Genealogy, Traditions and Downfall of the Ispocoga or Creek Indian Tribe of Indians.* Birmingham, AL: Birmingham Public Library Press, 1989.

Suarez, Annette McDonald. "The War Path Across Georgia Made by Tennessee Troops in the First Seminole War." *Georgia Historical Quarterly* 38 (1954): 29–42.

Sugden, John. "The Southern Indians in the War of 1812: The Closing Phase." *Florida Historical Quarterly* 60 (1982): 273–312.

"Third U.S. Infantry." War of 1812 / First Creek War. ADAH.

Thompson, Lynn Hastie. *William Weatherford: His Country and His People.* Bay Minette, AL: Lavender Publishing Company, 1991.

Thompson, Mattie Thomas. *History of Barbour County, Alabama.* Eufaula, AL: by author, 1939.

Twyman, Bruce Edward. *The Black Seminole Legacy and North American Politics, 1693–1845.* Washington, DC: Howard University Press, 1999.

Walker, Anne Kendrick. *Backtracking in Barbour County: A Narrative of the Last Alabama Frontier.* Richmond, VA: Dietz Press, 1941.

Wallace, Anthony F.C. *The Long Bitter Trail: Andrew Jackson and the Indians.* New York: Hill and Wang, 1993.

White, George. *Historical Collections of Georgia.* New York, 1854.

Wilkins, Thurman. *Cherokee Tragedy: The Ridge Family and the Decimation of a People.* Norman: University of Oklahoma Press, 1986.

Willoughby, Lynn. *Flowing Through Time: A History of the Lower Chattahoochee River.* Tuscaloosa: University of Alabama Press, 1999.

Woodward, Grace Steele. *The Cherokees.* Norman: University of Oklahoma Press, 1963.

Woodward, Thomas S. *Woodward's Reminiscences of the Creek or Muscogee Indians.* 1859. Reprint. Mobile, AL: Southern University Press for Graphics, 1965.

Wright, J. Leitch. *Creeks and Seminoles: The Destruction and Regeneration of the Muscogulge People.* Lincoln, NE: University of Nebraska Press, 1986.

Index

Copyright Acknowledgments

The author and publisher gratefully acknowledge permission to use the following material:

Excerpts from the Frank L. Owsley papers, Department of Special Collections & Archives, Auburn University Libraries, Auburn University, Alabama. Reproduced with permission.

Excerpts from the Thomas J. Peddy papers, Department of Special Collections & Archives, Auburn University Libraries, Auburn University, Alabama. Reproduced with permission.

From the Alabama Department of Archives and History, Montgomery, Alabama, the following materials: "Choctaw War Customs," F#18, Box 2—Henry Sale Halbert Collection; "3rd U.S. Infantry," F#10-SG13378—Letter Milton to McKee 5/16/1814; "Misc. Battles," F#6SG13377—Returns; "Choctaw/Chickasaw Indians," F#7-SG13377—Journal of John McKee, McKee Letters: 9/14/1814; "Horseshoe Bend—First-Hand Accounts," F#4-SG13377—John Reid Letters 4/1/1814, 4/5/1814, John Coffee Letter 4/25/1828. Reproduced with permission.